Studies in Anglo-Saxon History IX

KINGS, CURRENCY AND ALLIANCES

History and Coinage of Southern England in the Ninth Century

The ninth century was a period of upheaval in England, as the kingdoms of Mercia and Wessex vied for supremacy, and East Anglia and Kent sought to regain their independence; the arrival of the Vikings introduced a further element of unrest. This interdisciplinary collection of papers by historians, numismatists and philologists considers fundamental aspects of the period's political and economic history. Alliances and treaties are a central theme, political and monetary; relationships are explored between a number of kings and leaders (Frankish and earlier English parallels are adduced), arguing that these culminated in a distinct 'Kingdom of the Anglo-Saxons' representing the people of Wessex and English Mercia from about 880 to 927. A radical reassessment of events in London in the later ninth century is presented, prompted by a detailed examination of the numismatic evidence marshalled here along with the written sources; it is argued that the Vikings were not in control of the city prior to Alfred's 'reoccupation' in AD 886. The volume includes an illustrated corpus of the coinage of Berhtwulf and another for the middle years of Alfred's reign; moneyers are identified as witnesses to charters, and the forms of their names are analysed according to the Old English dialects they represent. A listing of some 500 single coin-finds forms the basis for a discussion of the nature and extent of monetary use in ninth-century England.

Dr MARK BLACKBURN is Keeper of Coins and Medals at the Fitzwilliam Museum, Cambridge, and DAVID DUMVILLE is Professor of Palaeography and Cultural History in the University of Cambridge, and a Fellow of Girton College.

STUDIES IN ANGLO-SAXON HISTORY

General Editor: David Dumville

ISSN 0950–3412

Already published

I. A LOST ENGLISH COUNTY: WINCHCOMBESHIRE IN THE TENTH AND ELEVENTH CENTURIES
Julian Whybra

II. WORCESTERSHIRE ANGLO-SAXON CHARTER-BOUNDS
Della Hooke

III. WESSEX AND ENGLAND FROM ALFRED TO EDGAR
David N. Dumville

IV. ANGLO-SAXON EXETER: A TENTH-CENTURY CULTURAL HISTORY
Patrick W. Conner

V. LITURGY AND THE ECCLESIASTICAL HISTORY OF LATE ANGLO-SAXON ENGLAND
David N. Dumville

VI. ENGLISH CAROLINE SCRIPT AND MONASTIC HISTORY: STUDIES IN BENEDICTINISM, A.D. 950–1030
David N. Dumville

VII. SLAVERY IN EARLY MEDIAEVAL ENGLAND, FROM THE REIGN OF ALFRED UNTIL THE TWELFTH CENTURY
David A.E. Pelteret

VIII. ANGLO-SAXON GLASTONBURY: CHURCH AND ENDOWMENT
Lesley Abrams

KINGS, CURRENCY AND ALLIANCES

History and Coinage of Southern England in the Ninth Century

Edited by

MARK A. S. BLACKBURN *and* DAVID N. DUMVILLE

THE BOYDELL PRESS

First published 1998
The Boydell Press, Woodbridge

ISBN 0 85115 598 7

The Boydell Press is an imprint of Boydell & Brewer Ltd
PO Box 9, Woodbridge, Suffolk IP12 3DF, UK
and of Boydell & Brewer Inc.
PO Box 41026, Rochester, NY 14604–4126, USA

A catalogue record for this book is available
from the British Library

Library of Congress Cataloging-in-Publication Data

Kings, currency, and alliances : history and coinage of southern England in the ninth century / edited by Mark A. S. Blackburn and David N. Dumville.
p. cm.
Includes bibliographical references (p.) and index.
ISBN 0–85115–598–7 (hc. : alk. paper)
1. Great Britain – History – Anglo-Saxon period, 449–1066. 2. Anglo-Saxons – England, Southern – Kings and rulers. 3. Anglo-Saxons – England, Southern – History. 4. Coins, Anglo-Saxon – England, Southern. I. Blackburn, M. A. S. (Mark A. S.) II. Dumville, D. N.
DA152.K47 1998
941.01 – dc21 98–15873

This publication is printed on acid-free paper

Printed in Great Britain by
St Edmundsbury Press Ltd, Bury St Edmunds, Suffolk

CONTENTS

PLATES ILLUSTRATING COINS

(between pp. 150 and 151)

THE CONTRIBUTORS AND EDITORS

Paul Bibire is Lecturer, Department of Anglo-Saxon, Norse and Celtic, University of Cambridge

Mark Blackburn is Keeper of Coins and Medals, Fitzwilliam Museum, University of Cambridge

Michael Bonser is a fruit farmer at Wimbish, Essex

James Booth is Reader, Department of English, University of Hull

Thomas Charles-Edwards is Professor of Celtic, University of Oxford, and a Fellow of Jesus College, Oxford

David Dumville is Professor of Palaeography and Cultural History, University of Cambridge, and a Fellow of Girton College, Cambridge

Simon Keynes is Reader in Anglo-Saxon History, University of Cambridge, and a Fellow of Trinity College, Cambridge

Michael Metcalf is Keeper of Coins and Medals, Ashmolean Museum, Oxford; Professor of Numismatics, University of Oxford, and a Fellow of Wolfson College, Oxford

Lord Stewartby, a banker, is a former Minister of State and a Fellow of the British Academy

PREFACE

It was Sir Frank Stenton who, in the 1950s, inspired and nurtured a new generation of Anglo-Saxon numismatists led by Christopher Blunt and Michael Dolley. He impressed on them and on his fellow historians the mutual benefits of close co-operation between the two disciplines, and the friendships which they then enjoyed are happily still shared among their successors forty years later. This book is in a very real sense a further product of Stenton's vision and encouragement.

For the ninth century, above all others, the coinage has a fundamental contribution to make to our knowledge of political history. It provides the names of East Anglian kings not recorded in other sources, gives corroboration to slight accounts such as that of King Egbert's conquest of Mercia in 829 or the brief reign of Redwulf of Northumbria, and challenges our interpretation of events. This is nowhere more evident than in the reign of Alfred. The account of events in London, as propounded by Stenton in 1945, could not readily be reconciled with the evidence that began to emerge from a detailed study of the coinage, yet numismatists were reluctant to challenge the judgement of a scholar of Stenton's standing. He would, I am sure, have welcomed Simon Keynes's willingness here to look again at this question and to weigh the new numismatic evidence with that of written sources, prompting a fresh and we hope more satisfactory interpretation.

Yet this is but one example of the benefit that can flow from the interdisciplinary approach to Anglo-Saxon studies that has motivated this volume. Paul Bibire's analysis of the forms of moneyers' names shows how they provide evidence for dialects that are otherwise absent from the written record, while in turn helping numismatists to understand the way in which instructions were transmitted to the die-cutters. Similarly, Lord Stewartby's demonstration that a number of moneyers are to be found among the witnesses to charters sheds light on the composition of both groups of people. The coin finds assembled by Michael Bonser and interpreted by Michael Metcalf provide information about the monetary economy and use of coinage that one cannot begin to approach from the documentary side, but which is important for our understanding of how society functioned.

The subject of alliance and treaties is addressed by several contributors from different viewpoints. Thomas Charles-Edwards brings into play Frankish and earlier English parallels in order to tease out the significance of the terms of the peace agreed between Alfred and Guthrum. James Booth presents a detailed analysis of the coinage of Berhtwulf of Mercia, from which he examines the political implications of a period of collaboration between the mints of Rochester and London in the early 840s. My own paper and another with Simon Keynes lays out the coin evidence for Alfred's relations with Ceolwulf II, as well as the London question referred to above. But the key essay in this volume, which pulls together strands from many different sources, is Dr Keynes's wide ranging review of relations between the West Saxons and the Mercians and of Alfred's concept of a 'Kingdom of the Anglo-Saxons'.

Most of the papers published here were originally presented at a symposium held in Cambridge in April 1988. That the book has taken so long to appear is a matter of regret to both editors, and we thank the contributors for their patience. The symposium and accompanying volume were conceived and arranged by us jointly, and in subsequent years we each advised contributors on drafts of their papers. The final editing has, however, been carried out while David Dumville was on sabbatical, and he cannot be held responsible for any infelicities of style or errors of fact or judgement that have found their way into the printed text. We are very grateful to Clare Orchard for preparing the bibliography, and to Ruth Johnson and Eleanor Smith for retyping some of the manuscripts.

Mark Blackburn
September 1997

KING ALFRED AND THE MERCIANS

Simon Keynes

On his deathbed in 1014, the ætheling Æthelstan, eldest son of King Æthelred the Unready, bequeathed to his brother Edmund Ironside 'the sword which belonged to King Offa'.[1] It is a pleasant exercise in wishful thinking to imagine that this was the 'Hunnish sword' given to Offa by Charlemagne in 796,[2] and that it was of some use to Edmund when fending off the Danes in 1016. It is no less of a pleasant diversion to wonder how a Mercian royal heirloom had come into the possession of the West Saxon royal family, and to ponder its potency as a symbol of the relations which developed between the rulers of each kingdom. Perhaps Offa had bequeathed the sword to his son-in-law Beorhtric, king of Wessex (786–802); and perhaps, when Beorhtric was accidentally poisoned by his wife, the sword passed with other treasures into the hands of his successor Ecgberht, and so on down the line; or perhaps it remained for a while in the custody of Offa's successors, and passed into West Saxon possession in the context of some later association between the two kingdoms.[3] Whatever the case, the sword should be a symbol of something, and with a bit of luck it could be a symbol of the subject which I am about to address.[4]

The subject in question is the unfolding nature of King Alfred's relationship with successive rulers of Mercia, initially King Burgred, thereafter King Ceolwulf, and latterly Ealdorman Æthelred; but not only with the rulers themselves,

1 S.1503 (*Anglo-Saxon Wills*, ed. Whitelock, no. 20; trans. *EHD*, no. 129). In references to Anglo-Saxon charters, S. = Sawyer, *Anglo-Saxon Charters*, with number of document.

2 *Epistolae Karolini aevi*, ed. Duemmler, no. 100 (trans. *EHD*, no. 197).

3 The 'Saxon sword with a gold scabbard', said to have been given by King Alfred to his grandson Æthelstan (William of Malmesbury, *Gesta Regum*, § 133 (ed. Stubbs, I.145; trans. *EHD*, no. 8, p. 305)), was presumably not the same thing.

4 This paper was written in the first instance for the purposes of a symposium on King Alfred held at the University of Reading on 2 July 1986, under the gaze of a portrait of Sir Frank Stenton. It became obvious that much would depend on a proper understanding of the numismatic evidence; and I should like to express my gratitude to Marion Archibald, Mark Blackburn, and the late Christopher Blunt for their help in assembling a rough corpus of *Cross-and-Lozenge* pennies, and most especially to Dr Blackburn for his memorable display of expertise in arranging the index cards in meaningful piles. I am also grateful to Stewart Lyon and Michael Metcalf for further guidance; to Jeremy Haslam, Janet Nelson and David Hill for allowing me to read papers of their own covering the events of 886; and to Tony Dyson and Pamela Taylor for valuable comment. I am particularly grateful to Patrick Wormald for sustaining a correspondence which always helps to keep these matters fresh, and in their place. The map which accompanies this paper was drawn by Reginald Piggott, working from a much less elegant draft.

for one must also consider King Alfred's attitude to the Mercian people as a whole, whether in regard to the 'Mercian' city of London, or to the process by which he came to presume on the leadership of a people whose affection for a West Saxon king could hardly have been taken for granted. It is a subject which depends upon the correlation of evidence derived from chronicles, charters, and coins; and while the evidence is assuredly imperfect, difficult to handle, and capable of all manner of different interpretations, it will be suggested that the exercise gives rise to a perception of political development in the 870s and 880s which offers a key to our understanding of the reign of King Alfred the Great. The received view of events during this period proceeds from an assumption that the kingdom of Wessex and the kingdom of Mercia were 'rival' political orders, or polities, which endured into the first quarter of the tenth century; it is supposed, more particularly, that following the partition of Mercia in 877 London fell under Viking control, and that it remained so until King Alfred took it by force in 886, whereupon he entrusted it to Æthelred, ruler of the Mercians; and it is presumed furthermore that it was Edward the Elder, having succeeded his father as king of the West Saxons, who extended his authority over the Mercians in the second decade of the tenth century. It will be suggested, however, that the position in the 870s was more complex; that in the early 880s there emerged what amounts to a new political order, which subsumed the kingdom of Wessex and whatever was left of the former kingdom of Mercia, including London, and which was understood by contemporaries to embrace the whole of 'English' England; and that it was this polity, dignified in court circles as the kingdom 'of the Anglo-Saxons', that was Alfred's abiding political legacy to Edward the Elder.

Wessex and Mercia before the accession of King Alfred

It is important to emphasise at the outset that the relationship between Mercia and Wessex was quite obviously other than one of simple antagonism. The two kingdoms could be classified as ancient enemies, at least on the basis of the recorded instances in the seventh and eighth centuries when they are known to have come to blows; but by the time of King Alfred's accession in 871 much of their past enmity must long since have been forgotten. During the reigns of Æthelbald and Offa, when Mercia was the dominant power south of the river Humber, the kingdom of Wessex was ruled by a succession of kings who stand in no known genealogical relationship to each other or to the attested dynastic lines; yet despite this apparent sign of internal weakness, there is no reason to believe that Mercian overlordship extended over them in any of the different ways that it extended over the rulers of the Hwicce, Kent, Sussex and East Anglia.[5] A link between the two kingdoms was established in 789, when Beorhtric, king of the West Saxons (786–802), married Eadburh, one of Offa's plentiful supply of daughters; but the link was one intended to bring political advantage to both parties, and is certainly not indicative of West Saxon subjection to Mercia.[6]

5 In Stenton's view, for most of the period between 726 and 802 Wessex 'was little more than a large, outlying province of the Mercian kingdom' (*Anglo-Saxon England*, pp. 203–4; see also pp. 209–10 and 225). For a different view, see Keynes, 'England, 700–900', pp. 31–5.

6 See Keynes and Lapidge, *Alfred the Great*, p. 236, n. 30. It has been suggested that Beorhtric was

Charter-evidence suggests that Offa's son Ecgfrith was on amicable terms with his brother-in-law Beorhtric,[7] and in a charter of Cenwulf, king of Mercia, dated 799, we find an intriguing reference to a peace established in that year between the Mercians and the West Saxons, under kings Cenwulf and Ecgberht.[8] Any goodwill felt by the West Saxons towards the Mercians may have been impaired in 802, when Queen Eadburh contrived (albeit inadvertently) to poison her husband Beorhtric, and was driven from the land;[9] for according to Asser's account (given on the authority of King Alfred himself), it was her action which gave rise to the custom which prevailed thereafter among the West Saxons, whereby kings' wives were denied the dignity appropriate to their station.[10] One senses, however, that the custom expressed popular feelings and served to place a restriction on the king, and that it may not have found favour with the kings themselves.

For much of the first quarter of the ninth century the rulers of Mercia and Wessex seem to have left each other to their own devices: Ecgberht was doing what historians are wont to describe as 'consolidating his position', and Cenwulf was probably preoccupied with maintaining his interests in Kent. Presently, however, the Mercian polity began to come apart at the seams. There are signs of dissension within Mercia itself in the years following the death of King Cenwulf in 821; and in 825 King Beornwulf was defeated by Ecgberht at the battle of *Ellendun* (Wroughton, Wilts.), precipitating the collapse of Mercian authority in the south-east.[11] Four years after *Ellendun*, in 829, Ecgberht is said to have 'conquered the kingdom of the Mercians', and whatever the chronicler may have

a '(?) Mercian nominee to the throne of Wessex' (Collins, *Early Medieval Europe*, p. 334); cf. below, p. 11, n. 40.

7 See S.148 (from Worcester) and S.149 (from Malmesbury); on the latter, see Edwards, *The Charters of the Early West Saxon Kingdom*, pp. 121–3.

8 S.154 (from Worcester), perhaps implying that Ecgberht was in some way recognised as king before the death of Beorhtric in 802; cf. Stenton, *The Latin Charters*, pp. 27–8. It has been suggested (Scharer, 'The writing of history at King Alfred's court', pp. 183–5) that the ninth-century line of West Saxon kings – Ecgberht, Æthelwulf, Æthelbald, Æthelberht, Æthelred, Alfred – was in fact of 'Kentish' origin, because Ecgberht's father Ealhmund is known to have reigned in Kent in the early 780s, because the people of Kent (and Surrey, and Sussex, and Essex) considered themselves to have been wrongfully forced away from Ecgberht's kinsmen, and because the names 'Ecgberht' and 'Æthelberht' had been borne by eighth-century Kentish kings; it is suggested further that Ealhmund and his descendants were subsequently intruded into the 'main' West Saxon dynasty (through a 'brother' of King Ine) in order to establish their necessary credentials as descendants of Cerdic (reflected in the Alfredian Chronicle, and, for that matter, in Alfred's description of King Ine, in his law-code, as his kinsman). Anything of this nature is possible; and of course it might help to account for the favourable reception of Ecgberht and his line in the south-east. The question is whether a member of a 'West Saxon' line (Ealhmund) had been able to gain a foothold in Kent, in a period of political confusion, or whether a member of a 'Ken- tish' line (Ecgberht) was able to establish himself in Wessex, and start a new dynasty. The fact that Offa seems to have required Beorhtric's help to rid himself of a threat from the ætheling Ecgberht, apparently in 789, suggests to me that Ealhmund and Ecgberht were genuinely West Saxon (cf. Keynes and Lapidge, *Alfred the Great*, p. 236, n. 30; Keynes, 'England, 700–900', pp. 34–5); and the names alleged to be redolent of a Kentish connection are hardly unusual.

9 Asser, §§ 14–15. For H. Becher's suggestion that Eadburh is to be found in the *Liber Vitae* of Reichenau at the head of a community of nuns in northern Italy, see Keynes, 'Anglo-Saxon entries in the *Liber Vitae* of Brescia', p. 115, n. 71.

10 Asser, § 13; see further Keynes and Lapidge, pp. 235–6.

11 The crucial document which exposes the disintegration of the Mercian regime in the early 820s is

intended to convey by this phrase is also attested by the London coinage issued in Ecgberht's name, as king of the Mercians,[12] and by a Mercian regnal list which assigns him a reign of one year.[13] We are told, however, that in the following year Wiglaf 'again obtained the kingdom of the Mercians', in circumstances which are far from clear; but for various reasons it seems likely that Ecgberht relinquished his rule in Mercia of his own volition, and was thereafter prepared to respect Wiglaf's sovereignty as an independent ruler.[14]

From the 830s onwards, the presence of marauding Vikings in the country seems effectively to have obliged the English to bury any residual differences. It is apparent, however, that the West Saxons were by now very much the dominant political force south of the Humber, and that the rulers of the Mercians were but shadows of their former selves. A reader of the *Anglo-Saxon Chronicle* would certainly be left in no doubt as to the leading role which the West Saxons took in the struggle against the Vikings, perhaps because that was precisely the impression which the chronicler intended to create, or perhaps even because it was true. It emerges from analysis of ninth-century charters that there may have been significant differences between the political orders in Wessex and Mercia, which might have contributed in some way towards the apparently uneven balance of power. In Wessex, the rule of King Æthelwulf (839–858) was firmly established; the south-eastern provinces of Kent and Sussex, with Surrey and Essex, were brought within the orbit of the West Saxon kings (perhaps more effectively so than they had been brought within the orbit of the Mercian kings in the previous dispensation);[15] and the whole of the extended kingdom 'of the southern peoples'

S.1435 (*Charters of Selsey*, ed. Kelly, no. 15); see also Keynes, 'The control of Kent', pp. 119–20.

12 See Blunt, 'The coinage of Ecgbeorht', pp. 472–3; Blackburn, in *MEC*, p. 292; and Pagan, 'Coinage in southern England', p. 47.

13 London, British Library, MS Cotton Tiberius A.xiii, fo. 114v; printed in *Hemingi Chartularium*, ed. Hearne, I.242.

14 It is simply a matter of how one chooses to read the evidence. Stenton considered it unlikely that Wiglaf was restored to the Mercian kingdom by Ecgberht, and more likely that he was brought back to power by a revolt in Mercia (*Anglo-Saxon England*, p. 233); he also regarded Wiglaf's charter issued at the council of Croft in 836 (S.190; trans. *EHD*, no. 85) as a sign not only of Wiglaf's independence, but of 'the revival of Mercian authority over the southern episcopate' (*Anglo-Saxon England*, p. 234). It should be noted, however, that according to the chronicler Wiglaf *onfeng* the kingdom of the Mercians in 830; the verb is used of archbishops receiving the pallium (e.g. in the annals for 806 and 834), and does not necessarily convey a sense of obtaining by force. Moreover, it is striking that it was Ecgberht who in 830 reduced the Welsh to submission, hardly the action of one whose authority in Mercia had recently been compromised (or was about to be so); and it would assuredly be dangerous to read much of political moment into the fact that West Saxon and Kentish bishops attended a church council convened in Mercia. It is also interesting that there was apparently no new coinage in Mercia in the 830s (see Pagan, 'Coinage in southern England', pp. 47 and 55), and that earlier Mercian issues were complemented in Mercian pockets by West Saxon coins of the 830s (for the most part minted at Rochester and Canterbury); thus, the Middle Temple hoard (Blackburn and Pagan, 'A revised check-list', pp. 294 and 302 (no. 50)), deposited *ca* 842, shows a striking lack of 'Mercian' (London) coinage of the 830s. Regnal years in Wiglaf's charters are calculated from 830–1: S.188, dated 831, in the first year of his 'second reign' (Canterbury diplomatic); S.190, dated 836, in his seventh year (Mercian diplomatic).

15 Keynes, 'The control of Kent', pp. 120–30. The distinctive polity created in the central decades of the ninth century is represented, from a Kentish perspective, by the use in Kentish charters of

(designated 'Greater Wessex' by some modern historians) seems to have been governed at the local level by ealdormen who were the king's appointees in each shire.[16] The fabric or nature of secular authority was arguably rather different in Mercia, where power seems to have resided in the collective body of the ealdormen (who appear to have been leaders of local peoples, as opposed to royal appointees), and where the king was one of their own number set up to rule over themselves, in such a way that no single dynasty was able to establish or maintain control.[17] In short, the 'rise of Wessex' was not a matter of one kingdom passing into the shadow of another, by dint of superior military might; nor was it a matter

royal styles which present Æthelwulf as king 'of the southern peoples' (e.g. S.287, dated 839, and S.291, dated 842), or, more regularly, as king 'of the West Saxons and of the men of Kent' (e.g. S.293, dated 843, and S.316, dated 855).

16 The particular impression formed of the West Saxon polity in the eighth and ninth centuries arises in the first instance from a reading of the law-code of King Ine (cf. Keynes, 'England 700–900', pp. 26–7), and otherwise from analysis of eighth- and ninth-century West Saxon charters. For discussion of the terminology of high office, see Thacker, 'Some terms for noblemen', esp. pp. 211–12 (*prefectus*); see also Keynes, *An Atlas of Attestations*, Tables XII and XXI. The profusion of *prefecti* in late-eighth- and early-ninth-century charters, especially of King Cynewulf (757–86), King Beorhtric (786–802), and King Ecgberht (802–39), is striking. The term *prefectus* appears to have been superseded thereafter by *dux*. The *duces*, or ealdormen, seem in their West Saxon manifestation to have been men placed by kings in control of particular shires, and are thus to be found leading shire levies in the 840s and 850s. It should be noted in this connection that the shires of Wessex may have come into being under different circumstances: Dorset and Somerset, in the west, took their names from the people who lived in proximity to (or were governed from) the royal estates at Dorchester and Somerton; Wiltshire and Hampshire, to the east, denote the territories dependent upon or governed from the royal estates at Wilton and Southampton. See also Brooks, 'The administrative background', pp. 133–4, and Campbell, 'The late Anglo-Saxon state', p. 43, n. 9. It may be significant, furthermore, that thegns (*ministri*) are conspicuous by their presence in ninth-century West Saxon charters, as if the kings encouraged the development of a hierarchy of lesser office-holders.

17 The particular impression formed of the Mercian polity in the eighth and ninth centuries arises in the first instance from a reading of the Tribal Hidage (cf. Keynes, 'England 700–900', pp. 21–5 and 27), and otherwise from analysis of eighth- and ninth-century Mercian charters. For terminology, see Thacker, 'Some terms for noblemen', esp. pp. 204–5 (*princeps*); see also Keynes, *An Atlas of Attestations*, Tables X and XVII. It should be noted, in the first place, that the kingdom of the Mercians was inhabited by a number of ealdormen (generally styled *dux*, a term apparently synonymous with *princeps*), and that the charters give rather little sense of the existence of a body of thegns serving the king. Secondly, those persons who rose to become rulers of the Mercians appear in several cases to have attested the charters of their predecessors, though not with any striking degree of prominence or consistency: this applies to Ceolwulf I (during the reign of Cenwulf), Beornwulf (during the reigns of Cenwulf and Ceolwulf I), Ludeca (during the reign of Beornwulf), Berhtwulf (during the reign of Wiglaf), Burgred (during the reign of Berhtwulf), and Æthelred (during the reign of Burgred); only Wiglaf and Ceolwulf II are nowhere to be seen. Thirdly, in those (very few) cases where a Mercian ealdorman can be identified on the ground, as it were, we find that he was styled the leader of a people: Humberht, distinctively prominent during the reigns of Wiglaf, Berhtwulf and Burgred, was *princeps* of the *Tomsætan* (S.197), and Æthelred (Mucel) was ealdorman 'of the *Gaini*' (below, n. 34). It is true that the impression of a contrast between the structures of secular power in Wessex and in Mercia may in part be no more than a reflection of the fact that we have a chronicle for Wessex, and not for Mercia; it may be more to the point, however, that it is the charters, not the chronicle, which make the difference, and that the draftsmen of charters issued under each political dispensation may have worked from different positions. Perhaps one should add that the shire-system in Mercia is generally considered to have developed rather later than the shire-system in Wessex: see Stenton, *Anglo-Saxon England*, pp. 336–8; and Taylor, 'The origin of the Mercian shires'. Cf. Campbell, 'The late

of the emergent political order inheriting anything from the order which it displaced. Rather, a predatory power which had enjoyed its time of glory began to turn in on itself, and was presently eclipsed by a more structured form of political order with a stronger base, a different agenda, and what the prescient might see as a brighter future.

Relations between Wessex and Mercia in the central decades of the ninth century were certainly close, and apparently friendly. It is interesting, for example, that King Æthelwulf seems to have supplied technical assistance to King Berhtwulf in the mid-840s, in connection with Berhtwulf's attempt to revive the Mercian coinage after its (intriguing) interruption during Wiglaf's (second) reign: for it was presumably with official sanction that Æthelwulf's die-cutter in Rochester supplied dies to Berhtwulf's moneyers in London, and there also appears to have been some movement of moneyers between London and the Kentish mints under Æthelwulf's control.[18] It was during the 840s, moreover, that the land in the upper Thames valley which had long been disputed between Mercia and Wessex seems finally to have passed into West Saxon hands: a charter dated 844 and preserved in the Abingdon archives records that Ceolred, bishop of Leicester, gave 14 hides at Pangbourne in Berkshire to King Berhtwulf, and that Berhtwulf then gave the same land to Ealdorman Æthelwulf;[19] but by the end of the decade at least some part of the region was under West Saxon control, for Wantage was a West Saxon royal estate when Alfred was born there in 849,[20] and it transpires that Ealdorman Æthelwulf moved over to the West Saxon court at about the same time.[21] Nor should one overlook the charter by which Berhtwulf granted privileges to the minster at Breedon-on-the-Hill, Leicestershire, in 848: the community was freed from certain obligations, but not from the need to provide sustinence and accommodation for any ambassadors coming to the king from overseas, or for messengers from the West Saxons or Northumbrians.[22]

Anglo-Saxon state', p. 53: 'In the mid-ninth century Wessex certainly and Mercia probably had an ealdorman for each shire.'

18 See Booth, above, pp. 68–74; see also Blackburn, in *MEC*, pp. 292–3, and Pagan, 'Coinage in southern England', pp. 55–6. S.95 (trans. *EHD*, no. 66) is King Berhtwulf's confirmation, *ca* 844–5, of certain rights which the bishop of Rochester enjoyed in London.

19 S.1271 (trans. *EHD*, no. 87), marked on the map (Fig. 1). For discussion of the charter, see Stenton, *The Early History of the Abbey of Abingdon*, pp. 25–7, and *Anglo-Saxon England*, pp. 234–5; an interesting spin is applied by Wormald, 'The ninth century', p. 141.

20 Asser, § 1. Cf. Smyth, *King Alfred the Great*, pp. 3–9, and Keynes, 'On the authenticity of Asser's *Life of King Alfred*', pp. 535–6. Perhaps one should add that under the conditions which prevailed in the 840s, it is not inconceivable that Alfred's mother Osburh, herself of 'Jutish' extraction (Asser, § 2), should have been visiting a 'Mercian' royal estate at the critical moment in 849.

21 Ealdorman Æthelwulf attested Mercian charters in the early 840s (to *ca* 845), but seems thereafter to vanish from sight, until his reappearance in West Saxons charters in the late 850s and 860s; see Keynes, *An Atlas of Attestations*, Tables XVII and XXI. Ealdorman Æthelwulf died in 871, and his body was secretly taken to Derby (*The Chronicle of Æthelweard*, ed. Campbell, p. 37). A unique penny combining obverses of King Berhtwulf and King Æthelwulf was formerly regarded as a special issue struck to commemorate the transfer of Berkshire from Mercia to Wessex (Stenton, *Anglo-Saxon England*, p. 245, n. 1; cf. Dolley and Skaare, 'The coinage of Æthelwulf', p. 71); but the coin is now more plausibly regarded as an aberration (see Blackburn, in *MEC*, pp. 292–3, and Pagan, 'Coinage in southern England', p. 56).

22 S.197 (from Peterborough); see Hart, *The Early Charters of Northern England*, no. 34 (pp. 68–9), and Keynes, *Councils of Clofesho*, pp. 39–40.

None of this necessarily amounts to political alliance, but one could not think of a better phrase to describe the situation in the 850s and 860s. The chronicler records that in 853 'Burgred, king of the Mercians, and his council asked King Æthelwulf to help him bring the Welsh under subjection to him', and that Æthelwulf duly obliged. One might choose to believe that the natural sympathies of the chronicler have caused him to represent the Mercians as the weaker party, but whatever the exact basis on which the two kings collaborated, their relationship was consolidated in the same year by Burgred's marriage to King Æthelwulf's daughter Æthelswith, in a ceremony conducted at the West Saxon royal estate at Chippenham in Wiltshire.[23] These were also momentous times in Æthelwulf's kingdom 'of the southern peoples'. His eldest son Æthelstan, who had acted as king of Kent and the other south-eastern provinces throughout the 840s, fought against a Viking fleet in 851 (or thereabouts) – and then disappears from sight. This must have forced a change of intentions on the part of King Æthelwulf, matched by new arrangements within the royal family. The two eldest surviving sons, Æthelbald and Æthelberht, were accorded high office as ealdormen. The two younger sons, Æthelred and Alfred, also began to take a visible (if not at this stage much more than symbolic) place in public affairs: they were apparently despatched as a pair to Rome in 853 (though only Alfred reached the ultimate destination), perhaps because their father thought the experience would stand them both in good stead, and they attested the decimation charters of 854 in their own right. King Æthelwulf went to Rome in 855, though not before installing his son Æthelberht as king of Kent. During Æthelwulf's absence overseas, Æthelbald seems to have set himself up as king of the West Saxons; and on his return in 856, Æthelwulf was obliged to resume power in the 'eastern' part of his kingdom (apparently with reference to Kent and the other south-eastern provinces), leaving Æthelbald in control of the western districts. Æthelwulf made a formal arrangement at about the same time, whereby the bipartite kingdom would be divided after his death between his elder sons Æthelbald (in the west) and Æthelberht (in the east), with his younger sons Æthelred and Alfred expected to follow Æthelbald in the west. Æthelwulf's death in 858 put the plan into operation perhaps sooner than intended; and by marrying his step-mother (Judith), Æthelbald may have sought to strengthen his own hand. The early death of Æthelbald (in 860) benefitted Æthelberht, who re-united the kingdom though sometimes allowed Æthelred to act as king in Wessex; the early death of Æthelberht (865) benefitted Æthelred, who retained both parts of the kingdom and recognised Alfred as his prospective successor; and the early death of Æthelred (871) left Alfred in charge, and his nephews perhaps sorely disappointed.[24]

Links between the kingdoms of Mercia and Wessex had grown only stronger

23 Asser, § 9. S.206 (from Worcester; trans. *EHD*, no. 90) is a charter of Burgred, dated 855, granting lands on both sides of the Gloucestershire–Wiltshire border to the bishop of Worcester, as marked on the map (Fig. 1). S.210 (from Worcester) is a charter of Burgred and Queen Æthelswith, dated 864 and issued at Bath, on the border between Mercia and Wessex (see Keynes, 'King Athelstan's books', p. 161, n. 95), granting land at Eaton, Oxon, to the bishop of Worcester; Eaton is also marked on the map.

24 Keynes and Lapidge, *Alfred the Great*, pp. 14–16 and 314–16, with references. For the possibility that Æthelred, as well as Alfred, went to Rome in 853, see Keynes, 'Anglo-Saxon entries in the "Liber Vitae" of Brescia', esp. pp. 112–13.

in the 860s, and found expression in various ways. Some time between 852 and 874 King Burgred granted land at Binegar, near Wells in Somerset, to a certain Eanulf, probably to be identified as Eanwulf, ealdorman of Somerset (d. 867). The charter recording this transactions does not survive; but if we may assume that it was genuine, it is interesting not only that Burgred was empowered to make a grant of land in what one would expect to have been part of the kingdom of Wessex, but also that the beneficiary should seem to be a prominent West Saxon layman.[25] Another point of interest emerges from an examination of episcopal attestations to Mercian and West Saxon charters. Bishops of London had regularly attested those charters in the first half of the ninth century which were issued at councils of the southern English church, but in the second half of the century, when such councils seem no longer to have been held, they vanish almost completely from view; they never attest charters of the Mercian kings, and in fact the only appearances of a bishop of London are in a charter of Æthelberht, king of the West Saxons, issued in 860, and in a charter of Æthelred, king of the West Saxons, issued in 867.[26] Quite what to make of this is uncertain, but it looks as if the bishop of London, though he must technically have owed his political allegiance to the king of the Mercians, was already in the 860s tending to look towards the king of the West Saxons.[27] Numismatic evidence adds a further dimension to this picture of a political alliance (represented by the interdynastic marriage) and of the arguably ambiguous position of London (represented by the bishop's appearance in West Saxon charters).[28] Very few coins seem to have been minted in the name of the Mercian king in the 850s, probably a consequence of the Viking descent on London in 851; so presumably Burgred's Mercians initially made do with the coins issued in the names of earlier Mercian kings, perhaps with some West Saxon coinage mixed in. The London mint seems

25 The charter (S.1701) was preserved in the (lost) *Liber Terrarum* of Glastonbury Abbey (LT no. 93); see Keynes, 'The control of Kent', p. 128, and Abrams, *Anglo-Saxon Glastonbury*, pp. 58–9, 109–10, and 335–7. The place, Binegar, is marked on the map (Fig. 1). For Ealdorman Eanwulf, see Keynes, 'The Fonthill letter', p. 56, n. 19. King Burgred also gave land at Lydney, in Gloucestershire, to a certain Æthelred (S.1702: LT no. 87), who has been identified as Æthelred I, king of Wessex (865–71), or as the Æthelred who later became ealdorman of the Mercians; see Abrams, *Anglo-Saxon Glastonbury*, pp. 164–5, and below, n. 82. Lydney is marked on the map (Fig. 1).

26 S.327 (a grant of land in Rochester to the bishop of Rochester) and S.337 (a grant of land at Navestock, Essex, to St Paul's, London), marked on the map (Fig. 1). Seen in a wider context (Keynes, *Atlas of Attestations*, Tables XIV and XIX), these two charters appear to have emanated from special kinds of assembly, attended by a wider range of ecclesiastics and laymen than was usual; for further discussion, see Keynes, 'The control of Kent', pp. 128–30.

27 While London itself had remained under Mercian control, a substantial part of the diocese of London (comprising the former kingdom of the East Saxons) had fallen under West Saxon control in the second quarter of the ninth century. It is the case, therefore (as Pamela Taylor reminds me), that the bishop would have found himself serving two political masters. What is so striking is that the bishop seems so rarely to have set foot in the Mercian camp, and attended the 'West Saxon' court on special occasions. One should add that the archbishops of Canterbury, although technically owing political allegiance to the kings of Wessex, occasionally attested Mercian charters in 840s, 850s and 860s; cf. Keynes, 'The control of Kent', pp. 123–4 and 127–8. On the 'Kentish', as opposed to 'Anglian' or 'West Saxon' features of the dialect of the moneyers' names at London, see Bibire, above, pp. 159–61.

28 For surveys of the numismatic evidence, see Pagan, 'Coinage in the age of Burgred', esp. pp. 12–14; Lyon, 'Historical problems (2)', pp. 229–34; Blackburn, in *MEC*, pp. 310–12; and Pagan, 'Coinage in Southern England', pp. 57–62.

to have been active again on Burgred's behalf from about 860 onwards, producing the *Lunettes* coinage in increasing quantity and decreasing quality as the decade wore on; and whereas the West Saxon coins of King Æthelberht minted at Canterbury in the early 860s were of different design, the bulk of coins of King Æthelred minted at Canterbury in the later 860s were of the same *Lunettes* type, creating what has been called 'a single uniform coinage for both Wessex and Mercia'.[29] It is possible, moreover, that some of Burgred's London moneyers minted the odd *Lunettes* penny in the name of King Æthelberht and of King Æthelred,[30] and if these coins are indeed official products their production would seem to reflect much the same development as the bishop of London's attestation of West Saxon charters; in other words, there were West Saxon interests in London, and London interests in the kings of Wessex, a good deal earlier than one might have expected.[31] One should add that hoards deposited in different parts of Wessex during the 850s and 860s show an admixture of Mercian, archiepiscopal, East Anglian and West Saxon pence, and that single finds of Mercian and West Saxon pence are widely distributed;[32] it may well be, therefore, that in certain respects the two kingdoms formed part of a 'single economic unit'.[33]

In 868 the alliance between Wessex and Mercia found further expression. In that year Alfred, younger brother of King Æthelred of Wessex, married Ealhswith, daughter of Æthelred (Mucil), ealdorman of the *Gaini*,[34] of Mercian royal stock on her mother Eadburh's side, and sister of one Æthelwulf who can perhaps be identified as the ealdorman (*dux or princeps*) of that name holding land in

29 Blackburn, in *MEC*, p. 311. For the suggestion that it was the king who benefitted from the debasement of the coinage, see Metcalf and Northover, 'Debasement of the coinage in southern England', esp. pp. 151 and 169.

30 See Lyon, 'Historical problems (2)', pp. 233–4, and Blackburn, in *MEC*, p. 311. Pagan, on the other hand, regards the coins in question as 'unofficial' issues ('Coinage in the age of Burgred', pp. 15–16; 'Coinage in southern England', p. 62; and Biddle, *et al.*, 'Coins of the Anglo-Saxon period from Repton', pp. 116–19).

31 Men with interests in London may have had dealings with the rulers of both Wessex and Mercia. The Ceolmund, 'prefect', to whom King Æthelwulf of Wessex granted land at Rochester in 842 (S.291) was perhaps the Ceolmund, 'prefect', who for 60 shillings sold a 'profitable little estate' in London, which had formerly belonged to the king of Mercia, to the bishop of Worcester, confirmed by a charter of King Burgred dated 857 (S.208 (trans. *EHD*, no. 92)).

32 For the hoards, see Blackburn and Pagan, 'A revised check-list of coin hoards', p. 294, esp. nos 54 (Sevington, Wilts.), 57 (Croydon (Old Palace), Surrey), 58 (Dorking, Surrey) and 59 (Trewhiddle, Cornwall); see also Pagan, 'Coinage in southern England', pp. 58–9. For single finds, see Bonser, 'Single finds', below, pp. 199–240.

33 Stenton, 'The Anglo-Saxon coinage and the historian', p. 374. The hoard of *Lunettes* pennies of Burgred, Æthelred and Alfred, found at Duddington, Northants, in December 1994, affords a good illustration of the coinage which circulated in the 870s.

34 Attestations of ealdormen called Mucel (Mucil) are found in ninth-century Mercian charters from 814 to 866 (Keynes, *An Atlas of Attestations*, Table XVII); there were at least two ealdormen of that name in the 830s and 840s, and it is difficult to tell them apart. A first Mucel, probably the son of Esne (cf. S.190), was perhaps active from the 810s to the late 840s. A second Mucel was perhaps active from the mid-830s to the late 860s, and may well be Æthelred Mucil of the *Gaini*. The Ealdorman Mucel who was present at meetings of the West Saxon court in 867 (S.337), 868 (S.1201, 340), and in the 870s (S.343), was conceivably King Alfred's father-in-law; but of course it is possible that these attestations relate to a West Saxon ealdorman of the same name. For further discussion, see Keynes and Lapidge, *Alfred the Great*, p. 240, n. 57, and Smyth, *Alfred the Great*, pp. 24–8.

Gloucestershire, in the mid-850s, and who may have taken a special interest in the affairs of Winchcombe abbey.[35] There appears to have been an understanding by this stage that Alfred would succeed his elder brother as king, and one has to suppose, therefore, that the marriage was of some political significance. It is striking, of course, that the nuptials were not mentioned in the *Anglo-Saxon Chronicle*; so it may be that the feelings engendered by the poisoning of King Beorhtric had persisted in certain quarters, and that there were people at court in the late ninth century who could not bring themselves to approve of their king's Mercian wife. Asser, on the other hand, gives the marriage great prominence, informing us that it took place amid all due ceremony and feasting in Mercia;[36] and one senses from Asser's obvious contempt for the custom which constrained the king from calling her his queen that the king himself might have shared the same opinion. The king later bequeathed to Ealhswith a group of three royal estates, at Lambourne and at Wantage, in Berkshire, and at Edington, in Wiltshire; she was instrumental in the foundation of the Nunnaminster, at Winchester; and after her death, on 5 December 902, she was commemorated in what seem to be most telling and appropriate terms, as 'Ealhswith, the true and beloved Lady of the English' (*uera domina Anglorum Ealhswythe cara*).[37]

A charter issued in 868, whether at the time of the marriage or on a subsequent occasion in the same year, affords another view of the close relationship which now existed between the Mercian and West Saxon ruling families. It is a grant by Burgred's (West Saxon) queen Æthelswith of an estate at Lockinge, near Wantage in Berkshire, to a certain thegn called Cuthwulf, attested by King Æthelred of Wessex, his brother Alfred, a group of West Saxon laymen, and by Burgred of Mercia and Æthelswith herself.[38] It should perhaps occasion no surprise that Æthelswith retained her power to make such a grant in her native Wessex, but if the grant was made on the occasion of Alfred's marriage, it is interesting that such a transaction should have been conducted from somewhere in Mercia. Also in 868, King Burgred and his councillors asked King Æthelred and the ætheling Alfred for military assistance against the Viking army which had taken up winter quarters in Nottingham; and whereas the chronicler plays it fairly straight, Asser

35 In 855 Alhwine, bishop of Worcester, leased land at Cutsdean in Gloucestershire (near Winchcombe) to Ealdorman Æthelwulf and his wife Wulfthryth (S.1273), as agreed by his oath on a gospel-book. Æthelwulf was described as a *uenerabilis dux* in 897 (S.1442), in the context of his dealings with Winchcombe; see further below, n. 130. He died in 901 (ASC). See also Hart, 'Athelstan "Half-King" ', p. 116, n. 1, and Keynes and Lapidge, *Alfred the Great*, p. 241, n. 58.

36 Asser, §§ 29 and 73–4. Asser's treatment of Ealhswith is discussed by Nelson, 'Reconstructing a royal family', pp. 65–6.

37 For the bequests in the king's will, see Keynes and Lapidge, *Alfred the Great*, pp. 177 and 323; and for a reference to Ealhswith's role in the foundation of the Nunnaminster, see *The Liber Vitae of the New Minster*, ed. Keynes, p. 81. For the commemoration of Ealhswith, in the context of a metrical calendar which originated in the early tenth century (a copy of which is incorporated in the 'Æthelstan Psalter'), see McGurk, 'The metrical calendar', p. 110; see also Dumville, 'The Anglo-Saxon Chronicle and the origins of English Square Minuscule script', pp. 74–7 and 105–6, and Keynes, 'Anglo-Saxon entries in the *Liber Vitae* of Brescia', p. 119.

38 S.1201 (from Abingdon), marked on the map (Fig. 1). The predominately West Saxon complexion of the witness-list is established by comparison with S.340 (from the Old Minster, Winchester), by which King Æthelred, in a meeting at Dorchester in 868, gave land in Hampshire to his thegn Hunsige.

elaborates by representing the Mercian request as a humble appeal for help, and by representing West Saxon aid as nothing short of magnificent.[39] Burgred was, of course, appealing to his two brothers-in-law, and they presumably responded in a spirit of friendly co-operation.[40]

Alfred and Burgred, 871–874

At the time of his accession in 871, King Alfred was already closely associated with the Mercian regime. In personal terms, his sister was queen at the Mercian court,[41] and he had a Mercian wife; and through his wife he would have had links with the Mercian nobility of which he would have been conscious at all times. In political terms, he inherited what can only be termed an alliance with the reigning Mercian king, in which Wessex was the stronger partner, and which had recently involved the West Saxons in the rendering of military assistance to the Mercians, against the common enemy. And in economic terms, he inherited a situation in which the coinages of Wessex and Mercia were all but identical in design, and in which coins of both Mercian and West Saxon rulers seem to have circulated side by side; moreover, London moneyers of Burgred may have struck a few coins in the name of the West Saxon king. The king of Wessex would thus seem already to have had interests in London, and it would also appear that the bishop of London was in some sense looking more towards him than to the Mercian king. The position in the opening years of Alfred's reign was thus just a continuation of the position established in the later 860s, which had itself grown out of a longer process of accommodation between the two kingdoms: barely any charters of Burgred or Alfred survive from the early 870s, but seen in numismatic terms, Burgred's moneyers were producing increasingly debased (and even diminutive) *Lunettes* coins from London, a small proportion of which were struck in the name of King Alfred,[42] and these 'Mercian' coins were matched by a similarly debased and diminutive series of *Lunettes* coins struck by King Alfred's moneyers in Canterbury.[43]

39 Asser, § 30.

40 A charter of King Æthelred, issued *c.* 868, is attested by 'Beorhtferd filius regis' (S.539). It is unlikely that this was a son of Æthelred himself, and one wonders, therefore, whether this Berhtferth was a Mercian ætheling on a visit to the West Saxon court, perhaps even a son of Burgred and Æthelswith; see Keynes, 'The West Saxon charters', pp. 1130–1. For the Mercian 'B-dynasty' of the ninth century, see Wormald, 'The ninth century', p. 138; see also above, p. 2, n. 6, and below, p. 39, n. 168.

41 Æthelswith presumably accompanied her husband Burgred to Rome in 874 (*Anglo-Saxon Chronicle, s.a.* 874; see also Asser, § 46, and Keynes, 'Anglo-Saxon entries in the *Liber Vitae* of Brescia'); she is said to have died in 888, and was buried in Pavia (*Anglo-Saxon Chronicle, s.a.* 888).

42 See Lyon, 'Historical problems (2)', pp. 233–4, and Blackburn, in *MEC*, p. 311; Pagan seems prepared to accept some of the London *Lunettes* coins struck in Alfred's name as official issues ('Coinage in the Age of Burgred', pp. 15–16, and 'Coinage in southern England', pp. 62–3). For the possibility that *Lunettes* coins continued to be struck in Alfred's name for a while after Burgred's deposition in 874, see below, p. 15.

43 Blackburn, in *MEC*, p. 311.

Alfred and Ceolwulf, 874–ca 880

In 874 Burgred of Mercia was deposed by the Vikings, and was replaced by their appointee Ceolwulf, described by the Alfredian chronicler as a 'foolish king's thegn'. It is pertinent to ask whether what we blithely call 'Mercia' was necessarily a coherent and stable kingdom, and whether, therefore, the appointment of a new king under such circumstances would immediately have been registered and recognised throughout the regions which had formerly given their political allegiance to Burgred. It is also important to bear in mind that a moneyer who struck a coin in the name of a particular king was not necessarily making a statement about his own political affiliation, and might simply have been serving someone else's commercial interests in the place where he worked. Strange things, therefore, may have happened in London in the wake of Burgred's fall: if some London moneyers were already accustomed to minting a few coins in the name of the West Saxon king, they might have continued to do so on much the same basis until such time as the situation in western Mercia, and Ceolwulf's position, became clear; and it is not inconceivable that for a time at least they might have regarded Alfred himself as their king.

Before considering the numismatic evidence which bears on these and related matters, it is necessary to review the evidence of charters and other written sources. It is well known that for all his appearance of being a puppet ruler nominated by the Vikings, Ceolwulf was nevertheless a king taken seriously by his English contemporaries, Mercian and West Saxon alike.[44] Two charters survive which serve to demonstrate the point. In one, dated 875, Ceolwulf grants exemptions from certain royal rights to the whole diocese of Worcester, and receives (in return for a payment of gold) the lease of an estate at Daylesford in Gloucestershire, for himself and three heirs, with reversion to Worcester; the charter is attested by the bishops of Lichfield, Worcester and Hereford, and by two Mercian ealdormen.[45] In the other, also dated 875, Ceolwulf grants certain estates in Worcestershire to the community of St Mary's, Worcester, again attested by Mercian bishops and laymen.[46] Another charter alludes to Ceolwulf's purchase of land at Water Eaton in Oxfordshire from the bishop of Worcester, and his grant of it to a certain Hungith, and so reveals that Ceolwulf had interests further afield.[47] In 877, however, the Vikings came to Gloucester and proceeded to divide Mercia between Ceolwulf and themselves. There can be little doubt that the western part of the kingdom remained under Ceolwulf's control, not least because the Mercian regnal list preserved in a manuscript from Worcester assigns him a reign of five years, which might be taken to imply that his authority was recognised in Worcester until about 879;[48] but it has usually been assumed that

44 See Stenton, 'Anglo-Saxon coinage and the historian', pp. 372–3, and *Anglo-Saxon England*, p. 252, n. 1.

45 S.215 (trans. *EHD*, no. 95), marked on the map (Fig. 1).

46 S.216, marked on the map (Fig. 1). The reference to the community of St Mary's indicates that the text is spurious in its transmitted form; but it would appear none the less to reflect the existence, in the Worcester archive, of an authentic charter of King Ceolwulf other than S.215.

47 S.361, marked on the map (Fig. 1).

48 London, British Library, MS Cotton Tiberius A. xiii, fo. 114v; printed in *Hemingi Chartularium*, ed. Hearne, I.242. According to the *Annales Cambriae*, Rhodri Mawr was killed by the English

London fell outside his share, and remained under Viking occupation until Alfred recovered the town from them by force in 886.[49] Certainly, the West Saxon chronicler describes how Alfred 'occupied' (*gesette*) London in 886, apparently with the implication that he was not previously in control of the town.[50] Moreover, the reference in annal '883' (in certain manuscripts) to an occasion when the English besieged the Vikings at London might be taken to indicate that the Vikings had been established there in some force; the fact that a Viking army wintered at Fulham, on the Thames, in 878–879, would perhaps be easier to understand if London itself were at the time in Viking hands; and it might be thought that the absence of the bishop of London from the two extant charters of Ceolwulf points in the same direction.[51] Yet this evidence and these considerations fall a long way short of establishing beyond doubt that London was under Viking control from 877 to 886, and one could not exclude the possibility that English authority continued to be maintained and recognised there during that period: the settlements of the Vikings in Mercia appear to have been concentrated more in the east midlands,[52] and, as we shall see, the written sources which seemed to put them in occupation of London between 877 and 886 are capable of a different interpretation, which would leave London for the greater part of that period under English control.[53] What became of Ceolwulf himself after 879 is far from clear. It may be significant that his apparent demise seems to coincide with the presence of Guthrum at Cirencester in 878–879; perhaps Guthrum's presence served as the catalyst which led to Ceolwulf's removal from office, and perhaps

('a Saxonibus') in 878 (*AC, s.a.* 877); an Englishman might have been disposed to assign the credit to King Ceolwulf. The same annals indicate that the Welsh got their revenge at the mouth of the Conway in 881 (*AC, s.a.* 880); perhaps it was Ceolwulf who was defeated on this occasion (in which case the regnal list might have underestimated the length of his reign), but for a late tradition to the effect that it was Ealdorman Æthelred, see below, n. 84.

49 See, for example, Stenton, *Anglo-Saxon England*, pp. 254–5 and 258–9, and Loyn, *The Vikings in Britain*, p. 43 (p. 59). This was also the view taken by the late Professor Whitelock in her (unpublished) biography of King Alfred, ch. 5, and it is implicit in the conventional dating of Alfred's treaty with Guthrum between 886 and 890 (on which see further below, pp. 31–4). See also Dyson, 'King Alfred and the restoration of London', pp. 100–101: 'On the other hand, the written notices for 886 make it plain that Alfred had not previously been in occupation of the town in any sense. . . . The conclusion is inescapable that its "occupation" essentially involved the replacement of a Danish presence by an English one.' For allusions to these events in more general accounts of the period, see Wormald, 'The ninth century', pp. 132 and 155; Stafford, *The East Midlands*, pp. 109–12; Yorke, *Kings and Kingdoms*, pp. 123 and 151; Kirby, *The Earliest English Kings*, pp. 214–18; Yorke, *Wessex in the Early Middle Ages*, pp. 110–11; and John, *Reassessing Anglo-Saxon England*, pp. 75–6.

50 Note, however, that in 878 the Vikings conquered (*geridon*) the land of the West Saxons before they settled (*gesæton*) there and drove (*adræfdon*) a great part of the people across the sea. Asser (§ 83) understood the chronicler to mean that in 886 Alfred 'restored the city of London splendidly . . . and made it habitable again' – *Lundoniam civitatem honorifice restauravit et habitabilem fecit* (ed. Stevenson, p. 69; trans. Keynes and Lapidge, pp. 97–8). See further below, pp. 21–4.

51 This last point is, however, beside the point; see above, p. 8.

52 For the possibility that Rutland remained under English control, see Keynes and Lapidge, *Alfred the Great*, p. 337, n. 36, and Cox, 'Rutland'. See also Hall, 'The Five Boroughs of the Danelaw', esp. pp. 150–2.

53 See below, pp. 21–4.

Ceolwulf returned to his former station or sought support elsewhere (if, indeed, he had not simply died).[54]

Whatever the case, it must always have been clear that any deeper understanding of Ceolwulf's position would have to proceed from analysis of his coinage, in relation to the contemporary coinages of King Alfred and Archbishop Æthelred; and in particular from a study of those types which Ceolwulf is known to have shared (in some sense) with Alfred himself, namely *Two Emperors* and *Cross-and-Lozenge* (the latter also known as *BMC* type V, or as the 'Ceolwulf' type). If the conventional reading of the written sources laid stress on Alfred's 'recovery' of London in 886, with the implication that the town had previously been under Viking control, numismatists have long suspected that the truth may not have been that simple. Thus Dolley and Blunt, in their preliminary study of Alfred's coinage (published in 1961), put forward the view that London was 'a species of "open city" ' in the years before 886, because they considered it likely that coins of what they called the 'Ceolwulf' type were minted there for both kings in the later 870s;[55] they also drew attention to the extraordinary fact that on certain coins of the 'Ceolwulf' type Alfred is styled 'rex A(nglorum)' or 'rex S(axonum et) M(erciorum)'.[56] The point was taken and developed by Pagan, who in a note appended to his study of Burgred's coinage (published in 1964) cited *BMC* type V as evidence that the London mint remained active on behalf of Ceolwulf and Alfred throughout the later 870s and 'right up to 886'.[57] But conventional historical wisdom, articulated above all by Sir Frank Stenton, proved too powerful an impediment to such uninhibited interpretations of the numismatic evidence. Stewart Lyon, for example, expressed his feeling (in 1968) that London 'could not have contained a major mint whether for Ceolwulf or Alfred before Alfred's occupation of the town in 886';[58] while Marion Archibald regarded the location of Ceolwulf's mint as 'uncertain', and seemed inclined to associate Alfred's coins of *BMC* type V with Canterbury (and possibly Rochester).[59] Historians, for their part, had reason to be a bit confused, and in the absence of any definitive

54 It is possible that Ceolwulf moved eastwards to London, and that the regnal list simply represents his rule as seen from Worcester; but it would be better practice to take the regnal list at face value, as evidence that Ceolwulf's activities did not extend beyond *ca* 879.

55 Dolley and Blunt, 'The chronology of the coins of Ælfred the Great', pp. 80–1; but in their chronological table, p. 95, they seemed to imply that Alfred's coins of the 'Ceolwulf' type were struck at a mint on or south of the Thames, and that Alfred did not start using the London mint until 886. See also Dolley, 'An unpublished hoard-provenance for a penny of Ceolwulf II', pp. 89–90 (published in 1963, and reiterating the case for London).

56 Dolley and Blunt, 'The chronology of the coins of Ælfred the Great', p. 80 (with all due hesitation about the expansion of the legends). The only coin which could be read as 'rex A' is Guthhere's, from the Canterbury mint (below, p. 136, no. 13); but the 'A' seems more likely to belong at the beginning of Alfred's name. For the coins apparently reading 'rex SM', see below, p. 18.

57 Pagan, 'Coinage in the age of Burgred', pp. 26–7; see also Pagan, 'An unpublished fragment of a coin of Ceolwulf II', pp. 14–15, and 'Coinage in southern England', p. 63, n. 33.

58 Lyon, 'Historical problems (2)', p. 237, citing Stenton (and proposing '*Cross-and-Lozenge*' as a better term for *BMC* Type V). Blackburn (in *MEC*, p. 312) similarly doubted that an official coinage could have been struck at London in Alfred's name while the town was under Viking control.

59 Archibald, 'An Alfred penny from Rochester'.

study of Alfred's coinage they equally had no particular cause to question their own assumptions.[60]

Yet this must be a case where the most natural interpretation of the numismatic evidence should be allowed to modify the received reading of the written sources. Understanding of the coinage in the mid-870s is hampered by the lack of hoards from the later 870s and early 880s, for the various types which appear to be in question survive in pitifully small quantity. There is, however, enough to show that the position in numismatic terms was far from straightforward, and that the position, in historical terms, may have been correspondingly confused. Alfred's moneyers were apparently still striking *Lunettes* coins for a while after Burgred's deposition in 874, but there are no surviving specimens in Ceolwulf's name (or, for that matter, in the name of Archbishop Æthelred, who was appointed in 870), and the likelihood is that the type was soon discontinued;[61] there are indications, however, that among Alfred's post-Burgred *Lunettes* coins there were some minted at London, and it is possible, therefore, that Alfred's authority was recognised there at least in the immediate aftermath of Burgred's departure for Rome.[62] The *Portrait-Quatrefoil* type (also known as the *Archbishop Æthelred* type), represented by two specimens minted in the name Archbishop Æthelred (nos 2–3 in the corpus assembled elsewhere in this volume) and by one minted in the name of King Alfred (no. 4), appears to have followed the *Lunettes* type at Canterbury, though it is (at present) unknown for Ceolwulf;[63] while the *Geometric-Quatrefoil* type, known only from a unique specimen in Alfred's name and also presumed to date from this period (no. 1), was minted, interestingly enough, by a moneyer who had previously worked for Burgred.[64] Mention should also be made of a fragment of a coin apparently of Ceolwulf (no. 8), considered to be 'early' but from a mint which may be thought to defy identification.[65]

60 Hence, it must be admitted, the position adopted in Keynes and Lapidge, *Alfred the Great*, pp. 20 and 266.

61 For Alfred's *Lunettes* type, see Dolley and Blunt, 'The chronology of the coins of Ælfred the Great', pp. 78–80; Lyon, 'Historical problems (2)', p. 234; Blackburn, in *MEC*, pp. 311–12; and Pagan, 'Coinage in southern England', pp. 62–3.

62 It should be borne in mind, of course, that London monyers had also struck some *Lunettes* coins in the names of Alfred's predecessors Æthelberht and Æthelred; see above, p. 9 and n. 30.

63 For the *Portrait-Quatrefoil* type, see Blackburn and Keynes, 'A corpus of the *Cross-and-Lozenge* and related coinages', below, pp. 130–1; see also Dolley and Blunt, 'The chronology of the coins of Ælfred the Great', p. 82; Blunt, 'The coinage of Æthelred, archbishop of Canterbury'; Lyon, 'Historical problems (2)', pp. 236–7; and Blackburn, in *MEC*, p. 313.

64 For the *Geometic-Quatrefoil* type, see Blackburn and Keynes, 'A corpus of the *Cross-and-Lozenge* and related coinages', below, pp. 129–30; see also Dolley and Blunt, 'The chronology of the coins of Ælfred the Great', p. 84, and Blackburn, in *MEC*, p. 313. The coin was minted by Luda, a London moneyer of Burgred in the *Lunettes* type. A man called Luda attests a charter of Ealdorman Æthelred, dated 883 (S.218); but the context suggests that this Luda was a member of the community of Berkeley abbey.

65 See Blackburn and Keynes, 'A corpus of the *Cross-and-Lozenge* and related coinages', below, p. 133, and Pagan, 'An unpublished fragment of a coin of Ceolwulf II'. The early date of the fragment is suggested by the fact that the portrait is in an inner circle (as in *Lunettes*); and the reverse inscription is read in such a way as to include the word '(Lin)co(lla)', for Lincoln. It would be hazardous to stake too much, however, on what is, after all, no more than a quarter of a coin. See also Blackburn, in *MEC*, p. 313.

Still more remarkable is the *Two Emperors* type, of which only two specimens survive (one in the name of each king). The coin of Alfred (no. 5) appears to be the product of the London mint, and that of Ceolwulf (no. 6) may be so too, although a West Mercian origin is also possible; both are thought to belong somewhere between the main series of *Lunettes* and *Cross-and-Lozenge* pennies (perhaps *ca* 875).[66] It has not escaped attention that on Alfred's coin, the king is styled 'rex Anglo(rum)', for 'king of the English', whereas on Ceolwulf's coin the king is 'rex', pure and simple. It would seem to follow that Alfred was recognised, at some time before Ceolwulf's demise and even in Mercia (or at least in London), as the one of the two kings who had superior authority. It might, on the other hand, be wiser to resist altogether the temptation to invest *Two Emperors* with great political significance: the 'Two Emperors' design on the reverse is copied from 'a fairly common Roman *solidus* of a type often found in this country',[67] the significance of which may not have been obvious to an Englishman; its particular rarity could be explained in terms of its being an aborted as opposed to a special issue; and since the dies for the two surviving coins were cut by different hands, the apparent difference in the standing of the two kings could be attributed to the die-cutters' individual preferences, or to nothing more than the fact that Alfred had the shorter name, allowing space for a longer style; moreover, it should be noted that the (?)*Two Emperors* obverse muled with a *Cross-and-Lozenge* reverse (no. 7), found at Southampton, appears to read '(E)lferd rex S(ax)'.[68] Of course the situation would be quite different if *Two Emperors* were to be regarded as a minor type first issued during the currency of *Cross-and-Lozenge*, and if Alfred's coin could be seen as later than, not strictly contemporary with, Ceolwulf's; for then the historian could overcome his inhibitions, and seize on the coin as an indication of Alfred's assumption of power after Ceolwulf's demise.[69] But all that is a heavy burden for one coin to bear, and perhaps on reflection what Stenton called 'the mystery of the two emperors'[70] should be allowed to remain just that, wrapping its riddle inside an enigma.

The small corpus of *Cross-and-Lozenge* pennies (comprising eleven specimens of Ceolwulf, about thirty-eight of Alfred, and four of Archbishop Æthelred) constitutes a body of evidence whose importance is out of all proportion to its

66 The 'early' dating of the *Two Emperors* type depends partly on the observation that the obverse portrait, within an inner circle, associates it typologically with the *Lunettes* series, and partly on the fact that both of the two moneyers in question (Cenred for Alfred, and Ealdulf for Ceolwulf) are known for Burgred's *Lunettes*, whereas only the latter is known in *Cross-and-Lozenge* (for Alfred); see Pagan, 'Coinage in the age of Burgred', p. 14, Lyon, 'Historical problems (2)', p. 236, and Blackburn, in *MEC*, p. 313. Dolley and Blunt, 'The chronology of the coins of Ælfred the Great', pp. 81–2 (and their Appendix, p. 95), had implied a date in the early 880s, following *Cross-and-Lozenge*, and put the mint on or south of the Thames.

67 Dolley and Blunt, 'The chronology of the coins of Ælfred the Great', p. 82; see also Blackburn, below, p. 113 (and in *MEC*, pp. 312–13).

68 Blackburn and Keynes, 'A corpus of the *Cross-and-Lozenge* and related coinages', below, p. 133. See also Blunt, 'A new type for Alfred'; Dolley and Blunt, 'The chronology of the coins of Ælfred the Great', p. 81; Lyon, 'Historical problems (2)', p. 236; and Blackburn, in *MEC*, p. 313.

69 Cf. Keynes and Lapidge, *Alfred the Great*, p. 228. It has to be admitted, however, that Alfred's coin is much closer to its Roman model than Ceolwulf's, and if anything is likely to be the earlier of the two.

70 Stenton, 'The Anglo-Saxon coinage and the historian', p. 373.

size.[71] The coins themselves are listed and classified elsewhere in this volume,[72] and are discussed in most instructive detail by Dr Blackburn;[73] but I cannot refrain from attempting myself to put them in a wider historical context. In view of the large number of moneyers involved in *Cross-and-Lozenge*, there can be no doubt that despite its rarity the type was a major issue, and indeed it is clear that it represented nothing less than a reform of the coinage, involving a significant increase in the weight of the coin and the fineness of its content. It might be supposed that such a reform could only have been contemplated after the victory over Guthrum's Vikings, at Edington in 878; in which case one might wish to believe that the 'joint' coinage in some way reflected an assumption by Alfred of rulership over Ceolwulf's Mercians and his own West Saxons alike, or even (as Professor Nelson has suggested) a celebration of the battle of Edington as a victory won by the West Saxons and Mercians together.[74] But one would then be left with something of a hiatus in the coinage in the mid-870s, and (more seriously) with the difficulty of explaining how Ceolwulf himself could have participated in the reform, given Guthrum's disturbing presence at Cirencester in 878–879 and the evidence that Ceolwulf's reign ended in 879.[75] I for one should prefer to imagine, therefore, that the reform was undertaken by Alfred and Ceolwulf some time between *ca* 875 and 878, despite the activities of the Viking army; after all, they might have trusted the Vikings, and were not to know that Guthrum would return. One could then argue that if *Two Emperors* were roughly contemporary with the inception of *Cross-and-Lozenge*, both types might have reflected the political circumstances of the mid-870s, with Alfred and Ceolwulf established in mutual (if unequal) respect as rulers of English England; but since King Æthelred and King Alfred had previously shared the *Lunettes* type with King Burgred, it would be dangerous to invest the coinage with too much significance in terms particular to Alfred and Ceolwulf.

The point of greatest interest is that a substantial proportion of Alfred's coins of the *Cross-and-Lozenge* type was minted at London (nos 20–31 in the corpus),[76] and that these coins seem on stylistic grounds to be earlier, as a group,

71 For discussion, see Dolley and Blunt, 'The chronology of the coins of Ælfred the Great', pp. 80–1; Blunt, 'The coinage of Æthelred, archbishop of Canterbury'; Dolley, 'An unpublished hoard-provenance for a penny of Ceolwulf II of Mercia'; Lyon, 'Historical problems (2)', p. 236; Archibald, 'An Alfred penny from Rochester'; Metcalf and Northover, 'Debasement of the coinage in southern England', pp. 164–5; and Blackburn, in *MEC*, pp. 312–13.

72 Blackburn and Keynes, 'A corpus of the *Cross-and-Lozenge* and related coinages', below, pp. 125–50.

73 Blackburn, 'The London mint in the reign of Alfred', below, pp. 105–23.

74 See Nelson, 'Wealth and wisdom: the politics of Alfred the Great', pp. 40–3, and Nelson, ' "A king across the sea" ', p. 60. Professor Nelson acknowledges that there is, of course, no clear evidence that Edington was anything other than a West Saxon victory. For her more recent opinion, see Nelson, 'The political ideas of Alfred of Wessex', p. 148, placing the reform of the coinage *ca* 875.

75 Obviously, if one chooses to disregard the evidence of the regnal list (above, nn. 48 and 54), the more serious difficulties evaporate: one could argue, quite simply, that Ceolwulf was active in London for a while after 879. See Pagan, 'Coinage in southern England', p. 63, n. 63.

76 An Alfredian *Cross-and-Lozenge* trial-piece or weight was discovered (in 1840) in the churchyard of St Paul's, providing tangible proof that coins were minted in Alfred's name at London in the period before 886. The trial-piece or weight is no. 32 in the corpus; see also Dolley, 'A piedfort

than the London *Cross-and-Lozenge* coins struck in the name of King Ceolwulf (nos 33–41).[77] If the reform is to be regarded as a joint economic venture, it was thus one which might have been planned in the first instance by Alfred alone, and in which he was able to persuade Ceolwulf to participate. Moreover, it is remarkable that on one of the 'earliest' Alfredian coins from the London mint, the king is styled 'rex SM',[78] apparently in an attempt to signify that he was king of both Saxons and Mercians, perhaps with the implication that the coins were struck before Ceolwulf's position was fully recognised in London.[79] It can be shown, furthermore, that *Cross-and-Lozenge* coins were minted at various other places. Some of King Alfred's coins, and all those of Archbishop Æthelred, were plainly the products of the royal and archiepiscopal moneyers at Canterbury (nos 9–15, for the king; nos 16–19, for the archbishop), while others would appear to be associated with Winchester (nos 42–51, for Alfred; no. 52, more remarkably, for Ceolwulf). The remaining coins of the type can be resolved into perhaps three 'West Saxon' moneyers (nos 53–8) and one conceivably 'Mercian' moneyer (no. 59) operating for Alfred, and another 'Mercian' moneyer for Ceolwulf (no. 60). The critical question, however, is whether London itself was an active mint for Ceolwulf and/or Alfred after the division of Mercia in 877, and for Alfred after Ceolwulf's apparent demise in 879. It is a matter which cannot be addressed solely with reference to the *Cross-and-Lozenge* type, for it is likely to involve some understanding of the chronology of the succeeding *London Monogram* and *Two-Line* types.[80] The numismatic evidence should be allowed to speak for itself, not least because it would be hazardous to rule out either possibility on historical grounds alone: our knowledge of how commercial activity in a place like London was organized is too imprecise to preclude the notion that the moneyers remained active despite the changes in political circumstances, or indeed that they could serve two masters simultaneously;[81] and besides, if London had been left in English hands after the division of Mercia in 877, it may well have remained so during the early 880s. One can but emphasise, at the same time, that this need not detract in any way from the intended and perceived significance of the new measures which Alfred took for the defence and restoration of London in 886.

It only remains to ask how one is to reconcile the chronicler's disparaging reference to Ceolwulf as a 'foolish king's thegn' with the evidence (a) that he was plainly recognised as king by the Mercians themselves, and (b) that he was also recognised as such by King Alfred. My only suggestion, if we must accept the

lead trial-piece of Edward the Confessor', pp. 175–6, and Vince, *Saxon London*, pp. 113–15 (with fig. 59).

77 Blackburn, 'The London mint in the reign of Alfred', above, pp. 117–19.

78 The coin in question is no. 27 in the corpus, by the prolific moneyer, Liafwald.

79 The potential significance of the style 'rex SM' must be judged in the context of the styles employed on all coins of the *Cross-and-Lozenge* type which accord a royal style to the king. Ceolwulf is 'rex M(erciorum)', for 'king of the Mercians'; and Alfred is 'rex S(axonum)', for 'king of the Saxons'; see below, pp. 134–49. This is perhaps no more and no less than we should expect.

80 Blackburn, 'The London mint in the reign of Alfred', below, pp. 120–2.

81 Smyth, *King Alfred the Great*, pp. 48–50, finds it impossible 'to envisage Alfred having any kind of autonomous hold on Mercian London' in the 870s, and prefers to interpret the numismatic evidence as an indication that, in London, both Alfred and Ceolwulf operated as sub-kings of the Danes.

chronicler's statement that Ceolwulf was indeed a Viking appointee, is that the remark does not represent the West Saxon attitude to Ceolwulf which was current in the 870s. Alfred may have regretted his brother-in-law Burgred's departure, but in 874 he would have had little option other than to accept the situation. In retrospect, however, Ceolwulf could be held in contempt, for his behaviour when first appointed in 874 or when Mercia was divided in 877 or when he was displaced in 879; and the harsh judgement of him could have arisen from the desire in Alfredian court circles to justify a turn of events which had ousted Ceolwulf from power. In short, the remark need not be construed as anti-Mercian, and might rather be construed as pro-Alfredian interests in Mercia.

Alfred and Ealdorman Æthelred, ca 880–899

I turn now to King Alfred's assumption of direct authority over Mercia in the wake of Ceolwulf's displacement, and his relations with the man who was henceforth the effective ruler of the Mercians, namely Ealdorman Æthelred. Nothing is known of Æthelred's background. He may have been of the royal stock of the Mercians (and distinct in this respect from Ceolwulf himself), and is conceivably the Æthelred who attested two Mercian charters issued in the late 860s (though not the two extant charters of Ceolwulf).[82] His occurrence at the end of the Mercian regnal list, following Ceolwulf, could be taken to imply that he gained power in Mercia after the end of Ceolwulf's five-year reign (in about 879), and is one of several signs that he was regarded in certain quarters (and perhaps at certain times) as a king.[83] He first makes an appearance in 881, when he is said to have conducted a raid into north Wales, only to be repulsed by Anarawd ap Rhodri at the mouth of the Conway.[84] Certain remarks in Asser's *Life of King Alfred*

82 S.212 and 214 (charters of King Burgred, dated 866 and 869); see also Keynes, *An Atlas of Attestations*, Table XVII, and Stenton, *Anglo-Saxon England*, p. 259, n. 2. For a grant by King Burgred to a certain Æthelred, see above, n. 25. The Æthelred included among the witnesses in S.1278 (a charter of Wærferth, bishop of Worcester, dated 872; trans. *EHD*, no. 94) was perhaps a member of the Worcester community.

83 London, British Library, MS Cotton Tiberius A.xiii, fo 114v; printed in *Hemingi Chartularium*, ed. Hearne, I.242. The length of Æthelred's 'reign' is not specified. He is called 'King of the Saxons' in an Irish source (*Fragmentary Annals of Ireland*, ed. Radner, pp. 166–73), and 'King of the Mercians' in Æthelweard, *Chronicon* IV.3 (ed. Campbell, pp. 49–50; Keynes and Lapidge, *Alfred the Great*, p. 190).

84 The *Annales Cambriae*, *s.a.* 880 (for 881), simply record 'Gueit Conguoy. Digal Rotri a Deo' ('The battle of the Conway. Rhodri avenged by God'); cf. above, n. 48. The involvement of Ealdorman Æthelred depends on a late-recorded story of quite uncertain authority, which may have originated at Bangor (Lloyd, *A History of Wales*, I.328, and n. 30): 'The Britains having returned their thanks to Anarawd, presently fell to work, and Necessity giving edge to their valour, they easily dispossessed the Saxons who were not yet warm in their seats. For some time they continued peacably in this part of Wales; but Eadred Duke of Mercia, called by the Welsh *Edryd Wallthir*, not being able any longer to bear such an ignominious ejection, made great Preparations for the re-gaining of the said Countrey. But the Northern Britains, who had settled themselves there, having intelligence of his Design, for the better security of their Cattel and other Effects, removed them beyond the River Conwey. Prince Anarawd in the mean time was not idle, but drawing together all the strength he could raise, encamped his Army near the Town of Conwey at a place called Cymryt, where himself and his Men having made gallant resistance against the pressing Efforts of the Saxons, obtained a very compleat Victory. This Battel was by some called

throw further light on his activities.[85] The kings of Glywysing and Gwent, in south-eastern Wales along the Severn estuary, are said to have been driven 'by the might and tyrannical behaviour of Ealdorman Æthelred and the Mercians' to seek King Alfred's protection, and it would appear that this took place some time in the early 880s; it is uncertain, however, whether they sought this protection because Alfred already had some authority over Æthelred, or simply because they hoped that the reciprocal obligations of lordship would induce him to bring pressure to bear on the Mercian ruler. Asser also mentions the eventual submission of Anarawd himself to Alfred, 'on the same condition as Æthelred with the Mercians, namely that in every respect he would be obedient to the royal will' – which leaves us in no doubt as to the general terms of Æthelred's submission, though none the wiser about when it took place. Asser's remark to the effect that Alfred 'summoned' four men to him from Mercia might be taken to suggest that Alfred's status as overlord of English Mercia was recognised in the early 880s, since it was about then that his Mercian helpers arrived at his court.[86] Two charters afford some further clues, albeit of the cryptic variety. One, dated 883, is a grant of privileges by Ealdorman Æthelred to Berkeley abbey in Gloucestershire, made in exchange for land at Stoke Bishop, which Æthelred then leased to a certain Cynwulf with reversion to Worcester.[87] Æthelred himself is styled 'by the inspiration of God's grace endowed and enriched with a portion of the realm of the Mercians' ('inbryrdendre Godes gefe gewelegod ⁊ gewlenced mid sume dæle Mercna rices'), clearly acknowledging the division of Mercia in 877, and he is said to act 'with the permission and witness of King Alfred and of all the councillors of the Mercians, ecclesiastical and lay' ('mid Ælfredes cyninges leafe ⁊ gewitnesse ⁊ mid ealra Myrcna witena, godcundra hada ⁊ woroldcundra'), indicating that his submission had taken place by this time, in 883. The second charter, dated 884, is a grant of land at Himbleton in Worcestershire to a certain Æthelwulf: Æthelred is 'by gift of divine grace supported in the rule and lordship of the Mercian people' ('divina largiente gratia principatu ⁊ dominio gentis

Gwaeth Cymryt Conwey, by reason that it was fought in the Township of Cymryt near Conwey. But Prince Anarawd would have it called Dial Rodri, because he had there avenged the Death of his Father Rodri. In this Battel Tudwal Rodri's son received a wound in the Knee, which made him be denominated Tudwal Gloff ever after; but for his signal service in this Action his Brethren bestowed upon him *Uchelogoed Gwynedd*.' Dr Powel, *The History of Wales, comprehending the Lives and Succession of the Princes of Wales, from Cadwalader the last King, to Lhewelyn the last Prince, of British Blood*, augmented and improved by W. Wynne (London, 1697), pp. 37–9; *The History of Wales, written originally in British, by Caradoc of Lhancarvan, Englished by Dr. Powell and Augmented by W. Wynne* (London, 1774), pp. 37–9.

85 See Asser, § 80; see also Keynes and Lapidge, *Alfred the Great*, p. 262, n. 183.

86 See Asser, § 77. The verb is *advocaverat*; and one has to admit that the same verb is used of Alfred 'summoning' Grimbald from Frankia (Asser, § 78). It would be tempting to attach significance to the statement in a twelfth-century Worcester source, to the effect that following Ceolwulf's death Alfred recovered (*recuperavit*) London and its surrounding territories, and acquired (*acquisivit*) the part of the Mercian kingdom which Ceolwulf had held (*Chronicon ex Chronicis*, ed. Thorpe, i. 267, and *The Anglo-Saxon Chronicle*, ed. Whitelock, *et al.*, p. 52, n. 6; cf. *The Chronicle of John of Worcester* II, ed. Darlington and McGurk, p. lxvi); but the statement may be no more than an inference from known events, drawn with the historian's advantage of hindsight.

87 S.218 (*Select English Historical Documents*, ed. (and trans.) Harmer, no. 12, pp. 20–2 and 53–4), marked on the map (Fig. 1). The transaction is similar in nature to one of the two charters of King Ceolwulf (S.215; above, p. 12).

Merciorum subfultus'), and in this instance he acts without reference to King Alfred.[88] The chief interest of the Himbleton charter is, however, that it is said to have been drawn up at a meeting where certain 'statutes' (*statuta*) of the Mercians were under consideration, held at Risborough in Buckinghamshire,[89] which implies that the English share of Mercia extended quite far south-eastwards towards London (see map).[90] In short, it is conceivable that King Alfred gained or assumed direct authority over the kingdom of Mercia not long after the demise of Ceolwulf in 879, and that Æthelred, if briefly regarded by the Mercians as their king, was thereupon obliged to acknowledge Alfred's overlordship. King Offa himself had been renowned for demoting those who fell under his sway, from kings to ealdormen; now the boot, as it were, was on the other foot.

Whatever the precise date of Æthelred's submission to King Alfred, it had certainly taken place by 883, and so by the time that Alfred took measures to secure his position in London. The *Anglo-Saxon Chronicle* refers to King Alfred's 'occupation' of London in 886, without any indication that the act involved the exercise or display of force;[91] it was left for others to create for themselves the impression that the event was the glorious climax of a military campaign, and that it marked, in effect, the first move in the capture or recovery of those parts of England which had previously fallen under the control of the Danes.[92] Modern historians have taken their cue from two different sources. The first is the passage found in the annal for 883 in the version of the *Chronicle* which underlies MSS BCDE (but not present in MS A,[93] or in the manuscripts used by Asser and Æthelweard), which describes how Pope Marinus sent some wood of the Cross to King Alfred, how in the same year two men took to Rome, and 'India', alms which Alfred promised thither 'when they (the English) were

88 S.219 (trans. Jones, *Anglo-Saxon Worcester*, pp. 87–8), marked on the map (Fig. 1).

89 'Acta est in Hrisbyri ubi tunc ipsorum conventio publica fuerunt conloquentes sibi invicem de necessariis gentis prædictæ statutis', which I take to mean '. . . where those conversing with him in turns about the necessary *statuta* of the aforesaid people were then in their public meeting' (cf. Jones, 'where at that time the Witanagemot met and discussed with him the necessity of this decision'). Patrick Wormald advises me that *statuta*, in this context, is most likely to signify 'judgements'; Dr A. H. J. Baines would prefer 'decisions', of whatever character.

90 Among the witnesses to this and other charters of Ealdorman Æthelred is Ealdorman Æthelferth (or Æthelfrith), who would appear to have been a person of West Saxon origin appointed presumably by King Alfred to look after his interests in south-eastern Mercia: see Hart, 'Athelstan "Half-King" ', pp. 116–18 (pp. 569–72); Keynes, 'A charter of King Edward the Elder for Islington', pp. 307–9; and Keynes, *An Atlas of Attestations*, Table XVII. Part of the estate at Risborough is known to have belonged to Ealdorman Æthelferth in the early tenth century (S.367): see Hart, 'Athelstan "Half-King" ', p. 116, n. 3 (p. 570, n. 3); Baines, 'The boundaries of Monks Risborough'; Hart, *The Danelaw*, pp. 460–2; and Baines, 'Monks Risborough: new light from Islington'.

91 *Anglo-Saxon Chronicle* 886 ABCDE (ed. Plummer, I, 80–1; trans. *EHD*, no. 1, p. 199). See also Asser, § 83; and Æthelweard, *Chronicon* IV.3 (ed. Campbell, p. 46). It should be noted that Æthelweard renders the chronicler's *gesette* as *obsidetur*, 'besieged'; but see *Asser's Life of King Alfred*, ed. Stevenson, p. 289, n. 2.

92 The historian's imagination can be seen at work in Roger of Wendover's account of the events of 886, written at St Albans in the thirteenth century. He describes how in the course of a violent campaign Alfred laid siege to London, whereupon all the English people came to give him their help; preparations were then made for an assault on the city, but the 'citizens' (presumably the inhabitants of London) chose to submit rather than fight.

93 See *Anglo-Saxon Chronicle, MS A*, ed. Bately, p. cvii.

encamped against the (Viking) army at London' ('þa hi sæton wið þone here æt Lundene'), and how by God's grace their prayers were well answered after that promise.[94] The second is the remark in Asser's *Life of King Alfred*, to the effect that in 886 Alfred restored London, 'after so many towns had been burned and so many people slaughtered'.[95] The passage in the *Chronicle* has been regarded as a misplaced (and misdated) allusion to a campaign which immediately preceded Alfred's occupation of London in 886,[96] and Asser's remark is then interpreted as confirmation by a contemporary writer that the occupation of London had been attended by much shedding of blood.[97] The event might thus be represented as the opening stage in the long process by which the English recovered what had been taken by the Danes, though while the chronicler, and Asser, were clearly inclined to give Alfred all of the credit, it may well be that a greater role had in fact been played by Ealdorman Æthelred.[98]

It should be recognised, however, that the received view of the event, as the outcome of a military campaign mounted by the English in order to dislodge the Vikings from an established stronghold, is the product of the natural tendency among historians to create an extended and connected story out of the surviving scraps of information, or to make a drama out of a crisis. It seems rather obvious, on reflection, that the passage in the annal for 883 makes best sense if it is left as it stands: as material inserted in an early version of the *Chronicle*, and genuinely pertaining to that year. It would appear that the compiler of the *Chronicle* originally said nothing, under 883, about Marinus, alms-giving, and the siege of London, and satisfied himself with a reference to Marinus's gift of the Cross to Alfred in his brief obituary notice on the pope, entered under annal 885. An early redactor of the *Chronicle* (or perhaps the compiler himself, on second thoughts) then decided to place a proper reference to the gift under annal 883, and had reason to associate it with a reference to the sending of alms to Rome (foreshadowing the similar entries in the annals for the later 880s), which in turn suggested the allusion to the siege of London.[99] In other words, it seems that Alfred was known to have made a move of some kind against London in 883; and in view of the evidence suggesting that moneyers had remained active there after the division of Mercia in 877 (and after Ceolwulf's demise in 879), it is possible that the move was made not against Danes who had been established in London since the time of the division itself, but in response to a short-lived Viking 'occupation' of the city in 883.[100] No such attack is recorded in the *Chronicle*; but a casual reference in a charter, indicating that Alfred was out with his army at Epsom (in

94 *Anglo-Saxon Chronicle* 883 BCDE (ed. Plummer, I, 79; trans. *EHD*, no. 1, p. 197).

95 Asser, § 83.

96 Stenton, *Anglo-Saxon England*, p. 258, n. 3; Whitelock, in *EHD*, p. 197, n. 6; Keynes and Lapidge, *Alfred the Great*, p. 266, n. 198; Smyth, *Alfred the Great*, p. 101.

97 Stenton, *Anglo-Saxon England*, p. 258, n. 3, and Whitelock, in *EHD*, p. 199, n. 4.

98 Smyth, *King Alfred the Great*, p. 519.

99 Pope Marinus died on 15 May 884, and the chronicler had entered the record of his death under 885; so the addition, whether or not it is correct in its association of events, cannot have been *intended* to refer to 886.

100 There seems little to recommend the older view (*Two Chronicles*, ed. Plummer, II, 89 and 96) that the promise of alms to Rome was made on a much earlier occasion, when London was occupied by the Danes in 871–2 (see S.1278 (trans. *EHD*, no. 94)).

Surrey) in 882,[101] is a salutary reminder that we cannot expect the *Chronicle* to provide a comprehensive log of the Viking campaigns.

The siege of London in 883 was presumably a combined West Saxon–Mercian operation, and its success (immediate or eventual) is indicated by the chronicler's remark that English prayers were well answered after the promise of alms; yet it was not until 886 that Alfred had occasion to 'occupy' the city. It may seem improbable that Alfred would have waited for three years, after removing the Vikings from London in 883, before taking more positive action for the defence of the city, and preferable not least for this reason to persist in the belief that the siege mentioned in the annal for '883' in fact took place immediately before the 'occupation' of London in 886.[102] It is conceivable, on the other hand, that Alfred had reason to feel that London was secure and the Londoners safe, at least for the time being, and that he was only prompted to take more decisive action by the activities of the Vikings in 885. A force arrived in that year from the continent and laid siege to Rochester; but the Vikings were beaten off by Alfred, whereupon some of their number returned to the continent, leaving others to ravage the land south of the Thames (with support from the Danes in East Anglia). These Vikings then established themselves for a while at Benfleet on the north bank of the Thames estuary, before themselves going back to the continent. In other words, Viking activity in 885 would have brought home to Alfred the need for effective protection of London itself; and the point was apparently grasped by Asser, if we may now interpret his reference to the 'restoration' of London, 'after so many towns had been burned and so many people slaughtered', not as an allusion to a campaign in 886 but as one to the events of 885.[103] Against this background, and in the light of what is known generally about King Alfred's establishment of towns and fortifications,[104] the 'occupation' or 'restoration' of London would be best regarded as a strengthening of its defences, involving the re-organization of its internal plan (perhaps what Asser meant by saying that Alfred made London habitable again) and the provision of a permanent garrison.[105] This much could be inferred from the written sources, and it is certainly compatible with the view of London's archaeology which emerged in the mid-1980s: that in the eighth and ninth centuries, commercial activity in London was concentrated outside and to the west of the (Roman) walled city, along the Strand, Aldwych and Fleet Street, and that it was not until the latter part of the ninth century that the focus of such activity moved back within the walls for greater protection.[106] One should add that it was presumably in connection with

101 S.345 (from the Old Minster, Winchester), dated 882, 'in expeditione . in loco qui Hebbeshamm appellatur'; Keynes, 'West Saxon Charters', p. 1135.

102 This is the position adopted by Dyson, 'King Alfred and the restoration of London', cited above, n. 49; see also Vince, *Saxon London*, pp. 84–5.

103 Keynes and Lapidge, *Alfred the Great*, p. 266, n. 198.

104 Asser, § 91.

105 As implied by Æthelweard, *Chronicon* IV.3 (ed. Campbell, p. 46). One does wonder, at the same time, whether Alfred might not have been moved to secure London's defences in 886 by his memories of the Leonine City (cf. Keynes, 'Anglo-Saxon entries in the Liber Vitae of Brescia', pp. 116–17) in the 850s and by news of the siege of Paris in 885–6 (Keynes and Lapidge, *Alfred the Great*, pp. 265–6).

106 The precise location of Middle Saxon London was long considered to be something of a mystery:

the 'restoration' of London that a fortification was built opposite the walled city on the south bank of the Thames, at Southwark, effectively commanding passage along the river past the adjoining London Bridge.[107]

King Alfred's 'occupation' or 'restoration' of London in 886 was followed by an event which is arguably one of the utmost significance: the submission to King Alfred of 'all the English people that were not under subjection to the Danes' ('all Angel cyn . . . þæt buton Deniscra monna hæftniede wæs').[108] The question arises whether the reference was to *all* of the English people (Saxons, Kentishmen, and Mercians alike), apart from those living in areas which remained under Danish control, or whether the reference was, more particularly, to those people who had been freed from a state of subjection by Alfred's occupation of London. It is a moot point;[109] but my own preference would be to suppose that the submission in 886 involved nothing less than a general reaffirmation of loyalty to King Alfred, perhaps involving the taking of a special

see, e.g. Biddle, 'Towns', p. 116; Vince, 'In search of Saxon London', p. 37; and Schofield, *The Building of London*, pp. 22–5. The suggestion that it lay to the west of the Roman city was made in 1984 by Biddle, 'London on the Strand', and Vince, 'The Aldwych'. For further discussion, see Hobley, *Roman and Saxon London*; Tatton-Brown, 'The topography of Anglo-Saxon London'; Merrifield, 'The contribution of archaeology to our understanding of pre-Norman London', pp. 11–12; Vince, *Saxon London*, esp. pp. 13–25; Dyson, 'King Alfred and the restoration of London', pp. 101–2; Mills, 'Before King Alfred'; Clarke and Ambrosiani, *Towns in the Viking Age*, pp. 13–14; and Keene, 'London in the early middle ages', p. 11. Excavations in progress at Covent Garden and elsewhere, as reported in the national press, continue to add to the picture. London *within* the Roman walls can never, of course, have been wholly deserted in the period before 886; bishops presumably remained at St Paul's, and one should bear in mind that the Alfredian *Cross-and-Lozenge* trial-piece weight was found there in the churchyard.

107 Southwark was among the burhs listed in the Burghal Hidage: *Anglo-Saxon Charters*, ed. Robertson, Appendix II, no. 1 (pp. 246–9); Keynes and Lapidge, *Alfred the Great*, pp. 193–4; and Hill, 'Gazeteer of Burghal Hidage sites', pp. 218–19.

108 The chronicler's phrase (ed. Plummer, I, 80–1) means literally 'all the English who were without the captivity of the Danes', i.e. not under Danish captivity. Asser's translation (§ 83) is accurate, though it involves an awkward echo of the Old English idiom (*sine* for *buton*): 'omnes Angli et Saxones, qui prius ubique dispersi fuerant aut cum paganis sine captivitate erant' ('all the Angles and Saxons who formerly had been scattered everywhere or were without captivity with the pagans'), reading *sine* from the (burnt) manuscript and its earliest transcript (and John of Worcester); see Keynes and Lapidge, *Alfred the Great*, p. 266, n. 199. The word *sine* in the manuscript was soon emended to *sub*, presumably to 'improve' Asser's construction but seeming to change the meaning from 'without captivity with the pagans' to 'with the pagans under captivity'. Nelson (' "A King Across the Sea" ', p. 53, and n. 42) adopts the emended text (*sub* for *sine*), and would translate: 'all the Angles and Saxons who . . . had been with the pagans but not as captives', i.e. voluntarily. This translation might also work for the unemended text (*sine* for *sub*). The point would be that the Mercian inhabitants of London (who might have included Ceolwulf, if he had repaired there on being ousted from south-western Mercia by Æthelred, *ca* 879) were in cahoots with the Vikings, and had held the town against King Alfred. This idea certainly has its attractions; but the chronicler's original statement in the vernacular is surely to be preferred to a rather clumsy Latin translation made by a Welshman whose command of English was less than secure (see *Asser's Life of King Alfred*, ed. Stevenson, pp. lxxvii–lxxviii), however that translation is to be construed. In defence of Asser, one should add that the Englishman Æthelweard was completely thrown by the chronicler's construction (*Chronicon* IV.3, ed. Campbell, p. 46)

109 For one view, see Stenton, *Anglo-Saxon England*, p. 259; for another, see Smyth, *King Alfred the Great*, pp. 386–7 and 669–70. See also Foot, 'The making of *Angelcynn*', pp. 26–7.

oath.[110] On this basis, the event would mark the confirmation of Alfred's status as the leader of the English people against their common enemy, and would deserve comparison as a symbolic act with the (second) coronation of Edgar in 973, or with the Salisbury oath of 1086. It is now almost axiomatic that the concept of a single 'English' people had originated towards the end of the sixth century in the mind of Pope Gregory the Great, that it had been picked up and promoted in the seventh century by the church of Canterbury, and that it was adopted by Bede in the eighth century as an organising principle of the *Historia ecclesiastica gentis Anglorum*, to express the unity of a Christian people in the eyes of God.[111] Yet while all readers of Bede might draw strength and comfort from his brilliantly far-sighted construction of a common past for the *gens Anglorum*, and while it is abundantly clear that *Angelcynn* was one of the buzz words at King Alfred's court,[112] it seems likely that Alfred was driven by what was, in effect, a vision of a more distinctive kind. The term 'Anglo-Saxon' (or its equivalents) had been used on the continent in the eighth and ninth centuries to denote the 'English' Saxons, as opposed to their continental counterparts.[113] It would appear, however, that the term in its Alfredian manifestations was used to signify the amalgamation of two political entities, namely the 'Anglian' kingdom of Mercia (less the part already settled by the Danes) and the 'Saxon' kingdom of Wessex and its eastern extensions. The concept of the 'Anglo-Saxon' people may have originated *ca* 880, in connection with Alfred's assumption of power over the English Mercians, but it was apparently a while before it began to take

110 Keynes and Lapidge, *Alfred the Great*, p. 306, n. 6; Keynes, 'West Saxon charters', pp. 1148–9. On the importance of the oath, see also Wormald, '*Engla Lond*: the making of an allegiance', pp. 6–7.

111 This line of argument has been developed and articulated most effectively by Patrick Wormald, in a series of wide-ranging papers: 'Bede, the *Bretwaldas*, and the origins of the *Gens Anglorum*', esp. pp. 122–6; 'Anglo-Saxon society and its literature', pp. 7–8; 'The Venerable Bede and the "Church of the English" ', pp. 18–23; '*Engla Lond*: the making of an allegiance'; and 'The making of England'. For lines which lead in a similar direction, see Stephens, 'Bede's Ecclesiastical History', and Cowdrey, 'Bede and the "English People" '. Of course, collective terms were adopted and used in some contexts merely as a form of shorthand, and might not bear the burden that we wish to place upon them. These matters had been aired at a meeting of the Elizabethan Society of Antiquaries, on 29 June 1604; for papers by Camden, Holland, and others, see *Curious Discourses*, ed. Hearne, I, pp. 90–100.

112 Foot, 'The Making of *Angelcynn*', argues that it was Alfred who 'harnessed the word to his own particular ends' (pp. 29, n. 25, and 41–2). The interesting fact, of course, is that a term evoking the 'Angles' was employed so enthusiastically in what is ostensibly a 'Saxon' context. See Wormald, 'Bede, the *Bretwaldas*, and the origins of the *Gens Anglorum*', p. 123. It might reflect the particular influence of Bede's *Historia ecclesiastica*, or a creeping Anglian culture which was becoming increasingly pervasive (in a process which might also find reflection, for example, in Woden's apparent success in replacing Seaxnet as divine ancestor of the West Saxon kings); equally, the use of *Angelcynn* might reflect the pronounced 'Mercian' or Anglian element at King Alfred's court. Asser (§§ 23, 75, 76) appears to put emphasis on 'Saxon' language and literature, which has led to the suggestion that Alfred wished to stress 'a distinctive Saxon, vernacular and aristocratic cultural inheritance' and teach it to the Angles (Nelson, 'Wealth and wisdom', pp. 44–5, and 'The political ideas of Alfred of Wessex', pp. 135–7; cf. Foot, 'The making of *Angelcynn*', pp. 34–5); but it is not clear that Asser's 'Saxon' is anything more than a Welshman's idiom for what his subject would have called 'English'.

113 See Levison, *England and the Continent in the Eighth Century*, p. 92, n. 1.

hold,[114] and it may thus have been specifically in connection with the events of 886 that Alfred came to be hailed as 'king of the Anglo-Saxons'.[115] In other words, the designation of King Alfred in the late 880s and early 890s as 'king of the Angles and Saxons', or 'king of the Anglo-Saxons', sprang not from Bede but from a different source; and the question arises, therefore, whether Alfred was seriously or consciously intent upon the realisation of Bede's precocious vision of the unity of the English people,[116] whether indeed he was 'laying claim to the old status of *bretwalda*',[117] or whether Alfred's vision of a chosen people walking upon England's pastures green was in fact conceived in the more overtly political context of a wish to bring the 'Mercians' and the 'Saxons' together.[118] Again, it is a matter of judgement; but to my mind Alfred was just the kind of ruler who might be expected to have found his own way forward.

Alfred put the seal on these momentous developments by entrusting London to the control of Ealdorman Æthelred, thereby respecting London's status as a 'Mercian' town, and establishing Æthelred's responsibility for London which persisted until his death in 911.[119] The act may have represented the formal

114 This is admittedly no more than an impression derived from the very unsatisfactory evidence furnished by Alfred's charters: see Keynes, 'The West Saxon charters', pp. 1134–5, citing S.345, dated 882, in which the king is styled 'Saxonum rex'.

115 For the development, significance, and incidence of the style 'king of the Anglo-Saxons', see (e.g.) Stevenson, *Asser's Life of King Alfred*, pp. 147–52; John, *Orbis Britanniae*, pp. 45–6; Keynes and Lapidge, *Alfred the Great*, pp. 38–41 and 227, n. 1; Keynes, 'The age of Alfred', p. 255; and Keynes, 'The West Saxon charters', pp. 1147–9. The notion that the style was of the utmost significance draws its strength (a) from the quality of the evidence that it was 'official' usage in charters of the 890s (cf. below, n. 154), (b) from the correspondence between the diplomatic evidence and the evidence of Asser's *Life of King Alfred* (below, pp. 43–4, and n. 199), and (c) from the overall pattern of royal styles in charters issued between the mid-ninth and the mid-tenth century. Reynolds, 'What do we mean by "Anglo-Saxon" and "Anglo-Saxons"?', pp. 398–9, 405 and 414, acknowledges the usage in charters, but does not seem to be impressed by its particular significance in the Alfredian context; cf. Reynolds, *Kingdoms and Communities*, p. 266, and Campbell, 'The late Anglo-Saxon state', p. 47. Dumville, 'The treaty of Alfred and Guthrum', p. 20, n. 94, is troubled (not unreasonably) by the difficulty of establishing any clear sense of a chronological development.

116 Cowdrey, 'Bede and the "English People" ', pp. 521 and 523; Wormald, 'Bede, the *Bretwaldas*, and the origins of the *Gens Anglorum*', pp. 120–1; Foot, 'The making of *Angelcynn*'.

117 Wormald, 'The ninth century', p. 155; see also Scharer, 'The writing of history at King Alfred's court', pp. 181–2.

118 The term 'Anglo-Saxon' was never intended to embrace all of the 'English', in the sense given currency by Bede. For further discussion, see below, n. 165.

119 For Æthelred and London, see S.346 (from Worcester, dated 889) and 1628 (from Christ Church, Canterbury, dated 898 or 899), discussed further below; see also Dyson, 'King Alfred and the restoration of London', pp. 102–7. Æthelred was in charge of the region around London, but it was nevertheless regarded as part of Alfred's kingdom (*Anglo-Saxon Chronicle* 893A 894BCD (ed. Bately, p. 57; trans. *EHD*, no. 1, p. 203)). The consequence of Æthelred's death in 911 was that Edward the Elder 'succeeded to London and Oxford and to all the lands which belonged to them' (*Anglo-Saxon Chronicle* 911A 912BCD (ed. Bately, p. 67; trans. *EHD*, p. 211), perhaps reflecting an arrangement originally made in the 880s. For Æthelred and Oxford, see also Blair, *Anglo-Saxon Oxfordshire*, pp. 96–7. The question arises whether this has any bearing on the date of the Burghal Hidage; cf. Wormald, 'The ninth century', pp. 152–3. If Worcester, Warwick, and Buckingham are regarded (without especially good reason) as 'interpolations', the Burghal Hidage might be held to represent a conception of burghal organization which extended in the north along the rivers Avon and Thames (Bath, Malmesbury, Cricklade, Oxford, Wallingford, Sashes, Southwark), on which basis there could be something to be said for the notion that in its

confirmation of an existing situation; but if not, and if Alfred had indeed been in notional control of London in the early 880s, it would seem to follow that there had been some loosening of the territorial integrity of English Mercia after Ceolwulf's demise, with Alfred recognised in the vicinity of London and Ealdorman Æthelred further to the west. It may also have been at about this time that King Alfred gave Ealdorman Æthelred the hand of his daughter Æthelflæd in marriage. Her first appearance as Æthelred's wife is in a charter which can be dated 887,[120] but the marriage could have taken place two or three years before, and (one might add) has no necessary connection with the events of 886.[121] Surviving charters issued during the 880s and 890s afford some impression of Æthelred's position in relation to King Alfred, though it has to be admitted that the message is far from clear. We have already seen that in 883 Æthelred, 'by the inspiration of God's grace endowed and enriched with a portion of the realm of the Mercians' ('inbryrdendre Godes gefe gewelegod 7 gewlenced mid sume dæle Mercna rices'), and acting 'with the permission and witness of King Alfred and of all the councillors of the Mercians, ecclesiastical and lay' ('mid Ælfredes cyninges leafe 7 gewitnesse 7 mid ealra Myrcna witena, godcundra hada 7 woroldcundra'), granted privileges to Berkeley abbey in Gloucestershire; the charter was attested by King Alfred, Æthelred *dux*, and others.[122] We have also seen that in 884 Æthelred, 'by gift of divine grace supported in the rule and lordship of the Mercian people' ('divina largiente gratia principatu 7 dominio gentis Merciorum subfultus'), granted land in Worcestershire to Æthelwulf, without any reference to King Alfred; the charter was issued at Risborough in Buckinghamshire, and was attested by Æthelred, 'governing the leadership of the Mercian people' ('Merciorum gentis ducatum gubernans'), and others.[123] In 887 Æthelred, 'by gift of the abundant grace of the Lord *dux* and *patricius* of the Mercian people, with the permission and sign-manual of King Alfred' ('gratia domini largiflua concedente dux et patricius gentis Merciorum cum licentia et inpositione manus Ælfredi regis'), granted a pair of estates belonging to the church of Pyrton, near Dorchester in Oxfordshire, to the see of Worcester, and did so 'for the safety and also for the security of our kingdom of the Mercians' ('pro sospitate necnon et stabilitate regni Merciorum nobis'); the charter was attested by King Alfred, Æthelred *dux*,

earliest form the document represented a situation in the early 880s, before responsibility for Oxford and London was passed to Ealdorman Æthelred in 886. It is doubtful, however, that all the burhs were in place so early: Shaftesbury is said to have been built in 880, but Southwark may not have been built until the walled city of London was 'restored' in 886, and both the chronicler and Asser write as if burhs were still under construction in the early 890s. It is as difficult to date the Burghal Hidage as it is difficult to date the Tribal Hidage, and for similar reasons: the process involves making certain assumptions about the nature of the text which may or may not be tenable.

120 S.217 (from Worcester), dated '880', in the fifth indiction (887).

121 Alfred was married in 868, and Æthelflæd was his first-born child (Asser, §§ 29 and 75); so she might have been of marriagable age by *ca* 885. One would not know from Alfred's will that Ealdorman Æthelred was his son-in-law, even though the received text may date from the 890s (Keynes and Lapidge, *Alfred the Great*, pp. 173–8); but the ealdorman did receive special attention, in the form of a sword worth 100 mancuses.

122 S.218 (from Worcester), cited above, n. 87.

123 S.219 (from Worcester), cited above, n. 88. For Risborough, see above, n. 90.

Æthelflæd *conjux*, and others.[124] In 888 Æthelred, 'by gift of the grace of God *procurator* in the lordship of the kingdom of the Mercians' ('gratia Dei disponente procurator in domino regni Merciorum'), granted land at Walden, in Hertfordshire, to his thegn Wulfgar, in a meeting held at Droitwich in Worcestershire and without any reference to King Alfred; the charter was attested by Æthelred, Æthelflæd, and others.[125] Also in 888, King Alfred himself issued a charter concerning land at Pendock in Worcestershire.[126] In 889 Alfred, 'king of the Angles and Saxons' ('rex Anglorum et Saxonum'), and Æthelred, 'sub-king and *patricius* of the Mercians' ('subregulus et patricius Merciorum'), with the witness of both peoples, granted property in London to the bishop of Worcester; the charter was attested by Alfred 'rex Anglorum et Saxonum', Æthelred 'subregulus et patricius Merciorum', Æthelflæd, and others.[127] Some time in the 890s 'Æðeldred ealdorman ⁊ Æðelflæd' granted rights pertaining 'to their sovereignty' ('to heora hlaforddome') in the newly-fortified town of Worcester to the bishopric of Worcester, with the witness of King Alfred and of all the councillors of the Mercians.[128] In 896 Ealdorman Æthelred convened 'all the councillors of the Mercians' at Gloucester, 'and this he did with the witness and permission of King Alfred' ('⁊ ðæt dyde be Ælfredes cyninges gewitnesse ⁊ leafe'); a dispute between the bishop of Worcester and a rather well-to-do priest called Æthelwold was settled, and the settlement was duly attested by Æthelred and Æthelflæd, three Mercian ealdormen, and a few others.[129] In 897 Æthelred and others

124 S.217 (from Worcester), marked on the map (Fig. 1). The charter contains a remarkable clause to the effect that six men who had belonged to the royal estate at Benson (Oxfordshire), with their families, were henceforth to belong to the church (i.e. Pyrton), with the permission of the king (i.e. Alfred). The men are named as Alhmund, Tidulf, Tidheh, Lull, Lull, and Eadulf. For Benson as a royal estate, see Blair, *Anglo-Saxon Oxfordshire*, pp. 49–50, 108, and 140.

125 S.220 (from St Albans), marked on the map (Fig. 1).

126 S.1839 (a lost original, from Worcester), marked on the map (Fig. 1). It is most unfortunate that the text of this charter does not survive. It was perhaps related in some way to a grant which had been made in the first instance by King Ceolwulf (S.216). It is not clear what significance (if any) should be attached to the fact that the lost original of S.1416, a Worcester lease issued in 892, was endorsed 'Ælfred rex'.

127 S.346 (from Worcester). For further discussion of this charter, see Dyson, 'Two Saxon land grants for Queenhithe', pp. 205–10; Dyson and Scofield, 'Saxon London', pp. 296–7; Dyson, 'King Alfred and the restoration of London', pp. 102–7; and Ayre, *et al.*, 'Æthelred's Hythe to Queenhithe'.

128 S.223 (from Worcester); trans. *EHD*, no. 99. It should be noted that in this instance Æthelred appears to have acted jointly with Æthelflæd; but the general impression from the 890s, as from the 880s, is that he acted in his own right. For the situation after Alfred's death, see below, p. 37, n. 159.

129 S.1441 (from Worcester). The importance of this document as a reflection of proceedings in the 890s needs special emphasis; see *Select English Historical Documents*, ed. Harmer, no. 14, pp. 24–5, with translation, pp. 56–7. Ealdorman Æthelred convened the meeting of the Mercian councillors at Gloucester; but he did so explicitly with King Alfred's permission. There follows a perfect description of the business conducted at such a meeting: 'And then they deliberated there how they could most justly govern their people, both in spiritual and temporal matters, and also do justice to many men both clerical and lay, with regard to lands and other things in which they had been wronged.' The dispute between the bishop of Worcester and the priest Æthelwold concerned the former's claim to woodland belonging to Woodchester (south of Gloucester and west of Cirencester), which had been given to one of his predecessors by King Æthelbald (716–57). So Æthelwold's *geneat*, called Ecglaf, and a Worcester priest, called Wulfhun, went round the boundaries of the estate, as indicated in the old charters, and presumably reported back to the

unnamed gave judgement in a dispute which concerned Ealdorman Æthelwulf (for Winchcombe abbey) and the bishop of Worcester, and the settlement was made with the witness of King Alfred, Æthelred 'dux Merciorum', and all their councillors.[130] And in 898 King Alfred, Archbishop Plegmund and Æthelred, 'ealdorman of part of the province of the Mercians' ('dux partis regionis Merciorum'), met at Chelsea to discuss the 'restoration' (*instauratio*) of London.[131] In short, Æthelred usually acted with the permission of or in association with King Alfred, but occasionally he acted independently of him. Although sometimes described as a plain *dux* or ealdorman, his status was clearly quite different from that of other *duces*, for he is also accorded styles which aspire to divine grace and which appear to verge on the royal. In other words, there is no mistaking that the Mercians retained a conception of their ruler as a rightful successor to earlier kings, and a conception of their land as a kingdom with its own identity; but equally there is no mistaking that Æthelred moved in an Alfredian world.

Ealdorman Æthelred's powers were unusual enough, under King Alfred's dispensation, in extending to the issuing of charters; but his powers did not extend to the minting of coins.[132] It is possible that the *Cross-and-Lozenge* type remained in production for a short while after the demise of Ceolwulf, minted in Alfred's

meeting at Gloucester. The land was restored to the bishop, who leased it to Æthelwold and to Æthelwold's son Alhmund, on the understanding that Alhmund would maintain the 'friendship' which his father had had with the bishop. The witnesses include 'Eadnoth, Alfred and Werferth': Eadnoth was perhaps the prominent Mercian layman of that name, and one might presume that Werferth was the bishop of Worcester, so it is possible that Alfred was none other than the king himself.

130 S.1442 (from Worcester). An interesting aspect of this charter is the view it affords of the *uenerabilis* Ealdorman Æthelwulf, who was the brother of Alfred's wife Ealhswith and thus the son of Æthelred (Mucel), ealdorman of the *Gaini*; see above, pp. 9–10. Æthelwulf had perused the 'hereditary charters' of King Cenwulf, and had found that, after Cenwulf himself, no heir to the inheritance which belonged to the church of Winchcombe had the power to grant any part of that inheritance to any man for longer than one life. Accordingly, Æthelwulf instituted proceedings against Wullaf in respect of the land at Upton (in Blockley, Worcs.) which belonged to Cenwulf's inheritance, i.e. to Winchcombe. Wullaf responded that Cynethryth (presumably a mid-ninth-century abbess of Winchcombe) had given the land to his father for three lives, and Ælfflæd (presumably Cynethryth's successor) had given it to him on the same terms. Æthelred and the councillors gave judgement that matters should be as laid down by King Cenwulf; Wullaf handed over to Ealdorman Æthelwulf the charters which had been written by Cynethryth and Ælfflæd; and Æthelwulf ordered that a new charter be drawn up for Wullaf, giving him a lease for one life, with reversion to the church of Worcester–in order to restore good relations between the communities of Worcester and Winchcombe. 'Peace' (*pax*) was thus re-established between Bishop Werferth and Ealdorman Æthelwulf, with the witness of King Alfred and Ealdorman Æthelred; and the agreement with Wullaf was drawn up with the witness of members of the two communities of Worcester and Winchcombe. The natural inference is that Ealdorman Æthelwulf was responsible in some way for Winchcombe, which may have some bearing on his own origin, and on that of his father and sister.

131 S.1628 (from Christ Church, Canterbury). For further discussion, see Dyson, 'Two Saxon land grants for Queenhithe', pp. 201–5; Brooks, *The Early History of the Church of Canterbury*, p. 154; Dyson and Scofield, 'Saxon London', pp. 296–7; and Dyson, 'King Alfred and the Restoration of London', pp. 102–7.

132 An analogous arrangement may have existed in the period, from 957 to 959, when the kingdom was divided between Eadwig and his brother Edgar: the latter issued charters in respect of land in his own territory, but seems not to have minted any coins. See Blunt, Stewart and Lyon, *Coinage in Tenth-Century England*, pp. 278–80.

name, but if so none of the coinage appears to have survived since at those mints which struck for both kings the coins of Alfred seem to pre-date those of Ceolwulf.[133] It was apparently *ca* 880 that the weight-standard of the coinage was further increased, represented most notably by Alfred's *London Monogram* and *Two-Line* types, and also by the unique specimen of a penny minted in his name at Gloucester. The *London Monogram* type (Pl. 11, M, O, Q and R) tends to attract the attention, not least because the coins happen to survive in fairly respectable quantity. It seems to have been current for a short time only, and is normally regarded as a special issue to celebrate the recapture or restoration of London in 886; yet there is no reason why it should not have been issued some years before that event, as a local type of no particular 'historical' significance.[134] The *Gloucester* type (Pl. 11, S) is too easily overlooked; but its importance is great, since it was minted at what was undoubtedly Ealdorman Æthelred's principal centre of power.[135] Another distinctive group of coins was struck in Alfred's name at Oxford (*Ohsnaforda*) (Pl. 11, T),[136] which like London and Gloucester was also a borough in practice under Ealdorman Æthelred's control.[137] It is tempting indeed, therefore, to interpret the three mint-signed issues of the early 880s, from London, Gloucester and Oxford, as a distinctive and highly significant group, which reflected and which might even have served to advertise King Alfred's assumption of power and his control of commerce in 'English' Mercia after Ceolwulf's demise. Alfred's far commoner *Two-Line* type was introduced initially at Canterbury, Winchester, and perhaps elsewhere, including a mint or mints located in the West Midlands; it was subsequently produced at London too, probably from the mid 880s, after the *London Monogram* type.[138] In short, King Alfred's authority was evidently recognised throughout the Mercian regions of 'English' England: if the Mercian scribes who wrote Ealdorman Æthelred's

133 See Blackburn, below, pp. 117–19.

134 For the *London Monogram* type, see Dolley and Blunt, 'The chronology of the coins of Ælfred the Great', pp. 82–3; Lyon, 'Historical problems (2)', p. 237; and Blackburn, in *MEC*, pp. 313–14. See also Blackburn, below, pp. 110–11 and 120–2.

135 Ealdorman Æthelred convened a meeting of his councillors at Gloucester in 896 (S.1441, cited above, n. 129); he and his wife were instrumental in the foundation of the 'New Minster' (St Peter's, later St Oswald's); relics of St Oswald were brought there from Bardney, Lincs., in 909 (ASC [Mercian Register]); and both were buried there (Æthelweard, *Chronicon* IV.4 (ed. Campbell, p. 53); ASC [Mercian Register], *s.a.* 918). According to William of Malmesbury (*De gestis pontificum* IV.155, ed. Hamilton, p. 293), the monastery at Gloucester flourished in the tenth century and developed an especially close connection with Malmesbury, 'as may be seen in the archives of each church', perhaps indicating that King Æthelstan made a point of promoting its interests. See also Thacker, 'Chester and Gloucester', and Hare, *The Two Anglo-Saxon Minsters of Gloucester*, pp. 3–7. For the Gloucester coin itself, see Dolley and Blunt, 'The chronology of the coins of Ælfred the Great', p. 83, and Blackburn, in *MEC*, p. 314; interestingly enough, Alfred is not called *rex*.

136 See Lyon, 'Historical problems (4)', pp. 196–7; Blackburn, in *MEC*, p. 314; and Blair, *Anglo-Saxon Oxfordshire*, pp. 100–1. Hoard evidence now shows this also to have been an early issue, contemporary with the *London Monogram* type: see Blackburn, below, pp. 110–11 and 120, n. 49.

137 See S.217, and the *Anglo-Saxon Chronicle*, *s.a.* 911.

138 For the *Two-Line* type, see Dolley and Blunt, 'The chronology of the coins of Ælfred the Great', pp. 84–6; Blackburn, in *MEC*, p. 314; Metcalf, 'The monetary history of England', p. 139; and Blackburn, below, pp. 110–11.

charters had occasion to dig into their pockets, they would have come up with a handful of Alfredian coins.

Asser's remark, to the effect that Ealdorman Æthelred undertook in every respect to be 'obedient to the royal will',[139] leaves one in little doubt that Alfred was in the dominant position; yet the pleasure which Asser, as a Welshman, might have taken in Mercian subjection to the West Saxons should not be allowed to conceal the fact that a new polity had come into existence. It is not that Alfred, as king of the West Saxons, had managed to gain recognition from or impose his authority over Æthelred, as ruler of the 'English' Mercians; it is rather that Alfred, as king of the Anglo-Saxons, presided over a political order which subsumed Wessex, its eastward extensions, and 'English' Mercia. One reflection of this new political order is to be found in a charter which refers to an occasion (perhaps in the late 870s or early 880s) when Ealdorman Wulfhere was arraigned for deserting King Alfred and his country in spite of the oath which he had sworn to the king and all his leading men, and forfeited his lands 'by the judgement of all the councillors of the West Saxons and of the Mercians' ('cum omnium juditio sapientium Geuisorum et Mercensium').[140] Another is to be found in the famous treaty between King Alfred and King Guthrum, generally dated between 886 (when Alfred 'occupied' London) and 890 (when Guthrum died).[141] Both of the surviving versions of the treaty, preserved in a manuscript from St Paul's, London,[142] introduce it as the peace (*frið*) 'which King Alfred and King Guthrum and the councillors of all the English race (*ealles Angelcynnes witan*) and all the people who are in East Anglia have all agreed on and confirmed with oaths'. The version which seems to represent the 'official' text proceeds to describe the boundary between the two parties in the following terms: 'up the Thames, and then up the Lea, and along the Lea to its source, then in a straight line to Bedford, then up the Ouse to Watling Street'.[143] The conventional interpretation of this

139 Asser, § 80.

140 S.362 (trans. *EHD*, no. 100). The charter is dated 901; but Wulfhere probably committed his crime during the course of the Viking wars in the 870s (see Nelson, ' "A king across the sea" ', p. 53, and Keynes, 'The West Saxon charters', p. 1127), and this meeting of West Saxon and Mercian councillors may have been one of the earliest of such joint councils. Wulfhere's forfeiture has also been connected with later events; see Wormald, 'The ninth century', p. 155. The use of the ancient term 'Gewisse', for the West Saxons, was seemingly suppressed in the OE Bede; so it is interesting that it was used here in the early tenth century.

141 The treaty is ed. Liebermann I.126–9; trans. *EHD*, no. 34, and Keynes and Lapidge, *Alfred the Great*, pp. 170–1. For its date, see Stenton, *Anglo-Saxon England*, pp. 260–2; Whitelock, in *EHD*, p. 416; Keynes and Lapidge, *Alfred the Great*, p. 311; and Baines, 'The Danish wars', pp. 14–15. For discussion of the treaty, and Guthrum's kingdom, in wider contexts, see Baines, 'The origins of the borough of Newport Pagnell', pp. 133–4; Abels, 'King Alfred's peace-making strategies', pp. 29–31; and Hart, *The Danelaw*, esp. pp. 8–16 and 25–42.

142 Cambridge, Corpus Christi College, MS 383, pp. 6 and 83–4; *The Making of England*, ed. Webster and Backhouse, pp. 267–8 (no. 242), shows the text of the treaty in CCCC MS 383, p. 6. For accounts of the manuscript, see Ker, *Catalogue*, no. 65; Richards, 'The manuscript contexts', pp. 181–4; and P. Wormald, *The Making of English Law* (forthcoming).

143 In one version (CCCC MS 383, pp. 83–4), the clause begins 'up on Temese' ('up the Thames'), and is introduced as '*our* boundaries'; in the other version (CCCC MS 383, p. 6), the clause begins 'andlang Temese' ('along the Thames'), and is introduced as '*their* boundaries'. It is as if the second version has been recast from the point of view of a different party, already established on the Thames; and if the first version is the 'official' text, the second may be a copy made for

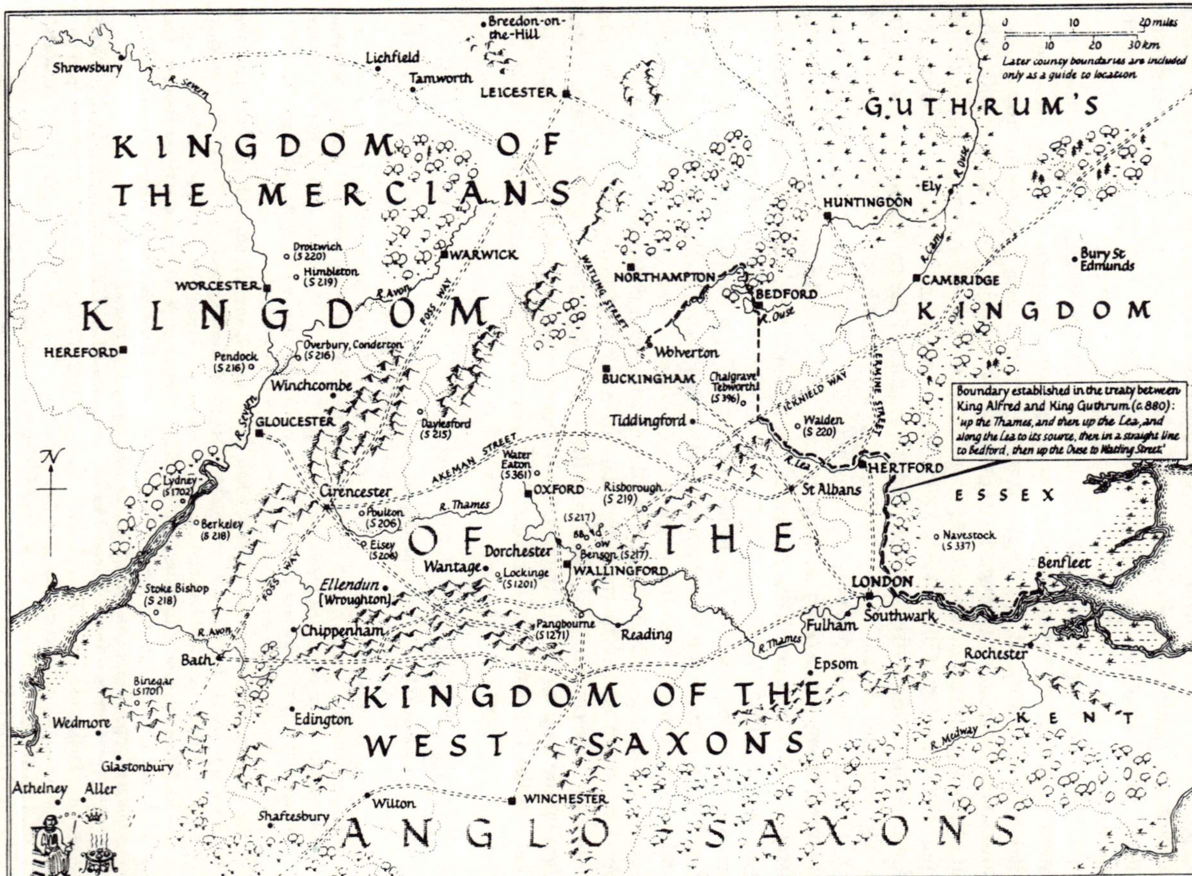

Fig. 1. The Kingdom of the Anglo-Saxons

boundary, running upriver from a starting-point in the Thames estuary and leaving London on the 'English' side, is marked on the map (Fig. 1); it is generally assumed, not without good reason, that the boundary would have continued along Watling Street (the A5) towards Tamworth. A more radical interpretation, proposed by Professor Dumville, takes the boundary to run along the Thames *downriver*, then up the Lea to Bedford, and along the Ouse to Watling Street, creating a line which is held to mark a boundary agreed between Alfred and Guthrum in 878 (at the so-called 'Treaty of Chippenham'), with Alfred left in control of the land south of the Thames but also east of the Lea (including part of Bedfordshire, east Hertfordshire, and Essex), and with Guthrum in control of a wedge of land extending south-eastwards through Oxfordshire and Buckinghamshire to London, with East Anglia thrown in for good measure.[144] The objections to this reading of the treaty are several and obvious;[145] and if we may set it respectfully to one side, we can revert to the more natural and straightforward interpretation. Since Alfred may well have assumed control of London not long after Ceolwulf's demise in 879, and since he may have retained interests there in the early 880s, it is conceivable that the treaty was in fact drawn up as early as 880 (when Guthrum first settled in East Anglia).[146] It is important to emphasise, however, that the treaty represents the boundary at a particular moment, and that just because it is our only contemporary evidence it does not follow that this was for all time the boundary between 'English' England and the Danelaw. If it was drawn up in 880, it may not have outlasted the Viking occupation of London in 883 (unless, perhaps, the Vikings in question were not from East Anglia); if peace-terms were renewed or remained in force, it may be that the extant treaty is

someone or some body in London. See further Keynes, 'Royal government and the written word in late Anglo-Saxon England', pp. 233–4.

144 Dumville, 'The treaty of Alfred and Guthrum', pp. 15–17. The interpretation has already attracted authoritative support (e.g. Blair, *Anglo-Saxon Oxfordshire*, pp. 96–7, and Williams, 'The Vikings in Essex', p. 94); and it cannot be doubted that it makes good sense of some of the political complexities of the age.

145 For the objections raised by the devil's advocate, see Dumville, 'The treaty of Alfred and Guthrum', pp. 19–23. I would grant Professor Dumville's response to the first (Alfred might well have presumed, in the late 870s, to act for the English: below, n. 146), but remain less than convinced by his responses to three others (that Guthrum would not be negotiating for the East Angles in 878; that 'up' the Thames, in what seems to be the 'official' version of the text, most naturally means 'upriver'; and that the boundary, if interpreted in this way, makes no separation between Guthrum's East Anglia and Alfred's Essex). If the Dumville Line is plotted on a map, it follows a course which seems, quite simply, to offend against common sense.

146 One might object that the reference to Alfred acting with the councillors 'of all the English race' most naturally points to the period following the general submission to Alfred in 886. The royal style on the *Two Emperors* coin is a reminder that Alfred might have been regarded as 'rex Anglorum' before then; but more to the point, it is entirely likely that following the demise of Ceolwulf *ca* 879 Alfred would have assumed leadership of the English for the purposes of such a treaty. He had, after all, already made terms with Guthrum at Chippenham in 878, standing sponsor to the Danish leader at his baptism at Aller soon afterwards, and also entertaining him at Wedmore. The extant treaty could not, however, represent whatever terms were agreed at Chippenham (since Guthrum's Danes were not then settled in East Anglia), nor could it represent what is so often called the 'Treaty of Wedmore' (for the same reason, and since there is no indication that there ever was such a thing); but there is no reason why it should not represent terms agreed in 880 (or thereafter), with Alfred acting in his own name as overlord of Mercia (cf. Davis, 'Alfred and Guthrum's frontier', pp. 806–7).

indeed none other than the 'peace' (*friþ*) between the (Danish) army in East Anglia and King Alfred which the Danes broke in 885;[147] and if the extant treaty was not drawn up until *ca* 886, it did not last much longer.[148] There is evidence, for example, that Ealdorman Æthelred, in council at Droitwich in Worcestershire in 888, felt empowered to grant land east of the boundary at Walden, in Hertfordshire, to his thegn Wulfgar;[149] while Alfred apparently made sufficient inroads into Essex in the 890s for him to have retained an ealdorman of that shire;[150] moreover, at some point the Danes acquired land west of the boundary, at Chalgrave and Tebworth in Bedfordshire, which had to be bought back from them in the early tenth century.[151] Even if the boundary had been constructed like the Berlin Wall, or the Maginot Line, which it patently was not, one should not be surprised if sooner or later it was overtaken by events. After all, the treaty envisages some traffic across the border, especially for purposes of trade, and that this took place is shown plainly enough by the evidence of coins: if we must give up the notion that *Two-Line* pennies were struck by the same (London) moneyers for both King Alfred and King Guthrum (under his baptismal name Athelstan), the very extensive imitation of the later Alfredian pence in the Danelaw presumably reflects contact of some kind.[152] Whatever the case, the treaty casts Alfred as one who operated in association with the councillors of all the English, and who established a boundary which made him responsible, implicitly, for a kingdom extending north as well as south of the Thames, down to and including London.

The 'kingdom of the Anglo-Saxons'

It may be helpful to reduce the reconstruction of events, proposed above, to its essentials, and to put it in the wider context of political developments in England from the seventh century to the eleventh. A basic distinction would appear to have existed in the seventh and early eighth centuries between the peoples who lived north and south of the river Humber; but it is arguable that it was during the period of Mercian supremacy, or more particularly during the reign of King Æthelbald (716–757), that the centre of gravity among the constituent peoples of England was drawn southwards from the Humber to the river Thames.[153] One

147 *Anglo-Saxon Chronicle s.a.* 885; Asser, § 72.

148 See Davis, 'Alfred and Guthrum's frontier', esp. pp. 803–6.

149 S.220, marked on the map (Fig. 1).

150 *Anglo-Saxon Chronicle s.a.* 896. See Keynes and Lapidge, *Alfred the Great*, p. 289; Hart, 'The ealdordom of Essex', p. 60 (pp. 116–17); Blackburn, 'The Ashdon (Essex) Hoard', esp. pp. 26–7; and Williams, 'The Vikings in Essex', p. 95. It would seem reasonable to assume that Ealdorman Beorhtwulf was responsible for southern Essex (perhaps extending to the line of the river Chelmer); on which basis it seems entirely appropriate that the Ashdon (north Essex) hoard, deposited in the early 890s, should comprise 'Danelaw' issues, and that the Leigh-on-Sea (south Essex) hoard, deposited in the late 890s, should comprise 'English' issues.

151 S.396 (trans. *EHD*, no. 103), marked on the map (Fig. 1). To judge from the general distribution of 'Scandinavian' place-names, Danish settlement in certain parts of what we are pleased to call the 'Danelaw' was of a kind which left much less of an impression in the longer term.

152 Blackburn, 'The earliest Anglo-Viking coinage', and Blackburn, 'The Ashdon (Essex) Hoard'; see also *MEC*, pp. 314 and 318–19.

153 For the Humber as a boundary between the 'Northumbrians' and the 'Southumbrians', see Stenton, *Anglo-Saxon England*, pp. 32–4. For the suggestion that the Humber (as opposed to the

outcome may have been to put relations between the Mercians and the West Saxons under greater pressure, initially in the region of the upper Thames valley; and it was during the course of the later eighth and ninth centuries that the tension worked itself out, in relation to the respective interests of the Mercian and West Saxon rulers in London and the south-east. The decisive change in the balance of power between the two kingdoms took place in the 820s, leaving King Ecgberht with the upper hand; a form of mutual accommodation began to emerge in the 840s and 850s, during the reign of King Æthelwulf; the guardians of ecclesiastical and economic interests in London appear to have been in the process of realigning themselves with Wessex in the 860s, when the western and eastern parts of the extended 'West Saxon' kingdom were beginning to coalesce; and, following the deposition of King Burgred in 874, Alfred himself was for a time recognised, in London, as king of both 'Saxons' and 'Mercians'. A certain Ceolwulf, of uncertain origin, was soon afterwards recognised as king of the Mercians, though it may be that he came to power in circumstances which at the time denied him the wholehearted support of all his people and which in retrospect would leave him open to ridicule. Between 874 and 879 Alfred and Ceolwulf maintained the appearance of an 'alliance' between Wessex and Mercia. When the kingdom of the Mercians was divided between English and Danes, in 877, London remained under 'English' control; but some time (perhaps not long) after the demise of Ceolwulf in 879, Alfred was able to assume authority over 'English' Mercia, gaining the submission of Æthelred, the new ruler of the Mercians, and gaining formal recognition at the same time in Gloucester and Oxford, but chosing to keep London itself under a more direct form of control. Londoners continued to recognise Alfred as their king during the early 880s, if only to judge from the fact that London moneyers struck coins in Alfred's name. In 883 a Viking force descended upon London; and since it would appear that the English commercial settlement was at this stage concentrated outside and to the west of the Roman walls, one might suppose, quite simply, that the Vikings had presumed to establish themselves within the city itself. King Alfred promptly responded by laying siege to the city, and sooner or later the Vikings were driven out. The weakness of London's position was exposed again when another Viking force entered the Thames estuary in 885; and in the following year Alfred decided to 'occupy' London and secure its defences for good. The chronicler's choice of words reflects the fact that London was already under English control, and that in 886 it was not necessary to eject any Vikings from the city itself, because there were none; defences were strengthened, and the existing commercial settlement was relocated within the city walls. The 'occupation' of London was followed soon afterwards by the formal submission to King Alfred of all of the English who were not under subjection to the Danes, reflecting the emergence by this time of a new political order. Alfred took the opportunity to entrust London into the hands of Ealdorman Æthelred; but English Mercia remained none the less an integral part of Alfred's kingdom, albeit retaining an identity of

Welsh March) was the boundary from which 'Mercia' took its name, see Hunter Blair, 'The Northumbrians and their southern frontier'; but cf. Brooks, 'The formation of the Mercian kingdom', p. 162. For the shift from the Humber to the river Thames, see Keynes, 'England 700–900', esp. p. 28.

its own under the 'Lord (and Lady) of the Mercians' and doubtless numbering among its people many who entertained aspirations to a renewal of its independence. The distinctively Alfredian political order which emerged in the 880s is implicit in the boundary established between Alfred and Guthrum; and in view of the royal styles employed in charters of the late 880s and early 890s, and adopted by Asser in his *Life of King Alfred* (893), there is no reason why it should not be described, unequivocally, as the 'kingdom of the Anglo-Saxons'. It is accordingly labelled as such on the accompanying map (Fig. 1).

The 'kingdom of the Anglo-Saxons' might be characterised as a political order which came into existence in the late ninth century, conceived at the court of King Alfred the Great, in opposition to the Danish invaders, as an expression of the common political interests of 'Anglian' and 'Saxon' peoples. The peoples were united rather than separated by the river which ran between them; and although, initially, they had two political centres, at Winchester and at Gloucester, the focal point of the kingdom in economic terms (and its future in political terms) lay towards the mouth of the river Thames, at London. The existence of the 'kingdom of the Anglo-Saxons' has passed largely unnoticed, yet the kingdom can be seen from the evidence of charters (and coins) to have endured for nearly fifty years (*ca* 880–927). It represented not so much the combination of the ancient kingdoms of Wessex and Mercia, as the creation of something different and wholly new; and since it proved to be nothing less than the political entity transitional between 'Wessex' (with its south-eastern extensions) and 'England', it must surely deserve to be given its due. In the last decade of his reign Alfred seems to have re-established control of Essex, perhaps as the natural extension of the positive steps taken at London. It is conceivable that Alfred's son Edward the Elder was anointed king in the late 890s, in an Alfredian manifestation of an established practice with well-known Carolingian, and Mercian, antecedents, though there is no reason to believe that Alfred's kingdom 'of the Anglo-Saxons' was in any sense diminished as a result.[154] It would appear that the order of service for a king's coronation, which might well have originated at about this time, was devised quite specifically for a kingship over two peoples (Angles and Saxons);[155] and it seems fitting that the royal estate at Kingston, on the river Thames, where King Ecgberht, King Æthelwulf, and Archbishop Ceolnoth had made a pact of friendship in 838, should have been chosen (perhaps by Archbishop

154 S.350, dated 898, is attested by Alfred, *rex Saxonum*, and by Edward, *rex*; the charter survives in what would appear to be its original single-sheet form (conveniently reproduced in Smyth, *King Alfred the Great*, pl. 21). It is arguable that Alfred's style ('king of the Saxons') represents not so much a 'loss of control during Alfred's very last years' (Nelson, 'The political ideas of Alfred of Wessex', p. 134, n. 42, and 'Reconstructing a royal family', p. 64), as a view of Alfred from a perspective other than that of the royal court (Keynes, 'The West Saxon charters', p. 1148, n. 1). In his will, in his law-code, and in one of his translations, Alfred styled himself 'king of the West Saxons', which is precisely what he was; and the usage is perhaps no more than a sign that for all his aspirations he never lost touch with reality. He was also styled *rex Saxonum* on coins minted at Exeter and at Winchester.

155 The operative prayer is 'Omnipotens sempiterne Deus', recited by the officiating (arch)bishop as he anointed the king and so before the king received the ring, sword, crown, sceptre, and rod. See Nelson, 'The second English Ordo', pp. 365–6; Keynes, 'A tale of two kings', p. 210; and Nelson, 'The political ideas of Alfred of Wessex', pp. 134–5. For a version of the prayer, see *The Claudius Pontificals*, ed. Turner, p. 91.

Plegmund, himself of Mercian origin) as the place for the coronation of kings of the new political order.[156] The essential truth, however, is that the Alfredian polity survived King Alfred's death: it was the kingdom of the Anglo-Saxons that passed in 899 to King Edward the Elder; it was as 'king of the Anglo-Saxons' that Edward would have been crowned, apparently at Kingston, on Whit Sunday (8 June) 900; and it was accordingly as 'king of the Anglo-Saxons' that he was known to the draftsmen of the majority of his charters.[157] The point needs to be emphasised, because if Edward had succeeded his father as king 'of the West Saxons' there would be more scope for supposing that the 'English' Mercians, under Æthelred and Æthelflæd, recovered a significant measure of political independence after Alfred's death.[158] Æthelred and Æthelflæd were still joint rulers of the Mercians in the opening years of the tenth century;[159] yet the evidence of charters,[160] and coins,[161] demonstrates clearly enough that they operated from the

156 For the pact of 838, see S.1438, and Keynes, 'The West Saxon charters', pp. 1112–14, with further references. For the suggestion that King Æthelwulf was anointed king at Kingston in 838, see Wormald, 'The ninth century', p. 140; and for the interesting observation that Kingston was the highest point of tidal flow on the Thames, see Wormald, 'Celtic and Anglo-Saxon kingship', p. 160, with p. 178, n. 42. For coronations at Kingston in the tenth century, see Keynes, *The Diplomas of King Æthelred*, pp. 270–1.

157 See Keynes, 'The West Saxon charters', p. 1148, n. 4. Leaving aside the more patently spurious charters, the exceptions are: S.365 (from the New Minster, Winchester), in which Edward is styled king 'of the Saxons'; S.374 (also from the New Minster), in which he is styled king 'of the English'; and S.372 (from the Old Minster, Winchester), in which he is styled king 'of the West Saxons'. In S.368 (from Wilton), an implicit distinction is made between Edward, king 'of the Anglo-Saxons', and Æthelwulf, king 'of the Saxons'; and in S.369 (from Abingdon) an implicit distinction is made between Edward, king 'of the Anglo-Saxons', and Æthelwulf, king 'of the West Saxons'. In S.375 (from the Old Minster, Winchester), the king is said to have ruled *Angul Saxonia*.

158 Cf. (e.g.) Stenton, *Anglo-Saxon England*, pp. 317–21; John, 'The age of Edgar', p. 161; and Stafford, *Unification and Conquest*, p. 26. Professor Dumville's list of Mercian rulers in the *Handbook of British Chronology*, ed. Fryde, *et al.*, pp. 17–18, ends provocatively with King Æthelred II, Queen Æthelflæd, and Queen Ælfwynn. To confuse the issue further, Henry of Huntingdon states that Æthelflæd was called 'not only lady, or queen, but even king' (*Henry, Archdeacon of Huntingdon, 'Historia Anglorum'*, ed. Greenway, p. 308). Of course it is scarcely surprising that Æthelred, Æthelflæd and Ælfwynn were considered royal or semi-royal by various observers; see *Two of the Saxon Chronicles Parallel*, ed. Plummer, II, 118–19.

159 In a charted dated 901, Æthelred and Æthelflæd are described as 'opitulante gratuita Dei gratia monarchiam Merceorum tenentes honorificeque gubernantes et defendentes' (S.221), and in a charter dated 904 they are 'Myrcna hlafordas' (S.1280); see also S.1282. They were empowered to issue charters without reference to Edward, but they remained none the less under Edward's control (see next note). Towards the end of his life Æthelred may have been incapacitated by illness (cf. *Fragmentary Annals of Ireland*, ed. Radner, pp. 168–9). The compiler of the 'Mercian Register' (incorporated in the *Anglo-Saxon Chronicle*, MSS BCD) calculated Æthelflæd's rule (*anweald*) from the time of her husband's death, in 911. She is described as 'domina Merciorum' in S.224, and as 'juvante superna pietate et largiente clementia Christi gubernacula regens Merciorum' in S.225 (with her daughter Ælfwynn following her in the witness-list, erroneously styled a 'bishop').

160 See Keynes, 'A charter of Edward the Elder for Islington', and Keynes, 'The West Saxon charters', p. 1149, n. 1. In S.367, dated 903, reference is made to King Edward, Æthelred, and Æthelflæd, 'who then held rulership and power over the people of the Mercians under the aforesaid king' ('qui tunc principatum et potestatem gentis Merciorum sub predicto rege tenuerunt'); the witnesses include Ælfwynn, presumably their daughter.

161 Blunt, *et al.*, *Coinage in Tenth-Century England*, pp. 34–43.

start under Edward's overall control. It seems entirely appropriate, under these circumstances, that the (West Saxon) chronicler should represent Edward as sending an army 'both from the West Saxons and from the Mercians' in 909 and 910; and one need not doubt, therefore, that it was Edward who orchestrated the military campaign to conquer the Danes of the southern Danelaw.[162] Nor is it surprising that Edward should have taken decisive action to secure his position in Mercia as the opportunities arose, first after Æthelred's death in 911 and again after Æthelflæd's death on 12 June 918.[163] One might be disposed to assume that Edward was succeeded, after his own death on 17 July 924, by his eldest son Æthelstan; but matters were hardly that simple. It may have been the intention of those in power to dismantle the kingdom 'of the Anglo-Saxons' and to reconstitute its separate components, under Ælfweard in Wessex and Æthelstan in Mercia; or it may be that the political establishment (at Winchester) intended Ælfweard to rule over both peoples, prompting another political establishment (at Gloucester?) to set up Æthelstan in opposition to him; or it may be that Ælfweard's early death, on 2 August 924, created an unexpected opportunity for the political establishment in Mercia to campaign for the recognition of Æthelstan as his successor.[164] It is apparent, however, that when Æthelstan was eventually crowned, at Kingston-upon-Thames on 4 September 925, he took his place, as his grandfather might have intended, as king 'of the Anglo-Saxons'.[165] As things turned out, the 'kingdom of the Anglo-Saxons' was soon overtaken by the turn of events. In 927 King Æthelstan took direct control of Northumbria, thereby

162 See Stenton, *Anglo-Saxon England*, pp. 319–63, and Wainwright, 'Æthelflæd, Lady of the Mercians'.

163 Æthelflæd was succeeded by her daughter Ælfwynn, who was probably the last of the line (cf. S.1280). Edward seems to have been determined not to allow Ælfwynn any semblance of political power, and in December 918 he seized her and took her back into Wessex. The compiler of the Mercian Register states in this connection that Ælfwynn was deprived of 'of all authority in Mercia' ('ælces anwealdes on Myrcum'). For the suggestion that Ælfwynn ended her days as a 'religious woman' with interests in Kent (S.535, dated 948), see Taylor, 'King Alfred and his family', p. 353.

164 For further discussion of these events, see (e.g.) Williams, 'Some notes and considerations', pp. 149–51; Wood, 'The making of King Aethelstan's empire', pp. 256–8; Keynes, 'King Athelstan's books', pp. 186–7; Yorke, 'Æthelwold and the politics of the tenth century', pp. 70–3; Keynes, 'England 900–1016'; and *The Liber Vitae of the New Minster*, ed. Keynes, pp. 19–21. For a connection between the establishment at Gloucester and a religious house intimately associated with King Æthelstan, see above, n. 135.

165 See S.394: *Charters of St Augustine's*, ed. Kelly, no. 26. In S.1417, a lease drawn up probably at Winchester, some time between 925 and 927 (*The Liber Vitae of the New Minster*, ed. Keynes, pp. 20–1), Æthelstan is styled 'king of the Anglo-Saxons and of the Danes', signifying authority not only over his English subjects but also over the 'Danes', i.e. the English, Danish, and Anglo-Danish inhabitants of the southern Danelaw; cf. Stenton, *Anglo-Saxon England*, p. 353, n. 1. He is styled 'king of the Anglo-Saxons' in two charters dated 926 (S.396 and S.397), from the archives of Abingdon and Burton respectively; for the former, see *EHD*, no. 103. The style 'king of the Anglo-Saxons' was applied to King Æthelstan in the MacDurnan Gospels, perhaps implying that the inscription was made between 925 and 927 (cf. Keynes, 'King Athelstan's books', pp. 153–9). The style 'king of the Anglo-Saxons and Mercians', applied to King Æthelstan in the Gandersheim Gospels (*ibid.*, pp. 189–90), was perhaps devised by a person who knew that Æthelstan was correctly styled king 'of the Anglo-Saxons', but was not properly conscious of the fact that the term 'Anglo-Saxons' was intended in court circles to subsume West Saxons and Mercians alike.

bringing into existence a kingdom 'of the English' (in a sense which would have appealed to Bede), and leading in the fullness of time to the emergence of the unified kingdom of England.[166] The problem was how to hold together a political order conceived on an even grander scale than the 'kingdom of the Anglo-Saxons'. In 939–940, Olaf Guthfrithsson gained control in York and pushed the border southwards to Watling Street, reducing Edmund's kingdom from that 'of the English' to that 'of the Anglo-Saxons', at least for a while; and although the kingdom 'of the English' was held as a unified whole from time to time during the 940s and 950s, a distinction was still recognised, in certain quarters, between the 'Anglo-Saxons' and the 'Northumbrians'.[167] When a division of the kingdom was effected between Eadwig and Edgar, in 957, the boundary between them was fixed along the line of the river Thames, suggesting (perhaps) that the point of balance still lay in the south; indeed, it was only following the death of King Eadwig, in 959, and the accession of Edgar to the re-united realm, that the kingdom of the English began to assume its most natural form. For while the river Humber duly recovered its former significance as the boundary between the north and the south, the political and economic interests of the kingdom were firmly disposed on the two sides of the river Thames, and London was set to come into its own.

'Anglo-Saxon' attitudes at the court of King Alfred

It should be clear from the above that in the 880s and 890s King Alfred's court would have been positively crawling with Mercians. Among them we can identify the king's wife Ealhswith, doubtless accompanied by her groupies and friends, and perhaps visited from time to time by her mother Eadburh ('from the royal stock of the king of the Mercians'), and by her brother, the Mercian ealdorman Æthelwulf; the king's son-in-law Ealdorman Æthelred, and any other members of the royal and noble houses of Mercia who needed to be present in Wessex on those occasions when 'all the councillors of the Gewisse and of the Mercians' met to deliberate on affairs of state;[168] distinguished churchmen, like Werferth,

166 The perceived grandeur of the new political order found immediate expression in the wholly remarkable series of charters produced in the name of King Æthelstan, between 928 and 935, by the royal scribe who has come to be known as 'Æthelstan A': see Keynes, *The Charters of King Æthelstan* (forthcoming).

167 In the seemingly 'Mercian' usage of the so-called 'alliterative' charters of the 940s and 950s (Keynes, 'King Athelstan's Books', pp. 158–9), Edmund was king 'of the Anglo-Saxons' in 940–2 (S.472–3 and 479), and Eadred was king 'of the Anglo-Saxons, Northumbrians, pagans, and Britons' (*vel sim.*) in 946 (S.520), 949–50 (S.544, 548–50, 552a), and 955 (S.569); so it would appear that 'Anglo-Saxons' had come implicitly to subsume the 'Danes' of the southern Danelaw, and was used to represent a people distinct from the Northumbrians.

168 See above, p. 31, n. 140. The *minister* Beorhtsige who attests a charter of King Alfred in 898 (S.350: above, n. 154) is positioned immediately after the ealdormen and ahead of Osferth *minister* and the remaining thegns; Osferth was a kinsman of the king (see Keynes and Lapidge, *Alfred the Great*, p. 322; Nelson, 'Reconstructing a royal family', pp. 59–61), and it is conceivable, therefore, that Beorhtsige was also in some sense royal, and, in particular, that he belonged to the Mercian 'B-dynasty' (above, p. 11, n. 40). A thegn called Beorhtsige attests charters of Edward the Elder in 901, and may or may not be the same man. The Beorhtsige who witnessed Alfred's charter is quite probably the Byrhtsige, son of ætheling Beornoth, who died fighting on the Danish side against Edward, in 902 (*Anglo-Saxon Chronicle* 904 A, 905 BCD), and who serves as a

bishop of Worcester, and Plegmund, who was appointed archbishop of Canterbury in 890;[169] the anonymous Mercian, perhaps, who was responsible for translating Bede's *Historia ecclesiastica* into English; priests like Æthelstan and Werwulf, and, if not one of them, the Mercian priest who seems to have been responsible for producing some of King Alfred's charters;[170] and perhaps some of the craftsmen whom the king had assembled 'in almost countless quantity from many races',[171] including the Mercian who seems to have devised the inscription on the Alfred Jewel.[172] The Mercians themselves had acknowledged Alfred's supremacy, and there were moneyers in 'Mercian' towns like London, Oxford and Gloucester minting coins in King Alfred's name; and while they might have harboured resentment towards the West Saxon people and their ruler, that is not the impression which one derives from the account of the campaign against the Danes in the 890s, in which West Saxons, Mercians and Welsh seem to have collaborated against the common enemy.[173] For his own part, King Alfred was doubtless pleased to be called 'king of the Angles and Saxons' or 'king of the Anglo-Saxons', but he seems to have taken to heart the responsibilities which such aspirations brought with them: he devoted one eighth of his annual revenues to the support of 'monasteries' throughout Wessex and Mercia,[174] and when framing his legislation he made a point of acknowledging the use which he had made not only of earlier West Saxon and Kentish laws, but also of the laws of Offa, king of the Mercians.[175] In short, Alfred would not have wished to offend Mercian sensibilities, any more than he could have afforded to do so.

Two literary works which emanated in the early 890s from the circle of scholars around the king will serve finally to illustrate different aspects of the 'Anglo-Saxon' attitudes then current at the court of King Alfred the Great. The *Anglo-Saxon Chronicle* is usually thought of as a fundamentally West Saxon work, celebrating the achievements of the West Saxon dynasty at the expense of their rivals, and cultivating the image of King Alfred himself as the heroic leader of English resistance to the Danes.[176] Of course the *Chronicle* offers a view of

reminder that some Mercians may well have resented the imperial pretensions of West Saxon rulers. For the suggestion that Beorhtsige was a kinsman of Byrhtnoth, ealdorman of Essex (956–91), see *Crawford Charters*, ed. Napier and Stevenson, pp. 85–6, with n. 4.

169 See Asser, § 77; see also Keynes and Lapidge, *Alfred the Great*, pp. 26 and 33.

170 Whitelock, 'Some charters in the name of King Alfred', pp. 88–90; Keynes and Lapidge, *Alfred the Great*, p. 330, n. 17; Keynes, 'The West Saxon charters', pp. 1135–7.

171 Asser, § 101.

172 See Keynes and Lapidge, *Alfred the Great*, p. 204.

173 See *Anglo-Saxon Chronicle* 893A 894BCD, with reference to the siege of Buttington; Keynes and Lapidge, *Alfred the Great*, pp. 43 and 116.

174 Asser, § 102.

175 Alfred's law-code, ed. Liebermann I.46; trans. *EHD*, no. 33, p. 409. For the basic conception of the law-code, as legislation for a new holy people, see Wormald, '*Lex Scripta* and *Verbum Regis*', p. 132, pending the appearance of his *The Making of English Law*. It is not clear what Alfred may have meant by the laws of King Offa: perhaps a vernacular code, in which case it is lost almost without trace (cf. Keynes and Lapidge, *Alfred the Great*, p. 305, n. 5), or perhaps a Latin capitulary issued in 786, in which case its substance is preserved, after all, in the report of the legates to Pope Hadrian (cf. Wormald, 'In search of King Offa's "Law-Code" ').

176 See, for example, Wallace-Hadrill, 'The Franks and the English', and Davis, 'Alfred the Great: propaganda and truth'.

history in which the West Saxons play the dominant role, and in which Alfred in particular comes out on top; after all, that is no more than we should expect of a work compiled by loyal subjects of the reigning king. It is arguable, however, that the chroniclers were concerned to do far more than beat a West Saxon drum; and that while they may not have been ready to join the draftsmen of the king's charters in a confident belief in the kingdom 'of the Anglo-Saxons', they knew themselves to be operating within a political order which embraced Wessex, Kent and Sussex, and whose ruler was looking beyond that horizon. Indeed, it is precisely this aspect of their work which places the compilers of the Alfredian *Chronicle* so comfortably within the court circle.[177] One should think twice, therefore, before reading into their account anything as crude as anti-Mercian bias, whether (for example) in their failure to record as much of Mercia's seventh-century history as we should have liked, or in their failure to do justice to such Mercian giants as Æthelbald and Offa. It is unfortunate that they did not manage to gather more material from elsewhere, but it seems that they did their best to record the traditions and royal genealogies of kingdoms other than Wessex, and that they restrained themselves from making hay of the difficulties which these other kingdoms faced in the ninth century, whether internally or from exposure to Viking attack. The only sour note remains the disparaging reference to Ceolwulf as a 'foolish king's thegn', best regarded, perhaps, as a judgement made after the event, and one which for all we know could have been music to the ears of Ealdorman Æthelred. There need be no doubt that all readers of the *Chronicle* would have been expected to admire the achievements and the strength of the West Saxon royal dynasty, and that West Saxons would have enjoyed it more than Mercians; yet it must be said that Mercians would have found nothing to give them offence, and only gentle reminders of the various occasions on which their people had received help from West Saxon kings.[178]

Asser's *Life of King Alfred* is a quite different matter altogether. For as long as the authenticity of the *Life* was regarded as suspect, attention was diverted away from its content; but there can be few now who would be inclined to challenge Dorothy Whitelock's reassertion of faith in the 'Genuine Asser', and the controversy has shifted to its credibility, and intended audience.[179] In the opinion of W. H. Stevenson, the *Life* was written for no purpose other than that of 'celebrating the doings and recording the life of a truly great man';[180] and perhaps it is best left at that, with the slight qualification that 'truly great' represents Asser's

177 Keynes and Lapidge, *Alfred the Great*, pp. 39–41, 217–18, 277–8, and 283, n. 14. Perhaps one should note that the chronicler refers to the 'alms of the West Saxons' in connection with the king's gifts to Rome in the 880s.

178 *Anglo-Saxon Chronicle* 839 (Beorhtric helping Offa, in 789), 830 (? Wiglaf's restoration), 853 (Æthelwulf helping Burgred) and 868 (Æthelred and Alfred helping Burgred).

179 This statement, written in 1986, proved to be wholly mistaken. The challenge was taken up by Smyth, *King Alfred the Great*. For a selection of reviews, see M. Lapidge, in *The Times Higher Education Supplement*, 8 March 1996, p. 20; Keynes, 'On the authenticity of Asser's *Life of King Alfred*'; D. N. Dumville, in *Cambrian Medieval Celtic Studies* 31 (1996), 90–3; D. R. Howlett, in *English Historical Review* 112 (1997), 942–4; and J. L. Nelson, in *Early Medieval Europe* 7 (1998).

180 *Asser's Life of King Alfred*, ed. Stevenson, p. cix; this might also have been the view of Asser himself (*ibid*. pp. lxxviii–lxxix, citing Asser, §§ 21 and 73).

opinion and should not determine unduly the formation of our own. Yet modern historians are almost expected to be more devious, and to find hidden purposes behind every work. Perhaps the most natural position would be to presume that the *Life* was aimed at an English audience, and indeed that the 'prime intended audience was the king himself'.[181] Alternatively, one might suppose that the *Life* was devised for the edification of the priests of the royal household, or as a form of *speculum principis* designed to show the æthelings at court how a king was expected to conduct himself.[182] All such options have particular attractions; but there seems to be more, overall, to recommend the view that the *Life of King Alfred* was intended for Asser's friends and associates in Wales.[183] Of course the *Life* is largely pious panegyric, but it is more questionable whether it really presents the king in a 'uniformly and intensely favourable light'.[184] True, it is dedicated to King Alfred, perhaps for reasons of the kind which lay behind the dedication of numerous volumes of county histories to Queen Victoria, and not with any presumption or expectation that the work would actually be read by the dedicatee; indeed, one might suppose that the dedication was intended primarily to advertise the subject's distinction and to establish the author's credentials.[185] Moreover, the *Life* was written in Latin, at a time when Alfred was translating everything from Latin into English, so it is difficult to believe that it was intended for an English audience of any kind.[186] Least of all does Asser's *Life* seem to have been intended for consumption at *court*, for it contains much that would not have been well received in the kind of milieu which I have been at pains to describe.[187] King Alfred's sensibilities might have been offended by the dwelling on the details of his illnesses;[188] by the critical references to his brother Æthelbald,

181 Campbell, 'Asser's *Life of Alfred*', esp. pp. 122–3 and 127–8. Davis, 'Alfred the Great', p. 177 (p. 41) took the view that 'while the Chronicle tells us what Alfred wanted us to know, Asser (if genuine) merely tells us what Alfred wanted to hear'. Kirby, 'Asser and his Life of King Alfred', pp. 26–33, develops the view that the *Life*, in its final form, was intended for English as well as Welsh readers.

182 Scharer, 'The writing of history at King Alfred's court', pp. 186, 189, and 204–5.

183 Schütt, 'The literary form of Asser's "*Vita Alfredi*" ', p. 210; Kirby, 'Asser and his Life of King Alfred', pp. 17 and 20–33; Thomson, 'British Latin and English history', p. 49; and Keynes and Lapidge, *Alfred the Great*, pp. 41–2, 56, and 250, n. 115. For discussion of this hypothesis, see Smyth, *King Alfred the Great*, pp. 362–3.

184 Campbell, 'Asser's *Life of Alfred*', p. 127.

185 Keynes, 'On the authenticity of Asser's *Life of King Alfred*', pp. 539–40. John Mitchell Kemble dedicated *The Saxons in England* (1849) to Queen Victoria, in the following terms: 'To the Queen's most excellent majesty, this history of the principles which have given her empire its preeminence among the nations of Europe, is, with her gracious permission, inscribed by the most humble and devoted of her servants.' He was, at the time, a candidate for the Regius Professorship of Modern History at the University of Cambridge.

186 Of course the point is merely rhetorical; at Alfred's school 'books in both languages – that is to say, in Latin and English – were carefully read' (Asser, § 75).

187 Patrick Wormald points out to me that the evidence might be approached in a different way. If we assume that Asser's *Life* was intended for court consumption, and might therefore reflect an 'official' view of events, it would follow that it constitutes powerful evidence of 'anti-Mercian' tendencies at the Alfredian court; and this in turn would tell *against* the interpretation of other, much weaker, evidence in terms of *entente cordiale* between Wessex and Mercia. See also Wormald, 'Bede, the *Bretwaldas*, and the origins of the *Gens Anglorum*', pp. 118–19.

188 Asser, § 74.

whose misdemeanours were so carefully suppressed (it seems) in the *Anglo-Saxon Chronicle* and (one might add) in the king's own will;[189] and by Asser's evident disapproval of the custom whereby the West Saxons did not allow the king's wife to sit beside him on the throne, or be called 'queen'.[190] The sensibilities of others at court might have been offended by the imputation of treachery to those involved in Æthelbald's plot against his father, including a former bishop of Sherborne and a former ealdorman of Somerset;[191] by Asser's comments about the excessive wealth of the English which brought about a disregard for the monastic life;[192] and by those of his stories which heap praise on the king for overcoming the stubbornness, stupidity and sloth of his ealdorman, reeves and thegns.[193] But above all, *Mercian* sensibilities might have been offended by Asser's vitriolic account of Offa's daughter Eadburh, who is represented as behaving 'like a tyrant (*tyrannice*) after the manner of her father';[194] by the suggestions of Mercian dependence on West Saxon help which go beyond what Asser found in the *Chronicle*;[195] by the statement that the rulers of Glywysing and Gwent were driven to submit to King Alfred 'by the might and tyrannical behaviour (*vi et tyrannide*) of Ealdorman Æthelred and the Mercians';[196] and by the remark that Anarawd of Gwynedd submitted to the king 'on the same condition as Æthelred and the Mercians, namely that in every respect he would be obedient to the royal will'.[197] Perhaps English readers could have taken it, but unless we are to suppose that Asser was singularly tactless it would seem easier to understand such remarks as representing the views of a Welshman who could afford to share his disapproval of certain things with his friends in St David's, and who could vent his feelings towards the Mercians in particular in the certain knowledge that such (characteristically Welsh) feelings would be most sympathetically received. At the same time, however, Asser could naturally voice his strong approval of the king himself, drawing attention to Alfred's distinctive qualities as a ruler, to the terrible hardships which the king had to endure in meeting the responsibilities of his office, and to the special benefits which all those who acknowledged his lordship could expect to enjoy at his hands.[198] It is important to emphasise, again and again, that while Asser calls Alfred's predecessors 'king of the Saxons', or 'king of the West Saxons', he represents Alfred himself invariably as 'king of the Anglo-Saxons'.[199] Asser evidently intended to suggest

189 Asser, §§ 12–13 and 17.
190 Asser, §§ 13–15.
191 Asser, § 12.
192 Asser, § 93.
193 Asser, §§ 91 and 106.
194 Asser, §§ 14–15.
195 Asser, §§ 7 and 30.
196 Asser, § 80.
197 *Ibid.*
198 Asser, §§ 76 and 80.
199 Keynes and Lapidge, *Alfred the Great*, p. 227, n. 1. If we may set aside the 'first' occurrence of the style, in a most conspicuous position (§ 1), and discount two other occurrences where Asser is clearly referring to the Alfred of his own day (§§ 13 and 21), it is striking indeed that the style is used in contexts which relate to the period 882–7 (§§ 64, 67, 71, 73, 83 and 87), as if Asser was conscious that the style was the product of political developments in the early 880s; cf.

by his terminology a significant distinction between Alfred and his predecessors; and in making this distinction, he was making a point. It seems that he was eager to promote the grandiose notions of Alfred which had emerged from the turmoil of the 870s and from the momentous political developments of the 880s; but he takes matters further, by representing Alfred's struggle as that of Christians against pagans, and in so doing he must have hoped to encourage his readers the more readily to embrace Alfred's cause.[200] Nor is it any less significant that Asser, as a loyal and devoted servant of the king, should represent Alfred to a Welsh audience as 'ruler of all the Christians of the island of Britain'. Several kings before Alfred – including Edwin and Oswald of Northumbria, Æthelbald and Offa of Mercia, and Ecgberht of Wessex – had been accorded the ultimate accolade of kingship throughout Britain, and for his successors, from Æthelstan onwards, the accolade might almost be taken for granted; but for King Alfred himself, to be described in such terms by a Welshman was high praise indeed.

The *Anglo-Saxon Chronicle* and Asser's *Life of King Alfred* may both have been produced by the court branch of Saatchi and Saatchi, but they were products of different departments and were intended for different audiences. The chroniclers constructed a view of English history which would accord with the conception of King Alfred as ruler of an amalgamated 'Anglo-Saxon' people, for the benefit of an English audience (perhaps at the king's court); whereas Asser produced an account of the king which was perfectly tailored for its intended Welsh readers, but which at court would have gone down like the proverbial lead balloon. In their different ways, therefore, both works reflect the *rapprochement* between the two kingdoms of Wessex and Mercia which had developed apace during the ninth century, and which found expression during Alfred's reign in so many other ways as well. Of course there would always be difficulties, but in the tenth century the long process was brought to fruition. It finds further expression, for example, in the co-operation between Ealdorman Æthelred, Æthelflæd and Edward the Elder, which made possible the re-conquest of the southern Danelaw; or (ironically) in the words of a Welsh poet, who foretold the day 'when the men of Wessex will come together in council, in a single party, of one mind with the Mercian incendiaries, hoping to bring shame on our splendid hosts';[201] or (more appropriately) in the words of the Anglo-Saxon poet who celebrated the heroism of both West Saxon and Mercian contingents at the battle of *Brunanburh*.[202] The two tenth-century West Saxon kings in whose reigns the political unification of England came closest to becoming a reality were undoubtedly Æthelstan and

Nelson, 'The political ideas of Alfred of Wessex', p. 155, n. 127, and Foot, 'The making of *Angelcynn*', p. 27, n. 12. Note also that *all Angel cynn* (ASC 886) was translated by Asser as *omnes Angli et Saxones* (above, n. 108).

200 See Keynes and Lapidge, *Alfred the Great*, pp. 41–2; and Thomson, 'British Latin and English history', p. 51.

201 *Armes Prydein*, ed. Williams and Bromwich, pp. 9 and 50–1.

202 *Anglo-Saxon Chronicle* 937 ABCD (ed. Plummer, I, 108; trans. *EHD*, no. 1, p. 219). An 'ealdorman of the Mercians' helped drive the Hiberno-Norse kings from York in 944 (Æthelweard, *Chronicon* IV.6 (ed. Campbell, p. 54)); but it is not clear who he was. The political identity of the Mercians died hard: Eadric Streona was appointed ealdorman 'of the kingdom of the Mercians' in 1007 (*ASC*).

Edgar, and it is significant that both had begun their careers in Mercia, and that both might therefore have commanded more than the usual affection which was accorded to a West Saxon ruler, north of the Thames.[203] Like King Alfred before them, gratefully might they have taken up 'the sword which belonged to King Offa'.

INDEX OF CHARTERS

Charters are cited above by their number in P. H. Sawyer, *Anglo-Saxon Charters: an Annotated List and Bibliography*, Royal Historical Society Guides and Handbooks 8 (London, 1968). A revised edition of Sawyer's list is in preparation, under the auspices of the British Academy / Royal Historical Society Joint Committee on Anglo-Saxon Charters.

[203] For the circumstances of Æthelstan's accession, see above, p. 38. When the kingdom of all England was divided in 957, Eadwig retained control of Wessex and the south-east, and his brother Edgar was assigned the land north of the Thames (becoming king of all England following Eadwig's death in 959); see above, p. 29, n. 132.

ALLIANCES, GODFATHERS, TREATIES AND BOUNDARIES

Thomas Charles-Edwards

Under the year 878 the *Anglo-Saxon Chronicle* describes a series of transactions designed to make peace between Alfred, Guthrum and their followers.[1] Alfred had won the battle of Edington and had confined the Danes to their fort, probably at Chippenham.[2] After a fortnight they came to terms. The Danish army gave Alfred hostages and swore great oaths. These oaths and hostages guaranteed two things: that they would depart out of the bounds of his kingdom and that their king would receive baptism. The *Chronicle* goes on immediately to set out in detail the fulfilment of the second promise. At the end of three weeks Guthrum came to Alfred at Aller as one of a company embracing thirty of the highest ranking men in the army. Alfred acted as Guthrum's sponsor receiving him from the font. From a later annal (890) we discover that he received at baptism a name favoured by the West Saxon royal family, Æthelstan. The loosing of the chrism bandage took place a few days later at Wedmore.[3] The Danes remained for twelve days with Alfred and the West Saxon king honoured both Guthrum and his companions with rich gifts.

The effect the annalist appears to be seeking is cumulative, with a series of transactions, one after the other, demonstrating both the firmness of the alliance made between the army and Alfred and the superiority which Alfred had obtained over the Danes and their king. The initial transactions are between the army on the one side and Alfred on the other. Guthrum, at the beginning, and the West Saxon people, throughout, occupy far less prominent positions: Guthrum's baptism is the fulfilment of an undertaking by the Danish army not by Guthrum. The army starts the process by offering the hostages (*foregislas*, Asser's *nominati obsides*[4]); but during the proceedings at the baptism and thereafter Guthrum is given a prominence almost the equal of Alfred's. The reason for the initial

1 For a detailed discussion see chapter 1 of Dumville, *Wessex and England.* A very general account is in Whitelock, *The Importance of the Battle of Edington*.

2 The reference to *þaet geweorc* is presumably Chippenham mentioned at the beginning of the annal: the annalist appears to be thinking in terms of two opposed armies each with their *geweorc*, for the Danes Chippenham, for Alfred the *geweorc æt Æþelingaeigge*.

3 Æthelweard adds the detail that it was Æthelnoth, ealdorman of Somerset, who washed off the chrism oil at Wedmore: Æthelweard, *Chronicon*, IV.3 (ed. and transl. Campbell, *The Chronicle of Æthelweard*, p. 43).

4 Asser, § 56 (ed. Stevenson, *Asser's Life*, p. 46). I take it that Asser was probably right in translating *foregislas* by *nominati obsides*, that is, they were hostages nominated in advance (hence *fore-*) by Alfred; for oathhelpers similarly nominated in advance see Downer (ed.), *Leges Henrici Primi*,

prominence of Alfred and the Danish army is, I suggest, not that the annalist wishes to slant his material so as to glorify Alfred but that he needs to emphasize that the Danish army, just as much as Guthrum himself, is bound by the alliance. The same desire to include the Danish army as well as their king is suggested by the way the annalist frames the baptism and the ceremony of loosing the chrism-bandage within his details on the arrival of the Danish company at Aller, thirty of the men of highest status in the army, and the final ceremony at which Alfred honoured the king with great gifts and honoured his companions *mid feo*, with precious things. This frame stresses both the dependence and the high status of the Danes: they come to the West Saxon king and depart honoured by him. Moreover Guthrum's position vis-à-vis his own army is seemingly enhanced by the baptism and his friendship with Alfred.

A first impression on reading this annal might be that here we have a diplomatic language with which both the annalist and his readership are familiar. Each act in the diplomatic ritual has a significance; and when combined together, they convey a definite message. I propose to test this first impression and thus to seek a firmer interpretation of the diplomatic exchanges between Alfred and the Danes. Again, while Alfred had made treaties with the Danes in 876 and in 877 – treaties by which the Danes obliged themselves to depart over the boundary of Wessex – those treaties had not included the element of baptism and thus spiritual kinship.[5] Moreover, the earlier treaties had not been faithfully observed by the Danes whereas the treaty of 878 appears to have lasted until 885.[6] It must, therefore, be asked whether the baptism of Guthrum and the consequent spiritual kinship between the two kings had the effect of shifting the diplomatic exchanges in Alfred's favour. Was it merely Alfred's victory at Edington and his ability to confine the Danes to their fort which brought about a radical change in the relationship between the Danes and the West Saxons or was it also the subsequent diplomacy? The baptism was not the first sacral element in the relationship between the two peoples: in 876 the Danes had sworn 'on the holy ring' that they would swiftly leave Wessex.[7] Although the annalist was happy to declare that they had never done such a thing for any other people, nevertheless that treaty had not secured their departure over the boundary. If the Danes were not constrained by their own gods in 876, why should they be constrained by the Christian God in 878? Professor Angenendt has argued that spiritual, and especially baptismal, kinship was perceived as the appropriate bond of that early mediaeval 'family of kings', headed by the emperor, the spiritual father of kings – a family

430–5; compare also Charles the Bald in a similar situation besieging the Northmen at Angers and securing *obsides quot et quantos quaesivit*, *Annals of St-Bertin*, *s.a.* 873.

5 *Anglo-Saxon Chronicle*, *s.a.* 876, 877; Asser, § 49 (for 876).

6 *Anglo-Saxon Chronicle*, *s.a* 885; Æthelweard's version of this annal, *Chronicon*, IV.3 (ed. Campbell, *The Chronicle of Æthelweard*, pp. 44–5), contains material not in the other texts of the *Chronicle*, including the statement that a detachment of the army that besieged Rochester that year received help from 'The foul people who then held East Anglia', who made an expedition to Benfleet in Essex. In Æthelweard's account, Alfred's dispatch of a fleet to the mouth of the Stour appears as a response to the East Anglian Vikings' expedition to Benfleet. See Plummer, *The Life*, p. 108, and Dumville, *Wessex and England*, pp. 8, 17–18.

7 *Anglo-Saxon Chronicle*, *s.a.* 876. On the ring and Asser's version of the annal, see Keynes and Lapidge, *Alfred the Great*, pp. 245–6 n. 90.

whose existence in Byzantine political thought was revealed many years ago by Dölger.[8] In England, too, according to this argument, baptismal kinship was employed as an element in an *imperium* as early as the reign of Oswald of Northumbria.[9] If this argument is accepted, Guthrum's baptism would then imply imperial claims on the part of Alfred, as well as Guthrum's inclusion within an insular family of Christian kings.

The background to the story is both continental and English, the continental being the more immediate of the two. The events at Edington, Aller and Wedmore occurred at the beginning of the worst decade for the Franks in their dealings with the Danes, culminating in the great siege of Paris.[10] For the course of the war in Francia the timing of Edington was critical. In the next year Guthrum's army moved to winter at Cirencester, just outside the West Saxon frontier; during the same year a new Viking army arrived in the Thames, wintering at Fulham.[11] Yet Alfred's alliance with Guthrum's army held, and the new army left for the continent in the course of 879, wintering at Ghent, while Guthrum's army entered East Anglia and settled there. Edington, therefore, and the alliance made by Alfred with the Viking army, probably averted a disastrous reinforcement of the forces attacking Wessex at the price of allowing the Vikings to acquire a recognised political control of much of eastern England north of the Thames. As long as Guthrum kept his side of the bargain, namely that he should remain out of Wessex, Alfred was committed to the treaty with his spiritual son. Before the attack on London in 886, it had to be claimed that the East Anglian Vikings had broken the treaty, though the chronicler fails to specify the offence.[12]

Edington and the subsequent alliance also had the effect of diverting the new Viking army to the continent. As it was a relief for the West Saxons, so it was disastrous for the Franks. It would be wrong, however, to blame West Saxon successes for all the misfortunes of the Franks. A crucial reason for the decision of the Fulham army to move to Ghent was the death of Louis the Stammerer, king of the West Franks, in the spring of 879; the consequent outbreak of a succession struggle embraced not only the West Franks themselves but also Louis III, king of the East Franks.[13]

The first theatre of operations for the army wintering at Ghent in 879 was

8 Esp. Angenendt, *Kaiserherrschaft und Königstaufe*; Dölger, 'Die "Familie der Könige" im Mittelalter'; and, on the background, Lynch, *Godparents and Kinship*.

9 Angenendt, *Kaiserherrschaft und Königstaufe*, pp. 183–4.

10 McKitterick, *The Frankish Kingdoms*, pp. 259–62, summarizes Frankish political history in the period.

11 For the next few years the *Chronicle* and Asser have the appearance of being a year in advance of the continental annals, in particular the *Annals of St Vaast*. The reason for this is that the *Chronicle* begins its year, in this period, in September, and it fixes the movements of the Vikings by their winter stations; these were taken up in the autumn and are thus placed in the following year; for this see D. Whitelock *apud* Plummer (ed.), *Two of the Saxon Chronicles* (rev. imp.), II, p. xli.

12 The last sentence in the *Anglo-Saxon Chronicle*, *s.a.* 885 A. The offence may be that mentioned by Æthelweard, *Chronicon*, *s.a.* 885 (ed. Campbell, *The Chronicle of Æthelweard*, pp. 44–5); see above n. 6. Note, however, the arguments of Keynes and Blackburn elsewhere in this volume that the Vikings had not been in control of London in the 880s.

13 The relationship between the succession struggle and the Viking move to Francia is explicitly stated by the *Annals of St Vaast*, *s.a.* 879 (ed. Rau, *Quellen*, II.294). For a detailed account of the Viking operations, see d'Haenens, *Les Invasions normandes*, 45–58.

Lotharingia, but they soon extended their harrying to include all the area between the Scheldt and the Somme.[14] In the summer of 882 a treaty was made which decisively shifted their operations into West Francia.[15] The Viking army was led by two kings, Godefrid and Sigefrid. On the Frankish side Louis III of the East Franks had just died (on Good Friday 882) and his brother Charles the Fat came north from Italy to take over his kingdom and to confront the Northmen. The Viking station for the winter of 881–2 had been Elsloo on the Meuse; here they were besieged by Charles. Attitudes to what then took place vary according to the standpoint of the annalist, but the sequence of events appears to have been as follows. The Frankish army was unable to continue the siege, according to some because of disease, according to others because of treachery.[16] A treaty was therefore made by which the Danish king Godefrid promised to accept baptism and to become Charles's godson; Charles, for his part, agreed to give Godefrid the Frisian lands which an earlier Danish leader Roric had held and to give him in marriage Gisla the daughter of Lothar II. It was also arranged that the other Danish king, Sigefrid, should receive a large payment of Danegeld and would undertake to depart from the territories of Charles as long as he (Charles) lived.

The resemblances between this treaty and that concluded by Alfred are striking, but so are the differences. We may take the resemblances first. The sequence of events is that of a formal contract and its fulfilment: first the giving of promises and hostages, secondly the performance of the acts promised. The latter consist of the baptism of a Viking king, his sponsorship by the Christian ruler, and a territorial settlement. There is also a promise, in both cases fulfilled, at least in the short term, to depart over the boundary of the Christian ruler's kingdom. Yet the differences are quite as remarkable. The two continuations of the *Annals of Fulda* (the continuation in the Vienna MS (MS 2) and the Bavarian Continuation in the Niederalteich MS) are alone in mentioning the giving of hostages: according to the MS 2 Continuation hostages were exchanged; according to the Bavarian Continuation only the Franks gave hostages since the Danish king Godefrid agreed to come out of his fort and travel six miles to meet Charles.[17] Alfred, however, gave no hostages to Guthrum's army and moreover received named hostages, as many as he wished. After Edington it was the Danes who sued for peace; but in 882 the initiative came from the Franks. In 882, also, the terms involved a split in the Danish forces: Godefrid would be baptized and receive lands in Frisia while the other king, Sigifrid, would receive Danegeld and depart from Charles's territory during his lifetime. As the aged Hincmar caustically observed, the East Frankish ruler was simply paying Sigefrid's Danes to do what they wanted provided that it was in West Francia[18] – a concession which came unworthily from one who bore the name of Charles and the title of emperor. Again, Alfred seems to have been extremely careful to involve the Danish army

14 *Annals of St Vaast*, *s.aa.* 879–81.

15 *Annals of St Vaast* and *Annals of St-Bertin*, *s.a.* 882 (ed. Rau, *Quellen*, II.300–2), *Annals of Fulda* (both continuations), *s.a.* 882 (ed. Rau, *Quellen*, III.116–18, 132–4).

16 For disease: *Annals of Fulda*, Bavarian Continuation, *s.a.* 882. For treachery: *Annals of Fulda*, MS 2 Continuation, *s.a.* 882. For the relationship between these texts, see Reuter, *Annals of Fulda*, 2–9.

17 *Ibid.*

18 *Annals of St-Bertin*, *s.a.* 882.

and not just the Danish ruler in the treaty, whereas in 882 the transaction was much more personal, between Charles and the Danish kings Godefrid and Sigifrid. It is symptomatic of this personal character of the 882 peace that it was to last during Charles's lifetime.[19] It also included an element quite absent from the treaty between Alfred and Guthrum, namely the marriage alliance between Charles and Godefrid by which the emperor gave his cousin Gisla as the bride of the newly Christian Danish king.

The annalists' verdicts on the 882 proceedings are, on the whole, hostile: exceedingly so in the case of the MS 2 Continuation of the *Annals of Fulda*, somewhat so in the *Annals of St-Bertin*, written at this stage by Hincmar, and also fairly hostile in the *Chronicle of Regino*.[20] Only the Bavarian Continuation of the Fulda annals refrains from condemnation.[21] One wonders, of course, what a hostile annalist, based in East Anglia perhaps, might have said about Alfred's treaty with the Danes, yet the differences between that agreement and Charles's treaty in 882 are sufficiently striking to suggest that, however hostile the observer, it would have been considerably more difficult to condemn Alfred than it was to condemn Charles. When we put the two treaties side by side, it is possible to see a common pattern with the baptismal relationship at its centre; yet the setting surrounding the baptismal sponsorship mattered and the variations in the setting were both numerous and crucial.[22] There is indeed a recognized diplomatic pattern, but the small print may be everything. The reactions of the annalists suggest that the baptismal relationship was far from being the decisive element: in 882 the *Annals of St Vaast*, otherwise a well-informed source, entirely omit to mention the baptism although the annalist does notice the marriage between Godefrid and Gisla.

It might be supposed that Charles's advisers in 882 were consciously imitating the negotiations between Alfred and Guthrum, yet this is improbable for the 882 treaty follows a pattern set much earlier in the century. In 882 Godefrid was given, according to the MS 2 Continuation of the Fulda annals, 'the counties and benefices which the Northman Roric, the vassal (*fidelis*) of the kings of the Franks had held in Kennemerland (Northern Holland)'. Hincmar, further removed, was more expansive: Godefrid was to receive 'both Frisia and the other honours which Roric had held'. Roric's career in Francia had extended for some forty years from the 830s when, with his brother Heriold (Harald Klak), he had held Dorestad as an imperial benefice, to the early 870s when he had become a *fidelis* of Charles the Bald.[23] In between he had been an adherent both of Lothar I and Louis the German.[24] His long career in Francia thus provides a thread which

19 *Annals of Fulda*, Bavarian Continuation, *s.a.* 882 (ed. Rau, *Quellen*, III.134, lines 2–3).

20 *Reginonis Chronica*, *s.a.* 882 (ed. Rau, *Quellen*, III.262–3).

21 This would be unsurprising if this continuation were, as seems possible, composed within the court circle: see Reuter, *The Annals of Fulda*, p. 9.

22 Calmette, *La Diplomatie carolingienne*, does not, in spite of the title, cover such issues, being directed at relationships between the sons of Louis the Pious after Verdun.

23 *Annals of Fulda*, *s.a.* 850 (ed. Rau, *Quellen*, III.38, lines 19–20). For relations between Franks and Danes in the first half of the ninth century, see Jankuhn, 'Karl der Grosse und der Norden', Ernst, 'Karolingische Nordostpolitik'; and, on the frontiers of the Carolingian Empire in general, Noble, 'Louis the Pious and the Frontiers'.

24 *Annals of Fulda*, *s.a.* 850.

binds the negotiations of the later ninth century with Franco-Danish relations under Louis the Pious. Indeed it stemmed from another alliance blessed by baptismal sponsorship, initially created in the last years of Charlemagne's reign – a period of intensive diplomatic exchanges between the Franks and the Danes.[25] At that stage the Franks were backing one faction in a Danish succession dispute, a faction called the *pars Herioldi*, against another, the sons of Godefrid I. The latter were themselves possibly supported by the Swedes.[26] The faction supported by the Franks eventually failed in its efforts to obtain supremacy in Denmark, although they were to try again as late as 855, after the death of Horic I.[27]

The lengthy negotiations between the Danes and the Franks between 812 and 827, in which the baptism of Heriold at St Alban's, Mainz, in 826 was only one incident, give several clues about the diplomatic language of the period. Frankish policy was hampered, partly by the weakness of Heriold's position within Denmark, partly by the intertwining of anti-Frankish moves among Danes and Slavs.[28] The combination of Frankish prestige, yet growing reluctance to embark on large-scale military enterprises, with Heriold's weakness within Denmark ensured that diplomacy rather than war occupied most of these years, whereas later, in the 830s, the disunity of the Franks encouraged the Danes to take military action.[29] Between 812 and 827 both factions in Denmark negotiated with the Franks, but they they did so in two different modes.

The first mode, adopted by the faction of the sons and nephews of Godefrid I who died in 810, revolved around treaties made on the boundary, *in marca*, namely on the river Eider. In 811 a temporary truce was made during the winter, *pax . . . in armis tantum iurata*, 'a peace sworn only upon weapons', until in the spring a full treaty was made by two high-ranking delegations and oaths were sworn by both sides each according to their own customs.[30] In 825 the sons of Godefrid were prepared to send an embassy to the assembly held at Aachen in August in order to arrange for a peace, but the treaty itself was made in October

25 *Royal Annals*, *s.aa.* 809, 811 (ed. Rau, *Quellen*, I.90–2, 96–8). Cf. Jankuhn, 'Karl der Grosse und der Norden', pp. 700–2.

26 *Royal Annals*, *s.a.* 813: 'the sons of King Godofrid and several of the leading men of the Danes, who had for some time been in exile among the Swedes'. Jankuhn, 'Karl der Grosse und der Norden', p. 702, assumes that the annalist was referring to a Swedish exile endured by the sons of Godofrid; but the use of *iamdudum* makes this unlikely since Godofrid had only been killed in 811. The exiled Danish *primores* may, before 811, have been hostile to Godofrid, but by 813 they had evidently thrown in their lot with his sons against the current kings, Heriold and Reginfrid.

27 *Annals of St-Bertin*, *s.a.* 855.

28 *Royal Annals*, *s.aa.* 808, 809, 810; the Abodriti were allied with the Franks, but the Wilzi, Linones and Smeldingi with the Danes; in 817, however, an intervention by Louis the Pious into an Abodritan dynastic dispute caused their temporary defection to the Danes (*Royal Annals*, *s.a.* 817). For the background see Ernst, *Die Nordwestslaven und das fränkische Reich*, esp. pp. 182–7 on the last years of Charlemagne.

29 On the reasons for Frankish reluctance to take the initiative militarily, see Reuter, 'The End of Carolingian Military Expansion', esp. pp. 403–5.

30 *Royal Annals*, *s.a.* 811. Cf. the later association between *hommage en marche* and *hommage de paix* in relations between Norman dukes and French kings; equality in power, inequality in status, and the need to make peace were all satisfied by making the homage (marking the subordination of duke to king) take place on the frontier (suggesting their virtual equality): Lemarignier, *Recherches sur l'hommage en marche*, pp. 81–5.

in marca eorum.[31] In 813 the other faction, the *pars Herioldi* had temporarily been in control of Denmark. At that stage it too made its agreement with the Franks *ad confinia Nordmannorum*; but as soon as Heriold and his brother Reginfrid were driven from Denmark later the same year and failed in 814 in an attempt to regain power, they adopted a second mode of negotiation, that proper to a client-king: according to the *Royal Annals*, Heriold, 'lacking confidence in his affairs, came to the emperor and commended himself into his hands'.[32] In 819 he was eventually established as ruler of part of Denmark with the help of the Abodriti.[33] In 823, again threatened with expulsion by the sons of Godefrid, Heriold himself came to an assembly held at Compiègne in November.[34] An embassy was then sent to negotiate between the two parties within Denmark; and, as a part of the embassy, Ebbo, archbishop of Rheims, went to evangelize the Danes.[35] The baptism of Heriold at Mainz in 826 was, therefore, the outcome of his dependence upon Frankish help, a dependence demonstrated not just by his homage in 814 but by his personal appearance at Compiègne in 823. Heriold, after 813, was in no position to make his treaties upon the boundary, *in marca*, even when he was in possession of Danish territory.

Much the most detailed account of the proceedings of 826 is given by the exiled Ermold in his long poem in praise of Louis the Pious.[36] Ermold's account is not accurate in all respects but he plainly had detailed information on which to work, he had a keen interest in court ritual, and his witness is that of an immediate contemporary. He is careful to link the baptism with the missionary efforts of Ebbo, and he provides a splendid picture of the successive ceremonies surrounding the baptism. The arrival of Heriold is immediately followed by the baptism itself and then by a solemn ritual of gift-giving.[37] The two are closely linked: as the emperor sponsored Heriold so he gives him presents; as the empress Judith sponsored Heriold's wife, so she gives her presents; the same was true for Lothar and Heriold's son. After the gift-giving the next acts in Ermold's sequence are a solemn mass, a feast and a hunt.[38] The series is concluded by an act of homage by Heriold and by the final gifts of the emperor, including, as we discover from the *Royal Annals*, the county of Rüstringen by the mouth of the Weser in Frisia.[39] For Ermold the baptism of Heriold was a crowning achievement:

> Quod nec Roma potens tenuit nec Francica jura,
> Tu retines Christi nomine cuncta, pater.[40]

31 *Royal Annals, s.a.* 825.
32 *Royal Annals, s.aa.* 813, 814.
33 *Royal Annals, s.a.* 819.
34 *Royal Annals, s.a.* 823.
35 *Ibid.*; Rimbert, *Vita Anskarii* (ed. Waitz), § 13.
36 Ermoldus Nigellus, *In Honorem Hludowici . . . Elegiacum Carmen*, lines 2028–2519 (ed. Faral, pp. 154–88). Hauck, 'Der Missionsauftrag Christi und Ludwig', pp. 289–93; Wood, 'Christians and pagans', pp. 31–8.
37 *Ibid.*, lines 2164–2279.
38 *Ibid.*, lines 2280–2447.
39 *Ibid.*, lines 2448–2503.
40 *Ibid.*, lines 2518–19.

> A land which neither powerful Rome nor the laws of the Franks subdued, you, father, entirely control in the name of Christ.

The viewpoint of the Royal Annals, however, was notably less sanguine. The county of Rüstringen was given to Heriold as a refuge should it be necessary.

In the very next year, in 827, the limitations of the new alliance were revealed.[41] Horic I, son of Godefrid, had promised to come himself into the presence of the emperor. To receive him Louis arranged a special assembly at Nijmegen, a royal palace not far from the *emporium* at Dorestad. This assembly was distinct from the normal one held at Compiègne later in 827 at which Louis received the annual gifts from his subjects.[42] It may be that Horic I insisted that his appearance was not to be at the assembly at which these annual gifts were presented in order to avoid seeming to have completely subjected himself to the emperor. In any case he failed to appear, and he and his brothers drove Heriold into exile. In 828 there is no talk of any appearance by the Danish king; negotiations are again held *in confinibus Nordmannorum*. From the *Royal Annals* it appears that before the two sides got down to talking, hostages had been given, apparently by both sides, in order to guarantee peace. The *pax* confirmed by hostages thus preceded the *foedus* which, together with the affairs of Heriold, was to be the subject of negotiation. Heriold, however, broke the peace by mounting a raid, an action of which the *Royal Annals* plainly disapprove.[43] Frankish diplomacy had thus been brought into a frustrating impasse: they had failed to give their client, Heriold, supreme power in Denmark; even his share of territory had been taken from him shortly after his baptism and sponsorship by Louis; the rival king, Horic I, had failed to appear at Nijmegen; and now Heriold had disrupted negotiations on the frontier, violating guarantees given by his Frankish patrons.

In spite of all this the link between the rulers of the Franks and the faction of Heriold endured. Heriold himself appears to have died about 830; but his nephews, one also called Heriold, and the other Roric, held Dorestad as a benefice together with other lands in Frisia during the 830s.[44] The younger Heriold was a

41 *Royal Annals*, *s.a.* 827.

42 For the importance of these annual gifts, see the *Ordinatio Imperii* of 817, §§ 4–5 (edd. Boretius and Krause, *Capitularia*, I.271).

43 *Royal Annals*, *s.a.* 828.

44 See *Annals of Fulda*, s.a. 850, for Heriold and Roric holding Dorestad and other land in Frisia during the 830s. It is necessary to distinguish (a) Heriold I who was a king in Denmark in the eighth century (mentioned in the *Royal Annals*, *s.a.* 812); (b) Heriold II, *nepos* of Heriold I, who is recorded in the *Royal Annals*, *s.a.* 812–28 and was baptized at St Alban's, Mainz, in 826; (c) Heriold III, *nepos* of Heriold II and brother of Roric (who died between 873 and 882) – this Heriold died before 850 according to the *Annals of Fulda* (*s.a.*) whereas the *Annals of St-Bertin* imply that he was still alive in that year; and (d) Heriold IV who was killed in 852. According to the excellent account of this family given by Vogel, *Die Normannen und das fränkische Reich*, pp. 405–9, Heriold II and Heriold III are identical. Vogel's case depends upon the Annals of Xanten, *s.a.* 850, which describe the Roric who died between 873 and 882 as *frater iamdicti Herioldi iunioris*, apparently referring to the only previously mentioned Heriold, namely Heriold II, baptized at Mainz in 826. On the other hand, the *Annals of St-Bertin*, *s.a.* 850, describe Roric as *nepos Herioldi*; and while in theory this could be Heriold I, it is not very likely that an annalist in 850 would describe Roric in terms of his relationship to the eighth-century Heriold rather than to Heriold II, who was well-known to the Franks; moreover, given Roric's dates, it is a little difficult, though not impossible, to identify Heriold III with Heriold II, himself *nepos* of Heriold I. Heriold

prominent supporter of Lothar in 840 but died within the next ten years.[45] With some intervals Roric was to hold on to Dorestad and part of Frisia until the 870s. It was these Frisian possessions of Roric which Godefrid III obtained in 882 when he received baptism and was sponsored by Charles the Fat. The Danish king was thus able to gain a hold of the territorial resources which had long supported an exiled line of Danish princes. It is not perhaps surprising that Notker's view of such baptisms and grants of territory in his Life of Charlemagne addressed to Charles the Fat is highly cynical.[46] Yet the cynicism is not entirely deserved: one Danish prince, probably of the *pars Herioldi*, died in 837 at the hands of his fellow-countrymen in an attack on Walcheren; from the addition to Thegan's Life of Louis the Pious he earned the epithet *dux Christianissimus*.[47]

From the negotiations between Christian and Scandinavian rulers in the ninth century, it is apparent that there were at least two modes of diplomacy. The first did not imply a dependence of one side upon the other; hostages and oaths were exchanged; the making of a treaty, and sometimes also the initial negotiations, occurred on the frontier, *in marca*. The oaths were sworn by each side according to its own custom: the pagan side was not compelled to adopt Christian or Frankish forms. In the other mode, dependence was shown by the appearance of one ruler as a guest in the palace of the other, by the adoption of Christian and also Frankish forms culminating in baptismal sponsorship, by homage and the grant of a benefice. On the basis of this survey of Frankish practice one can see that the *Anglo-Saxon Chronicle*'s account of the baptism of Guthrum follows traditional lines already entirely familiar to Danish as well as to English or Frankish rulers. Of course Guthrum's position in East Anglia made good political and economic sense when the Danes also hoped to control Dorestad and Frisia. In this way Danish rulers would be established at either end of cross-channel trade routes. Yet Guthrum's baptism also implied submission to Alfred and might be extended into West Saxon claims to overlordship over East Anglia. Sir Frank Stenton's judgment on the treaty between Alfred and Guthrum that there 'is nothing to suggest that Alfred claimed any supremacy over Guthrum or his followers' may be true of the surviving legal text which he dated to 886, but it is not true of the accounts in Asser and the *Chronicle* of the baptism of 878.[48] Once put into its right setting even the text of Alfred-Guthrum may not signify an equality between the two

IV may not have been related to the others. The relationships are obscured by the unfortunate imprecision of the term *nepos*: it means 'grandson' in the *Royal Annals, s.a.* 812 (Bernard son of Pippin is *nepos* to Charlemagne); 'nephew' in the *Royal Annals, s.aa.* 814 and 817 (Bernard son of Pippin is *nepos* to Louis the Pious); and in the *Annals of Fulda, s.a.* 881 *nepos* is used for a father's brother's son's son (Louis III of the West Franks, son of Louis the Stammerer, is *nepos* to Louis III of the East Franks, son of Louis the German). Vogel takes *nepos* to mean 'nephew' throughout, a convenient but insecure assumption. Cf. also Reuter, *The Annals of Fulda*, p. 30 n. 2.

45 Nithard, *Historiae* (ed. Lauer), III.7; *Annals of St-Bertin, s.a.* 841; Heriold seems to have been dead by 850: *Annals of Fulda, s.a.* 850.

46 Notker, *Gesta Karoli*, II.19 (ed. Rau, *Quellen*, III, 420–2).

47 Thegan, Addition in the Vienna MS (ed. Rau, *Quellen*, I.252); *Annals of St Fulda* and *Annals of St-Bertin, s.a.* 837.

48 Stenton, *Anglo-Saxon England*, p. 258; on the relation between the Treaty of Chippenham in 878 and the text of Alfred-Guthrum, see Davis, 'Alfred and Guthrum's frontier', and Dumville, *Wessex and England*, chap. 1.

parties; it defines boundaries but does not claim to be a treaty drawn up on the boundary.[49] There is, therefore, no evidence that it was in a different diplomatic mode from the peace of 878. Admittedly it cannot be identified with a text given a final form at the time of Guthrum's baptism for in the text of Alfred-Guthrum the Danish army is already settled in East Anglia which had not yet happened in 878; but it may well be a restatement, after the Danish settlement of East Anglia, of the relationship between Alfred and Guthrum initiated at Chippenham.[50]

In Asser there is also a further parallel to the 878 treaty which requires to be brought into the discussion, namely the submission of Anarawd of Gwynedd and his brothers to Alfred some time before 894.[51] They had previously been allied to the Vikings in Northumbria and had been exerting pressure on Hyfaidd, the king of Dyfed, and Elise ap Tewdwr, the king of Brycheiniog. According to Asser, Anarawd came into the presence of the king, was honourably received and was sponsored by him at confirmation. He was then given very great gifts and subjected himself and his people to Alfred's authority on the same terms as Æthelred and the Mercians. We have here a relationship of *amicitia* between two kings and their peoples sealed by the spiritual kinship of the rulers but plainly also marked by the submission of the sponsored king to the sponsor. Anarawd's arrival as a guest in Wessex and his reception of gifts from Alfred would show his dependence even if we were not told that he submitted to the king's lordship. Asser goes on to spell out what the Welsh kings gained from their submission to Alfred:

> Nor did all these rulers gain the king's friendship in vain. For those who wished to increase their worldly power were able to do so; those who wished an increase of wealth obtained it; those who wished to be on more intimate terms with the king achieved such intimacy; and those who desired each and every one of these things acquired them. All of them gained support, protection and defence in those cases where the king was able to defend himself and all those in his care.[52]

Friendship, *amicitia*, is the formal alliance; the intimacy brought about by living in the same household, *familiaritas*, is closer to what we would more naturally understand by the word 'friendship'.[53] *Amicitia* should bring concrete advantages to both sides, and Asser's portrayal of the benefits of alliance with Alfred is contrasted with the useless *amicitia* between Anarawd and the Northumbrian Vikings, 'from which he had got no benefit, only injury'.[54]

A further intriguing element in Asser's account of Anarawd is the statement that his submission was made on the same condition as that of Æthelred and the Mercians. This Asser summarizes by saying 'ut in omnibus regiae voluntati sic oboediens esset, sicut Æthered cum Merciis', 'that he would in all things be just

49 Ed. Liebermann, *Gesetze*, I.126–9.

50 According to the *Anglo-Saxon Chronicle*, *s.a.* 880 (referring probably to the autumn of 879; cf. n. 11 above), Guthrum's army left Cirencester for East Anglia 'and settled the land and shared it' a full year after it had left Wessex. The Great Army had taken winter stations in East Anglia in 865–866 and 869–870, but these did not constitute a full settlement.

51 Asser, § 80.

52 Asser, § 81 (the translation is that of Keynes and Lapidge, *Alfred the Great*, p. 96).

53 On *amicitia* see Althoff, *Verwandte*, pp. 88-119.

54 Compare the *familiaris dilectio* of Asser, § 76, line 40, with the *amicitia* between Anarawd and, first, the Northumbrians and then Alfred in § 80.

as obedient to the king's will as were Æthelred and the Mercians'. Asser's account of Welsh affairs suggests, therefore, that Æthelred had made a formal submission to Alfred on terms that were widely known in the 890s; it suggests further, by its mention of the kings of Glywysing and Gwent turning to Alfred's lordship to defend themselves from 'the might and tyrannical behaviour of Ealdorman Æthelred and the Mercians', that the policies of Alfred and Æthelred had not been in accord from the beginning.[55] The submission of Æthelred and the Mercians probably occurred after the submission of the kings of south-eastern Wales and before that of Anarawd. Finally, it suggests that the famous annal of 886 according to which 'all the English people that were not under subjection to the Danes submitted to him' should not be taken to reflect a policy by which Alfred put himself at the head of the English nation to the exclusion of the Welsh:[56] Alfred was attempting to gain lordship over all those not subject to the Danes whether English or Welsh. The *Chronicle*, written in English for an English readership, is naturally more interested in the English element in Alfred's lordship, but the importance of English nationality in his position can be exaggerated.[57]

Distinct from the relationship of god-parent to god-child is the spiritual kinship between a god-parent and the natural parent of the child. *Compaternitas*, as it was called, is almost as prominent in eighth- and ninth-century Frankish sources as god-parenthood itself.[58] It was similarly used to bind neighbouring rulers to their Frankish overlords: Salomon, the ruler of the Bretons, refers to Charles the Bald in one of his charters for Redon as his *compater*; the same relationship had existed between Charles and Salomon's predecessor, Erispoe.[59] An interesting variant on *compaternitas* is mentioned in the Parker Chronicle under 893. In 892 two Viking armies from the continent combined to attack 'the eastern kingdom', in particular Kent. One of these armies was the surviving part of the great army which had besieged Paris; the other was led by Hasteinn who had earlier been the chief of the Loire Vikings. In 893 Hasteinn's wife and children were captured by the English. They were returned to him because, we are told,

> one of them was his [Alfred's] godson and the other the godson of Ealdorman Æthelred. They had stood sponsor to them before Hasteinn came to Benfleet, and Hasteinn had given Alfred hostages and oaths; and likewise the king had given him generous gifts of money.[60]

Hasteinn was thus *compater* to both Alfred and Æthelred. It looks as though there had been a formal treaty when Hasteinn was still at Milton in Kent, before he moved to Benfleet in Essex. Judging by the agreement between Alfred and Guthrum in 878, as well as by earlier treaties between Christian rulers and the Danes, both in England and on the continent, Hasteinn should have promised to leave the dominions of both Alfred and Æthelred. Yet, although it may have

55 Asser, § 80.

56 *Anglo-Saxon Chronicle*, *s.a.* 886; Asser, § 83.

57 Cf. Stenton, *Anglo-Saxon England*, p. 256.

58 Cf. Lynch, *Godparents*, pp. 192–201, 285–88.

59 de Courson (ed.), *Cartulaire de l'abbaye de Redon*, no. ccxli (p. 190); Smith, *Province and Empire*, pp. 110–13.

60 *Anglo-Saxon Chronicle*, *s.a.* 894 A.

succeeded in getting Hasteinn out of Kent, the *compaternitas* between the English rulers and the Viking king failed to yield a full peace: Hasteinn continued to attack Mercia, from a base in Essex, and therefore within the Greater Wessex won by Alfred's grandfather.[61]

The three relationships of baptismal sponsorship, confirmation sponsorship and *compaternitas* are all variants of spiritual kinship. Yet they did not have exactly the same significance in Wessex, nor in Francia. The clearest argument for the difference between them stems, however, not from the *Chronicle* but from Alfred's lawbook, in particular from that part of the lawbook which he took from his West Saxon predecessor Ine. The relevant decrees form the final section of the extant text and thus the conclusion of Alfred's lawbook:[62]

> If anyone kills the godson or godfather of another, the compensation for the relationship is to be the same as that to the lord; the compensation is to increase in proportion to the wergild, the same as the compensation for his man does which has to be paid to the lord.
> If, however, it is the king's godson, his wergild is to be paid to the king the same as to the kindred.
> If however, he was resisting him who slew him, the compensation to the godfather is to be remitted, in the same way as the fine to the lord is.
> If it is a spiritual son at confirmation, the compensation is to be half as much.

We may take the decrees in turn. The first equates the compensation for killing baptismal kin, either godfather or godson, with the *manbot* paid to the lord of the slain man. This does not imply that a godfather is the lord of his godson for the godson also is entitled to the very same compensation if the godfather is killed. The effect of the decree is to put two artificial bonds, lordship and spiritual kinship, into the same category in terms of compensation. The second decree, however, shows that Ine was determined to place his own godparenthood on a special footing. Here the king is treated as if he were part of the natural kin of his godson. Spiritual kinship with the king is thus a much more serious business than spiritual kinship with one of his subjects. It is entirely consistent with the equation between the king's godparenthood and natural kinship that Guthrum received a baptismal name, Æthelstan, used by the West Saxon dynasty, so signifying his alliance with the West Saxon dynasty, not just with Alfred himself. In an age of conversion royal godparenthood could help to bind a Christian party among the aristocracy to their Christian king. The final decree, on the spiritual relationship created by sponsorship at confirmation, shows that its significance was definitely less than that of baptismal sponsorship. *Compaternitas* is not mentioned at all.

It is not surprising, therefore, if *compaternitas* with Hasteinn in 893–894 should have been less effective than baptismal kinship with Guthrum in 878. In

61 Cf. Dumville, *Wessex and England*, chap. 1, and Hart, 'The ealdordom of Essex', for the position of Essex at this period.

62 Ed. Liebermann, *Gesetze*, I.122–3, transl. Whitelock, *English Historical Documents*, i. 372. The syntax and style of Ine's laws are clearly different from Alfred's; I thus regard the likelihood of major revision of Ine's laws by Alfred before they were incorporated into the latter's lawbook as remote.

Frankish diplomacy *compaternitas* was used to cement an alliance between equals; it belongs naturally to the independent mode of diplomacy.[63]

As the decrees of Ine show, the background to Alfred's use of baptismal sponsorship is not only continental, for it reaches back to the beginnings of Christianity in Wessex. With the help of the *Chronicle* we can look back from the standpoint of Alfred's generation at the earlier, seventh-century, diplomatic uses of spiritual kinship. The *Chronicle*'s source is Bede but we need to notice what elements in Bede's story seemed worthy of record in a ninth-century West Saxon text. The three instances of baptismal sponsorship in the seventh-century part of the *Chronicle* are Oswald's sponsorship of the West Saxon king Cynegisl, Wulfhere's sponsorship of the West Saxon king Æthelwalh and Pope Sergius's sponsorship of the West Saxon king Caedwalla.[64] I shall take first Wulfhere's sponsorship of Æthelwalh.

At some date between 664 and 675 (and probably around 672–673) the king of the South Saxons was baptized in Mercia and was received from the font by the Mercian king Wulfhere. The story of this baptism appears to have come to Bede from Hexham and it forms a prelude to the missionary activities of Wilfrid in Sussex between 682 and 687.[65] Æthelwalh was already married to a Hwiccian princess Eafe and had thus contracted a marriage-alliance with a royal family subject to the Mercian kings. The story does not record who baptized Æthelwalh: it was presumably the bishop of the Mercians, perhaps either Chad or Winfrith. Bede says that Wulfhere gave to Æthelwald, *in signum adoptionis*, two provinces, the Isle of Wight and the land of the Meonware, situated within the *gens Occidentalium Saxonum*. The *Chronicle*, however, is careful to omit any mention of the Meonware and thus of Wulfhere's donation of a West Saxon province to Æthelwalh. It says simply that 'Wulfhere, the son of Penda, harried in the Isle of Wight, and gave the people of the Isle of Wight to Æthelwalh, king of the South Saxons, because Wulfhere had stood sponsor to him at baptism.' What it retains, therefore, is the grant of the Isle of Wight in virtue of baptismal sponsorship.

The grant of the Meonware, far more than of the Isle of Wight, was the most extreme instance of Wulfhere's domination of the southern English, a domination which came to an end about 673–674. The tactics are evident enough: the overlordship of the Isle of Wight, an object of West Saxon ambition, and even the lands of the Meonware, a West Saxon border province, are given to the weaker power, the South Saxons. In this way Æthelwalh and his people are made dependent upon Mercian support, for only with that support can they hope to retain their acquisitions and withstand the West Saxon counter-attack, which duly came in the 680s.[66] The dependence of Æthelwalh upon the Mercian king is further shown by his appearance in Mercia to be baptized. There is no meeting on the frontier and exchange of hostages. Æthelwalh is adopted into the Mercian royal kindred in a baptismal ceremony conducted within Mercia. Ine's decree

63 *Annals of St-Bertin*, *s.a.* 853; cf. Lynch, *Godparents*, p. 256 n. 88.

64 *Anglo-Saxon Chronicle*, *s.aa.* 635, 661, 688 (only the last date is credible).

65 Bede, *Historia Ecclesiastica*, IV. 13; on Bede's sources for Wilfrid's career I follow Isenberg, *Die Würdigung Wilfrieds von York*.

66 Bede, *Historia Ecclesiastica*, IV. 15.

showing royal godparenthood to be equivalent to natural kinship illustrates what Bede meant by *in signum adoptionis*. Moreover, they suggest that Wulfhere's manoeuvres should have been entirely intelligible to the primary victims, the West Saxons.

The baptism of Cynegisl by Birinus and the sponsorship of Oswald posed fewer problems for the *Chronicle*. In Bede this was associated, first, with a marriage alliance by which Oswald married Cynegisl's daughter, and, secondly, with the gift of a see at Dorchester by both Cynegisl and Oswald to Birinus. Birinus as baptizer and Oswald as sponsor were *compatres* and the dual grant of Dorchester thus corresponded to the three-way relationship between the bishop, Oswald and Cynegisl. It has been suggested by Hanna Vollrath-Reichelt that Oswald may have received land at Dorchester as a dowry along with his West Saxon bride, and further, that one can distinguish between a voluntarily accepted bretwaldaship in the case of Oswald and a domination founded on force as with Wulfhere.[67] I think both these suggestions are unlikely to be true. Oswald was undoubtedly exercising force in southern England in the late 630s. Æthelburh, the widow of Edwin, was compelled to send Edwin's son Wuscfrea and his grandson Yffi from Kent to Francia for fear of her brother Eadbald, king of Kent, and Oswald.[68] Penda killed another son of Edwin, Eadfrith, at the time his guest, during the reign of Oswald.[69] I suspect that Penda did so only after pressure had been applied by Oswald, for it was contrary to Penda's interests to strengthen the Bernician hold on Deira by killing a member of the Deiran royal kindred. Nor is Oswald likely to have received Dorchester as dowry, for dowry is not attested in early Anglo-Saxon England, only bridewealth.[70] It is more probable that Oswald was using the tactic later adopted by Wulfhere. The land north of the Thames was probably claimed by the Mercians and Oswald was perhaps associated with the grant to Birinus not just as *compater*, but because he had previously granted land north of the Middle Thames to his godson Cynegisl *in signum adoptionis*. As in the case of Wulfhere and the province of the Meonware, the land was not properly his to give; indeed it was given, I imagine, precisely because the Mercian claim to the land would be hard for the West Saxons to resist without Northumbrian aid.

Spiritual kinship may be associated with the confirmation or redrawing of boundaries, but the way in which the association works is quite different in different circumstances. The association in Wulfhere's case, and probably in Oswald's, is essentially aggressive, the act of a militarily dominant Christian ruler. Its legitimacy is dubious and it binds the recipient to the donor all the more effectively because it is dubious. The grants of Dorestad and other Frisian lands by Frankish rulers to Danish princes are defensive, initially a device to rescue a client-ruler expelled from his own kingdom, then a buffer against Danish onslaughts. Alfred's territorial dispositions, whether in 878 or in the written treaty with Guthrum, or in the presumed arrangement with Hasteinn in 892–893,

67 Vollrath-Reichelt, *Königsgedanke und Königtum*, p. 110.

68 Bede, *Historia Ecclesiastica*, II.20; on this see Stancliffe, 'Oswald', pp. 71–5.

69 *Ibid.*

70 Wallace-Hadrill, *Bede's Ecclesiastical History*, p. 231; but Clare Stancliffe is sceptical, 'Oswald', pp. 72–4.

seem to have been designed to protect the interests of Greater Wessex including Kent, Essex, Sussex and Surrey, which he had inherited from his brothers and his father.

Both Oswald and Wulfhere claimed an *imperium* which included several, at least, of the southern English peoples. Alfred's claims, like those of Oswald, extended to an authority not only over the English but also over the Welsh. Yet it remains unlikely that there was anything distinctively imperial about their use of spiritual kinship. The device was used by kings who cannot have had any claims to an *imperium*;[71] and, as the Laws of Ine show, spiritual kinship had a very real significance in bolstering political authority, but the authority was that of kings. Its use to strengthen an *imperium* was secondary. There may admittedly have been an *imitatio imperii* behind the use of such political rituals in the West, but the adoption of Byzantine practice did not of itself imply imperial claims.

Spiritual kinship was thus a flexible diplomatic device. It could be used both defensively and aggressively, and by mere kings as well as by emperors. In spite of the scepticism of observers such as Notker, it seems to have worked well within limits. It was, however, far from being unique. Another rite capable of creating artificial kinship, well attested on the continent and also in Wales, is the first cutting of the beard at the threshold between adolescence and manhood, *barbatoria*.[72] There was also a similar rite, with similar effects, involving the first cutting of the hair of an infant, *capillatoria*.[73] The two seem often to be confused, at least terminologically, in the sources.[74] In general this was a secular rite and thus less appropriate to missionary situations, but most western liturgies seem to have contained special prayers of blessing to be used on such occasions.[75] Its diplomatic uses are well illustrated by Paul the Deacon's story that Charles Martel sent Pippin to the Lombard king Liutprand for his hair-cutting, a ceremony which made Liutprand his ritual father.[76] The taking of arms was another rite of passage associated with the threshold between adolescence and manhood and also with adoption.[77] It could also be used in internal Frankish diplomacy, as when Louis the Pious marked Charles the Bald's entry into manhood and associated it with Charles's coronation and thus his acquisition of a status equal to that of Louis the

71 Wallace-Hadrill, *Bede's Ecclesiastical History*, p. 231.

72 Gregory of Tours, *Decem Libri Historiarum*, ed. Krusch and Levison, X.16; cf. Fredegar, *Chronica*, ed. Krusch, II.58, where Alaric only touches Clovis's beard; Bromwich and Evans (edd.), *Culhwch and Olwen*, pp. 3, 6–7 (given the age of Culhwch, the rite should be *barbatoria* rather than *capillatoria*); Paul the Deacon, *Historia Langobardorum*, ed. Waitz, IV.38.

73 A good example is *Historia Brittonum* (ed. Mommsen), § 39 (although the rite is not named and it also serves as an ordeal); rather less clear is *Liber Pontificalis*, ed. Duchesne, I.363.

74 Confusion between the two is probable in *Pactus Legis Salicae*, LXVII, ed. Eckhardt, where the natural father's role in bringing sons *ad capillaturias* is equivalent to giving a daughter in marriage); also in Paul the Deacon, *Historia Langobardorum*, VI.53 (Pippin was probably of an age for *barbatoria* rather than for *capillatoria*), and, similarly, in the Welsh example from the Mabinogion (above n. 72).

75 Deshusses (ed.), *Le sacramentaire Grégorien*, I.339, 340–1 (nos 991, 993); cf. Deshusses and Davragon, *Concordances et tableaux*, nos. 321, 898, 2310, and Bognetti, *L'età longobarda*, II, p. 104 n., discussing the pair of blessings *ad barbam incidendum* and *ad capillos incidendum* in *Manuale Ambrosianum*, ed. Magistretti, 497–8.

76 Paul the Deacon, *Historia Langobardorum*, VI.53.

77 Tacitus, *Germania*, § 13.

German and Pippin of Aquitaine.[78] Here the ceremony did not create an artificial kinship but rather asserted the rights of a natural kinship whose political consequences were nevertheless controversial. Marriage is, of course, a further source of artificial kinship. Each rite of passage marking the threshold between one period and another in human life was apparently capable of generating ritual kinship; and all forms of ritual kinship, not just baptismal sponsorship, were employed to forge or to strengthen alliances. In this sphere, the more the better.

Two strategies could be used: according to the first, a person moving through the various rites of passage would contract different alliances at each stage. They would not overlap, but would rather create a wide network of artificial kinship. According to the other strategy one alliance would be strengthened by another, as Louis the Pious gave arms and a horse to Heriold *Francisco more veterno* after his baptism and homage in 826,[79] or as Charles the Fat attempted to bind Godefrid to him both by baptismal sponsorship and by a marriage alliance; the same reinforcement is illustrated by the relationship between Cynegisl and Oswald. Pippin, however, was linked to the Lombards through one form of artificial kinship and, later, to the papacy through another. Baptismal kinship is especially prominent in seventh-century England or in the Viking age because Christian kings used it to attach pagan rulers to themselves. While it may, on occasion, have had imperial associations, it did not necessarily imply imperial claims; and, on the other hand, it was not the only form of ritual kinship to have such associations. Adoption by the giving of arms bound Theoderic the Ostrogoth's designated heir, Eutharic, to the emperor Justin; it also bound the Herule king to Theoderic in a quasi-imperial relationship, and it linked Gothic nobles within Italy to their king.[80] Baptismal kinship needs to be set within the wider context of ritual or artificial kinship. The latter was a widespread element in early medieval society and different forms of it were used as the need arose. The political uses of ritual kinship demonstrate how flexible early medieval diplomacy could be.

78 *Annals of St-Bertin, s.a.* 838.

79 Ermold, lines 2488–9.

80 Cassiodorus, *Variae* (ed. Mommsen), VIII.1; cf. IV.2 and VIII.9 (*ad finem*).

III

MONETARY ALLIANCE OR TECHNICAL CO-OPERATION? THE COINAGE OF BERHTWULF OF MERCIA (840–852)

James Booth

The reign of Berhtwulf (840–852) constitutes an intriguing phase in the sparsely documented twilight of Mercian decline. Having reached the height of its power under Æthelbald and Offa in the eighth century, the kingdom suffered a series of disasters in the 820s. Ecgberht of Wessex defeated the Mercians at *Ellendun* in 825, and his son, Æthelwulf, brought the former Mercian sub-kingdom of Kent, already in revolt against Mercian authority, under West Saxon control. In consequence Essex, Surrey and Sussex also submitted to Wessex. Then, at about the time of the accession of Wiglaf to the Mercian throne in 827, the East Angles, to judge from their coins, took the opportunity to assert their independence. Henceforth the power of Mercia was confined within its own borders, a reduction of authority driven home by Ecgberht's victory over Wiglaf in 829, when, according to the *Anglo-Saxon Chronicle*, he 'conquered the kingdom of the Mercians, and everything south of the Humber'.[1] Ecgberht followed his victory by exacting submission from the Northumbrians, the traditional rivals of Mercia to the north, and the foundations of a West Saxon hegemony, to replace that of Mercia, had been laid.

However, in the five decades between Ecgberht's victories and the fall of Mercia to the Danes in 873/4, Anglo-Saxon Mercia remained politically distinct, with its national identity uncompromised. Although Wessex now controlled the economically and politically crucial region of Kent, it clearly lacked the military means or political will (or both) to bring its northern neighbour into complete subjection. A period of adjustment and diplomatic manoeuvring seems to have followed Ecgberht's triumphs. Some observers have detected in the meagre evidence a sturdy reassertion of Mercian independence during the latter part of Ecgberht's reign, continuing through the reign of Æthelwulf and beyond. The *Chronicle* offers an unqualified celebration of Ecgberht's triumphs, as one would expect from a simplified West Saxon retrospect of the 890s. But, to judge from its laconic (perhaps grudging?) entry for 830 ('In this year Wiglaf again obtained the kingdom of the Mercians'),[2] Ecgberht was powerless to prevent the Mercian king from regaining power within a year of the conquest of 829. Attempting to redress the balance, Stenton asserted that 'it is doubtful whether [Ecgberht]

1 Whitelock, *English Historical Documents*, p. 186.
2 *Ibid.*

exercised any authority outside Wessex and its eastern dependencies during the last nine years of his reign', and surmised that by the time of Ecgberht's death 'the kings of Wessex and Mercia stood towards each other on terms of virtual equality'.[3]

It has been seen as significant, in this context, that on a surviving charter of Wiglaf's reign, concerned with land deep inside Mercia, the Mercian king's words are witnessed by all the ecclesiastical powers of the south of England, including the archbishop of Canterbury, and the bishops of Rochester, Selsey, and Sherborne, whose sees lay firmly within territory now under West Saxon control.[4] Indeed, the synod of 836 for which this charter was drawn up seems to have preserved all the features of the synods of the previous century, which have been counted the greatest administrative achievement of the Mercian ascendancy. However, the evidence of Wiglaf's synod is not perhaps as conclusive as it might seem, and the persistence of this superstructural institution may not demonstrate any real revival in Mercian fortunes at this time. Ecgberht's failure to obstruct the attendance of the non-Mercian bishops does not necessarily indicate anything as significant as acquiescence in the 'revival of Mercian authority over the southern episcopate'. And Wiglaf's reference to 'my bishops' in the charter, which Stenton saw as highly significant,[5] may perhaps be no more than a form of words. Ecgberht's respect for the Mercian synod, the most sophisticated and 'international' of English institutions so far evolved, need not have conflicted with his vigorous pursuit of West Saxon secular hegemony over all the English. And the coin evidence gives no hint of any revival in the Mercian economic base at this time. Until the reign of Ceolwulf (821–823), Mercia had controlled the principal mints in the south of England (Canterbury, Rochester, London, and a mint in East Anglia) and had produced a mass of coinage. But only a tiny number of coins is attributable (with some doubt) to Wiglaf's second reign, during which minting seems most probably to have ceased altogether in the kingdom.

Berhtwulf, Wiglaf's immediate successor, came to power in 840, the year after Ecgberht's son Æthelwulf succeeded to the throne of Wessex. Whatever the actual balance of power at this point, the evidence, both documentary and numismatic, seems to indicate the establishment of a new, more sophisticated political climate in relations between the two major southumbrian Anglo-Saxon kingdoms, replacing the crude military impositions of the 820s. No doubt both kings perceived their best interest, for the time being at least, to lie in consolidation and reconstruction. And the dramatically increased external threat from the Danes can be assumed to have provided a further encouragement to reconciliation. However, it may be doubted that Æthelwulf (839–858), the youthful conqueror of Kent, former jewel in Mercia's hegemonic crown, would have felt comfortable with the idea that he was on terms of 'virtual equality' with Berhtwulf. And no doubt suspicion of West Saxon intentions was never long dispelled in Mercia.

In contrast with the confident dynastic succession of Æthelwulf in Wessex, the nature of Berhtwulf's claim to the Mercian throne is unknown, and Cyril Hart has suggested that after the failure of the line of Offa 'the insecurity of the

3 Stenton, *Anglo-Saxon England*, pp. 233 and 235.

4 Whitelock, pp. 518–19.

5 Stenton, *Anglo-Saxon England*, p. 234.

reigning house was reflected in its lack of authority to rule the kingdom'.[6] There is, however, no evidence that Berhtwulf's position suffered from internally generated instability caused either by the dubiousness of his succession or other factors. The difficulties which actually figure in the record are more tangible and concrete. Two years into Berhtwulf's reign, in 842, London, the key to the Mercian kingdom's commercial prosperity, suffered the disaster of a Viking raid. The same army descended also upon the Kentish port of Rochester, which for fifteen years or more had been firmly under West Saxon control.

It is tempting, if speculative, to see the documentary and numismatic evidence from the mid-840s as testimony to a concerted plan by the Mercian and West Saxon kings to rebuild the fortunes of these two ports. A document dated two or three years after the raid shows Berhtwulf confirming a grant made by King Æthelbald over a hundred years earlier to the church of St Andrew in Rochester, remitting the toll on one ship at London.[7] Berhtwulf's renewal of the grant was witnessed by Ceolnoth, archbishop of Canterbury, and also by the bishop of Rochester and the bishop of Leicester, as is appropriate to an agreement affecting institutions in both Kent and Mercia. Thus the document has a similar 'international' form to that of the synodal decisions of the earlier period of Mercian ascendancy, though the current political realities were of course vastly different from those which had existed when Æthelbald had originally made it. This charter could be seen as offering evidence of the cordial relations between Mercia and Wessex in the 840s. The place in which it was signed, 'the royal residence *Werburgewic*', has been speculatively identified with Hoo in Kent, whose church was dedicated to St Werburh, and which is conveniently close to Rochester, in whose favour the grant was made. If this identification were to be trusted, we would need to picture the Mercian king sitting in a West Saxon royal residence, presumably in a joint council with Æthelwulf, his words being witnessed by ecclesiastics from both Kent and Mercia. Unfortunately, however, the identification of *Werburgewic* is doubtful, and the grant could have been renewed near London (where the privilege which it grants was exercised). It may represent no more than a limited transaction between Berhtwulf and the Church. Dorothy Whitelock concluded that *Werburgewic* was 'probably in Mercia'.[8]

However, the coin evidence does appear to give more substance to this tenuous documentary hint of political co-operation between the kings. There was a dramatic increase in monetary activity at this time. Mercian coinage was re-established – on a substantial scale – with what looks like a joint issue struck in the names of both Æthelwulf and Berhtwulf, and as we shall see minting seems to have begun again at London. It could be then that a meeting between the two kings took place in 844 or 845 (the date given on the charter), whose only decisions now visible to us are a joint issue of coin and this minor grant to St Andrew's.

Other documents of the period have been taken to suggest that a significant shift of power and control was taking place in favour of Wessex during this decade. But, on examination this evidence is inconclusive. A charter of 843 or 844

6 Hart, 'The kingdom of Mercia', p. 56.
7 Whitelock, *English Historical Documents*, pp. 491–2.
8 *Ibid.*, p. 492, note 2.

shows Berhtwulf disposing of land at Pangbourne, on the Thames in Berkshire, in territory which had formerly been part of Wessex.[9] The fact that Alfred was born, according to Asser, on 'the royal estate called Wantage in the district known as Berkshire' in 849 (or shortly before) has been thought to show that by the late 840s Berkshire as a whole had fallen into into West Saxon hands.[10] Perhaps some peaceful surrender or exchange of land did take place at this time. But it could be that Wantage, to the south of the Thames, remained throughout this period of comparative stability in West Saxon hands, while Pangbourne, which is actually on the Thames, remained under Mercian control.

In the event, any transfer of territory between the Anglo-Saxon kingdoms was superseded by the Danish onslaught, which presaged the destruction of the Mercian kingdom. It was indeed another Viking raid such as began Berhtwulf's reign, which is its last recorded event. As the *Anglo-Saxon Chronicle* relates, in 851

> 350 ships came into the mouth of the Thames and stormed Canterbury and London and put to flight Brihtwulf, king of the Mercians, with his army, and went south across the Thames into Surrey. And King Æthelwulf and his son Æthelbald fought against them at *Aclea* with the army of the West Saxons, and there inflicted the greatest slaughter [on a heathen army] that we have ever heard of until this present day, and had the victory there.[11]

We may speculate on the degree of nationalistic bias to be detected in this simple picture of Mercian humiliation followed by West Saxon triumph. It may be suspected that Berhtwulf's engagement with the Vikings played a part in weakening the invading force and ensuring the eventual West Saxon victory. It would also be interesting to know whether the apparent lack of co-ordination between the Mercian and West Saxon opposition was simply a result of the suddenness of the raid, or of distrust between the Anglo-Saxon kings – or even perhaps of a cynical strategy on the part of Æthelwulf. Berhtwulf's ultimate fate is not recorded. He must have died or been killed shortly after this defeat.

Possibly an important lesson was learnt from this engagement, since during the reign of Berhtwulf's successor, Burgred (852–874), military solidarity between the kingdoms is well in evidence. In 853 Burgred requested Æthelwulf's help in subduing the Welsh. The A text of the *Anglo-Saxon Chronicle* depicts the ensuing action as largely a West Saxon victory, while manuscripts D and E, with a different bias, speak of the campaign as waged by the Mercian king, 'with King Æthelwulf's help'. Later in the same year the *Chronicle* tells us 'King Æthelwulf gave his daughter in marriage to King Burgred, from Wessex to Mercia.'[12] The West Saxon annalist no doubt envisaged a future English unity in which Wessex would be the dominant partner. However, evidence of Mercian resilience is offered by the surviving coins. After Berhtwulf's defeat the Mercian coinage, which had apparently remained in a healthy state throughout the latter part of his reign, once more virtually ceased, and only a handful of coins can be attributed to

9 *Ibid.*, pp. 521–2.

10 Keynes and Lapidge, *Alfred*, p. 228.

11 Whitelock, *English Historical Documents*, p. 188.

12 *Ibid.*, p. 189.

the first decade of Burgred's reign. However in the 860s Mercian coinage re-established itself, and by the beginning of the next decade as many as thirty moneyers were at work in London. Indeed when an enduring unity of coin-type was finally accepted by the the two kingdoms, it was the Mercian *Lunettes* design, already in circulation, which was adopted.

THE COINS

The coins of Berhtwulf provide us with evidence concerning the economic conditions in Mercia at this time, and may cast light on political relations between the two kingdoms. However the insight they offer is compromised by the scarcity of extant specimens, and their low survival-rate. Eighty-six certain coins of Berhtwulf were located for the present study, of which eighty-one were in good enough condition, and well enough photographed, to allow of die comparison.[13] These eighty-one coins were struck from no fewer than seventy-two obverse and seventy-five reverse dies, which fact in itself establishes that very many more dies must have been used. It seems unlikely that each pair of dies would have produced less than several thousand coins, so the volume of actual coin must have been very large. There is also, as we shall see, internal evidence suggesting several recoinages. It seems then that once minting had been re-established in Mercia, there was a strong demand for coin, and effective measures to ensure that it circulated effectively. Historians assessing the importance of money in this period must take account of the huge quantities of coins suggested by the number of surviving dies. It may indeed be that Berhtwulf's coinage approached in circulating volume that of his successor Burgred, though the accidents of hoard survival (and Burgred's longer reign) have made it seem otherwise.

It is possible to make only provisional remarks concerning the weight standard and the metal quality of Berhtwulf's coins. Many of the specimens have clearly suffered weight loss through chipping or corrosion. Thirty more or less undamaged specimens[14] types yield an average weight of 1.25g, which compares with an average weight of 1.27g for thirty-four 'phase two' coins of Æthelwulf in the *British Museum Catalogue* (from both Canterbury and Rochester). Evidence as to metal quality is even more exiguous. Only one metal analysis is yet available, published by D. M. Metcalf and J. P. Northover.[15] The authors cite analyses which indicate that a standard of purity of 90% or more prevailed in Francia and England in the early decades of the ninth century, but that this was debased from the 840s onwards, apparently at different rates in the various kingdoms. The Berhtwulf coin which was analysed (no. 22 below) proved to be 76.11% 'silver', a comparable result to that yielded by a *Cross-and-Wedges* coin of Æthelwulf (moneyer Brid) of 73.99% 'silver'. Future analyses will no doubt further clarify the precise timing and circumstances of this debasement.

13 Nos 24, 30, 31, 59, 83, and 87 were excluded from the die-comparison.

14 Nos 1, 5, 17, 18, 22, 25, 26, 29, 33, 36, 38, 39, 41, 42, 43, 44, 52, 54, 55, 61, 66, 68, 69, 72, 76, 77, 79, 80, 81, and 86.

15 Metcalf and Northover, 'Coinage alloys'.

The classification of Berhtwulf's coinage is rendered difficult by the diversity of the surviving specimens. Both the style of the bust and the types of reverses vary greatly, and a dauntingly large number of specimens turn out to display unique features or combinations of features. Any classification must therefore remain, at some points, tentative and provisional. The situation is also complicated by the fact that the reverse types of the coins seem in most cases misleading as a guide to the sequence of issues. As J. J. North pointed out in his authoritative early analysis, a grouping by obverse style generally produces a more convincing arrangement.[16] North's basic classification in terms of busts is followed here, with some minor simplifications. For the purposes of discussion Berhtwulf's coinage can be divided into four sections. The first of these, the Rochester-connected group (bust A), and the third, North's 'late style' portrait group (here termed bust G), both survive in sufficient numbers to show that they form internally homogeneous emissions. However the second group, the intermediate portrait coins (busts B–F), is internally diverse, and seems to have had a very low survival rate. It probably represents a series of different issues, whose ordering and interpretation must remain at present uncertain. It is possible that the fourth group, the non-portrait coins, also represents more than one issue, but so few specimens have survived that their sequence and dating remain obscure.

1. The Rochester-connected group (bust A)

Fortunately the most historically intriguing group (nos 1–32) is clearly definable. Its coins show a distinctive bust (A) which is stylistically identical with that found on the 'phase two' portrait coins of Æthelwulf's four moneyers Biarnnoth, Ethelhere, Maninc, and Welheard. The reverse types of the Berhtwulf coins also largely correspond with those of coins struck for Æthelwulf by these same moneyers. The similarities are so close as to make it certain that the dies for this group came from the same source as those in Æthelwulf's name. Berhtwulf's moneyers are five in number: Brid, Burnwald, Deneheah, Oswulf, and Sigeheah. The actual complement of moneyers working at one time however may have been four. Oswulf is not represented in later issues and one of the other moneyers could have taken over his position during the course of the issue. It is possibly relevant here that Brid uses the same cross-crosslet reverse design.

Thirteen specimens of this issue in the name of Æthelwulf were located, struck from twelve obverse and thirteen reverse dies. The average weight of the five undamaged specimens (A, B, D, G, and I) was 1.25g. Thirty-two specimens in the name of Berhtwulf were found, of which twenty-nine could be subjected to die-comparison. They proved to be struck from twenty-seven obverse and twenty-eight reverse dies. The average weight of the eight undamaged coins was 1.28g. The relative numbers of specimens seem to suggest that more coins of this type were struck in the name of Berhtwulf than Æthelwulf, but since a more through search was made for the Mercian component of the issue it may be that this impression is misleading. On the other hand all the Æthelwulf coins are of

[16] North, 'The coinage of Berhtwulf', pp. 213–15.

identical style, while the Berhtwulf component shows two cruder variants (busts A2 and A3), which may indicate either that the type was issued for a longer period in Berhtwulf's name than in Æthelwulf's, or that a new die-cutter was employed late in the Mercian emission. However that may be, the negligible amount of die-duplication present in both the West Saxon and Mercian components certainly suggests that a much larger number of dies was originally used. This was in ninth-century terms a very substantial issue.

This group almost certainly constitutes the first issue in Berhtwulf's name. After the lapse of a decade in the production of Mercian coinage it seems to have been found necessary to bring in help from the nearest West Saxon minting centre. It would be difficult to account in any other way for the fact that the same die-cutter or die-cutters produced dies in both kings' names. But what level of official co-operation between Rochester and London, Wessex and Mercia, does this issue represent, and where was it struck? Our answers must depend to a large extent on our interpretation of the early issues of Æthelwulf, with which this group of coins belongs.

The currently accepted version of the Rochester coinage during this period is complicated, and there is still room for discussion at some points. Two groups of coins have been attributed in previous research to the period *ca* 839 – *ca* 842 ('phase one'), one with portrait (*BMC* ix and x) and one without (*BMC* va, attributed to Canterbury). The portrait coins (pl. 1, a) show a crude bust or head very similar to that on one group of Ecgberht's coins. It is the fact that the Ecgberht coins have the reverse legend SCS ANDREAS or SCS ANDREAS APOSTOLVS which is the strongest evidence that the whole group must belong to Rochester, whose church was dedicated to Saint Andrew. The absence of a moneyer's name on these particular coins of Ecgberht, and their religious legend, have been interpreted as indicating that a single episcopal moneyer was working in Rochester at this time, though this is conjectural.[17] Æthelwulf's coins of this group show no ecclesiastical affiliations. They bear the names of three moneyers, Beagmund, Dun and Wilheah, who can thus safely be assigned to Rochester. It could be that one of them was an ecclesiastical moneyer (by the time of the Grately Laws of Æthelstan about a century later, Rochester was assigned two regal moneyers and one episcopal moneyer). Because of the close similarity of style with the coins of Ecgberht it seems most likely that these coins were struck in the months immediately following Ecgberht's death in 839, though it is just possible that they were struck by Æthelwulf as king of Kent while his father was still alive.[18]

Also attributed to Rochester at this time is that group within the SAXONIORVM issue which replaces the moneyer's name with the word OCCIDENTALIVM around the reverse device (pl. 1, b). A new die-cutter seems to be at work here, whose neat style of lettering can be detected in subsequent issues at Rochester. This must therefore be a distinctive Rochester version of the Canterbury SAXONIORVM issue, which shows the moneyer's name. The legend of the Rochester coins makes it highly probable that the issue marks Æthelwulf's ascent to the West Saxon throne, which would indicate a date of 839 or shortly afterwards. It has

17 See Blunt, 'The coinage of Ecgbeorht', pp. 473–4.

18 Pagan, 'Coinage in southern England', p. 54.

been suggested that they were an ecclesiastical emission concurrent with the early portrait coins, and lack moneyers' names because the bishop of Rochester had only one moneyer.[19] However the coins show no signs of episcopal origin and their legend celebrates a secular event. It seems more likely that the SAXONIORVM OCCIDENTALIVM coins were a regal issue, and succeeded the cruder portrait coins, the moneyers' names being dispensed with simply to make space for the declaration of Æthelwulf's accession.

In 'phase two' (*ca* 842 – *ca* 848) the picture is similarly complicated. Again two Rochester issues are in question, one with portrait (the joint issue with Berhtwulf) and one without (*BMC* xviii–xxiii). No coins in either issue give any visible sign of episcopal authority, though it is possible that one or more of the moneyers was striking on the bishop's behalf throughout. The non-portrait issue (pl. 1, c–f) retains as obverse the *Cross-and-Wedges* design of the OCCIDENTALIVM SAXONIORVM issue, combining this with a variety of reverses largely identical with those on the 'phase two' portrait coins. Among those responsible for this issue are the established Rochester moneyers Beagmund, Dun and Wilheah, and since the first two of these are absent from the 'phase two' portrait issue, and also from succeding issues, it seems reasonable to place the *Cross-and-Wedges* coins immediately after the end of 'phase one'. The new moneyers, Brid, Ethelhere, Maninc and Welheard, make their appearance in this issue. An indication of the date of the new coinage is perhaps given by the absence of coins of this type (or any 'phase two' coins) from the Middle Temple hoard, from which many of surviving specimens of the earlier Rochester issues derive. The deposition of this hoard has been associated with the Viking raid on London of 842, and the new issue should presumably be dated after this. However, as Metcalf and Northover point out, the *Cross-and-Wedges* and later coins seem to be significantly debased compared with earlier issues. So it could be that the change of type had already occurred before 842, but that the coins of purer metal had deliberately been selected for the hoard.

All four of the new Rochester moneyers are also found striking in the shared West-Saxon/Mercian portrait issue which is our chief concern here: Ethelhere, Maninc and Welheard in the name of Æthelwulf, and Brid in the name of Berhtwulf. Since, as we have seen, the early moneyers, Beagmund, Dun and Wilheah, are now absent, it would seem reasonable to assume that the portrait issue immediately followed the *Cross-and-Wedges* issue, rather than being issued concurrently. This version is supported by the appearance of a new moneyer at this point, Biarnnoth, whose name is not found on any *Cross-and-Wedges* coins. He seems to have begun striking for Æthelwulf during the currency of the portrait type and then continued striking in the subsequent DORIBI/CANT issue of 'phase three' (*BMC* i), which probably began about 848. A difficulty in this arrangement is the absence from the portrait issue of coins in the name of Wilheah, who having struck early portrait and *Cross-and-Wedges* coins reappears in the later DORIBI/CANT issue. However in view of the very small number of surviving specimens of the joint issue (particularly in the name of Æthelwulf), it seems

19 Blunt, Lyon, and Stewart, 'The coinage of southern England', p. 25.

quite possible that Wilheah did strike coins of the type – in Æthelwulf's name, or just possibly Berhtwulf's – but that none has yet come to light.

Thus it is possible to replace the inhomogeneous 'phases' of previous accounts of the Rochester coinage of the 840s with a simple (if still tentative) sequence of unitary issues. If we take the view that the West Saxon coinage at this period was in regular continuous production, then it may be that each issue was struck for a period of approximately three years, and that the Rochester issues were synchronised with those of Canterbury. Only the initiation of the joint issue with Berhtwulf at Rochester would break this pattern, there being no corresponding change at Canterbury at this point (see Table 1).

TABLE 1. Possible sequence of issues at Rochester and Canterbury: *ca* 839 – *ca* 851
(All dates are approximate)

	Rochester	*Canterbury*
839:	Early portrait	(Ecgberht?) SAXONIORVM/moneyer's name
839–42:	OCCIDENTALIVM SAXONIORVM	SAXONIORVM/moneyer's name
842–45:	*Cross-and-Wedges*	'Phase Two' Portrait
845–48:	Portrait (with Berhtwulf)	'Phase Two' Portrait
848–851:	DORIBI/CANT	DORIBI/CANT

The joint issue with Berhtwulf is thus associated firmly with Rochester. The apparent career of Brid (see Table 2) might seem to suggest that the entire issue, in both kings' names, was actually struck, as C.S.S. Lyon formerly suggested, at Rochester.[20] It may be however that this was not the case. Hugh Pagan believes that the dies were more probably cut at Rochester and the Mercian component then transported to the kingdom's mint-town of London.[21] Such a system, with a single die-cutting centre supplying different mints, is evident at various points later in the Anglo-Saxon period, and it is possible that it can be seen here in embryo. This interpretation seems likely for several reasons. Berhtwulf's moneyers are different from Æthelwulf's. (The only exception, Brid, must be assumed to have moved for a time from Rochester to London and then returned.) Berhtwulf's other four moneyers have names new to the coinage, and after this issue the three survivors strike coins of different style from those of Rochester, the dies for which must certainly have been cut at London. It seems clear then that Berhtwulf's moneyers were London dignitaries rather than mint-officials in Rochester. It is just possible however that rather than purchasing dies from Rochester, the London moneyers employed the die-cutter himself, who moved, with

20 Lyon, 'Historical problems (2)', pp. 228–9. Both Lyon and Pagan assign all coins of busts A–F to a single 'Rochester style' group. However the stylistic identity with Æthelwulf's Rochester coins is only apparent in the case of bust A. Busts B, C, E and F are only distantly related to bust A and do not immediately declare an affinity with any Æthelwulf issue. Bust D is unrelated to bust A.

21 Pagan, 'Coinage in southern England', pp. 55–6.

his tools, from Rochester to London, less than a day's journey away. But whether it was the dies that moved, or the die-cutter, the arrangement must have been of some duration. Even if royal control was slight, security considerations would still surely dictate that a moneyer would not hold more than one or two pairs of dies at any one time. And the fact that twenty-nine surviving coins of Berhtwulf of this type were struck from twenty-seven obverse and twenty-eight reverse dies suggests that each of his four or five moneyers would have employed many more pairs of dies during the course of the issue.

TABLE 2. Moneyers using Rochester dies: *ca* 839 – *ca* 851
(All dates are approximate)

Early portrait (839)	*Cross-and-Wedges* (842–45)	Portrait (845–48)	DORIBI/CANT (848–51)
Æthelwulf	*Æthelwulf*	*Æthelwulf*	*Æthelwulf*
Beagmund	Beagmund		
Dun	Dun		
Wilheah	Wilheah		Wilheah
	Brid	*see below**	Brid
	Ethelhere	Ethelhere	Ethelhere
	Maninc	Maninc	Maninc
	Welheard	Welheard	Welheard
		Biarnnoth	Biarnnoth
		Berhtwulf	
		Brid*	
		Burnwald	
		Deheheah	
		Oswulf	
		Sigeheah	

We may see here perhaps an anticipation of the situation which occurred in the late 860s and 870s during the *Lunettes* issue of Æthelred I and Alfred. Although the *types* of the Mercian and West Saxon coinage were identical at this time, stylistic differences show that generally speaking coins were struck at West Saxon mints only in Æthelred's or Alfred's name, and at London only in Burgred's. Puzzlingly, however, a small number of West Saxon coins of the type are from dies of identical style to those of Burgred's London coins. The picture is obscured by imitations and irregular coins, but some West Saxon coins of London style are undoubtedly regular. It has been assumed that these must have been actually struck in London alongside those of Burgred,[22] or after his defeat and

22 Pagan in Biddle *et al.*, 'Coins of the Anglo-Saxon period from Repton', p. 118.

exile. It may be possible, however, that the die-cutters in London supplied some dies to the West Saxon mints, or alternatively that one or more die-cutters moved from London to Rochester or Canterbury at some point during the issue.

But the question of whether the coins in Berhtwulf's name were actually struck in Rochester, or in London from dies made by a Rochester die-cutter, is less important than that of the overall political significance of the issue. Unfortunately the coins themselves cannot provide conclusive evidence on this point. It is still possible to argue that Berhtwulf simply 'had minting rights'[23] at Rochester, and that coinage did not begin again in London until later. Moreover, even if we accept the probability of a transfer of dies and/or personnel, it is still conceivable that nothing more momentous was involved than a low-level commercial transaction between some London merchants and the Rochester moneyers or die-cutter. Nothing as significant as a 'joint issue' would then be in question, though no doubt such a transaction must have required at least the acquiescence of both kings. The evidence that anything more politically significant than this was involved is circumstantial only. However, when we consider this evidence: the probable parallelism in numbers of moneyers between the kings, the uniform, regulated appearance of the coinage, the vast wealth these coins must have represented – above all the large number of dies used, and the probability that a proportion of them was regularly transported, under conditions of strict security, from Rochester to London – it must seem extremely likely that we are in fact dealing with a royal initiative directed from above.

But it still remains difficult to imagine the economic or political significance of such a joint coinage at the time. On a simple level it may possibly have been felt to express English solidarity in the face of the Danes. Æthelwulf could also conceivably have contemplated some advantage in fostering the revival of London as a minting centre, bearing in mind its position as the old capital of the Roman province and England's principal port: already potentially the 'English' capital city. The LONDONIA issue of *ca* 829, on which Æthelwulf's father termed himself REX M ('King of the Mercians'), hints at the importance which Ecgberht attached to the city, as well as showing his awareness of the potential of coinage as an instrument of propaganda.[24] Later, Asser carefully insists on London's non-Mercian, 'East Saxon' status in his life of Æthelwulf's son. A maximalist interpretation of Æthelwulf's design in facilitating this issue might see an attempt on his part to engineer a limited monetary union and thereby begin to incorporate London into the larger money economy of Kent and Wessex. Clearly Mercia would be a subordinate partner in such a development. The West Saxon coinages continued uninterrupted at Rochester and Canterbury, while the only Mercian coinage at the time was this Rochester/London issue shared with Wessex. A maximalist might also see an expression of Berhtwulf's resentment at his dependence in the breaking off of the joint arrangement after this first issue. However this line of interpretation is uncomfortably hypothetical and may

23 Lyon, 'Historical problems (2)', p. 229.

24 Blunt, 'The coinage of Ecgbeorht', pp. 472–3.

overestimate the political and perhaps also the economic rôle of coined money at this period.

It might be hoped that the reverse types of the coins would give further clues as to the way the issue was organised. However their evidence, though suggestive, is ambiguous and very incomplete. In both Æthelwulf's *Cross-and-Wedges* issue and the shared portrait issue the production of each moneyer is generally dominated by coins with a single reverse type, and this could be interpreted as indicating that reverses were subject to administrative control. However this interpretation is seriously undermined by the not infrequent instances of one moneyer using two different reverse types, or two or more moneyers sharing the same reverse type. This is particularly evident in Æthelwulf's *Cross-and-Wedges* type. Most of the surviving specimens of Beagmund in this issue, for instance, have a cross-crosslet reverse, and those of Brid a large A. However one specimen of each moneyer shares the cross-with-two-limbs-moline reverse which is also used by Ethelhere and Welheard. Further examples of such apparently unregulated correspondences are easy to trace in the surviving coins, though it is possible that such anomalies are explicable in terms of systematic changes of reverse type which took different forms for different moneyers.

The portrait issue shows much greater consistency in this respect. A single distinctive reverse type is found on all the coins of each of Æthelwulf's moneyers except Maninc, and each of Berhtwulf's moneyers except Sigeheah. However one pair of moneyers within each group shares a reverse type (Ethelhere and Welheard; Brid and Oswulf), and two reverse types (cross-with-two-limbs-crosslet, cross-and-wedges) are shared by moneyers from both West Saxon and Mercian groups (Maninc and Burnwald; Maninc and Sigeheah). Any deductions from this evidence must however be provisional, since the small number of specimens surviving in both groups makes it very likely that more reverse-type/moneyer combinations will come to light in the future. All we can say at present is that though the *Cross-and-Wedges* coins remain problematic, the joint portrait issue does show some signs of a centrally administered system governing its reverse types. This seems a more probable interpretation of the general consistency of types than the arbitrary preference of the die-cutter as he supplied dies now to one moneyer, now to another.

2. *Intermediate portrait coins (busts B–F)*

The second group of portrait coins in Berhtwulf's name (nos 33–61) is far less homogeneous than the first, and seems to represent a series of distinct issues. Developments in the obverse legend match those in bust style. Coins with busts B and C differ from coins of bust A in that the letters HT in the king's name are ligatured, while coins with busts D, E and F have HT ligatured and also a double V in the king's name. Though the bust is of various styles (B–F), all of them except one (D) are apparently derived from bust A, and presumably followed it, coming before bust G which marks a new stylistic departure. The sequence of moneyers also supports this ordering. Oswulf disappears after the bust A issue, but otherwise the moneyers in the intermediate group remain as before, with the

TABLE 3. Reverse types of Æthelwulf's and Berhtwulf's moneyers, *ca* 842 – *ca* 848

	Cross-and-Wedges	Portrait issue	
	Æthelwulf	*Æthelwulf*	*Berhtwulf* (Bust A)
Beagmund	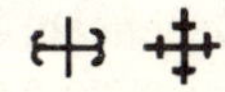		
Dun			
Wilheah	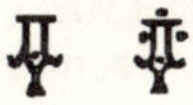		
Brid			
Ethelhere	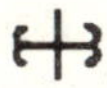	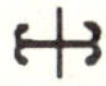	
Maninc		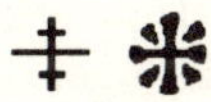	
Welheard	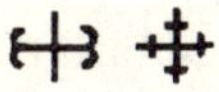	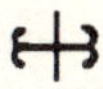	
Biarnoth			
Burnwald			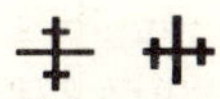
Deneheah			
Oswulf			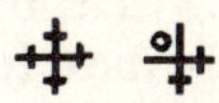
Sigeheah			

addition of Liaba and Eanred. As we shall see, other new moneyers make their appearance only in the bust G group.[25]

Three specimens with bust B have been located, struck from two obverse and three reverse dies (nos 33–5). Small and clearly defined in style though this group is, it shows some irregularities. One of the two obverse dies is paired with reverses in the names of two different moneyers. The first reverse, of the moneyer Brid, seems regular enough, but the other, of Deneheah, has a retrograde legend of irregular appearance. The other obverse die is even more anomalously paired – with a reverse bearing the name of King Æthelwulf (no. 35). At first sight this coin appears to offer dramatic proof that some attempt at monetary union was in fact being made at this time. But unfortunately its evidence is unconvincing. The obverse of the coin is struck from a neat enough Berhtwulf die. But the incompetent reverse die, which reproduces the *Cross-and-Wedges* design of the previous Rochester issue, appears to have been cut largely freehand rather than with punches, revealing its imitative, irregular nature.[26] How this anomalous coin came to be struck is a mystery, though speculation is irresistible. Both it and the coin of Deneheah with retrograde legend may simply be fraudulent forgeries, struck from stolen regular obverse dies. But conceivably, they reflect the confusion in London at the time when the supply of Rochester-cut dies ceased. It could be that as the last consignment of dies from Rochester wore out, the longer lasting obverse dies were for a time muled with reverse dies such as these, cut haphazardly by novice die-cutters, one of whom mistakenly copied from the wrong model. However, the slenderness of the evidence makes this no more than a hypothesis.

Several new London die-cutters seem to have been called into service at this time, either together or one after the other. It would appear most unlikely that a single craftsman could have modulated from the style of bust C to that of bust D or bust F, even if the production of coin had become intermittent and long intervals elapsed between issues. But it is impossible to tell whether some or all of the different styles of die were in fact supplied to the moneyers concurrently, or whether they represent sequential issues. It would be naively impressionistic to interpret this heterogeneity of style as proof in itself of economic instability, or of discontinuities in the emission of coinage. The C, E and F groups, which survive in slightly larger numbers than the others, show little die-duplication and must represent large volumes of coin. The seven coins with bust C which were located (nos 36–42) were struck from six obverse and six reverse dies, while the seven specimens showing bust E (nos 44–50) also yield six obverse and six reverse dies. One of the eleven specimens with bust F (nos 51–61) is too damaged for die comparison, but the remaining ten were struck from seven obverse and nine reverse dies. It seems quite probable then that the surviving intermediate group coins offer mere glimpses of a substantial and well administered coinage, though

25 North argued in 'The coinage of Berhtwulf' that the evidence of the Sevington hoard supported this sequence, since, as he believed, it contained only coins with intermediate and late bust styles and none with Bust A. However Hawkins's account of the hoard lists a coin of Æthelwulf of the shared West-Saxon/ Mercian issue (pl. 1, L below), and C. E. Blunt's notes indicate that a Berhtwulf coin of the issue (no. 22) was almost certainly present in the hoard (see below).

26 Pagan, 'Coinage in southern England', p. 56. Pagan suggests that the reverse derives from the OCCI DENTALIVM SAXONIORVM issue, which is less likely.

whether it took the form of a series of distinct issues or of one stylistically diverse emission is uncertain.

Nevertheless the smallish flans of a number of the coins might suggest a falling off in the weight standard of some or all of the intermediate subgroups. But once again the evidence is inconclusive. Only one coin each with busts B, D and E has escaped obvious weight loss, though the unique coin with bust D (no. 43) is broken in half. They weigh 1.12g, 1.05g, and 1.27g respectively. The five intact coins with bust C give an average weight of 1.23g, and the four intact coins with bust F give an average of 1.20g. It is *possible* therefore that weights were less well controlled during this phase of the coinage than they were earlier or later. But the evidence is inadequate, and no certainty is possible.

Previous commentators have seen significance in the fact that Liaba, who issues coins with busts D and F, has the name of one of Æthelwulf's moneyers at Canterbury, and it seems likely that this man somehow found his way to the London mint about this time. It has been suggested that we may be dealing with two men of the same name. Lyon remarks: 'The fact that one of Berhtwulf's moneyers, Liaba, shared the name of a Canterbury moneyer of Æthelwulf is probably coincidence, for there is no stylistic resemblance between their coins.'[27] However, this reasoning is not persuasive, since one of Liaba's surviving coins in Berhtwulf's name (no. 43) is of totally different style from the other two (nos 52 and 53), and was probably cut by a different hand. Moreover Liaba is not a common Anglo-Saxon name, and it seems more likely that the London Liaba was in fact the same man as the Canterbury moneyer.

3. The late portrait group (bust G)

The third group of portrait coins (nos 62–82) is far more homogeneous, at least as far as style is concerned. Although the busts vary greatly in minor detail, they are distinguished by a baroque floridity and confidence which makes them among the most distinctive aesthetic creations of the Anglo-Saxon series, and the reverses, though they sometimes preserve the basic designs of earlier coins, elaborate them into new ornamental forms. All this suggests strongly that the group comes last in the sequence of Berhtwulf's portrait issues. Moreover, changes in the mint personnel are evident. Burnwald, Deneheah, Eanred, and Sigeheah survive from earlier issues to strike coins of the new style, but they are joined by three apparently new moneyers, Eanbald, Eanna (or Eama), and Wine. We cannot necessarily presume from this that the establishment of moneyers was expanded, since the new moneyers may merely have replaced their older colleagues during the course of the issue.

The bust G group does however seem to mark a new start of some kind. The fact that only two styles of die-cutting are apparent, one extremely refined, the other cruder, suggests that it was produced by only two die-cutters, or even by a single man who became more casual during the course of a long issue. This could conceivably indicate a reassertion of central control after the diverse (concurrent or shortlived) issues of the intermediate group. Moreover the twenty-one

27 Lyon, 'Historical problems (2)', p. 228.

surviving specimens were struck by twenty obverse and nineteen reverse dies, which suggests that this emission could well have been of similar volume to that of the bust A group. It is also possible that the weight standard was restored in this issue – if it had in fact slipped. The nine intact coins of the group yield an average weight of 1.25g, and one of them (no. 81) is by far the heaviest known coin of the reign.

Despite the apparently undiminished volume of Berhtwulf's coinage in its later phase, however, the proliferation of minor variants on the same basic patterns might still be interpreted as indicating a certain weakness of central direction. In this respect the late portrait group offers a striking contrast to the earlier coinage of bust A. In the earlier phase the form and style of obverse were remarkably consistent, and the reverse type or types used by each moneyer gave evidence of being carefully regulated. In the late phase virtually every surviving coin shows a different combination of features in bust design, obverse legend and reverse type. It is tempting to contrast this variability with the neat uniformity of Æthelwulf's DORIBI/CANT coinage, struck from *ca* 848 at both Canterbury and Rochester. In Mercia it seems, after the end of the bust A issue, the same basic portrait type continued, generating minor variants, possibly at the whim of the die-cutter, through to the end of the bust G issue. However this interpretation of the evidence is by no means inevitable. There are far too few surviving coins for us yet to have a clear idea of the degree of systematic control operating in either the intermediate group or the bust G issue, and the discovery of more specimens may well dispel the impression of aimless variability. Moreover the non-portrait issue or issues, tiny though the number of surviving specimens is, should not for that reason simply be overlooked as insignificant. The discovery of a large hoard from *ca* 850 could easily transform our present picture of Berhtwulf's coinage out of all recognition.

4. *The non-portrait group*

The fourth group of Berhtwulf's coins, those without portrait, is represented here by only three indubitable specimens (nos 84–6), all from different dies. A possible fourth example (no. 87), an enigmatic fragment reading on the obverse +B[ ]VVLFRmX, and on the reverse +BEO[ ]VLF, must be provisionally disregarded, since it seems equally, if not more likely to be a solitary survival of a London issue of Beornwulf (823–5).[28] Admittedly no coins of Beornwulf are otherwise known without portrait, or of the London mint, but the unenclosed cross-crosslet reverse type is characteristic of London coins of the 820s. The fragmentary moneyer's name is of no assistance, since it does not correspond with that of any known moneyer of either Beornwulf or Berhtwulf. No more chastening lesson in the fragmentary nature of the surviving evidence from this period could have been devised than this enigmatic scrap of metal.

Of the three indubitable non-portrait coins of Berhtwulf, two (nos 84 and 85) are of similar style and fabric to the portrait coins, and were struck by moneyers whose names are recorded on portrait issues: Burnwald and Ean[ ]d (either

28 Blunt, Lyon, and Stewart, 'The coinage of southern England', pp. 35–6.

Eanred or Eanbald). The presence of the latter name implies that these coins came relatively late in the coinage, but otherwise they cannot be fitted into the chronological sequence.

The other non-portrait coin (no. 86) is however quite different from any other coin of the reign. The moneyer, Tatel, appears nowhere else in Berhtwulf's coinage, it is an unusually heavy coin, and its die-cutting technique suggests that it belongs to a quite distinct issue. The cutter, instead of using prepared punches, has marked out the design in pellets before working it into its final form with a cutting tool. Blunt, Lyon and Stewart parallel the style of this coin, and its cross-potent reverse type, with the London coins of the moneyer Redmudh, struck for Ecgberht of Wessex and for Wiglaf of Mercia in 829–30.[29] This would suggest that Berhtwulf made an abortive attempt to revive the coinage at an early point in his reign. The cross-potent reverse type however is found on a bust E coin of Berhtwulf (no. 47). And it must be noted that Tatel (not a common name) appears to have been the sole London moneyer during the first decade of the reign of Berhtwulf's successor, Burgred (852–74).[30] This convincingly places the coin not at the beginning, but at the very end of Berhtwulf's reign. The technical and stylistic parallel with the coins of Redmudh might result simply from the fact that both moneyers were working under circumstances of difficulty, without the usual mint equipment. It is difficult to resist the imaginative conjecture that this coin was issued in Berhtwulf's last months or weeks, during the aftermath of the Viking raid of 851.

The hoards

The patchy nature of the hoard evidence is in danger of seriously distorting our view of the coinage of this period. As the number of dies in the corpus located for this study shows, Berhtwulf's coinage was much more substantial than the actual number of surviving specimens might lead one to assume. But compared with the 860s and 870s from which several large hoards exist, the period of Berhtwulf's reign has been poorly served by the accident of discovery. More specifically the four hoards from which coins of Berhtwulf are recorded yield little in the way of evidence as to the ordering or dating of his issues. Of the two hoards probably deposited during his reign, one, Southampton (1837), yields only two identifiable coins of Berhtwulf, while the other, Sevington, contains a complete cross-section of his issues, and must belong late in the reign. The other two hoards, Dorking and Trewhiddle, though much larger, were deposited some time after Berhtwulf's death, and contain coins from both before and after his time.

The absence of coins of Berhtwulf from the Middle Temple Hoard, deposited *ca* 842, seems to show that the Mercian coinage was not revived until after that year, though, as mentioned above, it is just possible that newer, baser coins were deliberately excluded from this hoard, or even that, for some other contingent reason, no coins had been added to it for some months before its deposit.

29 *Ibid.*, p. 34.

30 Pagan, 'Coinage in southern England', p. 61.

Until recently commentators relied for information concerning the 'Hampshire hoard' on the account by John Lindsay, in which it now emerges that two separate finds, one deposited *ca* 850 (found in 1837) and the other *ca* 870 (found in 1836), were conflated into a single 'hoard' of forty-six coins dated to 1837.[31] Hugh Pagan has now convincingly disentangled the two finds by reference to a number of overlooked publications and private letters written by the collector Richard Sainthill, into whose hands coins from both hoards fell.[32] The hoard which concerns us here was deposited *ca* 850, almost certainly in Southampton.[33] By collating Sainthill's comments with Lindsay's account Pagan identifies fourteen coins from this find: one of Ecgberht of Wessex, six of Æthelwulf, and five of Berhtwulf, together with one each of Wulfred and Ceolnoth, archbishops of Canterbury. It is uncertain how many other coins were present, since Sainthill did not acquire the entire hoard. Two of the five Berhtwulf specimens mentioned are illustrated by Lindsay (nos 31 and 49 below). One or more of the other three (or other unrecorded specimens from the find) may remain hidden anonymously among the unprovenanced coins in the present list.

According to Edward Hawkins's contemporary account, the hoard found in 1834 at Sevington, Wiltshire, included some seventy coins,[34] most if not all of which passed into the possession of C. W. Loscombe. In 1868, Jonathan Rashleigh, presumably using the Loscombe sale catalogue of 1855 as his guide, listed by reign forty-seven coins from the hoard.[35] On the basis of these early sources C. E. Blunt, in the definitive modern account, was able to list forty-nine Sevington coins, the earliest being of Coenwulf of Mercia (796–822) and the latest of Æthelwulf (twenty-three coins) and Berhtwulf.[36] A similar date of deposit to that of the Southampton hoard seems likely: *ca* 850. Blunt's list includes nine coins of Berhtwulf (nos 22, 34, 42, 45, 48, 57, 63, ii and xiii). All the bust types, except D, were present, as might be expected in a hoard deposited towards the end of Berhtwulf's reign.

The find from Dorking, Surrey, uncovered in 1817, was probably deposited some five years after the end of Berhtwulf's reign, *ca* 857.[37] Taylor Combe's account of 1821 assigns one Frankish and 669 Anglo-Saxon coins to particular rulers, and refers to 'about 40 others' which he was unable to see.[38] The earliest coin mentioned is of Coenwulf, followed by one coin each of Ceolwulf I, Beornwulf, and Wiglaf. The sequence ends with 249 coins of Æthelberht of Wessex and a single coin of Burgred of Mercia, of the moneyer Tatel. Combe gives totals of 265 coins of Æthelwulf and twenty-three of Berhtwulf, though there were more among the coins which he did not see. More recent illumination has

31 Lindsay, *A View of the Coinage of the Heptarchy*, p. 123 and pl. 2.

32 Pagan, 'The older finds', pp. 64–70.

33 In Blackburn and Pagan, 'A revised check-list of coin hoards' (p. 294, no. 52) the date of deposit is given as '*c*.845?'.

34 Hawkins, 'An account'.

35 Rashleigh, 'An account', p. 150.

36 Blunt, 'The Sevington hoard of 1834'.

37 Blackburn and Pagan, 'A revised check-list', p. 294, no. 58.

38 Combe, 'An account'.

TABLE 4. The Dorking hoard (1817)

		No. of coins found	No. identifiable today (with list nos)
Ruding pl. 7.1 (Cross with two arms crosslet)	Burnwald	2	1 (19)
Ruding pl. 7.2 (Cross with two arms crosslet, two moline)	Deneheah	6	2 (20, 23)
Ruding pl. 7.3 (Cross crosslet)	Brid	2	2 (1, 2)
	Oswulf	1	1 (14)
	Sigeheah	1	1 (37)
	Wine	1	1 (64)
Ruding pl. 7.4 (Cross crosslet with annulet enclosing a pellet in centre)	Liaba	1	1 (53)
	Deneheah	1	0
Ruding pl. 7.5 (Cross with annulet in each angle)	Burnwald	2	1 (39)
Ruding pl. 27.3 (Monogram of alpha and omega)	Burnwald	1	1 (79)
New types (These are illustrated by Combe and included in later editions of Ruding)		5	5 (32, 38, 66, 72, 75)
Coins of Berhtwulf not on Combe's list		6	6 (29, 43, 47, 73, 80, 86)
	Total	29	

been cast on various aspects of the hoard by Dolley and Skaare,[39] by C. E. Blunt,[40] and by Hugh Pagan.[41]

Complications arise when Combe's list is collated with the twenty-two extant coins of Berhtwulf which can be attributed to the hoard, all of them in the British Museum. Seventeen came through Combe from G. Dewdney, the owner of the land on which the hoard was found, or from Robert Barclay who had bought over 500 of the coins. Four others (nos 2, 19, 80, and 86) can be traced back to Dewdney or Barclay, and one further fragment (no. 73) came to the Museum with a Dorking provenance reliably attached. Though sixteen of the twenty-three coins which Combe recorded are readily identifiable among these extant specimens, seven are not. Some of them may be among the unprovenanced coins in the

39 Dolley and Skaare, 'The coinage of Æthelwulf'.

40 Blunt, 'A small parcel from the Dorking (1817) hoard'.

41 Pagan, 'The coinage of the East-Anglian kingdom'.

TABLE 5. Hoard finds of coins of Berhtwulf

	Southampton (1837)	Sevington	Dorking	Trewhiddle
Bust A	1	1	8	1
Bust B		1		
Bust C		1	3	
Bust D			1	
Bust E	1	2	1	1
Bust F		1	1	3
Bust G		1	7	3
Bust type unknown	3(+?)	2(+?)	7(+?)	2(+?)
Non-Portrait			1	
Total	5(+?)	9(+?)	29(+?)	10(+?)

Moneyers:

Southampton A: Sigeheah; E: Burnwald

Sevington A: Deneheah; B: Deneheah; C: Deneheah; E: Burnwald, Deneheah; F: Deneheah; G: Eanred; Unknown bust type: Brid, Deneheah

Dorking A: Brid (2), Oswulf, Burnwald, Deneheah (2), Sigeheah (2); C: Burnwald, Sigeheah (2); D: Liaba; E: Burnwald; F: Liaba; G: Burnwald, Eanbald, Eanna (2), Sigeheah, Wine, uncertain moneyer (1); Unknown bust type: Burnwald (2), Deneheah (5); Non-portrait: Tatel

Trewhiddle A: Deneheah; E: Brid; F: Burnwald (2), Deneheah; G: Burnwald (2), Eanbald; Unknown bust type: Burnwald; Unknown type and moneyer (1)

current list, others may have been lost. Conversely six coins which are certainly or almost certainly from the hoard are not mentioned by Combe, namely nos 29, 43 (the only surviving Bust D coin), 47, 73, 80 and 86 (the non-portrait coin of Tatel). These were presumably among the coins which he did not see before writing his account. It seems then that there were at least twenty-nine coins of Berhtwulf in the hoard. The situation may be clarified by the modified and expanded version of Combe's original list set out in Table 4.

The numismatic component of the Trewhiddle (Cornwall) hoard, deposited *ca* 868 and found in 1774, comprised *ca* 115 English and continental pennies. Because of its early date of discovery and subsequent dispersal its exact composition remains uncertain. The hoard was briefly described by Philip Rashleigh shortly after it was found,[42] and subsequently his great nephew, Jonathan Rashleigh, listed some seventy-five coins from the find.[43] Many of these coins were illustrated in the Rashleigh sale catalogue in 1909, and can still be identified, while the distinctive Trewhiddle patina may be invoked to confirm other suspected attributions to the hoard. Using these sources and also early accounts by

42 Rashleigh, 'Account of antiquities'.

43 Rashleigh, 'An account'.

Rogers and Ruding, a reconstruction was made by D. M. Wilson and C. E. Blunt, and subsequently refined by Hugh Pagan.[44] The earliest coins were one of Offa (probably) and two of Coenwulf, the latest about fifty-two of Burgred and two of Alfred. Wilson and Blunt list ten coins of Berhtwulf (nos 26, 50, 51, 55, 56, 71, 78, 82, vii and xxv below). The bust types represented are A2, E, F (3), and G (3). It is possible that more coins of Berhtwulf were among the coins which were dispersed at the time of the discovery, and one or more of these may be among the unprovenanced specimens in the main list.

Acknowledgements

My thanks are due to Hugh Pagan for making available his extensive card index, on which the present corpus is based; to Lord Stewartby and Mark Blackburn for giving access to the late C. E. Blunt's notes on coins of the reign; and to Marion Archibald for her help with the British Museum specimens and others. Patrick Finn also provided invaluable assistance in bringing to light a number of elusive coins. I am greatly indebted to David Dumville and Mark Blackburn for their guidance at various stages in the preparation of the text, and to Michael Metcalf and David Sellwood for their advice on particular points. Photographs and permissions were supplied by the British Museum (d, e, f, A, D, E, H, J, L, and nos 1, 5, 14, 15, 20, 21, 25, 28, 29, 32, 33, 34, 35, 37, 38, 39, 43, 45, 47, 48, 51, 53, 54, 56, 57, 64, 66, 72, 73, 75, 76, 79, 80, 81, 82, 86); G. P. Dyer of the Royal Mint (no. 30); Edward Besly of the National Museum of Wales (no. 23); Michael Metcalf of the Ashmolean (no. 22); The Northampton City Museum (no. 61); Andrew Rogerson of the Norfolk Archeological Unit (no. 9); Mark Blackburn of the Fitzwilliam Museum (a, b, c, B, C,F, G, I, K, M, and nos 2, 3, 6, 7, 8, 10, 12, 13, 16, 17, 18, 19, 26, 27, 36, 42, 44, 46, 50, 52, 55, 62, 65, 68, 69, 71, 78, 84, 87); Michael Bonser (nos 11, 67, 74); Lord Stewartby (no. 70); Derek Chick (no. 85); Lawrence Stack (nos 40, 41, 60, and 77); Dr I. Schneider (no. 63); Peter Mitchell of A.H. Baldwin and Sons Ltd (nos 58 and 59); Patrick Finn, then of Spink and Son Ltd (no. 4); and Peter Clayton then of B. A. Seaby Ltd (no. 49).

44 Wilson and Blunt, 'The Trewhiddle hoard'; Pagan, 'Coinage in southern England', pp. 61–2.

LIST OF COINS

The numbering of coins on Plates 1–6 is the same as that in the list. For the collectors and auction sales cited see Manville and Robertson, *British Numismatic Auction Catalogues*.

Early Rochester Issues of Æthelwulf of Wessex (*ca* 839 – *ca* 848)

Six coins from the earliest issues of Æthelwulf are illustrated here for comparative purposes.

EARLY PORTRAIT (*ca* 839)
Moneyers: Beagmund, Dun and Wilheah

			Weight (g)	*Die-Axis*	*Where found*
a	EDELVVLF RE (crosspiece on curve of D) +BEAGMVND MO (ND ligatured)	Fitzwilliam Museum, ex C. E. Blunt coll., ex BM duplicates and Barnett	1.18	270°	?Middle Temple hoard

OCCIDENTALIUM SAXONIORUM (*ca* 839 – *ca* 842)
No indication of moneyer

b	AEÐELVVLF REX +OCCIDENTALIVM round the letters of SAXONIORVM	Fitzwilliam Museum, ex C. E. Blunt coll., ex ?Hanham, ex Grantley 979, ex Montagu 493, ex Shepherd 64, ex Dymock 107	1.43	270°	—

CROSS-AND-WEDGES (*ca* 842 – *ca* 845)
Moneyers: Beagmund, Dun, Wilheah, Brid, Ethelhere, Maninc, Welheard

c	+EÐELVVLF REX +BEAGMVND	Fitzwilliam Museum, ex C. E. Blunt coll.	1.24	90°	—
d	AEÐELVVL REX +BRID MONETA	*BMC* 78	1.39	270°	—
e	+EÐELVVL[ ]EX [ ]BRID MONET[ ]	British Museum, presented by L. A. Lawrence, 1950	1.02	270°	—
f	+EÐELVVLF REX +EÐELHERE	*BMC* 89	1.00	0°	Dorking hoard

NEW STYLE PORTRAIT (*ca* 845 – *ca* 848)
Moneyers: Biarnnoth, Ethelhere, Maninc and Welheard
All the coins of this type in *BMC*, *SCBI* and C. E. Blunt's collection are listed here. In addition Hugh Pagan drew my attention to coin J. No further search was made.

Obv. legend: EÐELVVLF REX or a fragment of this

i *Rev.: Ornamental A*

A	+BIARNNOÐ	*BMC* 36	1.26	0°	Dorking hoard
B	+BIARNNOÐ	*SCBI* Glasgow 536, Hunter 356	1.29	90°	—
C	+BIARNNOÐ	Fitzwilliam Museum, ex C. E. Blunt coll., ex Montagu 475, ex Crompton Roberts, ex Ryan 695	1.12	270°	—

ii *Rev.: Cross, two arms moline*

D	+EÐELHERE	*BMC* 61	1.29	270°	Dorking hoard
E	+EÐELHERE	*BMC* 62	1.07	0°	—
F	+EÐELHERE	*SCBI* Glasgow 537, Coats 292	1.21	270°	—
G	+EÐELHERE	*SCBI* America 283, ex Lockett 461, ex Mann 150	1.20	180°	—
H	+EÐELEHRE	British Museum, ex Barnett	—	0°	—
I	+EÐELERE	*SCBI* Mack 709, ex Ryan 703, ex Drabble 372, ex Montagu I 483, ex Londesborough	1.23	90°	—
J	+VVELMHEΛRD (same obv. die as K)	Massachusetts Historical Society, Stacks, NY, 17.9.1971, 837	—	270°	—
K	+[ ]LHEΛRD (same obv. die as J)	Fitzwilliam Museum, ex C. E. Blunt coll., ex A. H. F. Baldwin coll.	0.78	180°	—

iii *Rev.: Cross, two arms crosslet*

L	+MANINC+	*BMA* 428, ex Montagu 58	1.07	180°	Sevington hoard

iv *Rev.: Cross pattee*

M	+MANINC M	Fitzwilliam Museum, ex C. E. Blunt coll., ex Lockett 468, ex Carlyon-Britton 324, ex Rashleigh 207, Ruding (1840) App. pl. 27, 1	0.92	270°	Trewhiddle hoard

Berhtwulf of Mercia (840–52)

As complete a corpus as possible has been assembled, utilising the extensive researches of Hugh Pagan and the late C. E. Blunt, to whom acknowledgement and thanks are due. All the coins, with the exception of no. 83, are illustrated on plates 2–6. Coins recorded in early sources which cannot be identified with specimens now accessible are listed separately at the end of the main catalogue.

Note: The research for this paper was completed in April 1989; coins which have come to light since then are not included.

PORTRAIT COINS

GROUP I (*ca* 845)
Moneyers: Brid, Burnwald, Deneheah, Oswulf, Sigeheah

Bust A1: Double diadem; normally no hair on forehead. Drapery consists of four vertical lines, and the style is identical with that of Æthelwulf's Rochester coins A–M above

A2: As A1 but drapery of three lines only (nos 13, 25–7, 29)

A3: As A1 but drapery of two lines containing the X of REX (no. 14)

Obv. legend: BERHTVLF REX, or a fragment of this (except on nos 4 and 11)

i *Rev.: Cross crosslet*

Bust A1

1	+BRID MONETA	*BMC* 118	1.25	270°	Dorking hoard

2	[ ]BRID MONETA	Fitzwilliam Museum, ex C. E. Blunt coll., ex L. A. Lawrence (not in either Lawrence sale), = ?Barclay 18	0.96	0°	?Dorking hoard
3	+B[ ] MONETA (the back of the B in the obv. legend constitutes the fourth line of the drapery. Hair is indicated on forehead as on later busts)	Private coll., ex Elmore-Jones (1971) 25	—	270°	—
4	BIARHTVLF REX (HT ligatured and hair indicated on forehead) +BRID MONETΛ	Spink & Son Ltd ex L. Kenny coll. (acquired by him *ca* 1930–40)	1.30	0°	—
5	+OZVLF MONETA	*BMA* 135, ex Evans 47, ex Bergne 71	1.32	180°	—
6	+OZVLF MONETA (NE ligatured)	*SCBI* Glasgow 358, Hunter 238, Ruding (1840) pl. 7, 3	1.12	0°	—
7	+OSVVLF	*SCBI* Glasgow 359, Coats 144	0.98	0°	—
8	+OSVVLF	Fitzwilliam Museum, ex C. E. Blunt coll., ex Ryan 642, ex Brand (presumably ex Cuff 301)	1.27	90°	—
9	+O[ ]F MONETΛ (NE ligatured)	Archibald, in Challis and Cook, (1987) no. 115, p. 136	0.69	0°	Middle Harling, Norfolk, 1987 or earlier
10	+OSVLF MONETΛ (NE ligatured)	Glendining 13.3.1974, 65, = Rashleigh 66b, ex Astronomer 103	0.78	—	Found with a coin of Jænberht nr. Netley Abbey, 1861

11	BE[RH]TVLI REX (L upside down) +[ ]ZVLF MONETΛ (NE ligatured; irregular?)	Blackburn and Bonser (1985) no. 32	0.70	0º	Hoxne, Suffolk, 1985 or earlier

Bust A1 or A2?

12	+OZVVLF M	Blackburn, Dolley and Collier (1983) p. 7, 10	1.23	90º	Greetwell Crossroads, Scawby, Lincs., Oct 1982

Bust A2

13	+OZVVLF MONE	Glendining, 13.4.1988, 108	0.89	—	This or no. 60 probably found at Bawsey, Norfolk 1980–86

Bust A3

14	+OZVVLF M (annulet in one angle of cross)	*BMC* 131	1.21	180º	Dorking hoard

ii *Rev.: As i but crosslet on two arms of cross only*

Bust A1

15	+BVRNVVALD	*BMC* 121, ex Tyssen, ex Hodsall 121, Ruding (1840) pl. 7, 1	1.13	180º	—
16	+BVRNVVALD	*SCBI* Cambridge 406 (*MEC* 1: 1167), Duncanson, ex Smart	1.18	270º	—
17	+BVRNVVALD	*SCBI* Cambridge 407, (*MEC* 1: 1168), ex Young, ex Carlyon-Britton 283, ex Astronomer 102, ex Montagu 271, ex Shepherd 27	1.29	0º	—
18	+BVRNVVALD	*SCBI* Glasgow 355, ex Coats 141, ex Yorke Moore 38	1.26	90º	—

19	+BVRNVVALD	*SCBI* America 199, ex Lockett 2665, ex Napier 10, = ?Barclay 16	1.10	270°	?Dorking hoard

iii *Rev.: Cross with two limbs crosslet, two moline*

Bust A1

20	+DENEHEAH (HE ligatured; same obv. die as no. 21)	*BMC* 126	1.04	90°	Dorking hoard
21	+DENEHEAH (same obv die as no. 20)	British Museum, ex Barnett, ex Bruun 31, ex Gentleman 331, ex Montagu 11	1.08	270°	—
22	+DENEHEAH	*SCBI* Oxford 22, ex Lockett 390, ex Bliss 40, ex Montagu I 273, ex Brice, ex Lake Price 17, ex Murchison 99, = ?Loscombe 1035 (bt Webster)	1.36	270°	?Sevington hoard
23	+DENEHEAH	National Museum of Wales, Dykes (1976) no. 18, ex Grantley 866, ex Doulton 7	1.08	180°	—
24	[ ]DEHEHEᴧH	Rebello coll., Ruding (1840) pl. 7, 2 = Whitbourn 54	1.03	—	—

Bust A2

25	+DENEHEAH (same dies as no. 26)	*BMC* 125	1.32	180°	Dorking hoard
26	+DENEHEAH (same dies as no. 25)	*SCBI* Mack 603, ex Ryan 646, ex Watters 29, ex Rashleigh 60	1.17	0°	Trewhiddle hoard

27	+DENEHEAH	Fitzwilliam Museum, ex C. E. Blunt coll., ex Lawrence (not in either Lawrence sale) = ? Carlyon-Britton 887	0.93	0°	—

iv *Rev.: Cross with an annulet in each angle*

Bust A1

28	+ZIG[ ]HEAH	Lockett 2664, ex Drabble 337, ex Carlyon-Britton 1611 (?ex Marsham 836), ex Wigan	1.04	90°	—

Bust A2

29	+ZIGEHEΛH (?same dies as no. 30)	*BMC* 134	1.29 (Wt. in *BMC* transposed with that of *BMC* 133)	270°	Dorking hoard
30	+ZIGEHEΛH (?same dies as no. 29)	Rubbing made by James West in 1744, now in the archives of the Royal Mint. ?ex Cotton coll. (MS Cotton Titus B VI f. 239r lists a coin of this type with these legends), ?= Ruding (1840) pl. 7, 5 (but if not this would be a third specimen, probably from the same dies)	—	180°?	—

v *Rev.: Cross of eight limbs*

Bust A1

31	+SIGEHEΛH	Lindsay (1842) pl. 2, no. 46, Pagan (1988) p. 68	1.05	—	Southampton hoard, 1837

v *Rev.: Cross with two wedges in each angle*

Bust A1

32	+ZIGEHEΛH	*BMC* 135, Combe (1821) pl. 9, no. 7	1.18	270°	Dorking hoard

GROUP II (*ca* 848?)
Moneyers: Brid, Burnwald, Deneheah, Eanred, Liaba, Sigeheah

Bust B: Smaller head than A. Single diadem. Hair indicated on forehead. Drapery consists of three vertical lines, the outer two joined at the top by a curve, and the middle one ribbed.

Obv. legend: BERHTVLFREX with HT ligatured

i *Rev.: Cross crosslet*

33	+BRID MONETA (N reversed; same obv. die as no. 34)	BMC 119, ex Willett 5	1.12	90°	—

ii *Rev.: Cross crosslet with annulet in centre*

34	+DEHEHEΛH (retr.; same obv. die as no. 33; irregular?)	British Museum, transferred from British and Medieval Dept, 1937, ex Loscombe 1103	—	270°	Sevington hoard

iii *Mule between an obverse with Bust B and an irregular obverse of Æthelwulf showing a cross with wedges in angles*

35	+IΛEDEL VLF RE	British Museum, ex Ryan 641 ex Grantley 864, ex Lawrence (not in either sale)	1.04	0°	—

Bust C: Small head with single diadem and hair indicated on forehead. Drapery of four vertical lines, the two inner ones being longer than the outer two.

Obv. legend: BERHTVLFREX with HT ligatured. (No. 38 adds an initial Latin cross and no. 42 follows the king's title with M.)

i *Rev.: Cross crosslet*

36	+BVRNVVΛLD	Metcalf (1988) no. 135, pl. 7; Blunt (1954), p. 259, pl. II, no. 3	1.10	270°	Southampton, Grove St, 1946
37	+ZIGEHEΛH	*BMC* 132	1.10	180°	?Dorking hoard

ii *Rev.: Cross with three pellets in one angle and one pellet in each of the others*

38	+ZIGEHEΛH	*BMC* 133, Combe (1821) pl. 19, no. 13	1.24 (Wt. in *BMC* transposed with that of *BMC* 134)	60º	Dorking hoard

iii *Rev.: Cross with an annulet in each angle*

39	+BVRNVVΛLD (same dies as no. 40)	*BMC* 120	1.26	270º	Dorking hoard
40	+BVRNVVΛLD (same dies as no. 39	L. R. Stack coll., ex Mack (*SCBI* 600), ex Grantley 865, ex Boyne 1123, ex Christmas 29, ex Dymock 67, ex Addison 6, ex Pembroke 20	1.01	180º	—
41	+BVRNVVALD	*SCBI* America 200, ex Bareford 440, ex Lockett 3597, ex Bliss 41, ex Montagu 274, ex Brice, ex Bergne 73, (ex Murchison 101, ex Dymock 67a)	1.26	180º	—

iv *Rev.: Cross with voided centre; an annulet in each angle*

42	+DENEHEΛH	*SCBI* Norweb 100, ex Ryan 645, ex Reynolds 13, ex Rashleigh 67, ex Loscombe 1036, (illus. Hawkins, 'An account' pl. 23, no. 4)	1.27	270º	Sevington hoard

Bust D: Bust with curls and no diadem

Obv. legend: BERHTVVLF REX with HT ligatured and the X within the bust lines

i *Rev.: Cross with annulet enclosing pellet in centre and an annulet in each angle*

43	+LIΛBΛ MONET:	*BMC* 130, ex Mrs Combe	1.05	90°	?Dorking hoard

Bust E: Small head with double diadem and hair on forehead. Drapery variable but two dies have a row of pellets at the top

Obv. legend: BERHTVVLFREX with HT ligatured, or a fragment of this

i *Rev.: Cross crosslet with annulet enclosing pellet in centre*

44	+DENEHEΛH	*SCBI* Norweb 101, ex Drabble 815, ex Montagu 272, ex Marsham 82, ex Bergne 72, (ex Salt 9), = ?Cuff 305, Ruding (1840) pl. 7, 4 (Rebello coll.)	1.27	270°	—
45	+DE[ ]HEΛH (same obv. die as no. 46?)	British Museum, transferred from British and Medieval Dept, 1937, ex Loscombe 1103	—	270°	Sevington hoard
46	[ ]NEHEΛ[ ] (same obv. die as no. 45?)	*SCBI* Mack 602, ex Grantley 866a, ex Lawrence	0.71	0°	—

ii *Rev.: Cross potent*

47	[ ]BVRNVVΛ[ ]	*BMC* 123, ex Mrs Combe	—	90°	?Dorking hoard

iii *Rev.: Small cross pattee in saltire over cross crosslet*

48	[ ]RNVLΛLD (same rev. die as no. 49)	British Museum, transferred from British and Medieval Dept, 1937, ex ?Loscombe 1103	—	220°	Sevington hoard

49	+BV[ ]VVΛLD (same rev. die as no. 48)	Seaby *Bulletin*, Aug. 1981, E287, ex ?Sainthill 201, Lindsay (1842) pl. 2, no. 45, Pagan (1988) p. 68	0.84	0°	Southampton hoard, 1837

iv *Rev.: Ornamental A*

50	+BRID MONETΛ	Clonterbrook Trust 10, ex Lockett 3596, ex Carlyon-Britton 285, ex Rashleigh 63, Ruding (1840) App. pl. 27, 2	0.88	90°	Trewhiddle hoard

Bust F: Crude style with a large head and large round eye. Double diadem and hair on forehead. Drapery consists of five or more vertical lines with two rows of pellets above. (North designates the bust with simpler drapery on coin no. 51 a separate variety)

Obv. legend: BERHTVVLF REX with HT ligatured

i *Rev.: Cross crosslet*

51	+BVRNVVΛLD	British Museum, ex Barnett, ex Carlyon-Britton 1612, ex Rashleigh 66	1.10	90°	Trewhiddle hoard

ii *Rev.: Annulet surrounded by eight wedges; pellets between*

52	+LIΛBΛ MONE (same obv. die as no. 53)	*SCBI* Glasgow 357, Coats 143, ex Cuff 304, Ruding (1840) pl. C, 10	1.35	0°	—

iii *Rev.: Cross crosslet with annulet enclosing pellet in centre*

53	+LIΛBΛ MNO (same obv. die as no. 52)	*BMC* 129	1.07	0°	Dorking hoard
54	+DENENEAH (same obv. die as no. 55)	*BMC* 124, before 1838	1.25	270°	—

55	+DENENEɅH M (same obv. die as no. 54)	Private coll., ex Ryan 644, ex Bruun 32, ex Carlyon-Britton 886, ex Rashleigh 61	1.13	—	Trewhiddle hoard

iv *Rev.: Cross crosslet with annulet enclosing pellet in centre, small wedges between crosslets*

56	+BVRNVVɅLD	*BMA* 132, ex Rashleigh 62	—	30°	Trewhiddle hoard
57	+DEHEHEɅH	British Museum, transferred from British and Medieval Dept, 1937, ex Loscombe 1103	—	—	Sevington hoard
58	+DENEHE[ ]H	A. H. Baldwin and Sons (in stock 1988), in A. H. F. Baldwin coll. before 1958	—	270°	—
59	+DENEH[ ]	A. H. Baldwin and Sons (in stock 1988), in A. H. F. Baldwin coll. before 1958	—	0°	

v *Rev.: Cross with two limbs crosslet, two with crescents above and below (disconnected moline); a tiny wedge in each angle*

60	+EɅN+RED M (same dies as no. 61)	L. R. Stack coll.	—	—	This or no. 13 probably found at Bawsey, Norfolk 1980–86
61	+EɅN+RED M (same dies as no. 60)	Northampton City Museum, Archibald in Williams (1979) p. 244	1.15	270°	St Peter's Street Northampton, 1973–76

GROUP III (*ca* 850?)
Moneyers: Burnwald, Deneheah, Eanbald, Eanna (or Eama), Eanred, Sigeheah, Wine
Note: No satisfactory classification of the 21 located coins of this phase is yet possible, since variations in bust, legend and reverse type are so numerous that most of the coins show unique combinations of features. North classified the busts into three groups (A, B, C) according to whether the diadem was of one, two or three lines. He then subdivided these groups according to the variations in

drapery. However North's classification brings together coins with heterogeneous reverse types, and forces apart coins of similar obverse and reverse style. For this reason the classification preferred here is in terms of reverse type. Varieties of the bust (which is here designated Bust G) are noted as a secondary feature.

Bust G1: Single diadem.

G1a: Drapery of four lines, shoulders rounded. Neat hatching
G1b: As G1a but shoulders omitted. Hatching of crude horizontal curves
G1c: As G1b but hatching of diagonal curves
G1d: Thick bar at neck with cross below. Drapery consists of two crude diagonal lines each side
G1e: As G1d but without the cross and with drapery of four delicate lines each side

Bust G2: Double diadem.

G2a: Drapery of four thick lines with cross at centre. Shoulders rounded.
G2b: Elongated neck lines with horizontal hatching between. X in each shoulder
G2c: As G2a but below neck X with crescents in angles
G2d: Drapery a single line with curled ends. Two pellets each side. Latin cross upside down below neck

Bust G3: Triple diadem.

G3a: Drapery of three curved lines each side. Hatching between
G3b: Drapery similar to that on G2a, but more delicate style

i *Rev.: Cross crosslet*

Bust G1a

62	BERHTVLF REX (HT ligatured) +BVRNVVΛLD	*SCBI* Berlin 74, ex Murdoch 31, ex Nunn 49, ex Jersey	1.38	180°	—

Bust G1c

63	BERHTVLF REX M +EAN+RED	I. Schneider coll., ex Mack (SCBI 605), ex Ryan 643, ex Thorburn 27, ex Montagu I 270, ex Addington, ex Murchison 98, ex Dymock 65, ex Loscombe 1034 (illus. Hawkins, 'An account', pl. 23, no. 6	1.12	270°	Sevington hoard

Bust G1e

64	BERHTVLF REX (HT ligatured) +VVINE MONE	*BMC* 138		180°	Dorking hoard

Bust G2c

65	[ ]HTVLF REX +ZIG[ ]EAH	*SCBI* Mack 606, (ex Carlyon-Britton 887), ex Lawrence 207	0.98	270°	—

ii Rev.: Cross crosslet over quatrefoil

Bust G1a

66	BERHTVVLF REX EAHHA MONETⱯ (N reversed)	BMC 127, Combe (1821) pl. 9, no. 8	1.31	0°	Dorking hoard

Bust G1d?

67	BERHTVVLF[ ] [ ]ZIGEHEA[ ]	Publication by Blackburn and Bonser forthcoming	0.79	270°	Tilbury, Essex 1986/7

iii Rev.: Cross with two limbs crosslet, two moline

Bust G1a?

68	BERHTVVLF REX +DENEHEⱯH	Private coll., ex Drabble 336, ex Mann 146, ex Carlyon-Britton 284, ex Beaufoy 44	1.17	0°	—

Bust G2b

69	BERHTVVLF REX +DENEHEAH X	*SCBI* Glasgow 356, ex Coats 142, ex Yorke Moore 39	1.28	0°	—

Bust G2–

70	[ ]LF REX [ ]DENE[ ]	Lord Stewartby coll., bt Seaby *ca* 1948	0.64	180°	—

iv *Rev.: Cross moline*

Bust G1b?

No.	Legends	Provenance / references	Wt	Die axis	Findspot
71	BERHTVLF [ ] +BVRNV[ ]M	Fitzwilliam Museum, ex C. E. Blunt coll., ex Mack, *SCBI* 604, ex Matthews, ex Carlyon-Britton (not in sale), ex Rashleigh 65b, Ruding (1840) App. pl. 27, 4	0.65	0°	Trewhiddle hoard

Bust G2a

No.	Legends	Provenance / references	Wt	Die axis	Findspot
72	BERHTVVLF REX +EA+HH+ M	*BMC* 128, Combe (1821) pl. 9, no. 5	1.25	180°	Dorking hoard

v *Rev.: Seriffed cross with crosses in three angles and annulet in the fourth*

Bust G1a

No.	Legends	Provenance / references	Wt	Die axis	Findspot
73	[ ] [ ]OM[ ] (retrograde? irregular?)	British Museum, presented by Sir Henry Ellis, 1835	—	—	Dorking hoard

vi *Rev.: Monogram of A and cross*

Bust G1b

No.	Legends	Provenance / references	Wt	Die axis	Findspot
74	BERHTVL[ ]EX +SI[ ]EHEΛH (same obv. die as no. 75?)	Metcalf (1988) no. 136; Blunt (1954), p. 259, pl. II, no. 4	—	0°	Southampton, Kingsland, 1946/50
75	BERHTVLF REX +ΣIGEHEAH (rev. legend starts at 6 o'clock: same obv. die as no. 74?)	*BMC* 137, Combe (1821) pl. 9, no. 6	—	0°	Dorking hoard

Bust G1d

No.	Legends	Provenance / references	Wt	Die axis	Findspot
76	BERHTVLF REX (HT ligatured) +EΛ+H Λ+MO (rev. legend starts at 6 o'clock)	*BMA* 134, ex Sir John Evans, Smith (1850) I, pl. 23, 10 (Rolfe coll.)	1.15	270°	Richborough

vii Rev.: Monogram of alpha and omega

Bust G1a

77	BERHTVLF REX +BVRNVVɅLD (same dies as no. 78)	L. R. Stack coll., publication by Blackburn and Bonser forthcoming	1.08	—	Thetford, Norfolk, 1988
78	[ ]HTVLF REX [ ]RNVVALD (same dies as no. 77)	*SCBI* Mack 601, ex Carlyon-Britton (not in sale), ex Rashleigh 65a, Ruding (1840) App. pl. 27, 3	0.86	270°	Trewhiddle hoard
79	BERHTVLF REX (HT ligatured) +BVRNVɅLD (rev. legend starts at 6 o'clock)	*BMC* 122	1.28	0°	Dorking hoard

Bust G2d

80	BERHTVVLF REX +EANBALD MONET	British Museum, ex Lockett 391, ex Bliss 42, (ex Montagu 275), ex Marsham 24, ex Murchison 100, ex Dymock 66, ex Cuff 302, Ruding (1840) App. pl. 29, 20 (Dewdney coll.)	1.23	180°	?Dorking hoard

Bust G3a

81	+BERHTVLF REX M (HT ligatured; legend starts at 11 o'clock and is divided by the bust) +ZIGEHEɅH	BMC 136, ex Bank of England (1877), ex Austen (d. 1797)	1.54	90°	—

viii	*Rev.: Latin cross dividing TA (concluding Mone in the legend) with annulet beneath each letter*			

Bust G3b

82	BERHTVVLF REX (HT ligatured) +EΛNBΛLD MONE	*BMA* 133, ex Rashleigh 59, Ruding (1840) App. pl. 27, 1	0.97	0°	Trewhiddle hoard

COIN OF UNASCERTAINED BUST TYPE (A or G?)

Rev.: Cross with two limbs crosslet, two moline

83	BERHTVLF R[ ] +DEHEN[ ] *Not Illustrated*	Hermitage, St Petersburg, ex Reichel 57	—	—	—

NON-PORTRAIT COINS

GROUP IV (Uncertain date)
Moneyers: Burnwald, Eanbald or Eanred, Tatel and (doubtfully) Beo---ulf

i *Obv.: Chi-Rho monogram*
Rev.: Mercian M with bar above; one pellet each side

84	[ ]RHTVLF REX +EΛN[ ]M (rev. legend starts at six o'clock)	Fitzwilliam Museum, ex C. E. Blunt coll., ex Grantley 867, ex Boyne 1123, ex Murchison 102, ex Dymock 67b	0.85	90°	—

ii *Obv.: As last*
Rev.: As last but three pellets to left of M, and a small R to r

85	+BERHTVV[ ] REX BVRNVVΛLD [ ]O (rev. legend starts at 6 o'clock)	Private coll., publication by Blackburn and Bonser forthcoming	0.80	0°	Tilbury, Essex 1986/7

iii *Obv.: Cross potent with bars in angles*
Rev.: Cross potent

86	+BERHTVVLF REX M +TΛTEL MONETΛ	*BMC* 139, ex Cuff 303, ex Dimsdale 212, Ruding (1840) I, p. 120, App. pl. 29, 26 (Dewdney coll.)	1.45	320°	Dorking hoard

NON-PORTRAIT COIN OF DOUBTFUL ATTRIBUTION

iv *Obv.: Cross with rough wedges in angles in pelleted circle*
Rev.: Cross crosslet (no inner circle)
(Probably a coin of King Beornwulf, 823–25)

87	B[---]VVLF RmX +BEO[---]VLF	Fitzwilliam Museum, ex C. E. Blunt coll., bt Seaby, 1953, Blunt, Lyon, and Stewart (1963) pl.VII, C	0.93	90°	—

UNLOCATED COINS

The following coins and fragments, recorded in early sources, cannot be securely identified with any of the specimens in the above list, though further research may provide such identifications. Some references may be to the same coin. Hugh Pagan suggests, for instance, that nos. ii, iii, iv, and v could be the same fragment.

BRID

i Cuff (1854) 300 (BERHTVVLF REX / BRID MONETA, cross crosslet within a circle; a small portion of lower part of coin broken).

ii Loscombe (1855) 1037a (bt Webster), ex ?Sevington (BERHTVVLF REX / BRID MONET, cross crosslet within a circle).

iii Marsham (1888) 83a (*rev.*: +BRID MONET, cross crosslet in circle; fractured).

iv Sotheby, 6–7.4.1899 (bt Walters), ex Briggs (1893) 176b, bt Napier.

v Bascom (1914) 9.

vi *Spink Numismatic Circular*, Mar.–Apr. 1922, no. 3244 ('a little chipped, VF').

BURNWALD

vii Grantley (1944) 866a = ?Rashleigh 64, ex Trewhiddle (*rev.*: BYRNVVALD, cross with two limbs crosslet; chipped).

viii Combe, 'An account of some Anglo-Saxon pennies', p. 113 (cross with two arms crosslet), ex Dorking. (See Table 4 above).

ix Combe, 'An account of some Anglo-Saxon pennies', p. 113 (cross with an annulet in each angle), ex Dorking. (See Table 4 above).

DENEHEAH

x Barclay (1831) 17, ex ?Dorking.

xi Cuff (1854) 298, bt Webster (BERHTVVLF REX / DENEHEAN, cross crosslet within a circle, very fine, *cf.* Ruding pl. 7 no. 2).

xii Cuff (1854) 299, bt Cureton (as ix 'with some slight difference', very fine).

xiii Loscombe (1855) 1035 (bt Webster), ex ?Sevington (*rev.*: PENEHEAH, 'cross within a circle, two of the ends turned').

xiv–xvii Combe, 'An account of some Anglo-Saxon pennies', p. 113 (cross with two arms crosslet, two moline), ex Dorking. (See Table 4 above; ?one of these = no. 83).

xviii Combe, 'An account of some Anglo-Saxon pennies', p. 113 (cross crosslet with annulet enclosing a pellet in centre), ex Dorking. (See Table 4 above).

EANBALD

xix Montagu (1897) 2 (*rev.*: 'large A with curved ends').

OSWULF

xx Bergne (1873) 71 (bt Webster) (BERHTVLF REX / OSVLF MONETA, cross crosslet (*cf.* Ruding pl.7, no. 3).

xxi Grantley (1944) 866a (OSVVLF MONE [NE ligatured], *rev.*: cross crosslet; chipped), later Rose coll. (Devizes).

SIGEHEAH

xxii Barclay (1831) 18, ex ?Dorking.

xxiii Bateman (1893) 263.

UNSPECIFIED MONEYER

xxiv Astronomer (1906) 103 (*rev.*: cross crosslet; fragment).

xxv Rev. R. Hennah, ex Trewhiddle hoard (Wilson and Blunt, 'The Trewhiddle hoard', p. 118, no. 15; *rev.* type unspecified).

xxvi–xxviii Lindsay, *Coinage of the Heptarchy* (1848); Pagan 'The older finds', p. 68. (*rev.* types unspecified).

APPENDIX A

INDEX OF BERHTWULF'S MONEYERS

?Beo[--]ulf	87
Brid	1–4, 33, 50, i–vi
Burnwald	15–19, 36, 39–41, 47–9, 51, 56, 62, 71, 77–9, 85, vii–ix
Deneheah	20–7, 34, 42, 44–6, 54–5, 57–9, 68–70, 83, x–xviii
Ean[---]	84
Eanbald	80, 82, xix
Eanna (or Eama)	66, 72, 76
Eanred	60–1, 63
Liaba	43, 52–3
Oswulf	5–14, xx–xxi
Sigeheah	28–32, 37–8, 65, 67, 74–5, 81, xxii–xxiii
Tatel	86
Wine	64
[-]OM[-]	73

APPENDIX B

INDEX OF FINDS OF COINS OF BERHTWULF

Bawsey, Norfolk (1980–6)	13 *or* 6
Dorking Hoard (1817)	1, 2, 14, 19, 20, 25, 29, 32, 37, 38, 39, 43, 47, 53, 64, 66, 72, 73, 75, 79, 80, 86, viii–x, xiv–xviii, xxii
Greetwell Crossroads, Scawby, Lincs. (Oct 1982)	12
Hoxne, Suffolk (1985 or earlier)	11
Middle Harling, Norfolk (1987 or earlier)	9
Netley Abbey (1861)	10
Northampton, St Peter's St	61
Richborough, Kent	76
Sevington Hoard (1834)	22, 34, 42, 45, 48, 57, 63, ii, xiii
Southampton, Grove St (1946)	36
Southampton Hoard (1837)	31, 49, xxvi–xxviii
Southampton, Kingsland (1946/50)	74
Thetford, Norfolk (1988)	77
Tilbury, Essex (1986/7)	67, 85
Trewhiddle Hoard (1774)	26, 50, 51, 55, 56, 71, 78, 82, vii, xxv

IV

THE LONDON MINT IN THE REIGN OF ALFRED

Mark Blackburn

Despite the relative wealth of literary and documentary sources for the reign of Alfred (871–899), there is little that bears upon the status of London between the Viking wintering there in 871/2 and Alfred's 'occupation' of the city recorded in the *Anglo-Saxon Chronicle's* annal for 886. Interpreting these meagre sources,[1] most historians have thought that London either remained under Viking control from 871/2 or passed into Viking hands in 873/4 on the defeat of Burgred at Repton or in 877 on the partitioning of the Mercia. There it remained until Alfred captured it after a siege in 886.[2] For thirty years or more numismatists have been warning that coins in the names of Alfred and of Ceolwulf II of Mercia (873/4–878/9) appear to have been struck in London during the later 870s or early 880s.[3] However, in deference to the accepted reading of historical events a compromise was often sought which did less than justice to the weight of the numismatic evidence and which at times stretched credulity. Thus Dolley and Blunt in their classic study of the chronology of Alfred's coinage suggested that London may have been a species of 'open city' in which the Danes tolerated the minting of coins in Alfred's name.[4] Lyon went so far as to propose that the pre-886 coins attributed to London, including the substantial coinages of the Mercian

Acknowledgements. Enticed and frustrated by the observations of numismatists on the coinage of Alfred's middle years, in 1986 Simon Keynes decided to look at the evidence for himself and set about compiling a corpus of the *Cross-and-Lozenge* and related coins. He invited me to his rooms to discuss their die-cutting styles, and one afternoon we sat down together to play Happy Families with his card index. I do not remember now who won the game, but its results were far reaching, providing the inspiration for this paper which was originally intended to be one of joint authorship. With typical generosity, Dr Keynes insisted that I take credit (and responsibility) for the interpretation of the material presented here and that we should jointly publish the corpus which appears elsewhere in this volume.

Illustrations. In this paper references to coins by number are to the corpus of Blackburn and Keynes, below, and to the accompanying illustrations on Pls 7–11.

1 The evidence and its interpretations are surveyed by Keynes, 'King Alfred and the Mercians', above.

2 Stenton *(Anglo-Saxon England*, pp. 258–9) has been the most influential exponent of this interpretation of events, but a similar view has been adopted by most modern authors.

3 The arguments were clearly and succinctly put in Pagan, 'Coinage in the age of Burgred', pp. 26–7 ('Appendix A: London after 874'). He says 'The corpus of Ceolwulf II . . . is a salutary reminder that the London mint continued to operate' and later 'None of this suggests a major break in continuity caused by Viking occupation.'

4 Dolley and Blunt, 'The chronology', p. 81.

kings Berhtwulf (840–852) and Burgred (852–873/4), might have been struck at Rochester, i.e. within Greater Wessex.[5] Faced with this range of opinion and in the absence of a detailed study of the coinage of Alfred's middle years, historians have tended to ignore these issues, or merely noted them as a potential problem.[6] Yet in fact the coinage is probably our most direct and important source of evidence for London's status in this period, and when viewed independently it points to quite a different sequence of events from that traditionally accepted. It also sheds new light on aspects of Ceolwulf II's career of which no hint has hitherto been detected in other sources. Simon Keynes' paper, above, discusses further the historical background and the significance of the new interpretation of the numismatic evidence that is presented here.

Structure of the coinage

Alfred's coinage falls into three distinct phases, the divisions being marked by significant reforms in the fineness or weight of the penny, as well as changes in design.[7] During the opening years of his reign Alfred continued to strike the *Lunettes* type that his brother Æthelred I (865–871) had used and which was also being struck in parallel by Burgred of Mercia (Pl. 11, E–I). The *Lunettes* coins had already been debased considerably, and under Alfred they suffered further reductions in fineness and weight, so that by the end of the issue they contained less than a fifth of the silver of a typical penny of the earlier ninth century.[8] In the mid-870s Alfred set about restoring the quality of the coinage, just as his contemporary Charles the Bald (840–877) had done for the West Frankish coinage in 864. Initially, it would appear, Alfred intended to bring the English penny into line with the Carolingian denier, in terms of weight, fineness and value. Only one specimen of this coinage survives (*Geometric-Quatrefoil* type, no. 1), but its evidence is cogent, being struck to the Carolingian standard of *ca* 1.75g (27gr) rather then the traditional English standard of *ca* 1.35g (21gr). Moreover, it is the only coin type of this period to have a non-portrait design, as do the Carolingian issues. The coinage could have been struck in larger numbers than its rarity suggests, but this heavy standard failed to stick, for the remaining coins of Alfred's middle phase, although of fine silver, are struck to the traditional standard of *ca* 1.35g. The restoration of the silver fineness and weight alone was a remarkable achievement of government given the economic problems posed by such a reform and its concomitant price revaluation. People would have been expected to bring their *Lunettes* coins to the moneyers or exchangers and they would have

5 Lyon, 'Historical problems (2)', pp. 234, 236–7; Lyon's arguments are complex, but they include the observation that London could not have contained a major mint for Ceolwulf or Alfred during the Danish occupation of the city prior to 886. For other observations on the difficulty of fitting the coinage into the accepted framework of historical events, see Brooke, *English Coins*, p. 47; Dolley, *Anglo-Saxon Pennies*, pp. 19–20; Pagan, 'Coinage in the age of Burgred', pp. 26–7; Grierson and Blackburn, *Medieval European Coinage* 1, p. 312; Archibald, in Webster and Backhouse, *The Making of England*, pp. 35, 286.

6 E.g. Brooke and Keir, *London 800–1216*, pp. 19–20, 92–3; Dumville, 'The Treaty', p. 16 n. 79.

7 Dolley and Blunt, 'The chronology', provides the best general survey of Alfred's coinage, although it is now outdated in a number of respects.

8 Metcalf and Northover, 'Debasement of the coinage'.

received one new penny for perhaps every five old ones. This middle phase saw the use of several different coin types, struck for Alfred and Archbishop Æthelred (870–888), and also for Ceolwulf II of Mercia who adopted the same standards and some of the same types as Alfred. The principal coinage was the *Cross-and-Lozenge* type, but this was probably preceded by several smaller issues including the well-known *Two Emperors* type.[9]

The final and longest phase of Alfred's coinage was introduced by another monetary reform, in which the weight standard of the penny was again raised, this time not to the Carolingian standard but to an intermediate *ca* 1.6g (24.5gr). The significance of this particular weight is not understood. It may reflect a wider revision of weights and measures involving a 20 per cent increase in the weight of the pound, although no other evidence of this has come to light; alternatively it could have arisen from an adjustment of the value of the penny or level of the minting charge, reducing the number of coins struck from a pound of silver. Interestingly, the change was not adopted in the Danelaw when the Vikings began their own coinages, for these use the earlier *ca* 1.35g standard which must still have prevailed within the Anglian community there.[10] The coins of this third phase were principally of the so-called *Two-Line* type, but a number of special mint-signed issues were also produced at Canterbury, Exeter, Gloucester, London, Oxford, and Winchester (Pl. 11, M, O, Q–V). This last phase in fact continued for almost a century without any further reform or recoinage, although a number of new designs were introduced in addition to the basic *Two-Line* type and there was a gradual lowering of weight and silver standards.

The mint-signed issues provide direct evidence of another major innovation in the coinage for which Alfred was responsible, the extension of minting to a range of inland towns. Previously there had been only a few mints in England – essentially London, Canterbury, Rochester, an East Anglian mint (Ipswich?), and York – all located near ports on the Channel or the North Sea where bullion or foreign coinage would arrive in trade. Alfred's extension of minting, which was no doubt associated with his scheme for the development of the burghal system, was continued under Edward the Elder, and by the time of Athelstan (924–939) there were some thirty-five mints operating at towns throughout the country.[11] In tracing the development of the mint network we are hampered by the fact that before Athelstan's reign relatively few coins specify where they were struck and often the numismatist must rely on oblique methods of identifying their origin.[12] These involve recognising groups of coins that are the work of particular die-cutters from the style of the design and epigraphy and the form of inscriptions, then hoping to link these groups to moneyers who are associated with mint-signed coins. This will often enable us to identify the centre from which a moneyer drew his

9 For a description and corpus of the coins of this middle phase, see Blackburn and Keynes, 'A corpus', below.

10 Blackburn, 'The earliest Anglo-Viking coinage'.

11 The expansion of the mint system is discussed in Blackburn, 'Mints, burhs'. For Athelstan's coinage, see Blunt, 'The coinage of Athelstan', pp. 42–3.

12 Lyon has made an excellent analysis of Edward the Elder's coinage; see Blunt, Stewart and Lyon, *Coinage in Tenth-Century England*, pp. 20–96. A detailed study of Alfred's issues is in preparation by the present author.

dies, and it is likely that in many cases he would have been operating in the same town, but we cannot exclude the possibility that the moneyer could have had his workshop in another town nearby that possessed no die-cutter of its own. Thus, for example, if in this period there were a mint at Rochester which generally drew its dies from the Canterbury die-cutter we might be unable to identify it, unless perhaps occasionally it also looked to the London die-cutter for dies.

Alfred's coins survive in substantial numbers, but due to the pattern of hoarding they are very unevenly distributed across the reign.[13] There are probably some 150–200 *Lunettes* coins of Alfred and a similar (or perhaps larger) number of contemporary coins of Burgred, so that perhaps some 400 coins survive from the first five years of Alfred's reign; Burgred's pre-871 coins are even more numerous. They come from at least a dozen hoards giving us a fair picture of the coinage in the first few years of Alfred's reign, although our knowledge of the final year or so of the *Lunettes* issue is weak. The second phase is very poorly represented among the surviving material, with a total of only 61 coins for Alfred, Ceolwulf, and the archbishop.[14] This is because we have only two small hoards that are contemporary with the middle phase: four *Cross-and-Lozenge* coins found at Washington, Sussex in 1904, and three others, all of Ceolwulf II, found in Buckinghamshire in 1996. The majority of phase II coins come from the Cuerdale hoard deposited early in Edward the Elder's reign, *ca* 905. From the third phase some 1,300 coins survive of which perhaps half are official issues and half are Viking imitations. About 1,000 of these are from the Cuerdale hoard in which Alfred's latest coins, those of the 990s, were best represented. The five or six hoards contemporary with phase III were each dominated by local issues so that, while they illustrate the currency of their regions, they are of limited help in gaining an overall picture of the coinage or in constructing a chronology for the various types in this phase. Although then a total of some 1,500 coins of 'Alfred' are known, the majority belong to the opening or closing years of the reign, and for the critical period *ca* 875–890, encompassing the two coinage reforms and the initial expansion of the mint network, we have relatively few specimens and few hoards.

The London Mint

Under Burgred London appears to have been the most important minting place in England, with substantially more moneyers operating than at Alfred's mint in Canterbury. London is not named on any *Lunettes* coins, but Pagan has argued that the great majority, if not all, of Burgred's moneyers were working in the same place, sharing in common two prolific die-cutters (Pl. 11, E–F), and that this can only have been at London.[15] We cannot rule out the possibility that there were other smaller mints in Mercia, though as yet there is no firm evidence to

13 For hoards of Alfred's reign see Blunt and Dolley, 'The hoard evidence', and Blackburn and Pagan, 'A revised check-list'. For single-finds see Bonser, 'Single-finds of ninth-century coins', below.

14 See Blackburn and Keynes, 'A corpus', below, p. 128, where it is estimated that we know of only *ca* 17 per cent of the obverse dies and *ca* 10 per cent of the reverse dies originally used in phase II.

15 Pagan, 'Coinage in the age of Burgred'. Lyon's suggestion that it may have been at Rochester (n.

show that there were.[16] There is some confusion about the situation prevailing towards the end of the *Lunettes* issue, for there are a number of coins of anomalous style copying ones of Burgred, Alfred, and even Æthelred I, and there are other coins struck in the name of Alfred but by London moneyers and in what appears to be good London style (Pl. 11, I).[17] The date, origin and exact status of these groups have still to be determined. Nonetheless, we can be reasonably confident that most of Burgred's fifty-five or so moneyers were working in London (Table 1).

TABLE 1. Moneyers of Burgred of Mercia, *ca* 860–874

Beagstan, Beranh, Berheah, Berhtelm, Biornoth, Burghelm, Burgnoth, Cenred, Cethliaf, Ciallaf, Cunehelm, Cuthberht, Cuthulf, Dagelte/Dealge, Dealinc, Dela, Denewald, Diarulf, Diga, Dudda, Dudecil, Dudeman, Dudwine, Eadnoth, Eadulf, Ealdulf, Eanred, Ecgulf, Ethelheah, Ethelred, Ethelstan, Ethelulf, Framric, Guthere, Guthmund, Heawulf, Hereferth, Hugered, Hussa, Huthere, Lefle, Liafman, Liafwald, Luda, Ludig, Lulla, Osmund, Tata, Tatel, Tidehelm, Wine, Wulfeard, Wulfred

By contrast, the picture presented by the last phase of Alfred's coinage is very different from that at the beginning of the reign. England was by then partitioned between the Anglo-Saxons and the Danes, and large Anglo-Scandinavian coinages were being issued in the Danelaw, while in Greater Wessex and English Mercia Alfred was striking coins at a number of mints. The mint-signed coins represent a relatively small proportion of the coinage of phase III, and the majority consists of coins of the *Two-Line* type anonymous as to their mint, although they can be divided into several distinctive styles representing different regional groups.

The origin of the largest of these *Two-Line* groups is readily identified as Canterbury because it includes coins in the names of Archbishops Æthelred and Plegmund and because many of the moneyers of the simple *Two-Line* type also struck a variety in a related style bearing the mint-signature 'DORO' (*Dorovernia*, Canterbury). Some eighteen moneyers are associated with this Canterbury style during phase III. The second largest, with some eleven moneyers, is the London group, to which we will turn in more detail shortly. Then the next largest group is probably that associated with Winchester, which encompasses the work of nine moneyers, some of whom continued to operate in Edward the Elder's reign using a style of die that can be traced ultimately to Winchester mint-signed coins of Athelstan. The fourth major group, from west Mercia, is rather different, for it embraces five distinct styles of die-cutting that may represent the work of several

5 above) is not convincing. It depends in part on the attribution of Berhtwulf's coins to Rochester, on which see Booth, 'Monetary alliance', above.

16 Pagan and Stewart, 'A new Mercian moneyer', offers some evidence for a mint in the west Midlands.

17 H. E. Pagan in Biddle *et al.*, 'Coins of the Anglo-Saxon period from Repton', pp. 117–19; and in Biddle *et al.*, 'Coins of the Anglo-Saxon period from Repton, II', p. 18; Pagan, 'Two new coins'.

mints. The six moneyers involved are each in some way linked with the distinctive west Mercian coinage of Edward the Elder, which includes his pictorial issues. There are also a number of smaller stylistic groups to be found within the *Two-Line* issue, each associated with one or two moneyers and which presumably represent the work of other mints in Greater Wessex or Mercia, including one may suppose Exeter, Gloucester, Oxford, and perhaps Bath, attested from mint-signed coins of Alfred or Edward the Elder. Finally, there are some thirty *Two-Line* moneyers who have traditionally been treated as working for Alfred, but who were in fact operating exclusively in the Danelaw producing Anglo-Scandinavian coinages that emulate or imitate official West Saxon and Mercian issues.[18]

TABLE 2. *Two-Line* moneyers of Alfred, by style

Canterbury style	Burgnoth, Byrnwald, Denewald, Diarwald, Dunninc, Eadwald, Edmund, Elfstan, Ethelred, Ethelstan, Ethelwine, Ethelwulf, Garwine (?), Hereferth, Heremod, Hunfreth, Tirwald, Wine.
London style	*Early:* Beagstan, Bernred?, Dealinc, Della, Ealdwulf, Goda, Heawulf, Hereferth, Herewulf, Ludig, Tidweald, Tilewine. *Late:* Beagstan, Ludig.
Winchester style	*Early:* Beornmær, Dunna, Heremund, Wulfred. *Late:* Athelstan, Athelulf, Ælfstan, Æthered, Beornmær, Byrnhelm, Heremund, Wulfred.
West Mercian styles	*Style a:* Cuthberht. *Style b:* Buga, Cuthwulf. *Style c:* Wynberht. *Style d:* Dudig. *Style e:* Eadwald.
Other styles	Ælfwald, Boiga, Bernred, Ecwulf, Hunberht, Oswulf, Samson, Sigewald.

London's mint-signed issue, the *London Monogram* type (Pl. 11, M, O, Q and R), although quite plentiful today, was in fact produced on a relatively small scale,[19] and the bulk of the coins struck at London during phase III were of the *Two-Line* type (Pl. 11, U–V). There are a number of reasons for thinking the *London Monogram* coinage was produced early in phase III and probably preceded the issue of *Two-Line* coins there. It bears a portrait design, which was common in previous issues but abandoned in this phase, occurring only on the *London Monogram* type and on the unique mint-signed coin of Gloucester (Pl. 11, S) which is also regarded as early. An early date is also suggested by the

[18] Blackburn, 'The earliest Anglo-Viking coinage' (with a list of moneyers); *idem*, 'The Ashdon (Essex) hoard'.

[19] There is heavy die-linking among the extant coins, most of which derive from two hoards found in the City of London at Bucklesbury (1872) and Thames Street (*ca* 1880); known only from archive sources, it is possible that they are indeed the same find. Cf. Blunt and Dolley, 'The hoard evidence', pp. 234–5; Pagan, 'Two groups'. Evidence for the Thames Street hoard has recently come to light in a manuscript of T. Bliss; I am grateful to Edward Besly for allowing me to cite it.

composition of the Thames Street hoard, which consisted largely of *London Monogram* coins with only a few of the *Two-Line* type and one Oxford (*Ohsnaforda*) coin. It is notable that the only moneyer identified among the *Two-Line* coins is Wulfred, who operated at Winchester, which suggests that the London moneyers may not yet have embarked on the *Two-Line* issue. A third reason for regarding the *Monogram* issue as relatively early is that within the Cuerdale hoard the coins of this type were the most heavily pecked (i.e. tested) of all those of phase III, suggesting that they had been in circulation for longest.[20]

Most *London Monogram* coins have only the monogram on the reverse and omit the moneyer's name (Pl. 11, M, O and Q), but there are a number that include the name of the moneyer Tilewine (Pl. 11, R). A few other *London Monogram* coins in a distinctive but crude style, and which carry the names Ælfsan, Heahwulf, Herewulf, and 'Vinvrdat', are generally regarded as Viking issues of the Danelaw. However, since the coins are of good weight and two of the moneyers (Heawulf and Herewulf) struck *Two-Line* coins in the London style, it is probable that they are official issues, or imitations based on official coins that have not survived. If so their absence from the two City hoards would suggest that they were struck after those finds were put together, so perhaps in the mid-880s.

The *London Monogram* coins of Tilewine provide one of the crucial clues to the identification of the London moneyers under Alfred. Tilewine also struck coins of the *Two-Line* type, and these are in a distinctive style (Pl. 11, U). Ten other moneyers struck *Two-Line* coins in this same style, and they can tentatively be identified as colleagues of Tilewine at London, although there is the possibility that some of them may have operated from a neighbouring mint that drew its dies from London. Within this London style two phases of die cutting can be distinguished. On the earlier dies (Pl. 11, U) the lettering is made up of thin strokes composed of bars or shallow wedges without serifs, similar to the lettering on the *London Monogram* issue. The obverse legend is normally XEL FR ED RE or EL FR ED REX, with large spaces between the four sections. There is a degree of variation in the letter forms and the layout of the dies that is not found on the later group. The later dies (Pl. 11, V) have the reading EL (or ÆL) FR ED REX aligned symmetrically with the central cross and with lettering that is more consistent in form and positioning. The detailed criteria for identifying these styles and for distinguishing the substantial number of Danelaw imitations of them will be presented elsewhere.[21]

Tilewine is first named on the *London Monogram* issue,[22] but six of the remaining ten moneyers were also named on Burgred's coinage, which reinforces the attribution of this stylistic group to London and suggests a degree of continuity between phases I and III. It is notable that whereas all eleven *Two-Line* London moneyers were active during the period of the earlier style, only two (Ludig and Beagstan) produced coins of the later style. Ludig had been

20 Archibald, 'Pecking and bending', pp. 15 and 21.

21 Some of the criteria for identifying the imitations are set out in Blackburn, 'The Ashdon (Essex) hoard', pp. 16–18, 31.

22 Unless a *Lunettes* coin of Alfred in an anomalous style with a moneyer's name TILEFEINE (*BMC* 170) represents the same man.

active since Burgred's reign and appears to have stopped work during the later *Two-Line* style. Beagstan probably began his career as a moneyer mid-way through the *Two-Line* issue, since only one coin of his in the early style is known and the remainder of his work for Alfred is in the later style.[23] By the end of the reign he appears to have been the sole moneyer operating at London, and he alone continues under Edward the Elder. It is interesting to note that coins of the more prolific moneyers of the earlier style – Hereferth, Ludig, and Tilewine – were frequently imitated in the Danelaw, but there are no imitations of Beagstan, probably because by the time that he was active the southern Danelaw mints had turned away from copying the *Two-Line* type to strike the *St Edmund Memorial* issue. During the course of phase III then, the number of moneyers operating in London fell from at least nine at the beginning to just two, and by the end of the reign to only one.

Having seen the situation at the London mint at the beginning and the end of Alfred's reign, we may now turn to the critical coinage of phase II (all the known specimens of this phase are illustrated on Pls 7–10). The majority of coins in this phase are of the *Cross-and-Lozenge* type, and it is among these that a London group can be firmly identified. However, we should first look at the four minor types of phase II, two of which may also have been struck in London. The types have survived in so few specimens that we cannot be confident in our arrangement and interpretation of them. However, while they augment our knowledge, they are not critical to the overall thesis presented in this paper.

The first of these minor issues, the *Geometric-Quatrefoil* type, is known from a unique coin of Alfred (no. 1). The moneyer, Luda, had struck *Lunettes* coins for Burgred, so this coin is likely to have been issued at London. The moneyer is not known subsequently. As mentioned above, its weight (1.78g) is much heavier than any other penny struck during the reign and it is appears to represent a failed attempt to introduce the Carolingian weight standard. Arguably this belongs at the beginning of phase II and was followed by the *Portrait-Quatrefoil* and *Two Emperors* types, which both have similar obverse designs, i.e. a diademed bust of the king right, within a beaded inner circle.

The *Portrait-Quatrefoil* type (sometimes called the 'Archbishop Æthered' type) is known from three specimens, two of Archbishop Æthelred (nos 2–3) and one fragmentary piece of Alfred (no. 4). The moneyer of the Alfred piece, who has a name ending . . . ED, may be the same as that of the archiepiscopal coins, i.e. Ethelred, and it would thus be from Canterbury. However, the style of the bust is somewhat different and the inscription begins by the king's shoulder rather than above the head, so that it could be the product of another mint.

The *Two Emperors* type, with an obverse and reverse copied from a fourth-century Roman gold solidus (Pl. 11, J), is known in two specimens, one of Alfred (no. 5) and the other of Ceolwulf II (no. 6). The coins are in very different styles, that of Alfred being more naturalistic, carefully copying the draped bust of the Roman prototype, while Ceolwulf's dies are more schematized with a face

23 A moneyer Beagstan worked for Burgred, but only in the early and middle phases of the *Lunettes* issue, and this must be a different individual from Alfred's and Edward the Elder's moneyer. He is not counted in the six moneyers referred to above. The *Two-Line* coin of earlier style is *BMC* 202.

influenced by one of the Mercian *Lunettes* styles and the drapery perhaps by the *Cross-and-Lozenge* coinage. The coin of Alfred accords him the exceptional title REX ANGLO*rum*, to which we will return below. Both of the moneyers, Cenred for Alfred and Ealdwulf for Ceolwulf, had previously struck coins for Burgred suggesting that the mint(s) of both pieces lay in Mercia. For Alfred this is likely to have been London, but for Ceolwulf II it could have been elsewhere.[24] A fragmentary and corroded coin of Alfred from the Southampton excavations (no. 7) may be a mule or transitional issue struck from an obverse similar to the *Two Emperors* and *Portrait-Quatrefoil* types and a reverse of the *Cross-and-Lozenge* type. The *Two Emperors* reverse design also appears on a Danelaw coin of a King Halfdan (AIFDEN RX),[25] combined with the monogram reverse of the *London Monogram* type. For long this coin beguiled numismatists, who attributed it to Halfdan, the first Viking king of York (875–877), during his supposed occupation of London in 872–875, thereby introducing considerable confusion into the chronology of Alfred's issues.[26] Its status as a later imitative piece was recognised only in the 1950s.[27]

The reverse design of the *Two Emperors* type has often been seen as carrying some political significance, indicating an alliance between Alfred and Ceolwulf, Alfred and Halfdan, or a tripartite treaty, or even as marking the coronation of Alfred and Queen Ealhswith.[28] As Brooke pointed out,[29] this implies in Alfred a quite modern understanding of Roman coin types and a use of coin designs for propaganda purposes that is almost unprecedented in the Anglo-Saxon coinages. It is perhaps insufficiently appreciated by historians that the *Two Emperors* type is one of the most common designs on Roman solidi found in Britain, and that it had been copied previously on gold shillings of the mid-seventh century to which no such sophisticated interpretations have been applied. It is possible, then, that the type was used without any particular motive being attached to it. At this period there appears to have been a new interest in Roman coin designs, for no less than three new issues – the *Two Emperors* type (obverse and reverse), the *Cross-and-Lozenge* type (obverse), and the *London Monogram* type (three different obverses, two with the bust draped, the third cuirassed) – are copied carefully and directly from fourth- or fifth-century prototypes, rather than drawing on the common stock of contemporary coin types. One man must have been responsible

24 A west Midlands attribution is perhaps suggested by its style, which shares a number of features with the *Cross-and-Lozenge* coin by Cuthulf (no. 60), particularly the shape of the nose, the position of the eye, and the spelling of the king's name, CEOLVVLF, not CIOLVVLF as on 'London' style coins. However, in favour of a London attribution is the fact that a moneyer of the same name, Ealdwulf, struck the *Cross-and-Lozenge* lead weight found in London (no. 32) and *Two-Line* coins of Alfred in the 'London' style.

25 Brooke, 'Anglo-Saxon acquisitions – III', no. 300; Webster and Backhouse, *The Making of England*, no. 278.

26 E.g. Keary and Grueber, *A Catalogue*, II, p. xxxiv; Brooke, *English Coins*, pp. 33–4.

27 Grierson, 'Halfpennies and third-pennies', p. 489; Dolley and Blunt, 'The chronology', pp. 80, 81. On the dating proposed here, the Halfdan coin would be an issue of the 880s. If the obverse inscription refers to Halfdan I it must be copied from an earlier lost issue of his; alternatively one must postulate the existence of another Halfdan of whom no documentary record survives; Grierson and Blackburn, *Medieval European Coinage*, p. 319.

28 See the discussion in Nelson, 'A king across the sea', p. 60.

29 Brooke, *English Coins*, p. 45.

for choosing these new designs, and it may indeed have been he who provided the comment recorded in the *Anglo-Saxon Chronicle s.a.* 418 that 'In this year the Romans collected all their treasures which were in Britain and hid some in the ground, so that no one could find them afterwards, and took some with them into Gaul.'[30] The innovation in coin design is not limited to the choice of classical models. The *Geometric-Quatrefoil* type (no. 1) has an obverse inspired by the *Open Cross* type of Alfred's father, Æthelwulf (Pl. 10, D), and a reverse adapted from a coin of Offa (Pl. 10, A), while the *Cross-and-Lozenge* reverse borrows from another design of Offa (Pl. 10, B–C). Whoever was responsible for defining the coin types was a person with a lively interest.

The last of the minor issues attributed to phase II is but a small fragment, probably of Ceolwulf II (no. 8). It shows a right-facing(?) bust in a beaded border as on the *Two Emperors* and *Portrait-Quatrefoil* types, and on the reverse an outer inscription with . . . ANR . . ., probably a moneyer's name (Eanred?), and an inner inscription . . . CO . . ., which Pagan has suggested is from the mint-name *Lincolla* (Lincoln).[31] The attribution is speculative, for we do not know that Ceolwulf's authority was ever recognised in eastern Mercia, but alternative interpretations such as an earlier coin of Archbishop Ceolnoth (833–870) are still less convincing.

Dolley and Blunt placed these minor types after the *Cross-and-Lozenge* issue, assigning them to the early or mid-880s.[32] However, Lyon subsequently argued for an arrangement in which the minor types precede the *Cross-and-Lozenge* issue, and this has been adopted by subsequent authors.[33] There are several arguments in favour of this arrangement. All the known moneyers of the minor issues are recorded in the *Lunettes* coinage, whereas seven of the twenty-three *Cross-and-Lozenge* moneyers are new. Typologically the minor issues sit better at the beginning of the phase since they have affinities with the *Lunettes* type; in particular the three portrait types all have an inner circle as on the *Lunettes* coins while this is omitted from Alfred's *Cross-and-Lozenge* and later portrait issues. The lower incidence of the minor types within the Cuerdale hoard (3:24, minor: *Cross-and-Lozenge*) than among single finds (5:14) also points to an early date within phase II.

In the *Cross-and-Lozenge* issue (sometimes confusingly called the 'Ceolwulf' type) there are fifty-three extant coins struck by twenty-three moneyers. Of these, thirty-eight coins are of Alfred, eleven of Ceolwulf, and four of Archbishop Æthelred. Ten of the moneyers are known from only a single specimen each, and it is evident that our knowledge of this coinage is very incomplete. None the less it is also clear that it was struck on a larger scale than the minor issues of this phase and it appears to have been the principal type that demonitised the *Lunettes* coinage. Both Lyon and Archibald have commented on the diversity of styles among the coins and isolated two in particular which they attribute to Canterbury

30 Whitelock, *English Historical Documents*, p. 152.

31 Pagan, 'An unpublished fragment'.

32 Dolley and Blunt, 'The chronology', p. 81.

33 Lyon, 'Historical problems (2)', p. 236; Pagan, 'An unpublished fragment'; Grierson and Blackburn, *Medieval European Coinage* 1, p. 313; Archibald, in Webster and Backhouse, *The Making of England*, p. 284.

and another mint.[34] However, the extent of these groups and of the lesser styles has previously not been defined.

In the corpus below, the *Cross-and-Lozenge* coins are arranged in stylistic groups, and the criteria for distinguishing them are set out at the head of each section. There are three major groups and several minor ones. One large group comprises eleven coins (nos 9–19) by six moneyers and is clearly from Canterbury since it includes coins of the archbishop as well as Alfred. Another group with eleven coins (nos 42–52) by six moneyers appears to be based on Winchester, for two of the moneyers, Dunna and Wulfred, continued into the *Two-Line* issue

Table 3. Moneyers using London-style dies, *ca* 875–899

			Cross-and-Lozenge		*London*	*Two-Line*		
	Lunettes	Minor Types	Alfred	Ceolwulf	*Monogram*	Early	Late	Edward the Elder
Cenred	x(B)	x	—	—	—	—	—	—
Luda	x(B)	x	—	—	—	—	—	—
Ciolwulf	x(A)[2]	—	x	—	—	—	—	—
Dealing	x(B)	—	—	x	—	x	—	—
Dudecil	x(B)	—	—	x	—	—	—	—
Ealdwulf	x(B)	x?	x?	—	—	x	—	—
Hereferth	x(B)	—	x	—	—	x	—	—
Liafwald	x(B)	—	x	x	—	—	—	—
Beagstan[3]	x(B)	—	—	—	—	x	x	x
Bernred	x(A)[2]	—	—	—	—	x?	—	x?
Dealla	x(B)	—	—	—	—	x	—	—
Goda	—	—	—	—	—	x	—	—
Ælfstan	—	—	—	—	x?	—	—	—
Heawulf	x(B)	—	—	—	x?	x	—	—
Herewulf	x(A)	—	—	—	x?	x	—	—
Ludig	x(B)	—	—	—	—	x	x	—
Tidweald	—	—	—	—	—	x	—	—
Tilewine	x(A)[2]	—	—	—	x	x	—	—

Notes

1 In the *Lunettes* column, A = Alfred and B = Burgred.

2 The *Lunettes* coins of Ciolwulf, Bernred, and Tilewine, although in the name of Alfred, are in a Mercian or other anomalous style.

3 Burgred's moneyer Beagstan is unlikely to be the same individual as that who worked for Alfred and Edward the Elder (see n. 23).

34 Lyon suggested that the other mint was at either London or Rochester (Lyon, 'Historical problems (2)', pp. 236–7; Lyon, 'Some problems', pp. 180–1), while Archibald said that it could be at London or Rochester, or the style could represent a second group from Canterbury (Archibald, 'An Alfred penny'). Pagan had also proposed a London attribution for some coins; Pagan, 'Coinage in the age of Burgred', pp. 26–7.

striking with Winchester-style dies. However, the dies may have been supplied from there to neighbouring mints, including one in southern Mercia, as the group includes one coin of Ceolwulf II (no. 52). Oxford is a candidate for this since mint-signed coins were struck there early in phase III.

The third and largest group, comprising twenty-one coins and a lead weight (nos 20–41) by six moneyers, is evidently Mercian since it includes coins of both Alfred and Ceolwulf. Five of these six moneyers had struck coins for Burgred in a regular style attributed to London (Table 3), and a sixth, Ciolwulf, had struck *Lunettes* coins in the name of Alfred, but in an anomalous style, not that of the regular Canterbury die-cutter.[35] Looking on from the *Cross-and-Lozenge* type, three of these six moneyers are named in the *Two-Line* coinage and their coins belong to the major stylistic group that is attributed to London. This *Two-Line* group includes coins of Tilewine, the principal moneyer of the *London Monogram* issue, as well as Heawulf and Herewulf named on cruder-style *London Monogram* coins. It also includes several other moneyers who can be traced back to Burgred's London coinage, although no *Cross-and-Lozenge* coins from them are yet known. The lead weight found in St Paul's Churchyard bearing the impression of *Cross-and-Lozenge* dies, so far as one can judge in the 'London' style (no. 32), also supports the London attribution.

The body of evidence therefore points firmly to London as the source of these dies, and while, as in the case of Canterbury and Winchester, it is possible that some of them were made for mints elsewhere, we may assume that the majority of moneyers were working in London itself. Although Tilewine is the only moneyer named on the official *London Monogram* coins and this has been taken as indicating that he was the only moneyer operating at the beginning of the *Two-Line* type,[36] the London mint does not seem to have been reduced to this level. At least six of the earliest *Two-Line* moneyers can be traced back into Burgred's late coinage and so may well have been active during phase II although their coins do not survive. If one adds to this the three other moneyers recorded in the *Cross-and-Lozenge* issue of London-style and two in the *Geometric-Quatrefoil* and *Two Emperors* types, the complement of moneyers at London in the later 870s may have been ten or more, which compares well with the eleven or twelve moneyers recorded for the *Two-line* issue. Later, as we have seen, the London mint did contract dramatically, falling to just one by the end of the reign, and it was some years before it grew in importance again.[37]

Alfred and Ceolwulf

Alfred and Ceolwulf both struck the *Two Emperors* and the *Cross-and-Lozenge* types and, as has been shown above, both issued coins from the London mint. From this it has often been assumed that the kings had formally agreed on a

35 A moneyer Ciolwulf also struck *Two-Line* coins for Guthrum (880–890) at a mint in the Danelaw (*SCBI* East Anglian Museums 2). If this were the same man as Alfred's moneyer, he may have been operating from a mint in eastern Mercia or have moved from London.

36 Lyon, 'Historical problems (2)', p. 237. Pagan, 'Coinage in the age of Burgred', p. 27, had previously argued for a larger complement of moneyers.

37 Blunt, Stewart, and Lyon, *Coinage in Tenth-Century England*, pp. 30–2.

monetary alliance,[38] just as before them Æthelred I and Burgred appear to have done, but to what extent can we define the relationship between them? The *Anglo-Saxon Chronicle* in the annal for 874 records how the Viking army, after defeating Burgred and driving him into exile, 'gave the kingdom of the Mercians to be held by Ceolwulf, a foolish king's thegn; and he swore oaths to them and gave hostages, that it should be ready for them on whatever day they wished to have it, and he would be ready, himself and all who would follow him, at the enemy's service'. The only other time Ceolwulf is mentioned in the *Chronicle* is three years later when in 877, after the Vikings had stormed Exeter and been bought off by Alfred, 'then in the harvest season the army went away into Mercia and shared out some of it, and gave some to Ceolwulf'. Despite the chronicler's unkind remarks and his portrayal of Ceolwulf as a dependent of the Vikings, he was evidently accepted by the Mercians as their king since he granted charters and struck coins in his own name, and a Mercian regnal list from Worcester accords him a reign of five years after Burgred taking him to *ca* 879.[39] Beyond that we know virtually nothing of Ceolwulf – how readily he was accepted by the Mercians, what dealings he had with Alfred and Ealdorman Æthelred, or how his reign came to an end. But a detailed study of the coins can shed a little more light on events.

Only thirteen coins of Ceolwulf are known, all from the second phase of the coinage. Two belong to the minor types discussed above, and eleven are of the substantive *Cross-and-Lozenge* issue. Nine of these *Cross-and-Lozenge* coins are in the style attributed to London, one is from dies cut at Winchester, and the last could perhaps be from a mint in the west Midlands. The London coinage is thus the most substantial and informative, yet despite being a Mercian town, sixty per cent of its surviving *Cross-and-Lozenge* coins are in the name of Alfred and only forty per cent in that of Ceolwulf. Thirteen of the London coins are by a single moneyer, Liafwald, who worked for both rulers. At first sight this appears to be an alliance issue *par excellence*. But when one looks in detail at the coins, although they are sufficiently similar in their lettering, style of bust, and form of legends for us to be confident that they are the work of a single die-cutter, one notices that there are differences between the coins of Ceolwulf and those of Alfred which suggest that they were produced successively, not concurrently. In the corpus below the coins are arranged in their stylistic groups and within them alphabetically by ruler and moneyer but on the plates they are arranged in a way that demonstrates the stylistic progression. Of the twenty-one 'London' coins of Alfred and Ceolwulf (Pls 8 and 9), all but three are in the same style, and these three (nos 25 and 40–1), although perhaps the work of another die-cutter, are struck by moneyers of the London group.

On the best of Alfred's coins the form of the drapery is a tolerably good copy of the Roman prototype (Pl. 11, K). Nos 26–8 show the cloak falling from the annular brooch on the right shoulder and forming V-shaped folds on the breast. They also reproduce the double bands above the cuirassed arms. Alfred's other

38 Dolley, 'An unpublished hoard-provenance', pp. 89–90; Dolley, 'Ælfred the Great's abandonment', pp. 154–5.

39 MS Cotton Tiberius A.xiii, fo. 114v; a manuscript of *ca* 1000. Dumville, 'The Treaty', p. 7, n. 37, calculates Ceolwulf's reign as ending sometime between the latter half of 878 and late 879.

coins retain many of these elements, but they become progressively more stylised, although all but one (no. 21) retain the annular brooch. In contrast, on Ceolwulf's coins (nos 33–41) seven of the nine specimens lack the brooch, and on most the double arm bands have become single ones and the vertical lines representing the armour have been extended on to the shoulder. The two coins of Ceolwulf (die-duplicates) with an annulet brooch (nos 40–1) are anomalous in other respects,[40] and if not the work of another die-cutter must have been experimental. There is also a difference in the reverses of Ceolwulf's coins, for while they are all of a simple design without ornamentation in the lozenge or around the cross, most of Alfred's are decorated with a variety of symbols and only three (nos 22–3 and 29) have the plain form as on Ceolwulf's coins. Among Ceolwulf's reverses a development can also be discerned; only no. 36 has the central cross aligned at an angle and has the moneyer's name spelled LIAFVVALD, as on Alfred's coins, while Ceolwulf's other coins (nos 33–5 and 37–41) have the cross aligned with the vertical and where present the name is spelled LIOFVVALD.

Thus although there are enough common stylistic elements between Alfred's group and Ceolwulf's to show that they are the work of the same die-cutter, and the common moneyer, Liafwald, shows them to have been struck at the same mint, the differences between them and the stylistic progressions within each demonstrate that they must be successive, not concurrent coinages. Moreover, the degeneration in the obverse design away from the Roman prototype points surprisingly but firmly at Ceolwulf's coins coming *after* those of Alfred. To argue for the reverse order one would have to say that after a rather degenerate issue by Ceolwulf, Alfred took control of the mint and ordered the die-cutter to go back to the prototype, but that by the end of Alfred's coinage the die-cutter had once again reverted slowly to the form in which he had been engraving dies for Ceolwulf. Such a progression is highly improbable. Moreover, there is support for the sequence Alfred–Ceolwulf in the coins of the only other moneyer known to have worked for both rulers. This is Dunna, who used 'Winchester' style dies. Of his three extant coins, no. 42 (in the name of Alfred) is remarkably close in design to the likely prototype of Honorius (Pl. 11, K), while no. 43 (for Alfred) is more stylized, and no. 52 (for Ceolwulf) belongs even later in the series. How Dunna came to strike coins for Ceolwulf is uncertain. He may have been working at a south Mercian mint such as Oxford and drawing his dies from Winchester, or less probably he may have been a regular Winchester moneyer commissioned to strike coins for the Mercian king.[41] Whatever the explanation, Dunna's coins for Ceolwulf are amongst his latest products in this issue.

Ten of Ceolwulf's thirteen coins, therefore, belong relatively late in phase II, while the remaining three coins cannot be dated closely within the reign. The last of Ceolwulf's *Cross-and-Lozenge* coins, by the moneyer Cuthwulf, is in a distinctive style that is strongly influenced by one of the two main styles of Burgred's *Lunettes* coinage (Pl. 11, F),[42] and there are some grounds for attributing

40 Viz. the treatment of the drapery and the form of the central lozenge on the reverse, which is pelleted rather than a simple line as on all the other coins of this 'London' style.

41 The inscription on this die is CEOLVVLF M, but the lack of the royal style may simply be because the longer name left insufficient space and the ethnic *Merciorum* was considered more important.

42 Pagan, 'Coinage in the age of Burgred', style 'V'. Note particularly the almost vertical diadem,

the coin to a mint in the west Midlands.[43] For Ceolwulf's *Two Emperors* coin we cannot say whether it is contemporary with Alfred's or a later use of the type. Nor can we identify the mint with confidence.[44] Similarly, the fragment of an *Inscription-in-Field* type (no. 8) discussed above cannot be firmly identified, but if it was struck at Lincoln, as Pagan suggests, it should date from before the partition of Mercia in August 877.

The realisation that Alfred's *Cross-and-Lozenge* coinage at London preceded that of Ceolwulf requires some radical rethinking about the course of events following Burgred's exile in 873/4. The people in London, and possibly elsewhere in southern Mercia, would seem to have turned initially to Alfred rather than the Viking or west Mercian nominee Ceolwulf. There are even hints of this towards the end of the *Lunettes* coinage, for quite apart from the purely imitative groups that copy Æthelred I's and Alfred's coins in anomalous styles, there are better pieces struck by London moneyers in Alfred's name that seem to be official issues of the London mint (Pl. 11, I).[45] Further work on this difficult phase of coinage is required, but it seems likely that moneyers in London were issuing coins in Alfred's name towards the end of Burgred's reign and possibly for a period after his departure.[46]

Ceolwulf had been accepted as king in western Mercia by 875 when he granted two charters relating to estates in Worcestershire and Gloucestershire.[47] These were witnessed by the bishops of Lichfield, Worcester, and Hereford, but not the bishops of Leicester and Lindsey as Burgred's charters had been – the omission of the bishop of London from the witness lists of Ceolwulf's charters need not be significant, for he rarely witnessed Burgred's charters either. For the date at which Ceolwulf was recognised in London we are dependent on the dating of the *Cross-and-Lozenge* coinage. If we accept the evidence of the Mercian regnal list that Ceolwulf ruled – in western Mercia – for five years, and we have no grounds to doubt it, this implies that the *Cross-and-Lozenge* issue had ended by *ca* 879/80 since at London the latest coins are those in the name of Ceolwulf. The phase II coinage need not have been of long duration, but one should allow a few years for the implementation of this major recoinage with several early experimental types and followed by the substantive *Cross-and-Lozenge* issue first in Alfred's name, then in Ceolwulf's. It is sometimes said that the new coinage must belong after the battle of Edington in May 878 on the grounds that before this Alfred would not have been in a strong enough position politically or economically to institute a recoinage. But this is looking at the situation with hindsight, for there were periods between 875 and 877 when the Danes had been

the curved nose ending in a wedge, the curled strands of hair terminating in pellets, and the general triangular shape of the drapery.

43 A moneyer Cuthulf struck *Lunettes* coins in the names of both Burgred and Alfred in this Mercian style (Pagan and Stewart, 'A new Mercian moneyer'), and a Cuthulf struck Alfred's *Two-Line* type in a style that is associated with the west Midlands. If the moneyer was one and the same, the west Midland mint could already have been operating under Ceolwulf II and perhaps under Burgred.

44 See n. 24 above.

45 Pagan, 'Coinage in the age of Burgred', pp. 14, 17, and works cited in n. 17 above.

46 Pagan, in Biddle *et al.*, 'Coins of the Anglo-Saxon period from Repton', pp. 118–19.

47 Sawyer, *Anglo-Saxon Charters*, nos 215 and 216.

bought off and Alfred might reasonably have thought that his worst troubles were behind him. Weighing these factors, it probable that the recoinage was initiated by Alfred as early as 875 or 876, with Ceolwulf's London coinage starting *ca* 877/8. These dates are based essentially on the numismatic evidence, accepting Ceolwulf's reign as 873x874–878x880. If he in fact ruled longer, the chronology could be extended, but not beyond 883 when Ealdorman Æthelred was issuing charters.

On any reading of the evidence, we have to accommodate an initial period after Burgred's departure in which Alfred was recognised as the legitimate ruler in London and some other parts of southern Mercia, followed by an extension of Ceolwulf's authority to these areas in the later 870s. Since we have no evidence, beyond that of the coinage, for relations between Alfred and Ceolwulf, we can only guess at how this change might have come about. It is tempting to associate it in some way with the Mercian-Viking partition of Mercia in August 877 or with the West Saxon-Viking peace following the battle of Edington in May 878. But Alfred could have concluded a West Saxon-Mercian alliance promising mutual support at almost any time during Ceolwulf's reign, one term of which could have been that Alfred would recognise Ceolwulf's claim over southern Mercia.

This analysis of the political situation also makes more sense of the unusual title *rex Anglo[rum]* on Alfred's *Two Emperors* coin (no. 4), which has puzzled commentators for so long. This coin appears to have been produced at London in the mid-870s, that is at a time when people there regarded Alfred as their ruler in preference to Ceolwulf. It may be compared with the equally unusual *rex SM* which appears on one of Alfred's finest and earliest London *Cross-and-Lozenge* coins (no. 27), thus also of the mid-870s, and which was plausibly expanded by Dolley and Blunt as *rex Saxonum et Merciorum*. These need not necessarily be regarded as officially sanctioned titles evincing aspirations of Alfred to rule the whole of Mercia, for they may only reflect the political situation as viewed locally by one die-cutter in London. Similar claims are not made in charters or on any of the surviving coins struck at Canterbury and Winchester.

Date of the London Monogram and Two-Line types

Where does this leave the *London Monogram* coinage, which traditionally has been regarded as a special celebratorary issue to mark Alfred's rebuilding of the city after its capture from the Vikings in 886?[48]

It has been argued here that the *Cross-and-Lozenge* and minor associated issues ran from *ca* 875/6 until *ca* 879/80, and that during that period London was in Anglo-Saxon rather than Viking hands. On the demise of Ceolwulf, the Mercian mints reverted to Alfred – there are no coins known of Ealdorman Æthelred and the mint-signed coins of Gloucester and Oxford, from just this period, are in Alfred's name.[49] Alfred took this opportunity to implement his second monetary

48 Keary and Grueber, *A Catalogue*, II, p. xxxvii; Brooke, *English Coins*, p. 47; Dolley and Blunt, 'The chronology', p. 83.

49 Grierson and Blackburn, *Medieval European Coinage* I, p. 314. The presence of a specimen of

reform, replacing the *Cross-and-Lozenge* issue with the *Two-Line* type or in London with the *London Monogram* type and introducing the higher *ca* 1.6g weight standard and the new halfpenny denomination. There is no direct evidence to indicate how soon after Ceolwulf's demise he introduced the reformed coinage, but it is unlikely to have been long. There is reasonable continuity of moneyers at the three major mints from the two earlier phases into this third phase, and it is difficult to believe that Alfred would have wished to leave the London mint inactive for a number of years. As we have seen, the *London Monogram* coinage belongs to the beginning of the third phase, and on numismatic grounds one would wish to date it *ca* 880, rather than 886.[50]

There is one argument against an early introduction of the *Two-Line* type. Only seven coins of Archbishop Æthelred (870–888) are known, six of phase II and one of phase III, a *Two-Line* coin.[51] Yet *Two-Line* coins of his successor, Archbishop Plegmund (890–923), are plentiful. If there had been continuous and fairly even minting for the archbishops, the proportions in which Archbishop Æthelred's coins survive would suggest that the *Two-Line* type was introduced near to the end of his period of office. But this assumption cannot be made. Seven coins from an eighteen-year period of office itself suggests that production was very limited, and indeed there are no coins at all of the *Lunettes* issue, corresponding to the first five years or so of his office, when the royal moneyers at Canterbury were very active. Relatively little is known about Archbishop Æthelred, and his relations with the king or the Church,[52] but it would appear that his coinage was essentially limited to the middle years of his office. On balance, the archiepiscopal coinage cannot be relied upon as dating evidence, and the introduction of the *London Monogram* and *Two-Line* issues is best placed *ca* 880. The *London Monogram* type, then, does not celebrate the 'occupation' of London and the submission of all the English people to Alfred, but Alfred's assumption – or rather resumption – of control over the city from the Mercians after Ceolwulf's demise. This is one of six mint-signed issues of Alfred's reign, and it may be

the *Oxford (Ohsnaforda)* type in the London (Thames Street) hoard of *ca* 1880 shows that it was contemporary with the *London Monogram* issue (see pp. 110–11 above).

50 Archibald has also proposed a date earlier than 886, but suggests the year 878. She postulates that Alfred took over London as part of the deal with Guthrum after the battle of Edington, and that the *London Monogram* issue was struck to celebrate this. It is not clear what the nature of the agreement she envisages is. On the one hand she suggests that Alfred took over the city, not from the Danes, but from the Mercians (in which case what was Guthrum's role?), yet in the same piece she also refers to 'Alfred's taking over the Mercian city recently vacated by the Danes' (Archibald in Webster and Backhouse, *The Making of England*, pp. 286–7, nos 265 and 269; this dating is also cited, but not argued, in Archibald, 'Pecking and bending', p. 15). While a date as early as 878 might just be possible, the numismatic evidence does not point to this specifically, and there is a danger that, in postulating a West Saxon take-over of London in 878, and linking this coin issue with it, the one hypothesis will be used to justify the other. I would prefer the more neutral dating of *ca* 880, suggested by the numismatic evidence, allowing a range of historical explanations to be considered. Anyway, it is more likely that Alfred introduced the *Two-Line* and *London Monogram* types after Ceolwulf's demise, rather than following some special treaty relating to London, for had Ceolwulf still been ruling in western Mercia we might expect him to have issued *Two-Line* or *Monogram* coins there in his own name.

51 Blunt, 'The coinage of Æthelred'; and Blackburn and Keynes, 'A corpus', below.

52 Brooks, *The Early History*, pp. 149–52.

significant that the only other ones dated early in phase III – i.e. from the early 880s – are those of Gloucester and Oxford, where Alfred was similarly taking control of Mercian mints. Their purpose appears to have been to give publicity to Alfred's assumption of authority over Ceolwulf's former kingdom.

Whereas the coinage is surprisingly informative about events in London during the 870s, it is not at all helpful for the 880s. So the numismatist is unable to say whether there was an interruption in minting in 883, when the English were encamped against the Viking army at London, or whether Alfred's 'occupation' or 'restoration' of London in 886 affected coin production in any way. The *London Monogram* coinage would have lasted a relatively short time – perhaps a couple of years – and its replacement by the standard *Two-Line* type, probably already in use elsewhere, need not have had any political significance. There are no overt signs of an interruption in minting during the phase III issues, but one would not necessarily expect to discern any. However, it might be relevant that the only hoards found in or near London during the last quarter of the ninth century were deposited in the early 880s during the currency of the *London Monogram* issue,[53] and they could therefore have been associated with the siege referred to in the *Anglo-Saxon Chronicle*'s annal for 883.

Conclusions

To sum up, the coinage was one of the first arms of government to attract the attention of Alfred. Within the first ten years of his reign he had undertaken two major recoinages and monetary reforms and had started expanding the network of mints. Subsequent changes during the last twenty years or so the reign were of only minor importance. Unfortunately, it is from the critical period of these reforms that the surviving material is thinnest, and yet the coinage has most to offer the political historian.

A number of points have emerged in this paper from an analysis of the numismatic evidence which contradict the traditional interpretation of historical events in the 870s and 880s. Coins were struck in the names of Alfred and Ceolwulf II at London during the period *ca* 875–880. Within this period the coins of Alfred precede those of Ceolwulf, both at London and at one other mint, presumably in southern Mercia, which drew its dies from the Winchester die-cutter. At these two mints, after Burgred's exile in 874, Alfred's authority was recognised by the moneyers, and on some coins he was accorded the titles *rex Anglo[rum]* or *rex SM* (for *Saxonum et Merciorum*?). In the later 870s, the situation changed and the Mercian king was recognised as ruler of London. The *London Monogram* type, formerly associated with the events of 886, now appears to have been struck *ca* 880, shortly after Ceolwulf II's demise. The coinage thus shows that the Vikings were not in control of London during the later 870s and early 880s, as had hitherto been thought. This will have a significant influence on our understanding of Alfred's relations with Ceolwulf II and Guthrum. It would also allow the

53 Near Erith, Kent, *ca* 1840; London (Bucklersbury) 1872 (Blackburn and Pagan, 'A revised check-list', nos 81–2); and an unpublished hoard from London (Thames Street) *ca* 1880 (see n. 19 above). The next recorded hoard from London was deposited *ca* 945.

treaty between Alfred and Guthrum to be dated any time after 880, if one interprets its description of the Danelaw boundary in the conventional way, i.e. northwards up the river Lee, leaving London on the English-controlled side, and opens the way for a quite different understanding of the annals of the *Anglo-Saxon Chronicle* for 883 and 886.[54]

54 Discussed in Keynes, 'Alfred and the Mercians', above.

V

A CORPUS OF THE *CROSS-AND-LOZENGE* AND RELATED COINAGES OF ALFRED, CEOLWULF II AND ARCHBISHOP ÆTHELRED

Mark Blackburn and Simon Keynes

The sixty-one coins listed here are all the specimens known to have survived from the middle phase of Alfred's coinage. This distinct phase falls between two coinage reforms: that which removed the base *Lunettes* coins and restored the silver standard to over 90%, and that which raised the weight of the penny from *ca* 1.35g to *ca* 1.6g on the introduction of the *London Monogram* and *Two-Line* issues. These reforms have previously been dated to the later 870s and 886/7 respectively, but recent research suggests that they occurred somewhat earlier, *ca* 875 and *ca* 880.[1] This phase of coinage is under-represented in the extant material, yet its historical importance is considerable. To further our own researches we found it necessary to establish a definitive list of the coins of this period and organise them into stylistic groups; that work is the basis of this corpus.

In the catalogue below the coins are arranged by type, by issuing authority (king or archbishop), and alphabetically by moneyer. The sequence of the minor types is somewhat uncertain, although they are thought to precede the *Cross-and-Lozenge* type, and some arguments are put forward for placing the *Geometric-Quatrefoil* type first and seeing the *Two Emperors* and *Portrait-Quatrefoil* types as parallel issues of London and Canterbury respectively. The *Cross-and-Lozenge* type is sub-divided into four stylistic groups that indicate the sources of the dies and help to suggest probable mint attributions, which is necessary as none of the coins bear mint-signatures. The number of coins of each type and issuer is summarised in Table 1, and the *Cross-and-Lozenge* coins are summarised by style in Table 2.

Acknowledgements. We are grateful to the following for kindly providing information and photographs: Marion Archibald, the late Christopher Blunt, Martin Biddle, Michel Dhénin, Patrick Finn, Derek Hurt, Michael Metcalf, May Sinclair, Allan Williams and Antony Wilson. Stewart Lyon, Hugh Pagan, and Lord Stewartby have read and provided helpful comments on the typescript. Warren Esty kindly advised us on the estimation of dies.

1 See Blackburn, 'The London mint', above.

TABLE 1. Number of surviving coins by issuer and type

	Alfred	Ceolwulf II	Abp Æthelred	Total
Geometric-Quatrefoil	1	—	—	1
Portrait-Quatrefoil	1	—	2	3
Two Emperors	1	1	—	2
TE or P-Q/Cross-and-Lozenge mule?	1	—	—	1
Inscription-in-Field	—	1?	—	1
Cross-and-Lozenge	38	11	4	53
	42	13	6	61

All the coins in the catalogue are silver pennies; the first struck halfpence come from the third phase of Alfred's coinage. We have illustrated the fifty-nine specimens of which photographs exist,[2] and these are arranged on Plates 7–10 in a slightly different sequence from that of the catalogue in order to show stylistic developments within each group. Some Roman coins are illustrated as possible models for the designs on Plate 11. Short notes on the various types and styles are given in the catalogue, but for further discussion of these and their significance readers should see our respective papers above. We have not attempted to describe in the catalogue the designs or variety of ornamental features found, for example, on the reverses of the *Cross-and-Lozenge* coins. They can be seen from the plates. The find provenance and the collections or dealers through which each coin has passed are given under 'Provenance'.[3]

TABLE 2. Number of *Cross-and-Lozenge* coins by style

	Alfred	Ceolwulf II	Abp Æthelred	Total
Canterbury style	7	—	4	11
London style	13	9	—	22
Winchester style	10	1	—	11
Other styles	7	1	—	8
Uncertain	1?	—	—	1
	38	11	4	53

2 Illustrations are not available for nos 48 and 61, nor for the obverse of no. 57.

3 Details of the sales will be found in Manville and Robertson, *British Numismatic Auction Catalogues*.

The Finds

A summary of the coin finds for this phase of the coinage is given in Table 3, and after the catalogue there is an index to the individual coins. The most important source is the 1840 Cuerdale hoard, deposited *ca* 905.[4] The twenty-eight specimens that it contained were the oldest insular group among the 7,500 or so coins in the hoard, and their comparatively small number is evidence of the effectiveness of the recoinage of *ca* 880. The single specimen in the Morley St Peter hoard was similarly a chance survivor in a later hoard (dep. *ca* 925). Only two hoards deposited during the currency of this coinage have been discovered, and both are apparently small purse losses. The 1904 Washington (Sussex) hoard contained only four coins, all of the *Cross-and-Lozenge* type. The second find is very recent and information about it is, as yet, scant. Three *Cross-and-Lozenge* coins, all of Ceolwulf II and including a pair of die-duplicates, were reported to the Buckinghamshire Sites and Monuments Record in September 1996 (we are grateful to Julia Wise and Marion Archibald for information). They are said to have been found with the aid of a metal detector scattered in a field at Pitstone in Buckinghamshire, and they are apparantly the only finds of this period from the site. They were sold at auction in March 1997.

Of the remaining twenty-five coins from this phase, six were known prior to 1840 and may well have been single-finds. Thirteen are later provenanced single-finds, which include as many as five from post-War archaeological excavations (nos 7, 11, 20, 53, 57). By contrast, comparatively few have occurred among the many metal-detector finds of the last decade or so (nos 3, 16–17, 55).

TABLE 3. Sources of the coins

	Early types	Cross-and-Lozenge			Total
		Alfred	Ceolwulf II	Abp Æthelred	
Pre-Cuerdale finds	2	3	1	—	6
Cuerdale hoard	3	21	4	—	28
Washington hoard	—	3	1	—	4
Morley St Peter hoard	—	—	1	—	1
Pitstone hoard	—	—	3	—	3
Other finds	3	8	—	2	13
Unprovenanced (post-Cuerdale) finds	—	3	1	2	6
	8	38	11	4	61

4 For references to this and other hoards cited, see Blackburn and Pagan, 'A check-list'.

Survival rate

The fact that no substantial hoard contemporary with this period has survived in itself suggests that the coinage is rather poorly represented in the extant material, and this is indeed born out by a study of the dies. Of the sixty-one coins in the catalogue, we have been able to check the dies of fifty-eight obverses and fifty-nine reverses. Among these there are five die-linked pairs: nos 2–3, 38–9 and 40–1 are die-duplicates, and nos 17–18 and 49–50 share the same obverses. Thus there are fifty-three obverse and fifty-six reverse dies represented in this corpus, with forty-eight obverse singletons and fifty-three reverse singletons. Using formulae recommended by Esty,[5] we estimate the original number of dies used for the coinage:

Number of obverse dies: 447
Number of reverse dies: 811

These figures look very satisfactory, and suggest a typical 1:2 ratio of obverse:reverse dies. However, these are only point estimates (best guesses from a range of possible values), and because the sample is so small in comparison to the number of dies originally used, the 95% confidence intervals (i.e. likely ranges) are very wide:

Confidence intervals (obverse): between 225 and 1,145 dies
Confidence intervals (reverse): between 460 and 2,674 dies

Little reliance can therefore be placed on the point estimates when judging the size of the coinage. Indeed, a calculation of the coverage of the surviving sample shows just how inadequate our knowledge of this coinage is:

Coverage (obverse dies): 0.17
Coverage (reverse dies): 0.10

This indicates that only 17% of the original coinage was struck from the obverse dies that we know today, or that when a new coin is found there is an 83% probability that it will be from a new obverse die; or a 90% probability of it being from a new reverse die.

Of the twenty-five moneyers known in this phase of the coinage, twelve are recorded from only a single specimen, suggesting that many more remain to be discovered. Statistical estimates of the original number of moneyers would be even more uncertain than those for the number of dies, since moneyers evidently operated on very differing scales, for example, the London moneyer Liafwald is known from no less than thirteen specimens and he must have been far more prolific than anyone else.

5 Esty, 'Estimation of the Size of a Coinage'. The formulae used here are his J1 (coverage), H5 (point estimate), and C2, as approximated and simplified for us by Esty (confidence intervals).

Metrology

Twenty-five *Cross-and-Lozenge* coins in this corpus that are whole and show no apparent corrosion have an average weight of 1.32g. This will be influenced to some extent by leaching from the metal during their time in the ground, and the distribution (Fig. 1) suggests that the original standard was *ca* 1.35g or a little higher.

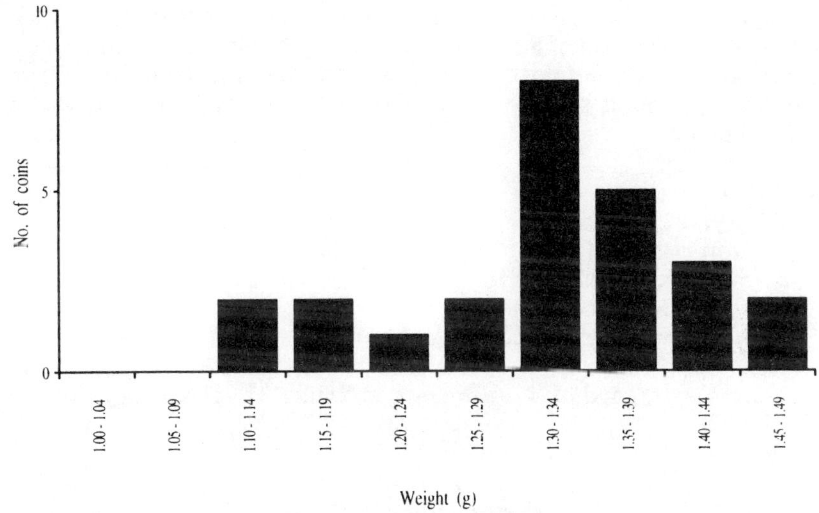

Fig. 1. Weight distribution of *Cross-and-Lozenge* coins

There are too few coins in the sample to justify a separate analysis of the weights by styles, but it is not unusual to find that slightly different standards were maintained at different mints. There is some sign of this in the two coins of Lulla of distinctive style (nos 53–4) which weigh 1.45g (although chipped) and 1.44g. With a larger sample one might be able to see more complex weight patterns within this phase of the coinage. Among the minor types, apart from *Geometric-Quatrefoil* (no. 1) weighing 1.78g, the reliable weights (1.30, 1.30, 1.42g) fall within the same distribution as those of the *Cross-and-Lozenge* issue and we may presume that a similar standard was intended.

***Geometric-Quatrefoil* type**

This superb piece is the only non-portrait coin of Alfred from this phase of the coinage. Its obverse design with a cruciform inscription is inspired by the reverse of Æthelwulf's last issue, *Open Cross* (Pl. 10, D). The central cross motif on the reverse seems to be based on one of Offa's coin designs (Pl. 10, A),[6] while the

6 Blunt, 'The Coinage of Offa', nos 50–1, 59–60, 73 (obverses).

quatrefoil frame is also found on the *Portrait-Quatrefoil* type (nos 2–4). Luda was a moneyer for Burgred, and this may, therefore, have been a London issue broadly parallel with the *Portrait-Quatrefoil* type at Canterbury. However, the heavy weight shows that it was struck to quite a different weight standard from that prevailing in either Alfred's early and middle phase (*ca* 1.35g) or his later phase of coinage (*ca* 1.6g), and it seems to have been intended to align with the Carolingian standard of *ca* 1.75g. The use of a non-portrait design could also be the result of Carolingian influence. This type appears, therefore, to be part of an intended reform of the coinage that either failed or was countermanded. We have thus placed it at the head of the minor types. It is possible that a comparable type was also struck at Canterbury on a heavy weight standard, and that the *Portrait-Quatrefoil* type was its successor there, when the *Two Emperors* type was being issued at London.

King Alfred

1. *Moneyer*: Luda
   Obverse: +AE/LFR/ÆD / REX
   Reverse: +/LV/DA/MO/N
   Weight: 1.78g (27.47gr). *Die-axis*: 180°.
   Provenance: British Museum (Assheton loan); ex Cuerdale hoard (1840).
   Reference: Hawkins, 'An account', p. 14, no. 27*; Haigh, 'Coins of Ælfred', p. 23 and pl. 1, 9; Dolley and Blunt, 'The chronology', p. 84 and pl. 9, 7.

***Portrait-Quatrefoil* type**

The obverse designs of this and the *Two Emperors* type are essentially the same, a diademed bust of the king right within an inner circle. The four known dies – two of each type – are executed in different styles. The *Two Emperors* coin of Alfred (no. 5) is a close copy of a fourth-century Roman coin. The bust on Archbishop Æthelred's *Portrait-Quatrefoil* type (no. 2), although in many respects a typical Anglo-Saxon coin portrait of the period, also has some classical features, notably the fine hair and long diadem, which may have come from the same Roman model or have been directly inspired by a coin of the Two *Emperors* type. In the *Cross-and-Lozenge* issue, a similar Roman model seems to have been distributed to the various mints or die-cutters, but the accuracy with which it was followed varied greatly, the Canterbury die-cutter(s) being more influenced by typical ninth-century coin portraits. The same may have been true of the minor types.

The reverse design is novel, although borrows elements from other types; the arrangement of the letters NETA of *moneta* is paralleled in Æthelwulf's *Open Cross* type (Pl. 10, D), and the quatrefoil frame occurs in Alfred's *Geometric-Quatrefoil* type (no. 1), which itself took other features from the *Open Cross* design. A similar quatrefoil frame was used by the Canterbury (style B) die-cutter in the *Cross-and-Lozenge* type.

The coins of the archbishop (nos 2–3) would have been struck at Canterbury, and the Alfred piece (no. 4) may have been too – possibly by the same moneyer –

although its style seems somewhat different and the obverse legend begins by the shoulder, rather than above the head.

Archbishop Æthelred

2. *Moneyer*: Ethered (cf. nos 3, 4 and 12)

Obverse: +EÐERED ARCHIEPI- (starting above head); same die as next coin.

Reverse: EÐ ER ED MO with N E T A in the margin; same die as next coin.

Weight: 1.42g (21.9gr). *Die-axis*: 0°.

Provenance: British Museum (*BMC* 61); ex Hollis (1817) 70 (and therefore presumptively from the collection of Thomas Hollis who died in 1774); unknown (pre-Cuerdale) find.

Reference: Ruding, *Annals of Coinage*, pl. 30, 5; Haigh, 'On the coins', p. 105; Blunt, 'The coinage of Æthelred', no. 3; Dolley, *Anglo-Saxon Pennies*, pl. 11, 32.

Comment: A nineteenth-century copy of this coin, struck from false dies, was published by Lawrence, 'Forgery', p. 404, no. 31 and pl. 2, 31. A second specimen from the same dies passed as genuine through the collections of Murchison 216; Shepherd 54; Montagu 327; Jenks; and Ryan 604, only to be condemned by Blunt and Thompson, 'Forgery', p. 23 and pl. 1, 13. The dies are now with A. H. Baldwin & Sons Ltd.

3. *Moneyer*: Ethered

Obverse: [+EÐERED] ARC[HIEPI-]; same die as last coin.

Reverse: [EÐ E]R ED [MO] with [N E] T [A] in the margin; same die as last coin.

Weight: 0.35g (5.4gr); fragment. *Die-axis*: 270°.

Provenance: Fitzwilliam Museum (CM.389–1995); bt M. J. Bonser 1995; found at Santon Downham, Norfolk 1994, possibly from soil removed from the site of the Thetford bypass and spread on this field.

King Alfred

4. *Moneyer*: [. . .]ed (Ethelred?, cf. nos 2–3 and 12)

Obverse: [ ]ED REX (starting at shoulder)

Reverse: [ ]E·D M·[ ] with [ ] A in the margin.

Weight: 0.51g (7.9gr); fragment.

Provenance: British Museum (*BMC* 179); pre-1838 acquisition; unknown (pre-Cuerdale) find.

Reference: Haigh, 'On the coins', p. 105; Haigh, 'Coins of Ælfred, p. 22 and pl. 1, 7; Dolley and Blunt, 'The chronology', p. 82, and pl. 9, 6.

***Two Emperors* type**

The two known coins of this type are in quite different styles. That of Alfred (no. 5) is more refined and closer to the Roman prototype, a late fourth- or early fifth-century gold solidus of a type that is often found in Britain (Pl. 11, J). The coin of Alfred was probably struck at London before the *Cross-and-Lozenge* issue. The unusual royal style (king of the English) and the iconography of the *Two Emperors* design have been the subject of much comment.[7] The coin of Ceolwulf has a more stylised bust, influenced by typical ninth-century coin portraits, and some features it shares with the *Cross-and-Lozenge* coin of Cuthulf (no. 60). The spelling of the king's name is in the form *Ceolwulf*, as found on his *Cross-and-Lozenge* coins attributed to West Mercian mints (nos 52, 60), rather than *Ciolwulf* used on all his *Cross-and-Lozenge* coins of London style (nos 33–41) and on those of the London moneyer Ciolwulf (nos 20–1). If contemporary with Alfred's coin, which seems likely, it was probably struck at a mint in western Mercia, although a London attribution cannot be ruled out since there was a moneyer of the same name, Ealdwulf, operating there in the *Cross-and-Lozenge* (no. 32) and *Two-Line* types. A third coin with the *Two Emperors* reverse design carries the name of a King Halfdan (*BMA* 300), but it is a slightly later Viking derivative for it combines this with the reverse design of the *London Monogram* issue; it is not, therefore, contemporary with the middle phase of Alfred's coinage.

King Alfred

5. *Moneyer*: Cenred

Obverse: +AELFRED REX ANGLO[ ] (square O)

Reverse: CENRED MON· ·ETA

Weight: 1.30g (20.1gr). *Die-axis*: 0°.

Provenance: British Museum (BM 1896–4–4–63) (*BMA* 476); ex Montagu I 545 ('dug up in the country'); bt Spink; found at Croydon Palace, Surrey, *ca* 1880.

Reference: *BMC* II, p. 34 (illustrated); Dolley and Blunt, 'The chronology', pp. 81–2 and pl. 9, 5; Dolley, *Anglo-Saxon Pennies*, pl. 11, 33.

King Ceolwulf II

6. *Moneyer*: Ealdwulf (cf. no. 32)

Obverse: +CEOLVVLF REX

Reverse: EALDOVVLF MENTA (ME ligatured)

Weight: 1.30g (20.1gr). *Die-axis*: 270°.

Provenance: British Museum (Assheton loan); ex Cuerdale hoard (1840).

Reference: Hawkins, 'An account', pp. 10–11, no. 17*; Hawkins, *Silver Coins*, no. 580; Haigh, 'On the coins', p. 106; Dolley, 'An unpublished hoard-provenance', pl. 8, 9.

Comment: The coin in the Assheton collection is unique. An electrotype copy of it passed through several famous collections, changing hands at high prices: Murdoch; ex Montagu I 282; ex Shepherd (not in sale); ex Yorke Moore (not in sale). It was thought to be the Assheton specimen, which might have been plausible since Yorke Moore had acquired another coin formerly in the Assheton family's Cuerdale parcel (no. 31). It was condemned as an electrotype before the sale of the Murdoch collection in 1903, and published as such by Lawrence, 'Forgery', p. 404, no. 24 and pl. 1, 24. It is now is the British Museum.

7 See the discussions in our papers above.

Two Emperors or *Portrait-Quatrefoil/ Cross-and-Lozenge* mule?

This coin has a *Cross-and-Lozenge* reverse but the portrait is enclosed in an inner circle as found on obverses of the *Two Emperors* and *Portrait-Quatrefoil* types. The coin is so poorly preserved that one cannot tell whether it is a mule between the two issues or merely a variant of the *Cross-and-Lozenge* type.

King Alfred

7. *Moneyer*: Ethe . . .?
    Obverse: [ ]LFERDREXS[ ] (starting at shoulder), *Two Emperors* or *Portrait-Quatrefoil* type?
    Reverse: E[ÐE?] MON E·TA, *Cross-and-Lozenge* type.
    Weight: 0.93g (14.4gr), badly corroded and fragmentary. *Die-axis*: 180°.
    Provenance: British Museum (BM 1950–2–1–1); ex Tudor Museum, Southampton 1950; found Southampton excavations 1949.
    Reference: Blunt, 'A new type' (with line drawings reproduced again here, Pl. 7, 7); Dolley and Blunt, 'The chronology', pl. 9, 3; Lyon, 'Historical problems . . . (2)', p. 236, n. 2; Metcalf, 'The coins', no. 147.
    Comment: The moneyer is perhaps the same as that of no. 45 (Ethelm . . .) of Winchester style, although the simple undecorated reverse of no. 7 has more in common with Lulla's distinctive coins (nos 52–4), which also have their obverse legends commencing at the shoulder as here.

Inscription-in-Field type

This type is recorded from a mere fragment – approximately a quarter of a coin – and is hence difficult to interpret. The obverse has the part of the ruler's name CEOL . . ., with traces of the curly hair of a profile bust within an inner circle. Pagan has suggested that it is a coin of Ceolwulf II and that the letters [ ]CO[ ] on the reverse may be part of the mint name *Lincolla* (Lincoln). Blunt, on the other hand, preferred to see it as a coin of Archbishop Ceolnoth (833–870) and the [ ]CO[ ] as part of his title *episcopus*. Although Pagan's interpretation seems preferable since the Cuerdale hoard contained no other coins as early as the 860s, the attribution is too uncertain to allow it to influence our interpretation of historical events.

King Ceolwulf II?

8. *Moneyer*: . . . anr . . . (Eanred, or less probably Beahred).
    Obverse: CEO[I], for *Ceolvvlf rex*?, bust right?
    Reverse: [ ]ANR[I] and [ ]CO[ ]; possibly for *Eanred moneta / Lincolla*
    Weight: 0.28g (4.3gr); small fragment.
    Provenance: British Museum; ex T. W. Armitage bequest 1956; ex Cuerdale hoard (1840).
    Reference: Pagan, 'An unpublished fragment'.

Cross-and-Lozenge type

Of this type fifty-three coins are recorded and it clearly is the main substantive issue of the phase. The obverse design is taken directly from a gold solidus of Honorius or another late fourth-century emperor (Pl. 11, K). A model must have been distributed to die-cutters at several centres, where it was copied with varying degrees of accuracy. The closest reproductions of the prototype were made by the die-cutters at Winchester (nos 42–52) and an unlocated centre which produced dies for the moneyer Lulla (nos 53–4). The London die-cutter's earliest work reproduces the drapery of the Roman model in some detail, but it became more stylised during the course of the issue (nos 20–41). At Canterbury there appear to have been two die-cutters both of whom interpreted the design rather freely (nos 9–19), and one was more influenced by the earlier *Lunettes* and *Portrait-Quatrefoil* types than the Roman model.

The reverse type was novel, though perhaps inspired by coins of Offa (Pl. 10, B–C).[8] A careful model of this appears to have been circulated, for there is a small detail present on the earlier coins from three different centres, namely the cross-arms that reach from the lozenge to the edge of the coin two of which are composed of pellets and two of plain lines (cf. nos 14, 21, 23, 27, 42, 45). This was a refinement soon ignored, and most coins have only pelleted or plain lines. From the outset the central lozenge on most coins was decorated inside and out with a variety of ornaments (pellets, trefoils, crosses, etc.). It seems likely that these details were of some significance administratively, and it remains to be seen whether any sense can be made of them.

Canterbury style

There are two distinct styles of die-cutting associated with Canterbury which appear to represent the work of two die-cutters. Certain features are common to both styles, namely (i) the obverse inscription (+(A)ELFRED REX or +EÐE(L)RED ARCHIEPI-) starts above the head; (ii) the moneyer's name on the reverse is preceded by an initial cross; and (iii) the word *moneta* or an abbreviation of it does not appear after the moneyer's name. The letter forms are also similar in both styles, with wedge-shaped punches as serifs and open top-barred As, but the lettering in style A is a little larger than in style B.

The distinguishing features of Canterbury Style A are: (i) hair enclosed by a curved line like a bonnet; (ii) diadem with tails that are often long and curled; (iii) a long narrow neck usually moulded, as on the *Portrait-Quatrefoil* type (nos 2–3); (iv) drapery which shows the cuirassed armour of the Roman prototype, though simplified and with no attempt at perspective; (v) the central motif within the lozenge on the reverse is aligned as a cross, rather than the saltire of most other styles; (vi) the outer limbs of the cross, between the lozenge and outer circle, are made up of pellets; (vii) the outer border on the reverse is either a plain circle or a circle broken by four crescents where the cross arms meet it.

Canterbury Style B has: (i) hair that is open, with the individual strands

8 Blunt, 'The Coinage of Offa', nos 37–9, 46 (with a central cross), or 87 (with a saltire).

sometimes ending in pellets; (ii) a short straight diadem, not extending behind the head; (iii) considerable variation in the portrait between the four known specimens, two having a long neck but less well defined than in Style A; (iv) the drapery also varies a lot, as the die-cutter seems to have copied various models – no. 13 shows influence from the *Lunettes* type, no. 12 the *Portrait-Quatrefoil* (nos 2–3), no. 15 the Roman prototype or perhaps Winchester style coins; (v) the central reverse motif is a saltire; (vi) the four limbs between the lozenge and the outer circle are simple lines; (vii) the outer border is either a simple beaded circle (no. 15), or a true quatrefoil (nos 11–13, 18). Style B shows greater variation than style A, and it is difficult to determine the sequence of the four known obverse and five reverse dies, but no. 12 shares a number of features with the *Portrait-Quatrefoil* coins of Archbishop Æthelred (nos 2–3), such as the drapery, eye, and construction of the reverse design, and should probably be placed first.

King Alfred

9. *Moneyer*: Burgnoth

Obverse: +···AELFRE D·REX (starting above head)

Reverse: +B VR GN OĐ, with a central small cross and cusps at ends of cross arms.

Weight: 1.30g (20.1gr). *Die-axis*: 0°.

Provenance: Ex Norweb 780 (*SCBI* Norweb 141); ex Lockett 2702; ex Carlyon-Britton 338; ex Murdoch 81; ex Montagu 559; ex Brice; ex 'Lady in the North' 4; ex Whitbourn 80; ex Norris 180; ex Kenyon; from the Cuerdale hoard (1840).

Reference: Haigh, 'On the coins', p. 106, no. 3; Haigh, 'Coins of Ælfred', p. 25, no. 22 and pl. 2, 12 (as formerly in the collection of J. Kenyon).

Comment: Canterbury style A.

10. *Moneyer*: Diarmund (cf. no. 11)

Obverse: +A···ELFRED REX (starting above head)

Reverse: +DI AR MV ND, with a central small cross and cusps at ends of cross arms.

Weight: 1.25 g. (19.3gr). *Die-axis*: 90°.

Provenance: British Museum (*BMC* 180); bought Mr Edwards (1839);[9] unknown (pre-Cuerdale) find.

Reference: Hawkins, *The Silver Coins*, pl. 13, no. 176; Haigh, 'Coins of Ælfred', p. 25, no. 21 and pl. 2, 11.

Comment: Canterbury style A. The three pellets on the breast echo those on the bust of the Archbishop in the *Portrait-Quatrefoil* type (no. 2), yet the

[9] H. E. Pagan has commented (pers. comm.) that the vendor to the British Museum was presumably William Edwards, later a coin dealer at 140 Aldersgate Street but in 1838 described in an MS note by Sir Henry Ellis as 'one of the boys who go about selling coins which they say they have found' (see also Hobler, *Records of Roman History* I, pp. 330–1, where in 1860 Hobler refers to 'young Edwards, who, with his brother long since dead, and Mr Eastwood, were the principal parties engaged in collecting antiquities from the Thames, and from excavations in London, for Mr Charles Roach Smith').

simplified drapery of this coin (no. 10) suggests that it does not belong early in the Canterbury A style.

11. *Moneyer*: Diarmund

Obverse: +A ELFRED +REX (starting above head)

Reverse: +DI AR MV ND, with central small cross and moline ends to the cross arms.

Weight: 1.40g (21.6gr), broken and repaired. *Die-axis*: 90°.

Provenance: Canterbury Museum, single-find from excavations at Canterbury, *ca* 1955.

Reference: *The Archaeology of Canterbury* VII, p. 125.

Comment: Canterbury style B.

12. *Moneyer*: Ethelred (cf. nos 2–4)

Obverse: +ELFRE DREX (starting above head)

Reverse: +E ÐE LR ED, with central saltire and quatrefoil border.

Weight: 1.15g (17.7gr), corroded. *Die-axis*: 80°.

Provenance: British Museum (BM 1960 5–5–5); ex Lockett 3631; ex Bruun 62 [the ticket has an inscription that is difficult to read but which has something like 'ex Sir J. G. Hob.., lot 79. 25/10/-'.].

Comment: Canterbury style B.

13. *Moneyer*: Guthhere

Obverse: A+ELFRE DREX (or +ELFRE DREXA) (starting above head)

Reverse: +G VÐ HE RE, with central saltire and quatrefoil border.

Weight: 1.24g (19.1gr), chipped. *Die-axis*: 80°.

Provenance: British Museum (BM 1904–6–3) (*BMA* 477); ex A. J. McEwan; from the Washington (Sussex) hoard (1904).

Comment: Canterbury style B.

14. *Moneyer*: Tirwald

Obverse: + ELFRE DREX (starting above head)

Reverse: +TI RV VA:· LD, with central small cross and circular border.

Weight: 1.16g (17.9gr). *Die-axis*: 180°.

Provenance: British Museum (Assheton loan); from the Cuerdale hoard (1840).

Reference: Hawkins, 'An account', p. 100 (Assheton parcel); Haigh, 'Coins of Ælfred', p. 25, no. 25 and pl. 2, 13.

Comment: Canterbury style A.

15. *Moneyer*: Torhtmund (cf. no. 19)

Obverse: ELFRE DREX (starting above head)

Reverse: +OT RH TM VND (ND ligatured), with central saltire and no border.

Weight: 1.10g (17.0gr). *Die-axis*: 180°.

Provenance: British Museum (*BMC* 184); ex Duchy of Lancaster 1841; from the Cuerdale hoard (1840).

Reference: Hawkins, 'An account', p. 12, no. 19; Hardy MS, no. 2; Haigh, 'Coins of Ælfred', p. 24, no. 14 and pl. 2, 4.

Comment: Canterbury style B.

Archbishop Æthelred

16. *Moneyer*: Ethelmund (cf. nos 17–18)

Obverse: EÐEL[ ]IEPI⁻ (starting above head), the fourth letter appears to be an L, rather than an R.

Reverse: +E[ ] ND, with central cross and circular border broken by cusps on long cross arms.

Weight: 0.47g (7.2gr); fragment. *Die-axis*: 0°.

Provenance: Allan Williams; found *ca* 1993.

Comment: Canterbury style A.

17. *Moneyer*: Ethelmund

Obverse: EÐERED ARCHIEPI⁻ (starting above head); same obverse die as next coin.

Reverse: +EÐ EL MV ND, with central cross and circular border.

Weight and die-axis: not recorded; bent and straightened.

Provenance: P. Finn list 8 (1996), no. 59; found Thames Exchange site, London early 1990s.

Comment: Canterbury style A.

18. *Moneyer*: Ethelmund

Obverse: same obverse die as preceding coin.

Reverse: +EÐ EL MV ND, with central saltire and quatrefoil border.

Weight: 1.33g (20.5gr). *Die-axis*: 90°.

Provenance: Maidstone Museum (*SCBI* South-Eastern Museums 629); provenance unknown.

Reference: Blunt, 'The coinage of Æthelred', no. 1.

Comment: Canterbury style A/B mule; i.e. not an original die pair, but a style B reverse used with a style A obverse.

19. *Moneyer*: Torhtmund (cf. no. 15)

Obverse: +EÐELRED ARCHIEPI⁻ (starting above head)

Reverse: +TO RHT MV ND:· (*HT* ligatured), with central small cross and a circular border.

Weight: 1.33g (20.5gr). *Die-axis*: 270°.

Provenance: Fitzwilliam Museum (*MEC* 1:1353; *SCBI* Cambridge 446); ex Young (1936); ex Carlyon-Britton 303; ex Murdoch 44; found near Tetbury, Glos. (before 1902).

Reference: Blunt, 'The coinage of Æthelred', no. 2; Keynes and Blackburn, *Anglo-Saxon Coins*, no. 51.

Comment: Canterbury style A.

London style

This group comprises twenty-one coins of Alfred and Ceolwulf plus a lead weight, of which nineteen are in one distinctive style and the remaining three (nos 25 and 40–1), although perhaps the work of different die-cutters, are by moneyers who also used the main style. The principal features of the main style are: (i) the obverse inscription starts above the head, normally without an initial cross (except no. 23), and reads ÆLFRED or ELFRED, and REX SM¯, REX SA, REX S or REX; CIOLVVLF REX M or REX; (ii) a tall narrow bust, emphasised by the vertical lines of the cuirassed drapery, which starts as a reasonable attempt to copy the Roman prototype, but becomes progressively more stylised; (iii) the profile of the hair is neatly rounded, without being bound by a line as it is in the Canterbury A style; (iv) the diadem extends well below the ear; (v) the reverse inscriptions do not begin with an initial cross and they usually end with moneta or an abbreviation of it; (vi) the central reverse motif is initially a saltire, but later under Ceolwulf it was normally a cross; (vii) of the large cross arms (between the lozenge and the edge of the coin) two or four are composed of pellets.

The attribution of this group to London is based on the careers of certain moneyers, which can be projected back into Burgred's coinage and on into Alfred's *Two-Line* type where a London group has also been identified.[10] Liafwald appears to have been more prolific than any of the other *Cross-and-Lozenge* moneyers, and he produced coins for both Alfred and Ceolwulf II. A clear stylistic progression can be discerned within this group, and Ceolwulf's coins (nos 33–41) belong at the end of it, showing that after Burgred's exile the mint struck coins in the name of Alfred and only subsequently used Ceolwulf's name. The historical implications of this are discussed in our respective papers above.

King Alfred

20. *Moneyer*: Ciolwulf (cf. nos 21–2)
    Obverse: ÆLFRE DREX:· (starting above head)
    Reverse: CIOL VLF MON ETA
    Weight: 0.55g (8.5gr), corroded and chipped. *Die-axis*: 150°.
    Provenance: Rochester Museum; excavation find, Rochester Castle, Kent (1976).
    Reference: Archibald, 'An Alfred penny'.

21. *Moneyer*: Ciolwulf
    Obverse: ELFR· EDRE· (starting above head)
    Reverse: CIOL VVLF MON ETA
    Weight: 1.34g (20.7gr). *Die-axis*: 130°.
    Provenance: British Museum (*BMC* 188); ex Duchy of Lancaster 1841; from the Cuerdale hoard (1840).
    Reference: Hawkins, 'An account', p. 12, no. 21; Haigh, 'Coins of Ælfred', p. 24, no. 16 and pl. 2, 6.

22. *Moneyer*: . . .lw. . . (Ciolwulf?).
    Obverse: [ ]DR[ ] (starting above head)
    Reverse: [ ] LVV [ ]
    Weight: 0.32g (4.9gr), fragment. *Die-axis*: 0°?
    Provenance: British Museum (*BMC* 186); ex Duchy of Lancaster 1841; from the Cuerdale hoard (1840).

10 Discussed further in Blackburn, 'The London mint', above.

23. *Moneyer*: Hereferth (cf. nos 24–5)
    Obverse: + ELFRE· DREX (starting above head)
    Reverse: HERE FERÐ MON ETA
    Weight: 1.28g (19.7gr), chipped. *Die-axis*: *ca* 135°.
    Provenance: Ex Mack (1977) 83 (*SCBI* Mack 730); ex Ryan 714; possibly that specimen 'found on the Downs near Wye', Kent (before 1849).
    Reference: British Archaeological Association's Sixth Annual Meeting, Chester, 1849. A Catalogue of the Museum of Antiquities exhibited at the King's School, Chester (1849), p. 27.

24. *Moneyer*: Hereferth
    Obverse: ÆLFRE DREX (starting above head)
    Reverse: hE RE FE RÐ
    Weight: 1.26g (19.4gr), chipped. *Die-axis*: 180°.
    Fineness: 92% Ag (Metcalf and Northover, 'Debasement', pp. 174–5, no. 106).
    Provenance: Fitzwilliam Museum (*MEC* 1:1352); ex Lockett 3632; ex Carlyon-Britton 1649; ex Murdoch 82; ex Montagu 557; ex Marsham 155; ex Wigan; according to Montagu, from the Cuerdale hoard (1840).
    Reference: Keynes and Blackburn, *Anglo-Saxon Coins*, no. 50.
    Comment: If this was a stray from the Cuerdale hoard, as asserted by Montagu, it remained undisclosed for several decades, since in 1880 *Cross-and-Lozenge* coins of this moneyer were not known to Haigh ('Coins of Ælfred').

25. *Moneyer*: Hereferth
    Obverse: +[E]LFRE DREZ (starting above head)
    Reverse: hER EF ER ÐM
    Weight: 1.14g (17.6gr), chipped. *Die-axis*: 350°.
    Provenance: British Museum (BM 1904–6–3–2) (*BMA* 478); ex A. J. McEwan; from the Washington (Sussex) hoard (1904).
    Comment: Not in the main 'London' style.

26. *Moneyer*: Liafwald (cf. nos 27–31, 35–41)
    Obverse: ÆLFRE·: DREXSI (starting above head)
    Reverse: LIA FVA LDM ONE
    Weight: 1.30g (20.1gr). *Die-axis*: 40°.
    Provenance: British Museum (BM 1896–4–4–64) (*BMA* 479); ex Montagu 556; ex Evans; ex Shepherd 70; ex Murchison 185; ex Martin 13; from the Cuerdale hoard (1840).
    Reference: Haigh, 'Coins of Ælfred', p. 25, no. 25 and pl. 2, 9 (as formerly in the collection of Rev. J. W. Martin).
    Comment: The final 'I' in the obverse inscription may be an upright for a letter M (cf. no. 27) for which there was insufficient room.

27. *Moneyer*: Liafwald
    Obverse: ÆLFRED REXSM⁻ (starting above head)
    Reverse: LIA FVA LDM ONE

Weight: 1.27g (19.6gr), broken and repaired. *Die-axis*: 180°.
Provenance: Fitzwilliam Museum (CM.1.347–1990); ex Blunt; bt London 1947; ex Drabble 384; according to Blunt's ticket, ex Carlyon-Britton (not in sales).

28. *Moneyer*: Liafwald
Obverse: ÆLFRED REXSA (starting above head; cross on either side of head)
Reverse: LIA FVA LD· MON
Weight and die-axis: not recorded.
Provenance: Bibliothèque Nationale, Paris; purchased in the nineteenth century; find-spot unknown.

29. *Moneyer*: Liafwald
Obverse: ÆLFRE· DREX· (starting above head)
Reverse: LIA FVA LD· MON
Weight: 1.32g (20.3 gr). *Die-axis*: 270°.
Provenance: British Museum (Assheton); from the Cuerdale hoard (1840).
Reference: Hawkins, 'An account', p. 100 (Assheton parcel); Haigh, 'Coins of Ælfred', p. 24, no. 11 and pl. 2, 2.

30. *Moneyer*: Liafwald
Obverse: ELFRE DREX (starting above head)
Reverse: LIA FVA LD· MON
Weight: 1.28g (19.7gr), broken in two and rejoined. *Die-axis*: *ca* 315°.
Provenance: Ex Mack (Glendining, 18 November 1975) 112 (*SCBI* Mack 731); ex North; ex Parsons 131; the two halves bt separately: (i) bt Seaby (1950); ex Mr Charnby of Preston; acquired with other coins of Alfred and Edward the Elder from a family who lived 6 miles from Cuerdale; (ii) bt Seaby (1952); ex man from Blackpool; from the Cuerdale hoard (1840).
Reference: P. J. Seaby, exhibit, *British Numismatic Journal* 26 (1949–51), p. 354; *SCBI* Mack, p. xii, note to no. 731.
Comment: C. E. Blunt noted in his card index that a manuscript of Rev. T. F. Dymoch (*ca* 1807–58) records a fragmentary *Cross-and-Lozenge* coin by the moneyer 'Fulda', which Mr Lyon has suggested to us may be the second piece here reading [ ]FVA LD·[ ]. It may, however, have been no. 31 below as communicated to Dymoch by General Yorke Moore (1806–90).

31. *Moneyer*: Liafwald
Obverse: ELFRE DREX (starting above head)
Reverse: LIA FVA LD MON
Weight: 1.16g (17.9gr).
Provenance: National Museum of Wales; ex Lockett 490; probably ex Montagu 558; ex Addington; ex York Moore 72 (as reading FYALD·MONETA); probably ex Assheton; ex Cuerdale hoard (1840).
Reference: Hawkins, 'An account', p. 100 (Assheton parcel); Dykes, *Anglo-Saxon Coins*, pp. 9 and 24.
Comment: This appears to be the second specimen of Liafwald described

by Hawkins as in the possession of Mr Assheton in 1841. The Assheton family had disposed of some other coins from their share of the Cuerdale hoard, including another *Cross-and-Lozenge* coin (no. 59) and some coins of Edward the Elder (Blunt, Stewart and Lyon, *Coinage in Tenth-Century England*, p. 25, n. 20).

32. Lead weight or trial piece.
Moneyer: Ealdulf? (cf. no. 6)
Obverse: +ÆLFRE DRE
Reverse: EAL DV· LF[ ] M[ ] (reading uncertain)
Weight: 163.1g (2517.0gr). *Dimensions*: 37 x 34 x 14 mm.
Provenance: British Museum; ex C. Roach Smith; ex E. B. Price; from St Paul's churchyard, London (1840).
Reference: *Gentleman's Magazine* 1841:ii, pp. 244–5, 498; Haigh, 'On the coins', p. 106; Roach-Smith, *Catalogue*, p. 107 (with the line drawings reproduced again here, Pl. 9, 32); Haigh, 'Coins of Ælfred', p. 24 and pl. 1, 10; Dolley, 'A piedfort', pp. 175–6, and pl. 6, 1; Stewart, 'A lead striking', p. 186 (suggesting it is a half-Roman-pound weight); Archibald, 'Anglo-Saxon and Norman lead objects', p. 338, no. 6, and fig. 4.13, 6.
Comment: The condition of this lead piece has deteriorated since it was found and we are reliant on the earlier publications for the readings and best illustrations of the piece. Stewart has suggested that it was intended to weigh half a Roman pound (*ca* 163.5g), but it may alternatively have been half a current £1 in money, i.e. the weight of 120 pennies, since coins of this issue appear to have been struck to a weight standard in the range 1.35–1.39g (see p. 129 above), and 120 pennies would have weighed between 162g and 167g. The two could of course be linked, for the monetary pound of the mid-ninth century may have been based on the Roman pound.

King Ceolwulf II

33. *Moneyer*: Dealing
Obverse: CIOLVVL FREX·: (starting above head)
Reverse: DE:· AL ING MON (Ns reversed)
Weight: 1.10g (17.0gr). *Die-axis*: *ca* 130°.
Provenance: Hunterian Museum (*SCBI* Glasgow 381); ex W. Hunter (d. 1783); ex M. Duane; found before 1758, reputedly in Ireland.
Reference: Simon, *An Essay*, Supplement pl. 3, 13 (headed 'Ancient coins found in Ireland in the possession of M. Duane, June 1758'); Ruding, *Annals of the Coinage*, pl. 7, 2 (as Ceolwulf I); Dolley, 'An unpublished hoard-provenance', no. 5, and pl. 8, 2.

34. *Moneyer*: Dudecil
Obverse: CIOLVVLF REXM (starting above head)
Reverse: DVD ECI LMON ETA (N reversed)
Weight: 1.42g (21.9gr). *Die-axis*: 150°.
Provenance: Fitzwilliam Museum (CM.1.226–1990); ex Blunt; bt London 1964; ex Bagnall; ex Ryan 648; ex Drabble 339; ex Montagu I 281; ex

Brice; ex Shepherd 29; ex J. Kenyon; ex A. Moore (1848) 305; from the Cuerdale hoard (1840).
Reference: Haigh, 'On the coins', p. 106; Dolley, 'An unpublished hoard-provenance', no. 7, and pl. 8, 3.

35. *Moneyer*: Liofwald (cf. 26–31, 36–41)
Obverse: CIOLVVL FREX:· (starting above head)
Reverse: LIOF VAL DMO NET (N reversed)
Weight: 1.37g (21.2 gr).
Provenance: Christies, 10 October 1989, lot 458; ex Stonyhurst College; from the Cuerdale hoard (1840).
Reference: Dolley, 'An unpublished hoard-provenance', no. 6, and pl. 8, 8.
Comment: The Christies cataloguer notes that the coin had been turned over in the die and struck twice, . . . FREX being visible in the first quarter of the reverse.

36. *Moneyer*: Liafwald
Obverse: CIOLVV FREX (starting above head)
Reverse: LI AF VA LD
Weight: 1.33g (20.5gr). *Die-axis*: 270°.
Provenance: Ex Mack (*SCBI* Mack 638); ex Lockett 407; ex Bruun (1925) 35.
Reference: Dolley, 'An unpublished hoard-provenance', no. 8, and pl. 8, 5.
Comment: Copies of this exist in silver and in lead struck from false dies made by Mr Trevor Ashmore of Devon in the 1980s or 1990s (specimen in Fitzwilliam Museum, CM.270–1994).

37. *Moneyer*: Liofwald
Obverse: CIOLVV LFREX (starting above head)
Reverse: LIO FV AL DMO
Weight: 1.37g (21.2gr). *Die-axis*: 30°.
Provenance: British Museum (*BMC* 403); ex Duchy of Lancaster 1841; from the Cuerdale hoard (1840).
Reference: Hawkins, 'An account', p. 10, no. 17 and pl. 1, 3; Dolley, 'An unpublished hoard-provenance', no. 1, and pl. 8, 6.

38. *Moneyer*: Liofwald
Obverse: CIOLVV LFREX (starting above head)
Reverse: LIOF VAL DMO NET (N reversed)
Weight: 1.32g (20.4gr), chipped. *Die-axis*: 350°.
Provenance: Spink sale, 4 March 1997, lot 81; found with nos 39 and 40 at Pitstone, Buckinghamshire, before September 1996, and evidently a small dispersed hoard.

39. *Moneyer*: Liofwald
Same dies as last coin.
Weight: 1.17g (18.1gr), chipped. *Die-axis*: 350°.
Provenance: Lord Stewartby; ex Spink sale, 4 March 1997, lot 82; found with nos 38 and 40 at Pitstone, Buckinghamshire, before September 1996.

40. *Moneyer*: Liofwald
Obverse: CIOLVVL FREX:· (starting above head); same die as next coin.
Reverse: LIOF VA LDM ONET (NE ligatured); same die as next coin.
Weight: 1.49g (23.0gr). *Die-axis*: 350°.
Provenance: Spink sale, 4 March 1997, lot 80; found with nos 38 and 39 at Pitstone, Buckinghamshire, before September 1996.
Comment: Not in the main 'London' style.

41. *Moneyer*: Liofwald
Same dies as preceding coin.
Weight: 1.21g (18.7gr). *Die-axis*: 40°.
Provenance: British Museum (BM 1915–5–7–702) (*BMA* 154); ex Morgan; ex Evans; ex Marsham 87; ex Boyne 62; ex Murchison 107; ex Dymock 70; ex Cuff 292; probably from the Cuerdale hoard (1840).
Reference: Dolley, 'An unpublished hoard-provenance', no. 3, and pl. 8, 7.

Winchester style

For the source of this third group Winchester is implied by the inclusion of the moneyer Wulfred, who can be associated with Winchester through a sequence of moneyers and styles down to mint-signed issues of Athelstan (924–939), and the moneyer Dunna, who used Winchester-style dies in the *Two-Line* type. This pushes the date for the establishment of a mint at Winchester back to the mid-870s.[11] The inclusion of a coin of Ceolwulf II in this group suggests either that Dunna's dies were being supplied to a mint in southern Mercia or that some coins were being struck on his behalf at Winchester.

The main features of this style are: (i) the obverse inscription starts above the head, with ÆLFRED (or ÆLFRÆD) REX SAX, REX SA, or REX S; CEOLVVLF R;[12] (ii) initially the die-cutter reproduced the Roman portrait rather faithfully, making a particular feature of the annulet brooches on the shoulder and long diadem ties, but it became progressively more stylised; (iii) in the reverse inscription there is no initial cross and *moneta* is usually included in full; (iv) the central motif is a saltire; (v) on the earliest dies two of the outer cross arms are pelleted and two are plain (nos 42, 46, 52), subsequently all four are pelleted (nos 43–4, 45?, 51), and finally all are plain (nos 47, 49–50, 52). The moneyer Dunna struck coins for both Alfred (nos 42–3) and Ceolwulf II (no. 52), and the Ceolwulf piece appears to be the latest of the three.[13]

11 It is uncertain whether the earlier West Saxon coinages of Beorhtric, Egbert and Æthelwulf were struck at Southampton or Winchester.

12 It should be noted that while the form *Ciolwulf* is found on coins of the London group (nos. 33-41), *Ceolwulf* occurs on the remaining three coins that are probably to be attributed to southern or western Mercia (nos 6, 52, 60). While this pattern is clear, the *Ciol*-form is not distinctive in terms of dialect; see Bibire, 'Moneyers' names: Philological approaches to some historical problems', below.

13 This corroborates the evidence of the London coins for the sequence of Alfred's and Ceolwulf's issues; see the discussion in Blackburn, 'The London mint', above.

King Alfred

42. *Moneyer*: Dunna (cf. 43, 52)
    Obverse: ÆLFR ÆDREXSA (starting to right of head)
    Reverse: DVN NA:· MON ETA (Ns reversed and O surrounded by four pellets)
    Weight: not recorded.
    Provenance: A. W. Morrison; ex Grantley 1000; ex Murdoch 79; ex Montagu I 554; ex Addington; ex Bergne 160; ex Cuff 454; from the Cuerdale hoard (1840).
    Reference: Haigh, 'On the coins', p. 106, no. 1; Haigh, 'Coins of Ælfred', p. 24, no. 13 and pl. 2, 3.

43. *Moneyer*: Dunna
    Obverse: +ÆLFRE DREXS (starting above head)
    Reverse: DVN NA:· MON ETA (Ns reversed)
    Weight: 1.30g (20.1gr), broken. *Die-axis*: 0°.
    Provenance: British Museum (*BMC* 181); ex Duchy of Lancaster 1841; from the Cuerdale hoard (1840).
    Reference: Hawkins, 'An account', p. 12, no. 18 and pl. 1, 4; Hardy MS, no. 3.

44. *Moneyer*: Eadelm
    Obverse: +ÆLFRE DREXS·: (starting above head)
    Reverse: EAD ELM MON ETA
    Weight: 1.32g (20.3gr). *Die-axis*: 130°.
    Provenance: British Museum (BM 1955–7–8–32); ex Lockett 488; ex Bliss 84; ex Murdoch 80; ex Montagu 555; ex Brice; probably from the Cuerdale hoard (1840).
    Comment: The Brice MS Catalogue (1881) in the Fitzwilliam Museum notes 'probably from the Cuerdale find', and the Montagu catalogue repeats this 'most probably' from Cuerdale.

45. *Moneyer*: Ethlem . . .
    Obverse: [ ] DREX·:·SAX (starting to right of head)
    Reverse: EÐLE M[ ] ETA
    Weight: 1.03g (15.9gr), fragment. *Die-axis*: 20°.
    Provenance: British Museum (*BMC* 182); ex Duchy of Lancaster 1841; from the Cuerdale hoard (1840).
    Reference: Hawkins, 'An account', p. 12; Hardy MS, no. 4; Haigh, 'Coins of Ælfred', p. 24, no. 17 and pl. 2, 7.
    Comment: The identity of the moneyer is uncertain. The only recorded Ethelm . . . moneyer in the second half of the ninth century is Ethelmund, who worked at Canterbury for Alfred in the *Lunettes* type and for the archbishop in the *Cross-and-Lozenge* type. However, the style of this coin makes it likely that it is the product of a different moneyer, possibly the same as that of no. 7.

46. *Moneyer*: Heahstan (cf. nos 47–8)
Obverse: +ÆLFRE DREXSA (or ÆLFRE DREXSAX) (starting above head)
Reverse: HEA HSTA NMO NETA (NE ligatured)
Weight: 1.39g (21.4gr). *Die-axis*: 0°.
Fineness: 96% Ag (Metcalf and Northover, 'Debasement', pp. 174–5, no. 105).
Provenance: Ashmolean Museum (*SCBI* Oxford 247); ex Lockett 489; ex Carlyon-Britton 929; ex J. H. Young 15; ex Bergne 161; ex Murchison 184; ex Huxtable 590; ex Kenyon; from the Cuerdale hoard (1840).
Reference: Haigh, 'On the coins', p. 106, no. 2.

47. *Moneyer*: Heahstan
Obverse: +ÆLFRE DREXSA (starting above head)
Reverse: HEA HSTA NMO NETA (HE and NE ligatured).
Weight: 1.40g (21.6gr). *Die-axis*: 320°.
Provenance: Fitzwilliam Museum (C. S. S. Lyon loan); bt Baldwin 1991; ex A. W. Morrison 1971; probably that specimen exhibited to the British Numismatic Society by P. J. Seaby on 24 May 1950, part of a parcel of eight coins evidently from the Cuerdale hoard (*British Numismatic Journal* 26 (1951), p. 234); from the Cuerdale hoard (1840).

48. *Moneyer*: Heahstan
Obverse: not recorded.
Reverse: 'HEI[ ] +STAN MONETA' (presumably for HEA HSTAN MON ETA?).
Weight: not recorded; 'in fragments soldered together'.
Provenance: Ex Grantley 1009 (part); possibly ex Kenyon 678 ('A similar lot, with head, broken in six pieces'); from the Cuerdale hoard (1840).
Comment: No illustration of this coin is known.

49. *Moneyer*: Luceman (cf. no. 50)
Obverse: +ÆLFR EDREXSA (or ÆLFR EDREXSAX) (starting above head); same obverse die as next coin.
Reverse: LVCE MA NMO NET
Weight: 1.37g (21.2gr). *Die-axis*: 350°.
Provenance: British Museum (BM 1904–5–10–1) (*BMA* 480); ex A. Sargent; from the Washington (Sussex) hoard (1904).

50. *Moneyer*: Luceman
Obverse: +ÆLFR EDREXS[ ] (or ÆLFR EDREXS[ ]X) (starting above head); same obverse die as preceding coin.
Reverse: L[ ]C [ ] NMO NETA (NE ligatured)
Weight: 1.03g (15.9gr), chipped and bent. *Die-axis*: 320°.
Provenance: Ashmolean Museum (Mr and Mrs A. Bagsett loan); single-find from Stanton St John, Oxon., *ca* 1985.

51. *Moneyer*: Wulfred
    Obverse: +ÆLFRE DREXSA (or ÆLFRE DREXSAX) (starting above head)
    Reverse: VVL FRE DMO NETA (NE ligatured)
    Weight: 1.45g (22.3gr). *Die-axis*: 200°.
    Provenance: British Museum (Assheton loan); from the Cuerdale hoard (1840).
    Reference: Hawkins, 'An account', p. 100 (Assheton parcel); Haigh, 'Coins of Ælfred', p. 24, no. 15 and pl. 2, 5.

King Ceolwulf II

52. *Moneyer*: Dunna (cf. nos 42–3)
    Obverse: +CEOLV VLFR (starting above head)
    Reverse: DVN NA MON ETA
    Weight: 0.76g (11.7gr.), corroded, broken and repaired. *Die-axis*: 320°.
    Provenance: British Museum (BM 1959 12–10–17; *SCBI* East Anglia 1); from the Morley St Peter, Norfolk, hoard (1958).
    Reference: Dolley, 'An unpublished hoard-provenance', no. 4, and pl. 8, 4; Dolley, *Anglo-Saxon Pennies*, pl. 11, 31.

Other styles

The remaining eight coins cannot be assigned to any of the three main groups described above. The coins of the moneyer Lulla (nos 53–5) form a distinct group on their own, in both the *Cross-and-Lozenge* and the *Two-Line* types. He was probably operating on his own at a mint in western England – possible candidates include Bath, Exeter and Gloucester, which later produced mint-signed issues, although it could have been elsewhere. Two of Lulla's *Cross-and-Lozenge* coins (nos 53–4) have the following features: (i) the obverse inscription starts by the right shoulder (as on the Roman prototype) and reads +AELFRED REX SAX; (ii) the portrait carefully follows the Roman original; (iii) the reverse inscription has no initial cross and includes *moneta* in full. They seem to be struck to a slightly heavier weight standard than other coins of this type. The third coin of Lulla (no. 55) is by a different hand and may be an imitation. Coins by the moneyers Regingild and . . . lf (nos 56 and 58) also have obverse inscriptions starting by the right shoulder and ending REX SAX, but they are in quite different styles and for the present remain unattributed. The same is true of the last two pieces. No. 59 by the moneyer Eadulf (a name formally distinct from the Ealdulf of no. 6) shows influence from Burgred's *Lunettes* type, although the drapery attempts to copy that of the Roman prototype. The final coin (no. 60), of Ceolwulf II, is possibly from a West Mercian mint. The moneyer Cuthulf struck *Lunettes* coins for Burgred and Alfred, but in a Mercian style, and in the *Two-Line* issue his coins are associated with a group of moneyers attributed to west Mercia.[14] The king's name, it may be noted, has the form CEOLVVLF. The style of bust and lettering has some similarities with Ceolwulf's *Two Emperors* coin (no.

14 Pagan and Stewart, 'A new Mercian moneyer'.

6), although that is more carefully produced and we would not press the association.

King Alfred

53. *Moneyer*: Lulla (cf. nos 54–5)
Obverse: +AELFREDREXSAX (starting at shoulder)
Reverse: LVL LA·:· MON ETA
Weight: 1.45g (22.4gr), chipped.
Provenance: Winchester Museum (CG64, 306); from Winchester, Cathedral Green excavations (1964).
References: Dolley and Blunt, 'Coins from the Winchester excavations', no. 2.

54. *Moneyer*: Lulla
Obverse: +AELFREDREXSAX (starting at shoulder)
Reverse: LVL LA·: MON ETA (lozenge O)
Weight: 1.44g (22.2gr). *Die-axis*: 40°.
Provenance: British Museum (*BMC* 183); ex Duchy of Lancaster 1841; from the Cuerdale hoard (1840).
Reference: Hawkins, 'An account', p. 12, no. 20; Hardy MS, no. 1.

55. *Moneyer*: Lulla
Obverse: EI·[ ]EX?A⁻ (reading uncertain, letters misformed; starting above head)
Reverse: LVL LA [ ]
Weight: 0.35g (5.4gr), fragment, pierced. *Die-axis*: 270°.
Provenance: Fitzwilliam Museum (CM.387–1991); bt S. Brown 1991; single-find from Bawsey, Norfolk, 1989.
Comment: The style of this coin is crude and quite unlike that of the other two coins of Lulla (nos 53–4). In view of its findspot, it could be a Danelaw imitation, and if so the first of its kind to be recognised.

56. *Moneyer*: Regingild (cf. no. 57)
Obverse: +ÆLFREDREXSAX (starting at shoulder)
Reverse: REGI NGIL DMO NETA (Ns reversed)
Weight: 1.28g (19.7gr), chipped. *Die-axis*: *ca* 225°.
Provenance: Allan Williams; ex Linzalone (Stacks, 7 December 1994) 2352; Mack (*SCBI* Mack 732); ex Ryan 713; ex Carlyon-Britton 339; ex Rashleigh 224; ex Cuff 453; unknown (pre-Cuerdale) find.
Reference: Ruding, *Annals of the Coinage*, pl. Supp. C, no. 17; Hawkins, 'An account', p. 12 (referring to a *Cross-and-Lozenge* coin of Alfred in Mr Cuff's collection before the discovery of the Cuerdale hoard); Haigh, 'Coins of Ælfred', p. 25, no. 20 and pl. 2, 10.

57. *Moneyer*: Regingild
Obverse: corrosion adhering and hence illegible.
Reverse: REG INGIL DMO+ NETA (distinctive design as no. 56)
Weight: not recorded, corrosion products adhering.

Provenance: Hereford and Worcester County Museum; transferred from the County Archaeological Service (HWCM 4575); found in excavations at Upwich, Droitwich, Worcs 1984.
Comment: This is presumably a coin of Alfred, although it could be one of Ceolwulf II. It was heavily encrusted when found, but having cleaned the reverse the conservator, Mr M. Read, did not feel that it was safe to clean the obverse. We are grateful to Miss M. M. Archibald for having drawn this find to our attention. The line drawing of the reverse is reproduced on Pl. 10, 57 courtesy of Hereford and Worcester County Archaeological Service (through Derek Hurst) and it is copyright of Hereford and Worcester County Council.

58. *Moneyer*: . . . lf
Obverse: . . . EDREXSAX (starting at shoulder)
Reverse: ... ..LF MON ETA (pelleted O)
Weight: 0.81g (12.5gr), fragment. *Die-axis*: 50°.
Provenance: British Museum (*BMC* 185); ex Duchy of Lancaster 1841; from the Cuerdale hoard (1840).
Reference: Hawkins, 'An account', p. 12; Hardy MS, no. 5; Haigh, 'Coins of Ælfred', p. 25, no. 18 and pl. 2, 8.

59. *Moneyer*: Eadulf
Obverse: +ÆLFRED REXZAX (starting above head)
Reverse: EAD VLF MON ETA (N reversed), no bars on arms of lozenge cross.
Weight: 1.38g (21.3gr). *Die-axis*: 40°.
Provenance: British Museum (*BMC* 187); bt Mr William Webster, coin dealer (1867); presumably ex Murchison (1866) 186; ex Dymock 116; ex Assheton; from the Cuerdale hoard (1840).
Reference: Hawkins, 'An account', p. 100 (Assheton parcel); Haigh, 'Coins of Ælfred', p. 23 and pl. 2, 1 (as formerly in the Dymock collection).
Comment: For other coins disposed of by the Assheton family, see no. 31.

King Ceolwulf II

60. *Moneyer*: Cuthulf
Obverse: +CEOLVV+LFREXM (starting at shoulder)
Reverse: CUD VLF MON ETA
Weight: 1.27g (19.6gr). *Die-axis*: 70°.
Provenance: British Museum (BM 1904–6–3–3) (*BMA* 153); ex A. J. McEwan; from the Washington (Sussex) hoard (1904).
Reference: Dolley, 'An unpublished hoard-provenance', no. 2, and pl. 8, 1.
Comment: Possibly from a west Mercian mint; see above.

Uncertain

61. *Moneyer*: not recorded.
Obverse: not recorded.
Reverse: not recorded.
Weight: not recorded, fragment.

Provenance: present location unknown; ex Sir John Twisden Bt (sale, May 1841), probably part of lot 154 (bt by the dealer Cureton); unknown (pre-Cuerdale) find.
Reference: Hawkins, 'An account', p. 12; referring to a *Cross-and-Lozenge* coin fragment in the collection of Sir John Twisden (d. 1 January 1841) before the discovery of the Cuerdale hoard.
Comment: Little is known of this piece, beyond that it was of *Cross-and-Lozenge* type; we cannot even be sure that it was of Alfred, although Hawkins thought that it was. The legends have not been recorded and it has not been illustrated, but it does not appear to be any of the fragments otherwise listed above.

ADDITIONAL ILLUSTRATIONS ON PLATES 10–11

Unless otherwise indicated, coins are in the Fitzwilliam Museum, Cambridge

A Offa, Light issue, moneyer Heaberht.
B Offa, Light issue, moneyer Eadhun (*MEC* 1.1126).
C Offa, Heavy issue, moneyer Ciolhard (Blunt, 'The coinage', no. 87).
D Æthelwulf, *Open Cross* type, moneyer Torhtulf (*MEC* 1.1309).
E Burgred, *Lunettes* type, London ('Horizontal') style, moneyer Cenred (*MEC* 1.1329).
F Burgred, *Lunettes* type, London ('Vertical') style, moneyer Dudwine (*MEC* 1.1333).
G Æthelred I, *Lunettes* type, Canterbury style, moneyer Bearhea (*MEC* 1.1342).
H Alfred, *Lunettes* type, Canterbury style, moneyer Sefreth (*MEC* 1.1350).
I Alfred, *Lunettes* type, London ('Horizontal') style or imitation, moneyer Biarnred (*SCBI* Glasgow 560).
J Valentinian II (375–392), solidus, Thessalonica, possible prototype for the *Two Emperors* type.
K Honorius (393–423), solidus, Ravenna, possible prototype for *Cross-and-Lozenge* type.
L Valentinian I (364–375), solidus, Trier, possible prototype for *London Monogram* type, M.
M Alfred, *London Monogram* type (*MEC* 1.1354).
N Constantius II, (as Caesar, 324–37), bronze, Lugdunum, possible prototype for diadem on *London Monogram* type, P.
O Alfred, *London Monogram type* (*MEC* 1.1355).
P Decentius (351–353), bronze, possible prototype for drapery on *London Monogram* type, R.
Q Alfred, *London Monogram* type (Fitzwilliam Museum, Lyon loan).
R Alfred, *London Monogram* type, moneyer Tilewine (*MEC* 1.1359).
S Alfred, *Gloucester* type (*BMC* 80).
T Alfred, *Oxford* type (*BMC* 127).

U Alfred, *Two-Line* type, London (early) style, moneyer Tilewine (*BMC* 377).

V Alfred, *Two-Line* type, London (late) style, moneyer Beagstan (*SCBI* Oxford 250).

INDEXES

Issuers

Moneyers

Finds

Collections

PLATES

1. Æthelwulf, Early Rochester Issues: Early Portrait (a); *Occidentalium Saxoniorum* (b); *Cross-and-Wedges* (c–f); New Style Portrait (A–M)

2. Berhtwulf, Group I, Bust A (1–19)

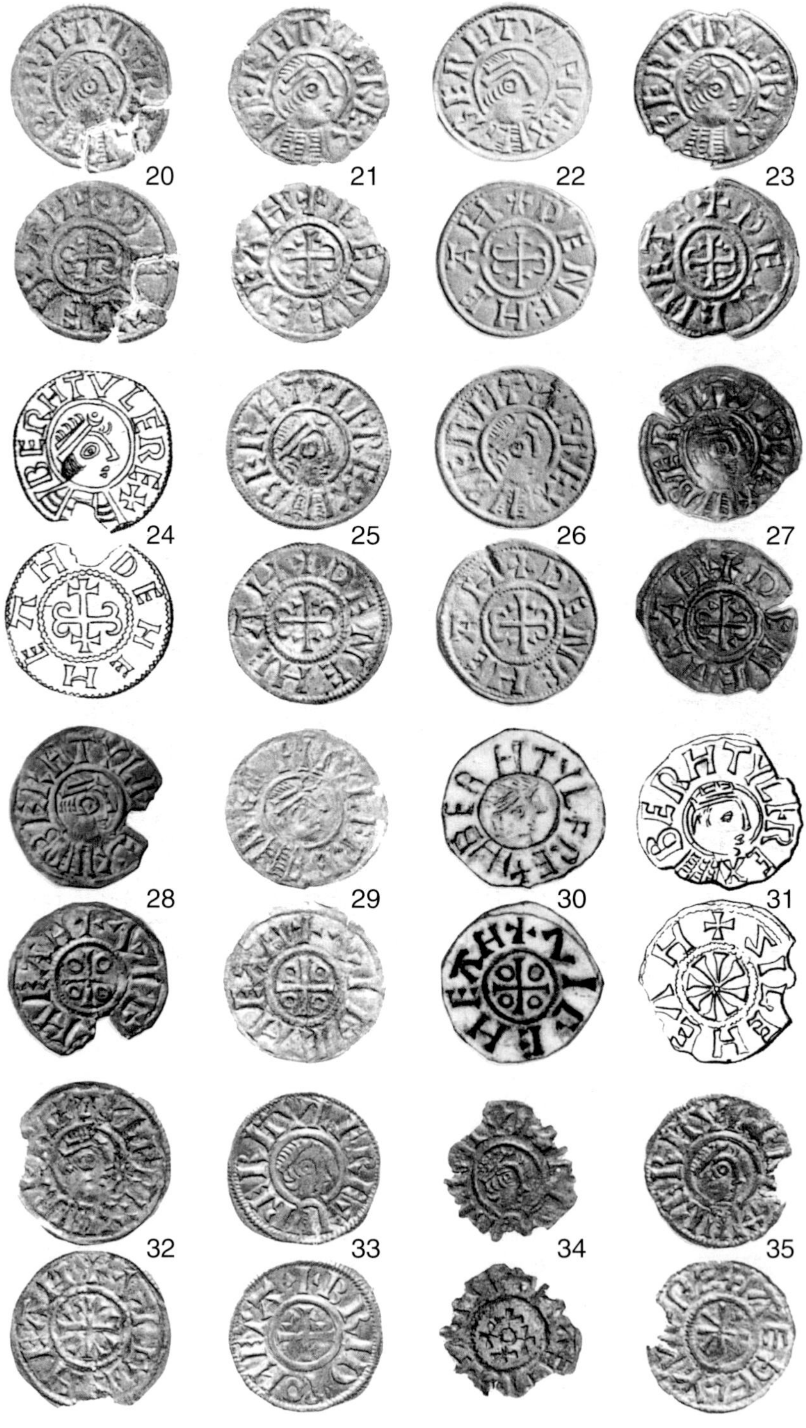

3. Berhtwulf, Group I, Bust A (20–32); Group II, Bust B (33–5)

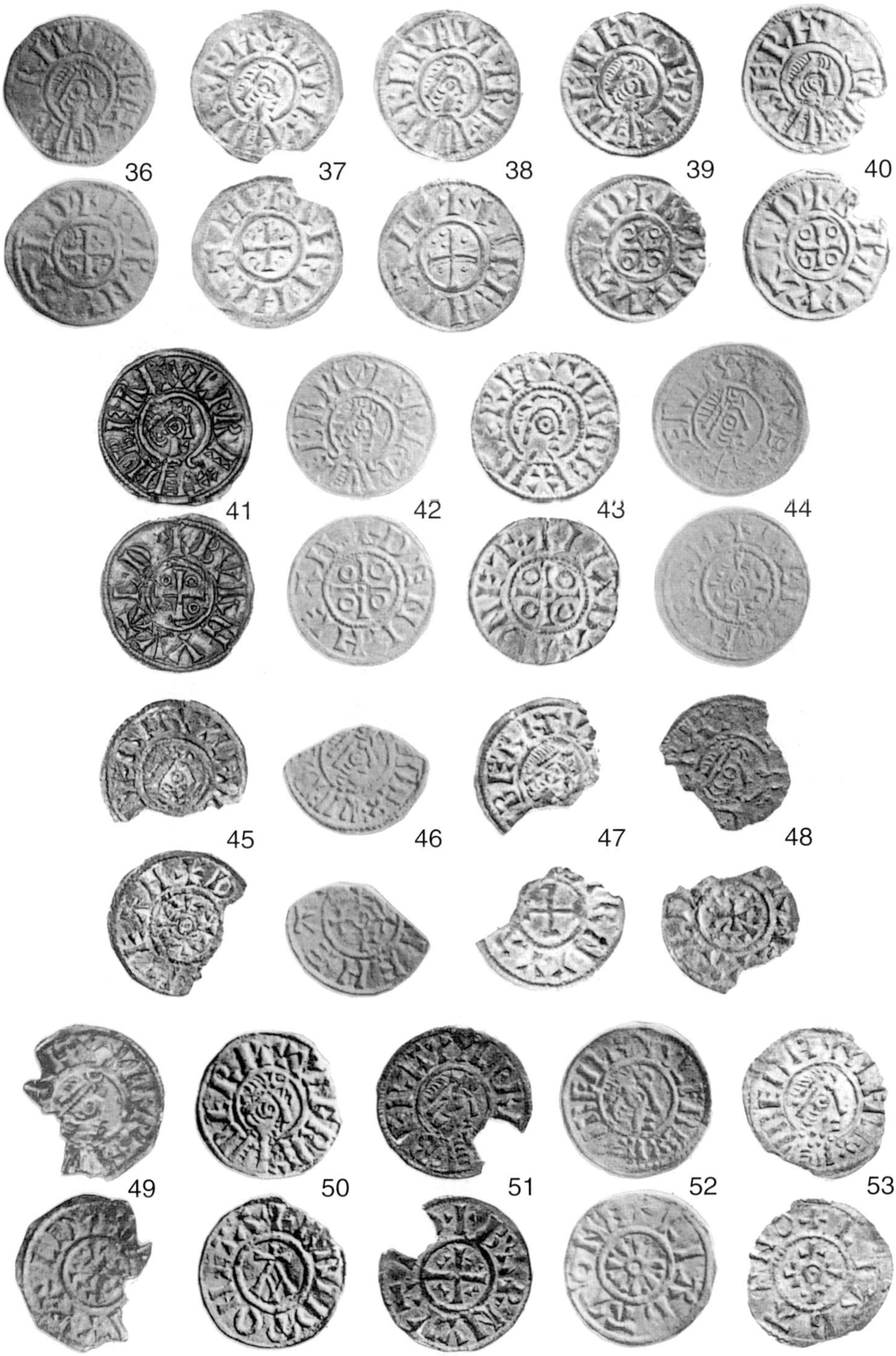

4. Berhtwulf, Group II, Bust C (36–42); Bust D (43); Bust E (44–50); Bust F (51–3)

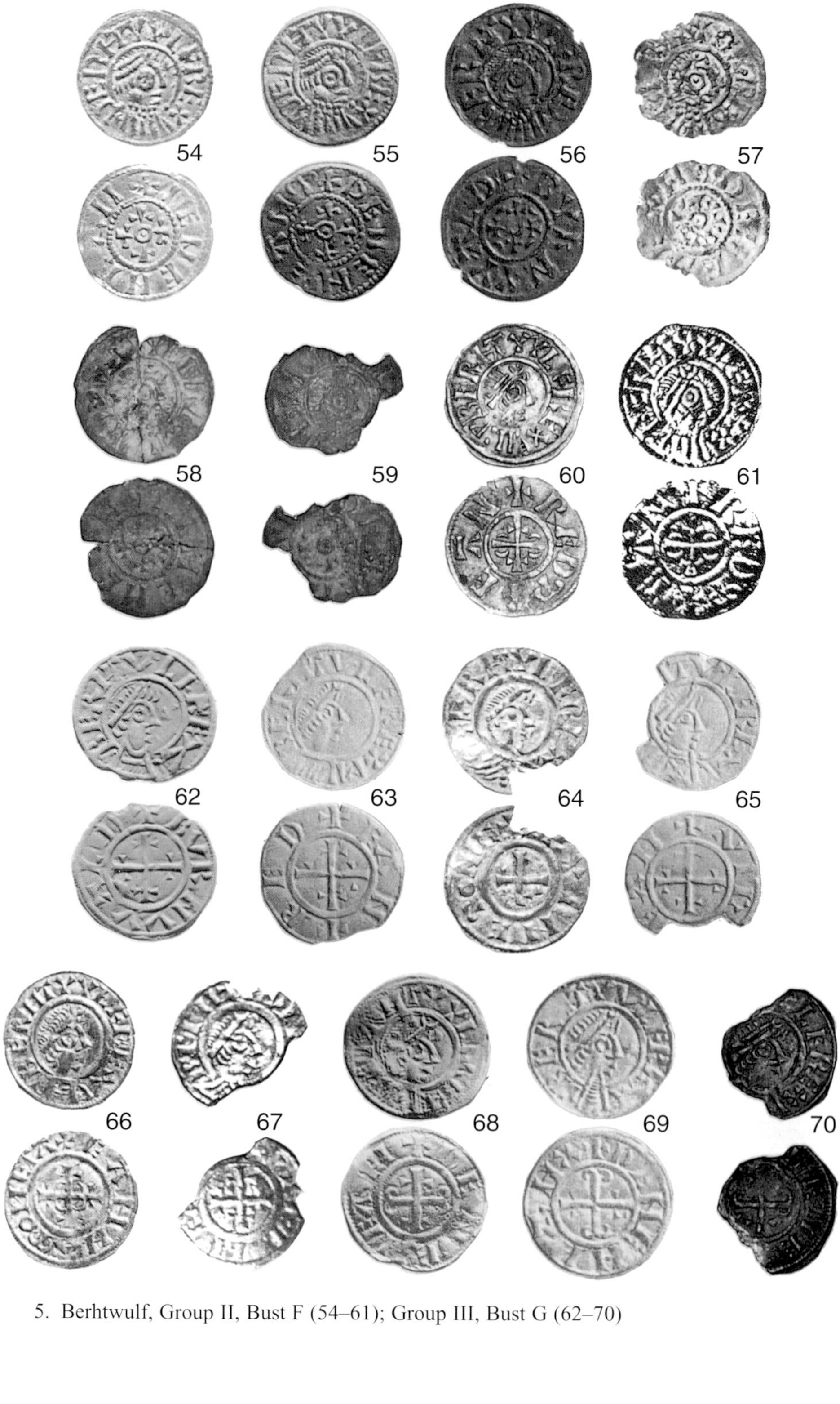

5. Berhtwulf, Group II, Bust F (54–61); Group III, Bust G (62–70)

6. Berhtwulf, Group III, Bust G (71–82); Group IV, Non-Portrait (84–7)

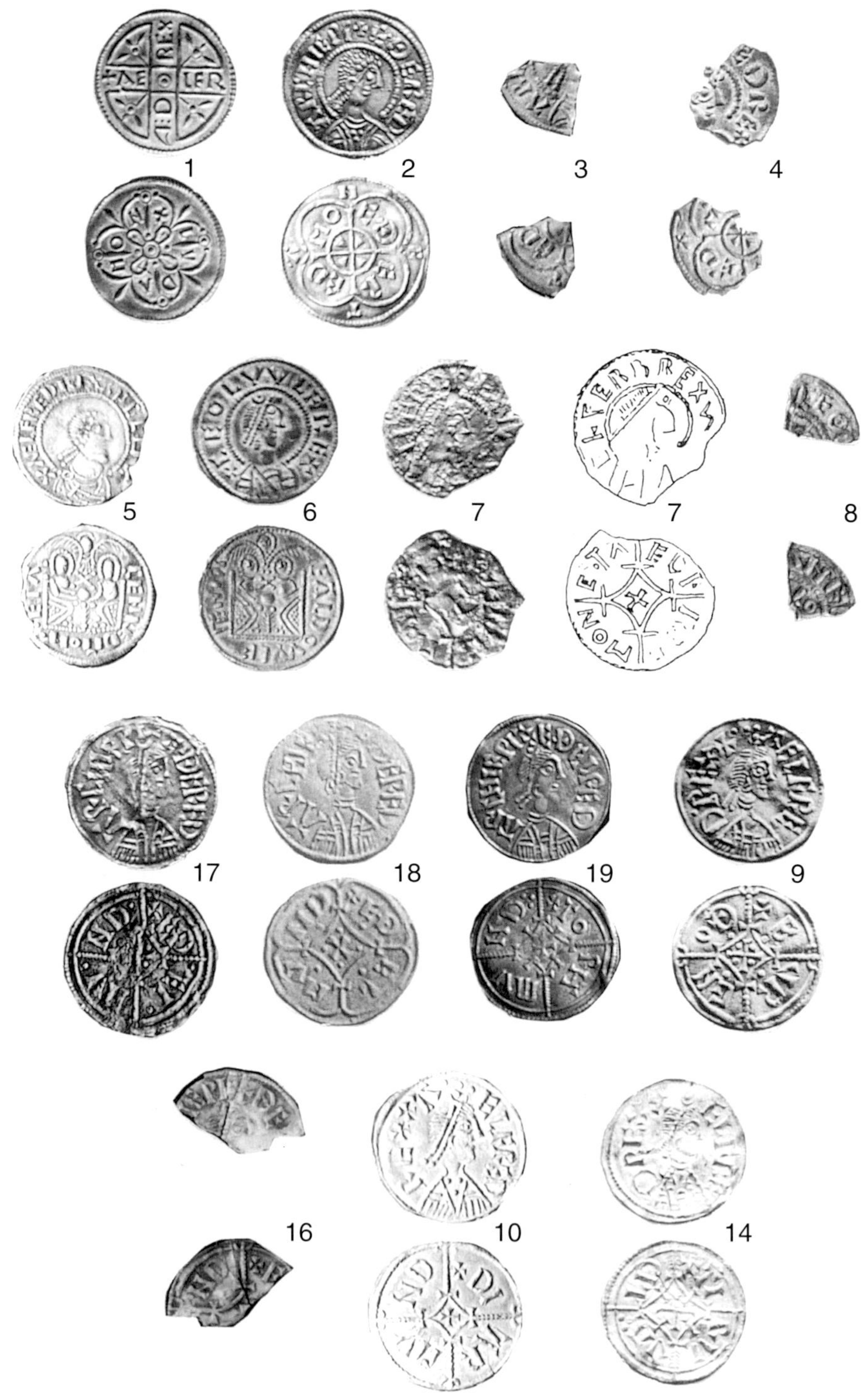

7. Alfred's reign, Minor types (rows 1–2); *Cross-and-Lozenge*, Canterbury A style (rows 3–4)

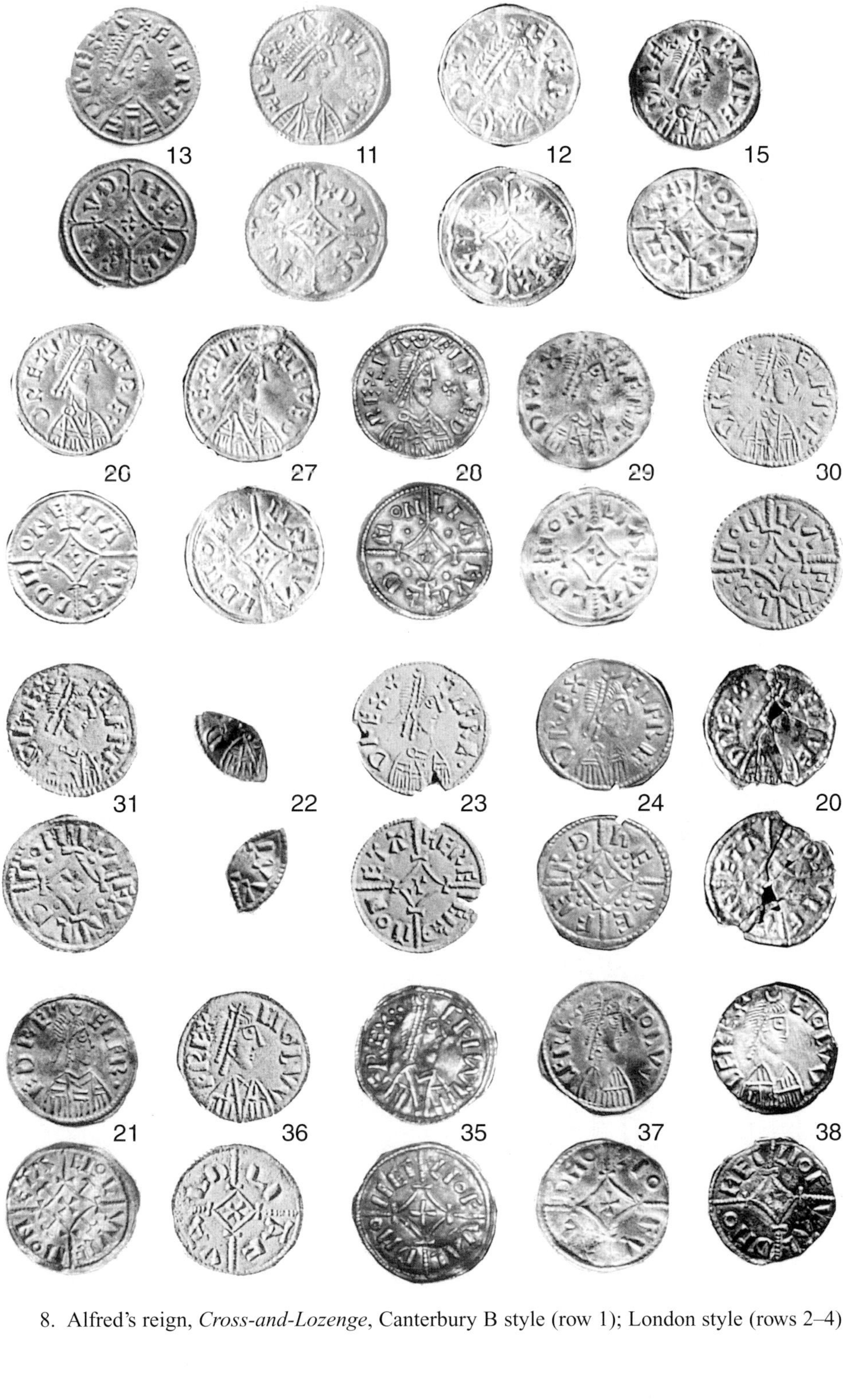

8. Alfred's reign, *Cross-and-Lozenge*, Canterbury B style (row 1); London style (rows 2–4)

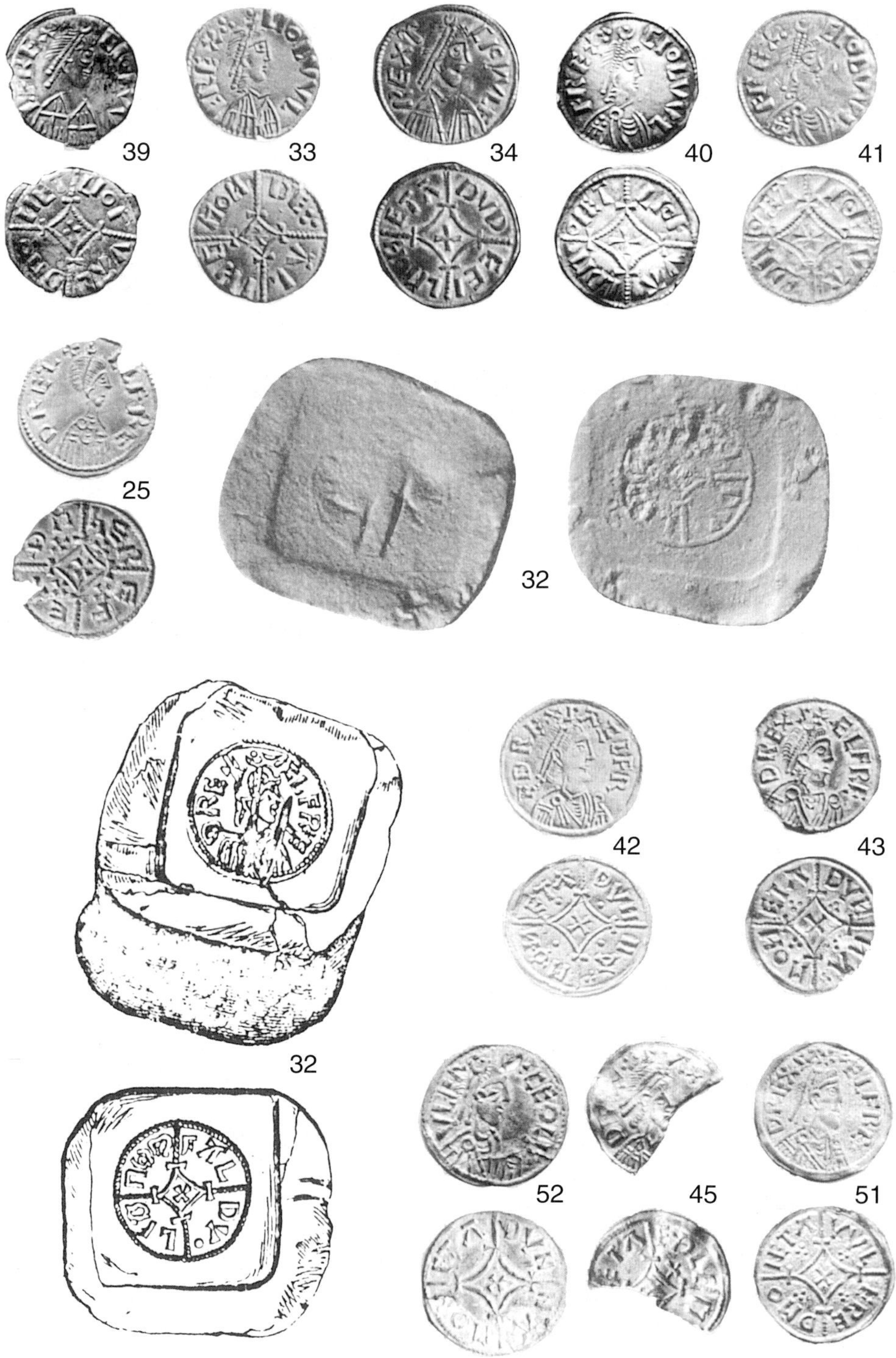

9. Alfred's reign, *Cross-and-Lozenge*, London style (rows 1–2); Winchester style (rows 3–4 right)

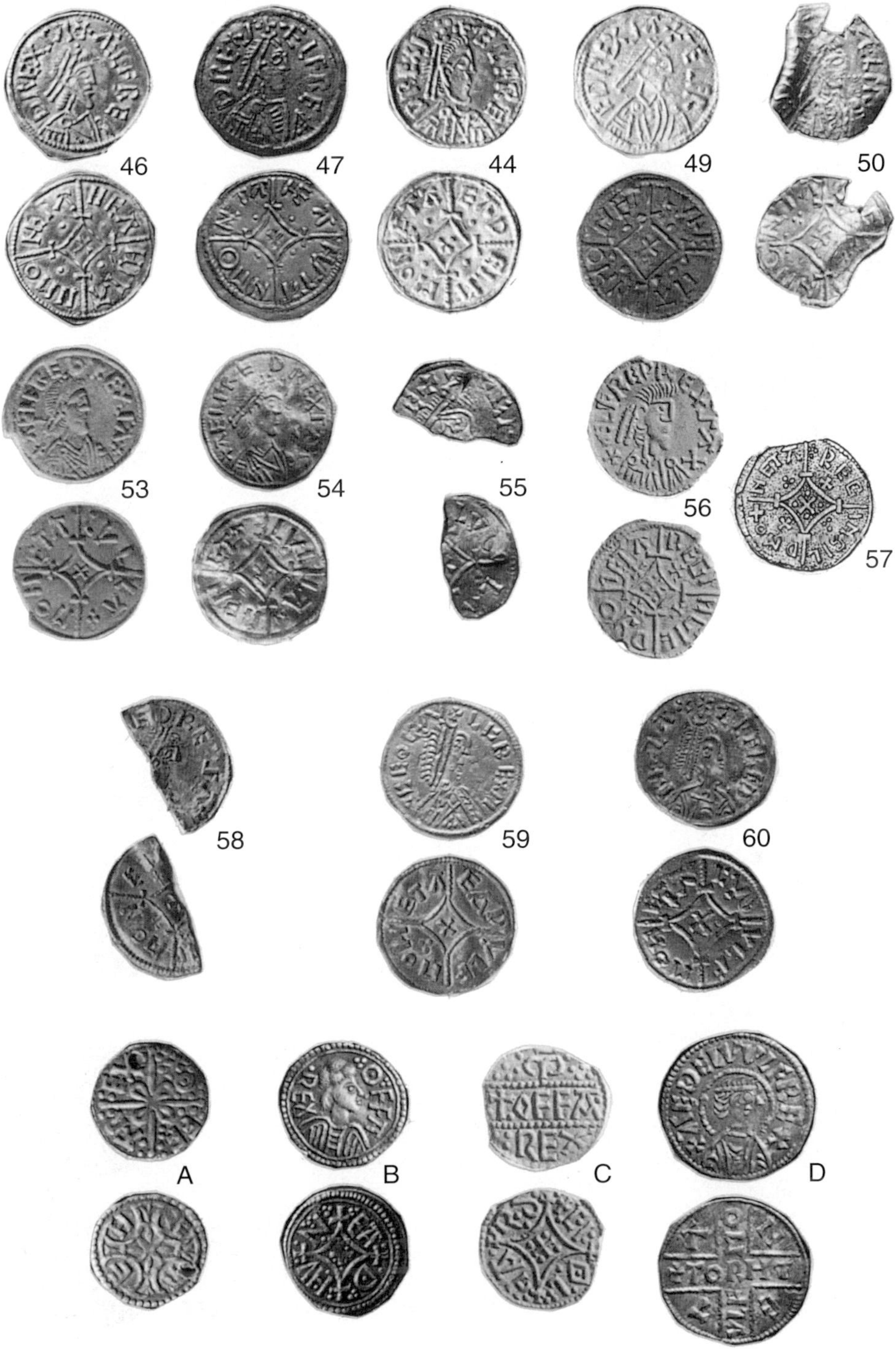

10. Alfred's reign, *Cross-and-Lozenge*, Winchester style (row 1); other styles (rows 2–3); prototypes for issues of Alfred (row 4)

11. Prototypes and other issues of Alfred (see pp. 149–50)

VI

MONEYERS IN THE WRITTEN RECORDS

Lord Stewartby

The number of moneyers in office at the mints of southern England increased dramatically in the middle of the ninth century, and it is natural to ask what kind of men they were. In another context I have suggested that likely identities can be found from the late eighth century to the eleventh between moneyers and persons named in Anglo-Saxon documents.[1] In several cases moneyers appear to be designated as *ministri*, or king's thegns, in written sources, and it therefore seems probable that the office of moneyer was generally held by men of relatively high rank. A systematic correlation of names on coins and in documents could be expected to yield more instances of probable identity, but here are a few to indicate possibilities in the period under review.

A charter between Æthelberht and one of his thegns relating to land in Kent, in 858, was attested by twenty-two witnesses including Dunn, Beagmund and Æthelhere.[2] The names of all these three occur on coins attributable to the mint of Rochester. In 855 King Æthelwulf had granted land near Rochester to Dunn, his *minister*, who bequeathed it to his wife with reversion to Rochester cathedral on her death.[3] Dunn's coins run from the later part of the reign of Coenwulf (796–821), through the reigns of Ceolwulf I (821–3), Baldred (*ca* 823–825), Ecgberht (802–839) and into Æthelwulf's (839–858). Although the earliest occurrence of Dunn as a moneyer and the charters in which the name appears span a period of some forty years or more, his presence as a witness in company with two of Æthelwulf's Rochester moneyers in 858 does suggest a likely identity between a long-serving moneyer and a king's thegn granted property towards the end of his life after many years of royal service.

Badanoth, described as the king's *apparitor*, was granted land near Canterbury by King Æthelwulf in 845 and the will of Badanoth Beotting from about this period also survives.[4] Both may refer to the same man who figures as Badenoth among the moneyers of Æthelberht.

1 Stewart, 'Ministri and monetarii', is based on my lecture to the 1986 International Numismatic Congress; it contains details and references additional to those given here. See also Stewart, 'English numismatics', for a suggested identification of the north-eastern moneyer Macus in the 950s.

2 Sawyer, *Anglo-Saxon Charters* ('S.'), no. 328.

3 S. 315 and 1514.

4 S. 296 and 1510.

One of the witnesses to a grant of land near Canterbury in 859 (?)[5] was called Diar, a name found on Canterbury coins of Æthelwulf.

Dudig, a moneyer in the 890s and in the very earliest phase of Edward the Elder's coinage, may be identified with the Dudig, Alfred's '*fideli ministro*', to whom he granted land in Wiltshire which passed to Malmesbury abbey in 901, having been obtained by Earl Ordlaf from Dudig '*viro venerabili*' in the interim.[6] The last appearance of Dudig in the documents is in a witness list to a charter of King Edward, also relating to land in Wiltshire, and dated 901,[7] just about the time when his career as a moneyer came to an end. Also very early in Edward's reign Dudig shares an obverse die with Buga, a moneyer of Alfred and Edward, and a fellow witness to the charter of 901. Another witness to this grant was Abunel, a rare Germanic name which occurs in similar forms on coins of the 890s in the names of Alfred, Guthrum-Athelstan and St Edmund (struck by the Vikings in Anglia).

The frequent close geographical association or identity of the places where the names of moneyers occur on coins and in documents is exemplified by the cases of Dunn, Beagmund and Æthelhere at Rochester and of Badanoth and Diar at Canterbury. Earlier instances include the name Bobba or Babba as a witness to Kentish charters of the late eighth century[8] and early ninth, and of Babba on coins of the Kentish and Mercian kings of similar period; Oba, a Canterbury moneyer of late Coenwulf to Ecgberht, whose name appears as witness to a charter of Archbishop Wulfred;[9] and Sigestef, a colleague of Oba, who (as Sigesteb) witnessed a Rochester charter of Ecgberht.[10]

From a later period there are five Exeter moneyers of Edward the Confessor (Ælfric, Dodda, Hunewine, Leofwine and Wicking) among witnesses to an agreement about land in Devon in 1046.[11] There was also an earlier moneyer Hunewine, who appears in documents of the late tenth century and of 1033,[12] also relating to land in Devon, and whose coins of Exeter and other mints in Devon and Somerset run from the 980s to the 1020s. Here again the names of several other Exeter moneyers accompany Hunewine's in the witness list to the earlier of the two documents, Cytel, Godwine, Wulfsige and Brun (described as '*preost*').

Some other tenth-century examples (if the identities are valid) suggest a tendency to move between adjacent counties. Byrthelm '*miles*', granted land in Staffordshire by Athelstan,[13] may have been moneyer for the same king at

5 S. 1196.

6 S. 356 and 1205.

7 S. 362; much earlier (871x877) he had witnessed a lease of land near Winchester by bishop Ealhferth, S. 1275.

8 S. 105 (Offa, 764); S. 35–6 (Ecgberht of Kent, 778 and 779); also S. 1264 (Abp Wulfred, 811). The last is presumably too late to be the same as the witness to S. 105, but could be the same Babba as the moneyer of King Eadberht Praen of Kent (796–798) and early Coenwulf.

9 S. 1268 (825x832).

10 S. 271 (823 or 828).

11 S. 1474.

12 S. 1452 (968x993) and 971. Brun is also the moneyer's name on the unique *Hand* penny of Launceston (early 980s).

13 S. 392.

Shrewsbury (Berhtelm) and the unlocated *civitas* of *Weardburh* (Byrhtelm). Maeglsothen, to whom ('*meo homini*') Eadwig granted land in Derbyshire,[14] coined at Chester for Edgar (Maelsuthan); and Elemod, a Chester moneyer of Æthelred II in the 990s, was later granted land by that king also in Derbyshire.[15] A southern case is that of Wihtsige, who received land in Dorset from Eadwig in 956[16] and minted for Edgar and Edward the Martyr at Winchester.

Against this pattern, the Wiltshire focus of the moneyer Dudig stands at first sight in contrast to the view that his coins, like those of Buga, belong to West Mercia. In the tenth century, certainly from the time of Athelstan, Chester and Shrewsbury were the principal mints of this region. But we may recall the existence of a mint-signed coin of Alfred from Gloucester, and it is not certain that minting had extended as far north as Chester, particularly before the Mercian campaigns of Æthelflæd in the 910s. Coinage at Gloucester by moneyers associated with land in Wiltshire would be unsurprising and it is worth considering whether a mint as far to the south as Gloucester could be a candidate for the coinage of Dudig and Buga at the turn of the century.

Abonel, whose coinage comes from the Danish eastern shires, is not a person we would expect to find deep into English Wessex; but men of the status of moneyer must often have travelled about the country by this date, and being witness to a charter, as opposed to a recipient of land like Dunn, Dudig or Hunewine, need not imply more than a single visit. So we do not have to rule out the possible identity of moneyer and witness even in this case. It would be valuable to have more evidence collated against which to measure such an apparent anomaly, particularly in view of the clear tendency for individual witness lists to contain the names of several moneyers.

14 S. 628.
15 S. 923 (1011).
16 S. 632.

VII

MONEYERS' NAMES ON NINTH-CENTURY SOUTHUMBRIAN COINS: PHILOLOGICAL APPROACHES TO SOME HISTORICAL QUESTIONS

Paul Bibire

In the context of this paper, the term 'philology' is used in its narrower sense, that of the history and development of a particular language, as evidenced in specific texts. This definition implies mastery of the texts as such. The evidence is only as good as the questions which can appropriately be asked of it. In dealing with the documentary evidence, for instance, all manuscript forms are by definition unique; it is only with the introduction of printing that mechanical reproduction reduces all copies of a single impression to a single value. By definition a scribe is literate, in the sense that he knows (or purports to know) how to write. Further, he is working in a place where writing-materials are available: parchment and vellum were expensive and required skilled preparation. The Anglo-Saxon scribe therefore normally works within an institution capable of providing writing-materials, normally a monastic scriptorium. He is therefore usually a monk, and will at the least have had a monastic education. A scribe may actually be the author of the text which he writes, or more frequently he may be copying from an exemplar which was possibly written in a different script, dialect or period and with a different set of scribal conventions, and which might itself be a copy of a copy. No scribe will copy exactly. The scribe may not understand what he is writing, either through ignorance (e.g. of Latin) or because of the difficulty of the text (e.g. poetry), the corruption of the text, or mere inattention. If so, he may make mechanical errors of eye and hand; he may mistake one letter-form for another, repeat or omit sections, or substitute familiar-looking forms for the unfamiliar. If he does understand his text, he may well begin to interpret, modify or even re-compose it. The time and place at which a scribe writes will affect him; his training at a given place or period will have taught him specific conventions of spelling and layout. The purpose of a text will affect its content and its copying: a glossary will be written differently from a charter or a Gospel-book; if a scribe is writing poetry, he may well use a variety of vocabulary and linguistic forms which he would not employ in prose. The conventions of manuscript presentation affect the forms which a scribe writes. If he is short of space, time or writing materials, he will abbreviate and compress, but if he is producing a display manuscript, he may well devise layout, ornament and wording to take up extra space. All such questions must be asked of each written document before it can be evaluated as linguistic evidence.

Different circumstantial questions may apply to the die-cutter. Coins are by definition produced by mechanical reproduction from single dies, and therefore multiple examples must each be examined to check whether they are produced from single dies or from separate dies which happen to contain the same forms. For this reason, among others, the raw data are not susceptible of direct statistical evaluation, and no such evaluation is attempted here. The die-cutter is presumably an artisan skilled in fine metalworking, either employed by the moneyer (unless in a small mint he is actually the moneyer himself) or employed at some central workshop supplying dies to different moneyers in different places. He is unlikely therefore to have had the same educational background as the scribe in a monastic scriptorium, and he may also have come from a different social background, and thus may not have been exposed to the same spelling conventions or used language of comparable formality. Informal usage could, for instance, lead to the appearance of less conservative linguistic forms, or of hypocoristic name-forms; these quasi-colloquial name-forms are in their turn less likely to be used of the king than of the moneyer. Coin legends could therefore give access to different strata of language-use, some of which are ill-represented in the documentary evidence. But again many questions, mostly unanswered, must be borne in mind in evaluating this evidence. How, for instance, did the content of the coin legend reach the die-cutter? If spoken, then the die-cutter was himself literate, and could attempt to reproduce the spoken words in letters. The coin legend would therefore be direct evidence of the die-cutter's linguistic competence. But he might have copied from a written (or cut) exemplar. If so, then he need not have been literate, and the language of the coin legend would reflect the language and literacy of the individual who wrote (or cut) the exemplar – the moneyer himself, or perhaps some official for whom the moneyer worked. Further, how will the layout of the coin, with its limited space, have affected the coin legend? The die-cutter may at times have had to abbreviate, use narrow in place of wide letter-forms, or use short forms of names; these short name-forms may well be hypocoristic. Answers to these questions are likely to vary from period to period, moneyer to moneyer, coin to coin, even legend to legend on single coins. There is for instance a marked discrepancy between the treatment of king-names and moneyer-names on individual coins.

Having at least asked, if not answered, these questions about the data, what can be learnt from philological examination of coin legends? First, for the philologist, the coin legends represent probably the last major body of linguistic evidence that has not been adequately incorporated into the general understanding of the history of English.[1] The coins have the very great merit of being fairly closely datable, and they can also frequently be assigned to a given geographic place of

1 W. G. Searle, as both a numismatist and a philologist, drew upon the evidence of moneyers' names in his *Onomasticon* (cf. pp. x–xi). However, the large number of errors, as he saw them, on the coins or in their published transcriptions discouraged subsequent students of onomastics from relying on these until Veronica Smart started working with them in the 1950s. It is largely through Smart's work on the moneyers' names of the tenth and eleventh centuries that this material has become accessible today; cf. Smart, 'Anglo-Saxons, Celts and Germans'; Smart, 'Moneyers of

origin.[2] Thus theoretically they can contribute very extensively to knowledge of areas of the English language, such as the East Anglian dialects, for which there is no documentary evidence whatsoever in the Anglo-Saxon period. Hitherto, the inherent difficulty of the material for scholars trained on documentary texts has discouraged its use. The progress of the *Sylloge* on its monumental course,[3] and in particular Veronica Smart's publication of Indexes to its first forty volumes,[4] give access to the coin-materials in collections other than the British Museum comparable to that of the *British Museum Catalogue*.[5] Anglo-Saxon numismatics is probably now, therefore, mature enough for philologists to be able to use the information which it can give. Scholars wishing to use the coins do not now have to reinvent the wheel: it is possible to rely for the most part on accurate transcriptions of most of the corpus, adequately and accessibly catalogued, analysed and discussed.

Secondly, the philologist can contribute evidence and arguments to debates conducted amongst numismatists or historians. Only rarely can the philologist resolve non-philological problems; philology is to some extent a closed discipline. Philological evidence and arguments can frequently be open to more than one historical interpretation. However, because philological evidence and arguments are inherently distinct from those of numismatics or history, they can be used to help to resolve problems in these disciplines without serious danger of circularity.[6]

Dialects of Old English

Philological method involves the comparison of a given name or word with those recorded in known documents (either originals or safely contemporary copies) more or less accurately dated and dialectally placed, and considered in the context of an overall understanding of the development of the Old English dialects. Many English dialects are not represented in surviving Old English sources at all, but they can to some extent be reconstructed by working backwards from Middle English documentary evidence, and from place-names, as well as working forwards from the common source of Old English. In the ninth century, there is direct and more or less datable documentation of Kentish, in a sequence of some ten vernacular charters (Sweet[7] nos 34, 37–42, and endorsements on 28, 30 and

the Late Anglo-Saxon Coinage: 973–1016'; Smart, 'Moneyers of the Late Anglo-Saxon Coinage: the Danish dynasty 1017–42'.

2 For a survey of the ninth-century English coinage, see Grierson and Blackburn, *Medieval European Coinage* 1, pp. 282–316. For a summary of the coin issues with their currently accepted mint-attributions, see North, *English Hammered Coinage*, vol. 1.

3 *Sylloge of Coins of the British Isles* 1–48 (London or Oxford, 1958–97).

4 Smart, *Cumulative Index of Volumes 1–20* (SCBI 27) and Smart, *Cumulative Index of Volumes 21–40* (SCBI 41). The latter was published after completion of this paper and account has not been taken of it.

5 Keary and Grueber, *A Catalogue*.

6 For example, in the 1890s Searle suggested that the dialectic form of the moneyers' names might serve as a means of distinguishing coins of West Saxon kings struck in Wessex from those struck at Kentish mints, although he did not pursue this line of research (*Onomasticon*, pp. x–xi).

7 Sweet, *The Oldest English Texts*.

44), each dated fairly precisely on internal evidence within the period 805–868 and all associated with Christ Church Canterbury. Also from the beginning of the ninth century there is one substantial text in a West Midland dialect, the gloss to the Vespasian Psalter (London, British Library, MS Cotton Vespasian A.i). This, although written in a manuscript with (apparently) exclusive Canterbury associations in a hand which is very similar to those of the early Kentish charters, appears to represent a dialect of Worcestershire or Herefordshire with great regularity and purity. On Old English grounds this dialect can be shown to be Mercian, with no apparent Kentish or West Saxon admixture; Middle English evidence enables its closer localisation. The Vespasian Psalter gloss is dated to approximately the first third of the ninth century on palaeographic and philological grounds, which are in agreement. The dialect of Surrey may appear in one charter (Sweet no. 45) dated 871x889 and the Codex Aureus inscription, but both these documents have strong Canterbury associations. Middle English and place-name evidence show that some specific features of Kentish extended west and north well beyond the present county boundaries. At the end of the ninth century, early West Saxon is represented in a number of Alfredian manuscripts, such as that written by the first hand of the Parker Chronicle (up to 891, and probably therefore written *ca* 892). Earlier West Saxon manuscripts are not written in that dialect. Other Old English dialects are not attested in the documentary evidence of the ninth century. However, Northumbrian is well represented in the eighth and tenth centuries; Kentish and Mercian are also represented, though not well, in the tenth century; and of course late West Saxon becomes largely universal throughout England in the tenth and eleventh centuries. The dialects of London, Essex, the East Midlands and East Anglia are not, as far as is known, documented in Old English at all, but are well represented in Middle English.

The documentary points of reference mentioned above reveal a number of diagnostic features in the ways in which the phonological structures of the different dialects are represented in writing during the Old English period. In the following discussion, forms which contain these diagnostic features are discussed in the alphabetic order in which they occur in the material for each reign. Forms which do not contain diagnostic features are disregarded, as are those which are ambiguous, unintelligible, or corrupt. Coin legends are given in CAPITALS, usual manuscript forms (employed as the basis for linguistic forms) are normally given in *italics*, and where a distinction between spelling representations and linguistic forms is useful, the graphs are given between angle brackets < >, while approximate phonetic reconstructions are given between square brackets [ ].

The coin legends used for the present study are those of the period *ca* 840–900 listed in the *Sylloge* vols 1–20, and in the *British Museum Catalogue* (taking account of subsequent reattributions).[8] King-names are drawn mainly from the *British Museum Catalogue*. Inscriptions that occur on Anglo-Scandinavian imitations of Alfred's coinage or on other contemporary copies have been ignored. It

8 I am more than grateful to Mark Blackburn for guiding me on the reliability of published attributions and in particular on the identification of Anglo-Scandinavian imitations of Alfred's coins. He has also helped me in drafting the conclusions, which seek to compare the dialectal evidence with current numismatic opinion.

should be stressed that this is a preliminary survey and is not based on a comprehensive corpus of ninth-century coin legends.

The Mercian kings

The coinage of the three Mercian kings minted in the period *ca* 840–879 – Berhtwulf, Burgred and Ceolwulf II – contains very few Anglian (Mercian and Northumbrian) linguistic features.

In the case of Berhtwulf (840–852), the king-name is spelled universally BERHTVLF or BERHTVVLF, with Anglian Smoothing of all diphthongs before *h* [χ] (i.e. monophthongisation, normally to the first element of the original diphthong), e.g. *eo* > *e*. But the moneyer-names never show Smoothing, e.g. DENEHEAH, EAHHA, SIGEHEAH. This indicates that the forms of the king-name and moneyer-names are in these instances derived from different dialects. One of the moneyer-names appears to show Anglian *a* instead of Southern (Kentish and West Saxon) *ea* before *l*+C,[9] BVRNV(V)ALD, but such forms are common in all dialects under low accent, as here in the second element of a compounded name. For the same reason, the second element of EANRED (containing an OE *ǣ*^{1}) need not be dialectally significant, since it may simply show reduction under low stress, instead of showing nWS *ē* contrasting with WS *ǣ*. No other possible Anglianisms appear in Berhtwulf's coinage.[10]

The form LIABA is decisively and distinctively Kentish, since all other dialects have *Lēofa*. Raising of the first elements of diphthongs and unrounding of their second elements eventually causes all long diphthongs to coalesce in Kentish as *īa*; the development also appears in short diphthongs. Other dialects lack the raising of first elements (other than in fairly rare back spellings due to coalescence elsewhere of *io* and *eo* as *eo*) and unrounding of second elements is sporadic. Instances of ordinary OE <ea> as Kentish <ia> are not safely attested until Middle English in the documentary evidence, but the spelling <ia> for <eo> is common in the Old English period. This development appears frequently but irregularly in the ninth-century Kentish charters (e.g. *biarn-*, Sweet no. 38; *agiaban*, *bebiade*, Sweet no. 39), but *eo*, *io* remain the normal forms in these charters. The <ia> form is universal in the moneyer-name. The <b>-spelling in LIABA for a voiced intervocalic fricative [ƀ] or [v], may also be significant. The spelling <b> for later universal <f> appears in very early texts, where an <f>:<b> contrast seems to be represented: *b* is used there for the sound derived from IE *bh* by Grimm's Law, or from IE *p* by Grimm's Law and Verner's Law; *f* is used for the sound derived from IE *p* when voiced between voiced sounds (*OEG*, para. 444).[11] Later, <b>-spellings appear only, fairly frequently, in the ninth-century Kentish charters, and occasionally in the Northumbrian *Liber Vitae Dunelmensis* (first half of ninth century, but probably preserving earlier name-forms); they are virtually completely absent elsewhere. They are universal in the moneyer-name. If this name actually represents the OE name *Lēofa*, and is not for instance

9 I.e. before *l* and a consonant as in *-weald*.

10 [Numismatists attribute Berhtwulf's coinage to the London mint. MASB]

11 Campbell, *Old English Grammar*.

a hypocoristic form of a name-form such as *Lēofbeald*, the *b*-spelling indicates that the form is probably Kentish. Cf. also LIABING, LIAFMAN, LIAFVALD / LIOFVALD.

In the coinage of Burgred (852–874) the number of forms is far greater, but the dialectal implications are almost identical.[12] The king-name invariably appears in the form BVRGRED, indicating that centralised standardisation has probably taken place (possible spelling variants could be e.g. <BURH-> or less probably <-RÆD>, beside more random forms). For the second element, cf. EANRED above. It contains no dialectally significant features. The moneyer-names do not show Smoothing before *h* [χ] or *g* [ʒ], e.g. BEAGSTAN, BERHEAH, EÐELHEAH, except in the second element of CVÐBERHT (one example only). Raising of first elements of diphthongs and unrounding of second elements appear variously in BIORHOÐ, CIALLAF, DIARVLF etc., LIAFMAN, LIAFVALD, though the diphthong *ea* is not yet affected by this change, e.g. BEAGSTAN, BEARHEAH, DEAL- etc., EADNOÐ, EADVLF, EANRED, HEAVVLF, VVLFEARD etc. Southern unrounding of long *ōē*, preserved intact in the Anglian dialects, to *ē*, appears in CENRED. OE *a/o*+N, which appears generally as *o* in Anglian dialects of the ninth century onwards, and is universally so in the Vespasian Psalter, appears as *a* in FRAMRIC. The name-element EÐEL- (in EÐELHEAH, EÐELLAF, EÐELVLF etc.) is particularly interesting. The normal OE form of this is *æðel-* 'noble', PrGer **aþuli(-)*; a cognate word Anglian *ōēðel* / Southern *ēðel* 'homeland' also occurs as a personal name-element. Only in two OE dialects could *æðel-* appear as *eðel-*: Kentish and Vespasian Psalter. In Kentish, all front vowels, long and short, other than *i* (i.e. long and short *e*, *oe*, *æ*, *y*, in approximately that chronological order) eventually coalesce as *e*. In the Vespasian Psalter dialect, by a sound change called Second Fronting, accented short *æ* > *e*, and short *a* > *æ* (sometimes later > *ea*), but all long vowels, and both long and short *oe* and *y* remain stable (cf. the discussion of CENRED above). The form EÐEL-, if, more probably, it is *æðel-* 'noble', could therefore be either Kentish or the particular variety of Mercian attested in the Vespasian Psalter; if it is *ēðel* 'homeland', it is Southern (Kentish/West Saxon), not Anglian. It is universal in these moneyer-names.

There are thus no forms amongst Burgred's moneyer-names which could not be Kentish, and several which must be Kentish; there are no forms which are unambiguously Mercian or generally Anglian.

The name GVÐHERE merits special mention. The name-element GUÐ- is listed in the Index to the *Sylloge* as of Norse origin.[13] If so, it might be rather striking to find an individual bearing a Norse name striking coins for Burgred. However, the Index to the *Sylloge* was not, of course, the proper place for a philological discussion of this element, which may represent several different words from both OE and ON. These are: firstly, OE *gūð* 'battle' (cognate with Frankish *gund-*, *gunt-*, cf. GVNTERE; ON *gunnr/guðr*); secondly, ON *gunnr*, which in its nom. sg. form only has a bye-form *guðr* (with a change of *nn* > *ð* before *r*); thirdly, ON *guð/goð* 'god' (cognate with OE *God*); fourthly, possibly even ON *góðr* 'good' (cognate with OE *gōd*) could contribute to the name-stock. In the case of GVÐHERE, the ancient heroic name, appearing in German as Gunter and Norse as Gunnarr,

12 [Burgred's coinage is also attributed almost exclusively to London. MASB]

13 Smart, *Cumulative Index of Volumes 1–20*, p. 44.

appears in English here as elsewhere in its phonologically regular form, *Gūðhere* 'battle-harrier'. Problems arise in the case of the Viking kings Guthrum and Guthfrith. The latter probably represents ON *Goðfrøðr*, *Guðrøðr*, roughly meaning 'one at peace with the god(s)', but may well have been Anglicised to *Gūðfrið*, 'war-peace, quarter given in war'. The name which appears in OE as *Godrum* or *Guðrum*[14] is probably related to ON *Guðþormr*, *Gormr*, itself probably **Goð-þorm-* 'divinely spared one', in which case the first element of *Godrum* has been correctly anglicised, and the second wholly misunderstood and re-structured, since no cognate of the **þurm*-root existed in English.

The coinage of Ceolwulf II (874–879) contains only two diagnostic forms: LIAFVALD beside LIOFVALD. The former shows Kentish raising of the first element of the diphthong *ēo* and unrounding of the second; the second form merely the Kentish raising without unrounding. The king's name takes two forms, CEOLVVLF and CIOLVVLF, the latter preserving the high first element of OE *īo*, which does not need to be Kentish.

The earlier West Saxon kings

The coinage of the earlier West Saxon kings, Æthelwulf (839–858), Æthelberht (858–865/6), and Æthelred I (865/6–871), can be taken together.

The coinage of Æthelwulf shows two forms of the king-name, AEÐELVVLF and EÐELVVLF, the latter slightly preponderant, with very little other variation (cf. the discussion of EÐEL- above). His moneyer-names do not generally show Anglian Smoothing, e.g. BEAGMVND etc., DEGBEARHT, DEIHEAH etc., HVNBEARHT etc., VVILHEAH etc. (beside one instance of VVILHEH, possibly showing reduction under low accent). Southern *ĕa* (Anglian *ă*) before *l*+C appears in EALGMVND etc., HEREBEALD, WEALHHEARD (but cf. EANWALD, TIRVALD, TORHTWALD in second elements). Kentish raising and unrounding in diphthongs appear in BIARNNOÐ etc., DEGBEARHT, DIAR, LIABA (beside one instance of LIVBA, possibly with an inverted A, or possibly an extreme archaism or a back-spelling). Normal OE short *æ* appears universally as *e*, e.g. DEGBEARHT, DEIHEAH etc., EÐELGEARD etc., EÐELHERE etc., EÐELMOD, EÐELNOÐ etc., and possibly in NEBECA (for HEBECA); no instances appear as *æ*. OE *a/o*+N appears as *a* in MANINC, MANNA; no instances appear as *o*. OE *ǣ*[1] appears as *ē* (i.e. nWS) in VERMVND, and also in all instances of -RED as second element, where it can also be explained as due to reduction under low accent.

The moneyer-names on Æthelwulf's coinage thus contain no forms which are specifically West Saxon, and no forms which are unambiguously Anglian, and a considerable number which can only be Kentish; the forms of the king-name show a slight preponderance of probably Kentish EÐEL- forms, but a large proportion of non-Kentish AEÐEL- forms also. In this context it is striking that coins struck for Æthelwulf by BIARNNOÐ, BRID, DEIHEAH etc., DIAR, EALGMVND, EANMVND, EÐELERD, HVNBEARHT etc., MANINC, NEBECA (for HEBECA), WEALHHEARD, VVILHEAH etc., show Canterbury mint-signatures.[15]

14 Björkman, *Nordische Personennamen*, pp. 48–9.

15 [All but one of Æthelwulf's moneyers have been identified by numismatists as working at the

The coinage of Æthelberht presents a similar picture. The king-name is almost invariably AEĐELBEARHT. This is a curious form, for it shows neither Anglian Smoothing in its second element, nor Kentish EĐEL- as its first; however, the diphthong in -BEARHT invariably shows Kentish unrounding of its second element, though never raising of its first element. It must be seen as a bastard form, therefore: neither Kentish nor West Saxon, but either a Kentish attempt to represent West Saxon or a West Saxon attempt to represent Kentish. Its invariability also suggests some degree of centralised administration, which prescribed a standardised form of the name.

The moneyer-names show retention of OE short *ă* in BADEMVND, BADENOĐ (cf. Vespasian Psalter Second Fronting in *beadu-*). They do not show Anglian Smoothing in BEAGMVND, DEGBEARHT, HEABEARHT, HVNBEARHT, OSBEARHT, VVNBEARHT, but cf. VIHTMVND (the form *wiht* appears as such in all dialects; it is a fem. *i*-stem, and this word may show failure of Breaking / *i*-mutation of a Broken diphthong ĭo > *i* in all dialects, cf. *OEG* paras 154,3, 201,1, but contrast para. 201,2; alternatively eWS, Kt *wiht* is explained *OEG* paras 304–6 as due to Palatal Mutation). They show Kentish raising and unrounding in diphthongs, e.g. BIARNMOD, BIARNVINE, DIARMOD, HEABEARHT, LIABINC, VVNBEARHT. They generally show Southern *ea* (for Anglian *a*) before *l*+C, e.g. CENVEALD, DEALLA, EALDRED, EĐELVEALD, HEREBEALD (but cf. BVRNVALD, one example in a second element). They show unrounding of Anglian *ōē* to Southern *ē* in CENRED, CENVEALD (first element). Kentish or Vespasian Psalter *e* for *æ* appears in DEGBEARHT, DEGLAF, EĐELGEARD, EĐELHERE, EĐELNOĐ, EĐELRED, EĐELVEALD, EĐELVLF. Kentish *b* for medial voiced *f* appears in LIABINC. OE *a/o*+N appears invariably as *a*, e.g. LVCEMAN, MANINC, VLANCEARD. OE long *ǣ*² may appear as *ē* in SEFRED (one example, if the first element is *sǣ* 'sea'): this sound-change is regular only in Kentish, though sporadic examples appear in Anglian, mostly before alveolars, which is not of course the case here. Among the moneyers' names on Æthelberht's coinage, therefore, no forms occur which cannot be Kentish, and there are many which must be.[16]

The coinage of Æthelred I again presents a similar picture. The king-name usually has the form AEĐELRED, though a few examples appear with EĐEL-. The moneyer-names show Kentish raising and unrounding in diphthongs, e.g. BIARNEAH etc. (beside BEORNNAE, one example), BIARNMOD, DIARVLF, LIABINC. Southern *ea* (Anglian *a*) before *l*+C appears in DEALLA, HEREBEALD (but cf. DENEVALD, one example in a second element). Kentish or Vespasian Psalter *e* for *a* appears in EĐELRED, ELBERE. Kentish *b* for intervocalic *f* appears in ELBERE, LIABINC. Anglian Smoothing does not appear in HEAHMOD. OE *a/o*+N appears invariably as a in MANN etc., MANNINC. Again, no moneyer-name presents forms which cannot be Kentish, and many must belong to that dialect.

Kentish mints of Canterbury or Rochester. Only a single coin of this reign is known from the West Saxon mint at Winchester or Southampton, and that, by the moneyer Eanwald, has the non-Kentish AEĐEL- form of the king's name. MASB]

16 [All the moneyers of Æthelberht and Æthelred I are attributed by numismatists to the Kentish mint(s) of Canterbury, and possibly Rochester. MASB]

The archbishops of Canterbury

As might be expected, the coinage of the archbishops of Canterbury during this period – Ceolnoth (833–870), Æthelred (870–889) and Plegmund (890–923) – show consistently Kentish forms.

Ceolnoth's name, surprisingly, normally appears in the form CEOLNOĐ, but instances with Kentish raising and unrounding of the diphthong are well attested: CEALNOĐ etc., CIALNOĐ, CIALNOĐ (beside two instances of CIVLNOĐ, possibly with inverted A, or an extreme archaism, or a back-spelling). Interestingly, the Kentish forms of the name occur mainly in his earliest coinage, and after *ca* 850 the standard form becomes CEOLNOĐ – another example of standardization of the obverse inscription. In contrast, a number of the moneyers' names on the coins from later in his archiepiscopate show Kentish raising and unrounding in diphthongs, e.g. BIARNRED, BIARNVLF, HEREBEARHT (but cf. BIORNMOD etc., with raising but never unrounding), LIABINCG. The case of DIALA is particularly important and interesting, because it shows raising of the first element of *ea*, not attested in the documentary evidence until the Middle English period. Southern *ea* (Anglian *a*) before *l*+C appears in DIALA (for *Dealla*), but not in second elements in CENVALD, EĐELVALD. Unrounding of Anglian $\bar{oe}$ to Southern $\bar{e}$ appears in CENVALD. Kentish or Vespasian Psalter *e* for *æ* appears in EĐELVALD, probably HEBECA. Kentish *b* for intervocalic *f* appears in HEBECA, LIABINCG, SVEBHEARD etc. (beside SVEFHEARD, one example).

Of Archbishop Æthelred's coinage, only the form EĐERED is significant, showing Kentish or Vespasian Psalter *e* for *æ*.

Archbishop Plegmund's coinage (excluding imitations) again shows mostly Kentish forms, as one would expect. Kentish or Vespasian Psalter *e* for *æ* appears in EĐELSTAN, EĐELVLF, ELFSTAN, but cf. ÆĐELVLF (one example). Southern *ea* (Anglian *a*) before *l*+C appears in TIDVEALD (two examples, but also two examples of TIDVALD, both of course in a second element).

King Alfred

The coinage of King Alfred (871–899) presents a far more complex linguistic picture than those hitherto discussed. First, many of Alfred's coins were imitated at Danelaw mints, although an attempt has been made to exclude such imitations from the present study. Secondly, the presentation of name-forms is far more variable, sometimes to the point of being unrecognisable. This would seem to imply, among other things, a lack of centralised linguistic standardisation, but it may be due in part to the presence of Danelaw imitations. Thirdly, a number of new mints were opened and mint-signatures become more frequent, making it possible to localise linguistic features more precisely. Fourthly, for the first time in the coinage under discussion, moneyers with non-English names appear, e.g. Samson, Simun, Stefanus (?), Varolf, but of these all except Samson are attributed to mints in the Danelaw.

Forms of the king-name vary between AELBRED (with Kentish *b* for *f*, but without Kentish *e* for *æ*), AELFRED, ÆLFRED, ELFRED; *æ* and *e* forms seem to occur in more or less equivalent numbers. AELBRED is probably best interpreted as a bastard form between Kentish and the normal form Ælfred (with Anglian *æ*, see ELDA, ELFVALD below; cf. the discussion of AEÐELBEARHT above), though it could indicate that *b* was used more widely than other Kentish features. Other spelling variations seem random.[17]

Among the moneyers' names, Kentish or Vespasian Psalter *e* for *æ* appears in EÐELVLF (beside AÐELVLF), DEIGMVND (with king-name AELBRED), EÐELSTAN (one example with Canterbury mint-signature; beside ÆÐELSTAN), EÐELVINE etc., EÐELVLF, EÐERED (beside ÆÐERED), ELFVALD (beside ÆLFVALD etc.), probably HEBECA; also, in a second element, SIGESTEF etc. AELFSTAN only occurs with *æ*. Southern *ea* (Anglian *a*) before *l*+C appears in DEALINC etc., DEALLA, EALDVVLF, beside HALDBERE (one example); second elements almost invariably have *a*, e.g. ÆLFVALD etc., BVRNVALD etc., DIARVALD etc. (Canterbury mint-signature), EADVALD etc. (beside EADVEALD one example), ELFVALD, LIAFVALD, TIRVALD (Canterbury mint-signature), etc. Anglian Smoothing is often absent, e.g. BEAGSTAN (beside one example of BEGSTAN), BEORHMÆRN etc., BIORHRED, HEAVVLF etc. (for Heah-wulf), HEAHSTAN, but BERHTERE, CVÐBERHT etc., ECBERH, HVNBERHT, VVNBERHT etc. only appear with Smoothing. Kentish raising and unrounding in diphthongs appear in BIARNRED, BIARNVLD, CIALVLF (beside CIOLVVLF, one example each), DIARVALD (Canterbury mint-signature), LIABING, LIAFVALD; but raising only appears in BIORHRED etc. In ELDA (Danelaw), ELFVALD and the king-name ELFRED, there appears the nWS *i*-mutation of the Southern diphthong which when unmutated appears as *ea* before *l*+C: these forms are at this period therefore exclusively Kentish; the name-form ÆLFRED in fact shows *i*-mutation of Anglian *a*, and is therefore itself Anglian, not West Saxon! Kentish *b* for *f* appears probably in HEBECA, certainly in LIABING (beside LIAFVALD), but *f* is universal in all moneyer-names in ÆLF-, ELF-, VVLFRED etc. OE *a/o*+N appears as *a* in MANNINC. OE long $\bar{æ}^2$ appears as $\bar{æ}$ in SÆFREÐ but as Kentish $\bar{e}$ in SEFRED (one example each).

The moneyers' names of Alfred's coinage therefore show a considerable mixture of Anglian, Kentish and undifferentiated forms. The only dialects not unambiguously represented in these names are West Saxon and Northumbrian!

A slightly clearer picture emerges when the coins with mint-signatures are examined by mint. There is a fairly large number of blundered Canterbury coins, but of legible moneyer-names, DIARVALD shows Kentish raising and unrounding, EÐELSTAN, EÐELVINE, EÐERED, ELFSTAN all show Kentish or Vespasian Psalter *e* for *æ* (beside no examples of *æ*); forms of the king-name as ELFRED are dominant (ten examples, beside two as AELFRED).

In contrast, TILEVINE, the moneyer named on coins from London, shows no certain Kentish feature, and the king's name on the London Monogram issue mostly has forms with Anglian *æ* (twenty examples, beside six with *e*). The two Winchester examples also have *æ* in the king's name.

On this basis it is reasonable to assume that the non-Kenticisms in Alfred's coinage, even where the coins lack mint-signatures, are to be attributed to mints outside Kent.

17 [In the first phase of Alfred's coinage (*ca* 871–875) Canterbury was the principal mint, but thereafter coins were also struck at London and elsewhere in Wessex and English Mercia. MASB]

The East Anglian kings

The East Anglian kings represented in the coinage are Æthelstan I (*ca* 825–*ca* 845), Æthelweard (*ca* 845–855), Edmund (855–869), and the Viking Guthrum /Æthelstan II (880–890). Shadowy figures such as Oswald (*ca* 870) are disregarded.[18]

On Æthelstan I's coinage, the king-name appears mostly with Kentish or Vespasian Psalter *e* for *æ* (twelve instances, beside one form AEÐILSTAH). One moneyer-name appears with the *e*-form: EÐILHELM. OE *a/o*+N appears exclusively as *o* in MONN etc. (some ten examples).

Under Æthelweard, the king-name appears with both *æ* (five examples), and with *e* (seven examples). Among the moneyers' names, AEÐELHELM and RAEgENHEBE (for Rægenhere, with runic *g*) occur only with *æ*. No other diagnostic features appear.

On Edmund's coinage, the king-name is virtually always EADMVND, with very little spelling variation. OE *æ* appears in AEÐELHELM etc., but as *e* in EÐELHELM and EÐELWULF etc. Anglian Smoothing may appear in BAELHELM, BELHELM (if these are for Bæghelm), BEORNHAEH, and EADBERHT. Anglian *a* before *l*+C may appear in EADWALD etc. (but this is of course in a second element).

The coinage of the Viking king Guthrum, who used his baptismal name Æthelstan, strikingly contains a number of non-English moneyer-names, e.g. GVNTERE (an Upper Frankish or High German form), probably ABENEL, probably ENODAS, and probably IVDELBERD. The king-name is standardised to a curious form EDELIA (perhaps produced by illiterate corruption of EDELTAN, with omission of the final *-n* to reduce the name to six letters as required by the design, and then omission of the bar of the top of the T, due to confusion with forms of A with a cross-bar at the top), beside a few instances of EDELSTAN, EDELTAN. These king-name forms at least all show Kentish or Vespasian Psalter *e* for *æ*. Anglian Smoothing appears in BERTER (if for Berhthere); Kentish e for the i-mutation of Southern *ea* (Anglian *a*) before *l*+C appears in ELDA. Kentish raising and unrounding of diphthongs is not visible in CIOLVVLF (which has original *īo*).

The East Anglian coins therefore show no certain Kentish forms, other than irregularly but frequently *e* for *æ*. However, the sample is too small, and too few diagnostic features appear, for any certain conclusions to be reached about them.

Conclusions

This paper has sought to present an overview of the evidence of the kings' and moneyers' names on the coinage of the period *ca* 840–900 and to show some of the lines of inquiry that could usefully be pursued. Before a comprehensive analysis can be undertaken it will be necessary to establish a full listing of the variant name forms on the coins, ensuring that it is not confused by the inclusion of names drawn from Viking imitations or contemporary forgeries. Already certain trends are apparent from a purely philological analysis. For the purposes of

18 [The coins of the East Anglian kings were all struck at a mint or mints in East Anglia, but some of those of Guthrum may have been produced in the East Midlands or Five Boroughs. MASB]

this paper I have quite intentionally avoided relying upon the numismatic attributions of various coin series to particular mints, so that the philological and numismatic arguments should not be seen as interdependent and hence circular. However, the conclusions reached here are in general consistent with the numismatic findings, and if the two are put together the pattern that emerges provides evidence for dialects for places, most notably London, that is not otherwise available for the ninth century.

In general there is more consistency in the forms of the kings' or archbishops' names than the moneyers' names, and it seems probable that some degree of central standardization of the obverse inscription took place as part of the instruction defining the coin design. This is particularly evident in the coinage of the Mercian kings Berhtwulf and Burgred, the West Saxon kings Æthelwulf and Æthelberht, and Archbishop Ceolnoth.

For the Mercian kings, Berhtwulf, Burgred and Ceolwulf II, the moneyers' names, where dialectically distinctive, are almost exclusively Kentish in language, which might be surprising, but numismatists would attribute virtually all of the Mercian coins to the mint of London. We have very little evidence for the London dialect in the Anglo-Saxon period, but when London English is at last unambiguously attested in the Middle English period, it appears to be an Essex dialect, with some although by no means all Kentish features. There are a number of possible explanations for the use of Kentish moneyer-name forms on the London coins. The London die-cutters may themselves have been of Kentish origin, although the fact that a consistent pattern can be observed over a period of forty years makes this less likely. Alternatively, Kentish may have been regarded as the most appropriate form for use in an official medium such as coinage. A third explanation could be that London English was in fact similar to Kentish, as the Middle English evidence would also suggest. To test this theory one ought to look at the name forms appearing on the coinage over a longer period – back to the late eighth and on to the tenth/eleventh centuries. It is interesting that the king-names show Anglian (i.e. potentially Mercian) traits, suggesting that while the die-cutters or their informants were free to chose the form used for the moneyer-name, the king-name was perhaps stipulated by the Mercian court.

Within the earlier West Saxon coinage most moneyer-names have Kentish forms, which is entirely consistent with the numismatists' attribution of the majority of coins to the mints of Canterbury and Rochester. The king-names again follow a different pattern, in this case showing some aberrant West Saxon traits. The East Anglian names for both kings and moneyers display more variety in their forms, with both Anglian and Kentish features present.

The ninth-century coinage thus presents a rich source of dialectal evidence for the philologist. There are many more questions that could be pursued based on a more thorough analysis of the material than has been possible here. I hope that this paper has drawn attention to the potential that exists and that it may inspire further research in this field.

VIII

THE MONETARY ECONOMY OF NINTH-CENTURY ENGLAND SOUTH OF THE HUMBER: A TOPOGRAPHICAL ANALYSIS

D. M. Metcalf

If we map all the single finds of ninth-century coins from England south of a line from the Mersey to the Humber (Fig. 1), the pattern which emerges is of a plentiful scatter almost everywhere in southern and eastern England and in the east Midlands (excluding the Fenlands and the Weald) but with virtually nothing from Wales or the Marches or from the south-west beyond Exeter, and very little in the Severn Basin or the west Midlands.

Each symbol on the map represents, as accurately as possible, a site where one or more ninth-century coins have been found: it is a map of sites, rather than of individual coin-finds. Thus, the single symbol at the site of *Hamwic* (Southampton) reflects over forty single-finds. There are between three and ten finds from many sites.

In numerous instances the actual field or plot of ground where the coin was found is reliably known, and for the great bulk of the material the record of the find-spot is accurate to within a mile or so – which is a perfectly acceptable degree of accuracy for the purpose of most of the arguments that will have to be considered – and is very trustworthy. Where only the name of the nearest village is recorded, the uncertainty need not be exaggerated. The symbol itself in Fig. 1 is roughly the size of a parish. Only a dozen finds, from eighteenth- or nineteenth-century records, are described so vaguely as to be said merely to be from a particular county. Even they are useful enough to be worth including; but they have had to be mapped arbitrarily.

The data-base for the study covers a 'long' ninth century, from the death of Offa in 796, to various dates between 899 and *ca* 910, depending on the coin series. It includes, for example, the varieties of St Edmund Memorial pence represented in the Cuerdale hoard (and errs on the side of including those of which the variety is uncertain), and one or two other coinages which may in fact be from the early tenth century. Coins from hoards have not knowingly been included. Within this definition, some 450 separate finds are now (summer, 1991) on record from south of the Humber. North of the Humber, extremely few silver pennies from southern mints have been found. Such few as there are, mostly from York, have been included in the data-base for the sake of

Acknowledgements. It would have been quite impossible to undertake this study without the generous cooperation of Mr M. J. Bonser, whose ready help was given unfailingly.

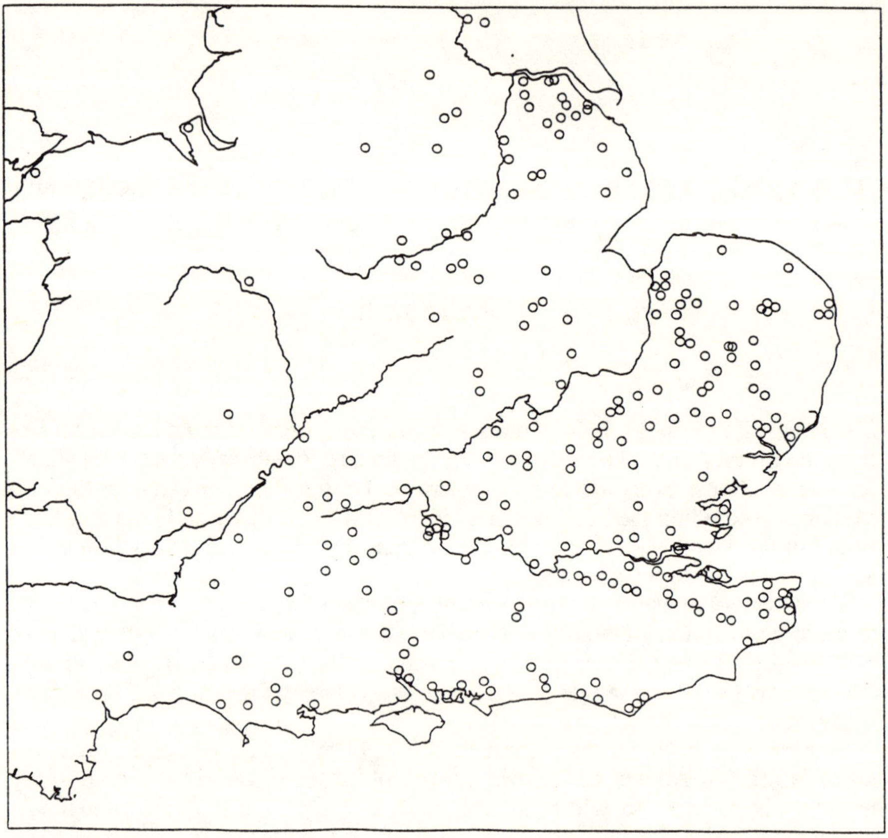

Fig. 1. All find localities of ninth-century coins, south of the Humber-Mersey line (southern English coins found north of the line are also shown, within the area mapped)

completeness. They are, of course, only a small proportion of all the ninth-century finds from the north.

Over forty coins, or about 10 per cent of the total, are (as already mentioned) from *Hamwic*, which because of its long history of excavations is the richest site for ninth-century coins.[1] Ipswich bids fair to rival it, with over thirty finds now recorded. The London area has yielded twenty-one coins, of which a gratifyingly high proportion are closely provenanced. Other urban sites have produced relatively few coins – Canterbury, nine, Rochester, four, Lincoln, four, and so on. Most of the 450 coins are chance finds or metal-detector finds from fields or the open countryside, with no evidence that they are *in situ* losses from an inhabited site. We may suspect that a good many of them were accidentally lost amid domestic rubbish in a nearby settlement and were eventually carted out among the rubbish, to be spread on the fields as manure. In that case they may have been

1 Pagan, 'The older finds'; Metcalf, 'The coins'.

found a mile or two from where they were lost; but that will not materially affect their evidence for the question of the distances over which coins circulated from their mint of origin.

Urban vs. rural finds

When one takes account of the relative intensity of searching on excavated sites (mostly urban), the urban contribution to the total seems quite modest. Among rural finds, a new type of site is beginning to come to our attention. The activity of metal-detector enthusiasts has begun to reveal a small number of richly productive sites in the open countryside, which are not yet fully understood, but which might possibly be interpreted as the sites of regular periodic fairs. One such location, near Royston, has so far produced seven ninth-century coins, as well as a much larger total from the seventh and eighth centuries.[2] The pattern as a whole, with its modest emphasis on the coastal *wics* and on such other towns as already existed, and its very plentiful scatter of finds in the countryside, belongs largely to the age before the Alfredian *burhs* were created.

The overall extent and the broad regional balance of the pattern of finds are virtually identical to what may be seen already in the middle decades of the eighth century, and as it still was in the eleventh century. The founding of towns resulted in a small increase – but only small – in the proportion of single finds coming from urban sites, and the Viking assaults upon the coasts helped to rob the trading *wics* of their earlier importance. The establishment of numerous mint-places from the early tenth century onwards, with moneyers in office in eventually some sixty or more towns throughout the area defined by the stray finds, is in sharpest contrast with the pre-Alfredian arrangements, which seem to have grown out of a scheme of one mint-place for each kingdom, and which meant in practice that minting was almost restricted to the southern and eastern coasts. But the radical change in the distribution of minting did not alter the extent of the territory over which coinage was in regular use. The map of finds reveals, in short, a perennial pattern of monetary circulation in lowland England, first visible to us in the mid-eighth century, although arguably present already from the mid-seventh, and recognizable thereafter throughout the middle ages. Money was drawn into the Midlands in the ninth century even though coins were not being minted there, presumably because there was a need locally, which was sufficiently strong to cause people to travel, and to transfer resources from one region to another, and to use money to such an extent that the odd coins which were occasionally lost by accident provide us today with a blanket coverage of the inland as well as the coastal regions of England.

Finding common ground on monetization

The monetization of the economy at this period has been a matter of historical controversy for the last thirty years and continues to be so. Documentary and other written sources are largely silent about the everyday, widespread use of

2 Blackburn and Bonser, 'Single finds of Anglo-Saxon and Norman coins'.

coinage, and historians have traditionally been inclined to accept that silence as negative evidence. Archaeological evidence of inter-regional transfers of goods does not lend itself very well to quantification and has tended to focus attention on high-status objects.[3] The numismatic evidence therefore has to stand on its own feet. The large claims that have been made for it, namely that it reveals an aspect of the country's economy about which we should otherwise be ignorant, and indeed that it should radically alter our estimate of the economy with its implication that there was a lively money economy geared to inter-regional and international trade, cannot look for any precise confirmation from other historical approaches. If the numismatic arguments are to gain acceptance, therefore, they have to be seen to be not just possible but inescapable. That is what gives the debate its special flavour. The conclusions that can be drawn from the numismatic evidence are outwardly quite simple and straightforward, but we need to scrutinize the steps by which they are reached with the greatest care, as if we were philosophers rather than historians, in order to satisfy ourselves that there is no incoherence in the argument, that there are no ambiguities in the reasoning, and that the evidence is sufficient in quantity and spread to avoid statistical imprecision.

On this last point, regarding the sufficiency of the evidence, it is only proper to say that until recently there was hardly enough. We owe the opportunities for study now open to us to the recent publication of the finds from Southampton, including a careful reassessment by Hugh Pagan of the nineteenth-century finds; to the energetic rescuing of information about stray finds by archaeologists in the museums service and in archaeological units throughout the country; to Miss Elizabeth Pirie for the example she has set in recording finds of stycas;[4] and most of all to the dedication and the considerable diplomacy of Mr M. J. Bonser. By winning the confidence and co-operation of numerous detectorists he has over the last few years rescued reliable information about a staggering number of single finds. These in particular have tended to be from the open countryside, and they complement the evidence from controlled excavations in important respects. One of the pleasures of numismatics is that stimulating new evidence can come to light year by year, in a way that new texts do not. As regards ninth-century monetary history, we can now reach much firmer conclusions than would have been possible even as little as six or seven years ago.

At the end of a recent symposium on ninth-century monetary history north of the Humber, Professor Nicholas Brooks undertook to provide the epilogue, which he did with his accustomed skill and judgement. In the course of his remarks, he expressed hesitations over the scale of the styca coinage, which were no doubt in line with the sentiments of many other historians. He pointed out that estimates based on numbers of dies were controversial, and suggested that more cautious formulas might be better in accord with the view that the primary function of the coinage was to serve an aristocratic elite.[5] This minimalist interpretation of the function and scale of the currency (with which I unhesitatingly disagree) makes

3 See, for example, Astill, 'Medieval ceramics and urban development'.

4 Pirie, 'Finds of "sceattas" '.

5 Brooks, 'Epilogue', pp. 398–9.

so radical a challenge to the historical assessment of the coinage that there is very little point in side-stepping it and simply preferring one interpretation or the other. One's choice will influence one's views on all the rest of the evidence. With Professor Brooks' kind indulgence, therefore, let us use his comment as a focus for debate, and try to find arguments which are not simply *parti pris*.

Let us concede that there is no way of directly rebutting the argument which runs as follows: 'Although the numbers of dies can be estimated within margins of statistical uncertainty and should in practice be a matter for consensus, the average number of coins struck from each die may have been far below the technical capacity of the die. The volume of mint-output may therefore, after all, have been much smaller than has been claimed by those on the other side of this debate, and the uses of money may, so far as this particular argument goes, have been restricted to the higher levels of society and even to purposes which served to reinforce their status.' There is no way of proving what the average output of a die was. An unwillingness to believe that it was at least half what it was in the thirteenth century (for which we have very exact information) is thus invincible.

The observations that follow are presented in full awareness of this reluctance, and the main thread of argument has deliberately been formulated as independently as possible of any assumption about the volume of the currency. One has to say, however, that the detailed topographical pattern of the finds, namely their widespread occurrence in villages and in the open countryside, with no obvious patterns or concentrations such as could be interpreted in terms of privileged or restricted access to the use of money, is strong *prima facie* evidence of widespread monetization at ordinary social levels. By analyzing the evidence of the single finds topographically one may hope to persuade the sceptical that that view is not only possible but inescapable – or, at the very least, one may hope to put the ball firmly into the other court.

Randomness particularized

The argument depends crucially on the proposition that the single finds in the available sample, of some 450 coins, are approximately random in respect of whatever characteristic we seek to consider. Randomness is all. It does not have to be completely true in order to provide us nevertheless with a useful starting-point, what the French call *un modèle aléatoire*, a model which we can work on, and accept or modify. If people lost their coins accidentally, then obviously they did not exercise any kind of selection: they did not choose to lose coins by one moneyer rather than another, or coins of one king rather than another. Randomness in these respects is an entirely reasonable assumption, and if there is no evidence to the contrary we can compare the quantities and the distribution patterns of, for example, Mercian as opposed to West Saxon coins in the sample with some confidence. When we encounter Northumbrian brass stycas in East Anglia, we may begin to feel less confident of equal loss rates, and entertain the doubt whether such coins were not discarded rather than accidentally lost, because of their low intrinsic value. Perhaps, at least, one did not sweep the house as diligently if one lost a styca. Carolingian coins, on the other hand, were made of good silver, and were as heavy as an English penny, if not heavier. There is no *prima-facie* reason to hesitate over supposing that they are accidental losses

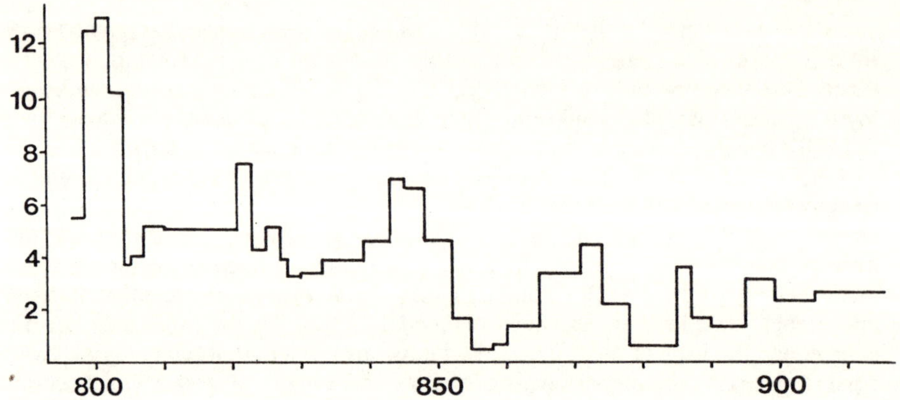

Fig. 2. Coin-finds per year throughout the ninth century (smoothed profile as explained in the text)

which can enter into numerical comparisons more or less on a par with English coins.

If we try to compare town and country it is another matter. The chances of losing a coin may have been different within the setting of a town – one was pulling out one's purse more often; and the chances of our finding a lost coin, after centuries of building and rebuilding on the same sites, road-making, rubbish disposal, and so on, are difficult to assess. On this comparison we must sharply question the hypothesis of randomness.

What about coin losses in troubled times? Might some of these single finds have been lost in adversity, or even concealed and not recovered? Might we expect to see an upsurge in the annual rate of single finds, matching the years of King Egbert's conquests, or the years when the great heathen host was ravaging far and wide? – a swathe of finds, even, in its path? Hoards, of course, behave differently from single finds, and there is a large number of hoards that are very plausibly dated to the years 865–875, both north and south of the Humber. The single finds of coins of Burgred make a somewhat different pattern from the normal one, with a more northerly emphasis. Perhaps some of them were lost in circumstances connected with the great host. The comparability of losses of coins of Burgred and of earlier rulers may thus be less than random.

The main point is that we can return over and over again to our data-base, with different questions, for each of which we ought to think separately about the randomness of the sample in respect of the particular question we are asking.

The circumstances of stray losses: accident – or warfare?

Let us begin our analysis, then, by distributing all our single finds according to their date, to see whether there is a sudden mortality of coin in the 820s or in 865–875. Unexpectedly and quite convincingly, they show a long decline in the course of the ninth century (Fig. 2). So without more ado we can say that it would be very difficult to sustain the argument that the Viking assaults led to greatly increased losses of single coins (as distinct from non-recovery of hoards). The graph has been smoothed by transferring a third of the total for each short period forward to the next period, cumulatively, on the grounds that coins continued in circulation for some time before they were lost. The smoothing does not affect the longer trends. Maybe there is a small upward tendency in the graph for the third quarter of the century, and some of our coins were lost in a context of violence: but this cannot be a major factor. One should not seek to be too precise about it, because the coins will have been lost a varying number of years after they were minted. Thus the sharp little peak in the early 820s should not be taken as evidence of a sudden change in the loss-rate in those years. An inspection of the find-spots of the coins in question gives no encouragement to look for special circumstances. A sudden brief increase might be explicable, but it is inherently unlikely that the loss-rate should then as suddenly dip below the trend-line. We know from other sources (namely hoards) roughly what the age-structure of the currency was in successive decades of the ninth century, and we can say that the average life-time of a coin was such that the decline indicated by the graph is real enough. But what exactly does it reflect? The chances of a coin's being accidentally lost were presumably much greater when it was in use than when it was put safely away. The coins that were being carried about and exchanged were the ones that were at risk. A long-term trend in the annualized number of stray losses is thus presumably an index essentially of the changing volume of transactions rather than of the scale of the currency. Burgred's later coins, certainly, were minted in relatively very great quantities, without any matching increase in the numbers of coins lost.

Monetary recession, without geographical retreat

Given the downwards trend through the ninth century, we might do well to ask ourselves next whether the dwindling numbers of finds were accompanied by any sort of retreat in the area over which currency was freely in use. It is clear that in the late seventh and eighth centuries there were periods of monetary recession, e.g. the earlier part of Offa's reign, when coinage was plentiful only in Kent and the extreme south-east.[6] The fluctuation is a basic argument for associating the use of coinage at that date predominantly with cross-Channel trade, and is not the sort of pattern we should expect to find if coinage had been predominantly at the service of an aristocratic elite. The map comparing finds from the later ninth century with those from the century as a whole (Fig. 3) gives no encouragement whatever to postulate a retreat in the monetized area. The find spots are just as widely scattered in the Midlands and the West as they were during the first half of the century.

There is, however, a substantial shift in the relative importance of the mints, away from Canterbury, and in favour of London and East Anglia (see Figs 8 and 9, below). The over-all figures for the second half of the century are heavily influenced by Burgred's plentiful *Lunettes* coinage, and by the St Edmund Memorial coinage, but even so it seems clear that the mints south of the Thames

6 Metcalf, 'Monetary expansion'.

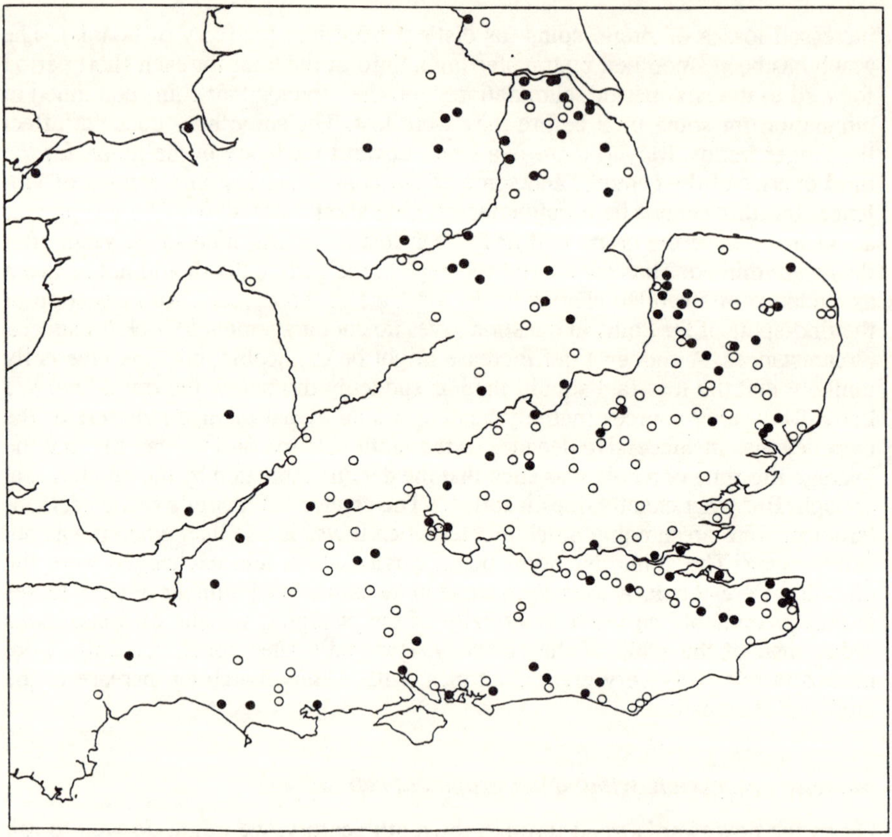

Fig. 3. Find localities of coins minted from *ca* 850 onwards (including stycas)

went into decline. The onset of debasement at Canterbury has been tentatively dated to *ca* 842, by which time the Viking threat to Kent was already growing serious. In 835 Sheppey had been ravaged; in 838–839, Archbishop Ceolnoth reached an accommodation with the West Saxon kings, under pressure from the Viking threat to the coasts; in 850 or 851 Canterbury was sacked and in 851 a heathen army wintered on the Isle of Thanet. A decline in minting is presumably symptomatic of the commercial risks of trading into the Wantsum Channel and, more generally, of plying across the North Sea and across the Channel.[7] The pattern of single finds suggests, however, that a down-turn in the amounts of bullion brought to the mints, in particular Canterbury, did not interfere noticeably with the dynamics of monetary circulation inland, into the Midlands.

7 Metcalf and Northover, 'Coinage alloys', pp. 112ff.

Instructive special cases: 1. Carolingian coins

Let us next return to the questions raised by the Carolingian and Northumbrian coins found in southern England. What one can do in order to gain a more confident understanding of them is to look at how they fall in relation to the pattern of finds as a whole. The Carolingian coins include issues in silver and in gold, which are best considered separately in the first instance, since their monetary uses and their loss-rates are liable to have been very different. There are now some twenty silver deniers and oboles on record, which thus make up about 4 per cent of all the finds in our list. Many of them are from the last quarter of the ninth century, and they will have made up a substantially higher proportion than 4 per cent of the losses from that period. They are, moreover, unevenly distributed through the country. They are conspicuously absent from Kent, London, and the Thames valley (Fig. 4). On the other hand they are relatively plentiful in Wessex, where it seems that money coming across the Channel to south-coast ports was sometimes able to pass into use in the region, escaping the normal procedure of being melted down and recycled into official English money. The finds from Culm Davey and Pins Knoll (1, 2) are a long way from a mint-town: if they arrived in England through Dorset or Devon ports, it is easily understandable that they were not promptly reminted. At *Hamwic* (3) there are two excavation coins from the middle decades of the century (when the West Saxon mints were in Kent), to set alongside eighth-century (pre-reform) coins of Charlemagne and Pepin from *Hamwic* and from Hod Hill. At Chichester there is an excavation coin (4). Again, reminting may have been inconvenient.

In East Anglia, a greater number of Carolingian silver coins has been found, but the total number of finds from the region is greater still, so that the proportion is somewhat less. The coins of Charles the Bald could well have been in use in the years after the Danish conquest and before the introduction of the St Edmund Memorial coinage. There is also a Danish coin among the finds, from Lavenham (5), and several Islamic dirhems or fragments (6, 7) which no doubt reached England by way of Scandinavia. Again it seems, therefore, that there may have been a 'window of opportunity' for foreign coins to enter East Anglia at a time when minting locally was in abeyance, or when political control of the region had been disturbed. The four excavation finds from Ipswich (8–11) are particularly instructive: they are from different sites in the town (Buttermarket, School Street, St Peters Street), and are all of Charles the Bald. The mints of the coins are directly across the North Sea, in Saint-Quentin, Beauvais, and Quentovic; and there is another Quentovic coin in the name of Charles from Thetford (12), and an obole from Bardwell (13). The four Ipswich coins are among a total of thirty-two from the town on our list: 12 per cent. As also at *Hamwic*, it is safe to assume that they are typical losses in a busy commercial town – whereas the circumstances of an isolated loss in a village, considered by itself, are inevitably uncertain.

The Norfolk finds from Downham Market and Beachamwell (14, 15) are too few to support any specific hypotheses. They may have arrived in England via the Wash.

At York (16) the picture looks much the same: well-authenticated finds

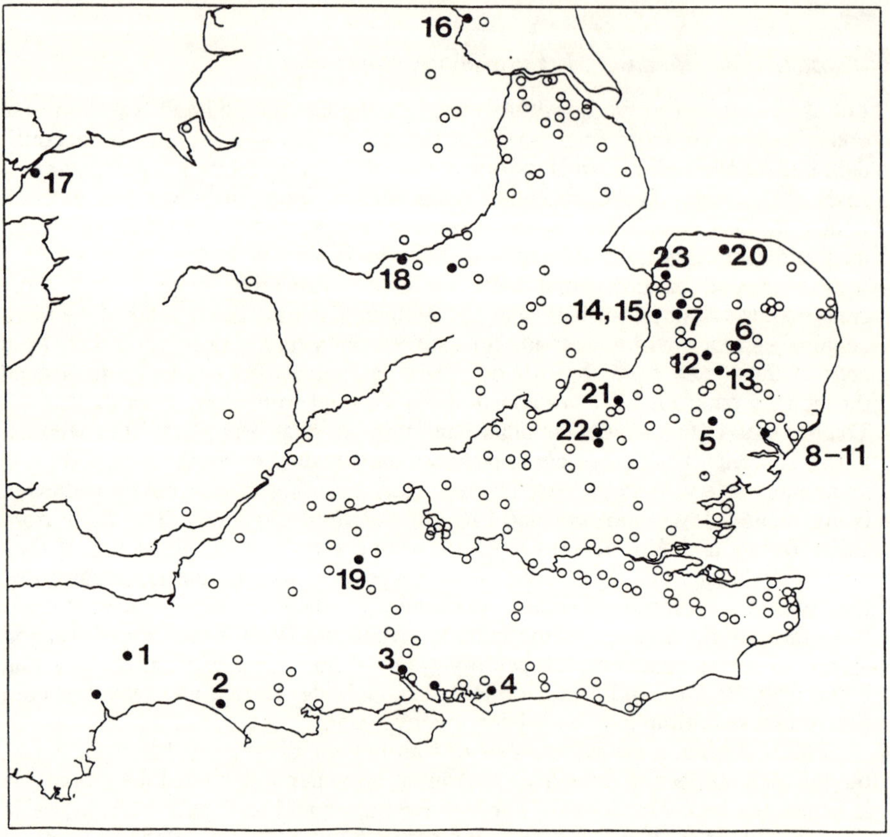

Fig. 4. Find localities of Carolingian coins in silver and gold (including possibly English imitations of the gold). Numbered finds are referred to in the text

forming a significant fraction of the ninth-century assemblage, and a 'window of opportunity' before the minting of the Anglo-Viking series in York began. There are outlying finds from Coxwold and Settle (beyond the northern margin of the map) which repeat a distribution-pattern observable in the second half of the eighth century.

Finds from Caernarfon (17) and near Repton (18) are very peripheral. That from Caernarfon is from an Aquitanian mint, thus conforming with a tendency for westerly finds to be from westerly Carolingian mints. The fact that the Preshute find (19) is from Rouen makes it seem more likely that it came directly across the Channel to Wessex. One of the Southampton finds, similarly, is from Toulouse. There are, however, plenty of exceptions.

The gold imitations of Louis I, minted either in Frisia or in some cases probably in England, are surprisingly plentiful among the finds. We see again a south-coast distribution (Exeter, Southampton, Portchester) and a Norfolk/Wash distribution (20) extending inland to Cambridge (21) and near Royston (22). A unique gold coin from near Kings Lynn (23) is struck from a denarius die of the mint of Chartres. There is a more northerly find from Stamford Bridge, and others from beyond the fringe, in the Isle of Man and at Elgin.

In the tenth century there is of course a good deal of evidence for the use of gold, in wills and charters, and the question arises whether the gold coins in the name of Louis I might in some cases be substantially later losses. The distinctive distribution-pattern offers some sort of argument against that idea, in that if the coins had been in English hands for long periods, a more even scatter of finds might have been expected. The distribution evidence is, however, very open-ended, because an English or British origin has been canvassed for so many of the finds.[8] The Carolingian silver coins are certainly imports; with the gold, it is difficult to be sure where one stands.

Gold presumably had a significantly lower loss-rate than silver because people took greater care with it. The total of seven or eight such coins among 450 is impressive, even if the numbers are small compared with what was to be found in Frisia. The main points that emerge from a consideration of the Carolingian finds in Britain are (1) the sheer volume of such coins that were in circulation (if we assume that the loss-rate was similar for deniers and pennies); (2) their concentration in Wessex and in the Danelaw; and (3) the hypothesis of 'windows of opportunity', when there was no English mint available nearby, or when political control over the currency had been weakened.

If the losses were random as between deniers and pennies, they would imply that the numbers of Carolingian coins passing from hand to hand in England, taking the ninth century as a whole, were equivalent to the output of about 4 per cent of the output of the dies used in England. One should be very chary, therefore, of special explanations – remembering the web of romantic fancy which Michael Dolley and Norman Shiel spun around the find from Culm Davey, involving Queen Judith's morning gift.[9]

And the finds of which we have records reflect only those that got away. It seems likely that a great deal more Carolingian money crossed the sea, but entered the country before the Danish onslaught, or via Canterbury or London, and was promptly recoined.

Instructive special cases: 2. Northumbrian stycas

In the same way that there is a southern and eastern fringe of Carolingian coins in England, so also there is a northern and eastern fringe of stycas found south of the Humber. Most of them are coins containing less than 10 per cent silver in their alloy. The brass that made up the remainder was itself a metal with a higher value than copper; but it is questionable whether a styca could have been received, outside Northumbria, at a face value as high as that of a good silver

8 Pagan, 'The imitative Louis the Pious solidus'; Stewart, 'A solidus from Yorkshire'. Both studies adduce the evidence of die-duplication. The two varieties for which Grierson originally suggested a British origin are G.I (which includes finds from Stamford Bridge, Hon (Norway), and Elgin), and G.XVI (which includes the finds from Cambridge, Royston, and Lewes). The stylistic similarity to each other of the Southampton and Porchester finds has been noted.

9 Dolley and Shiel, 'A Carolingian *denarius*'.

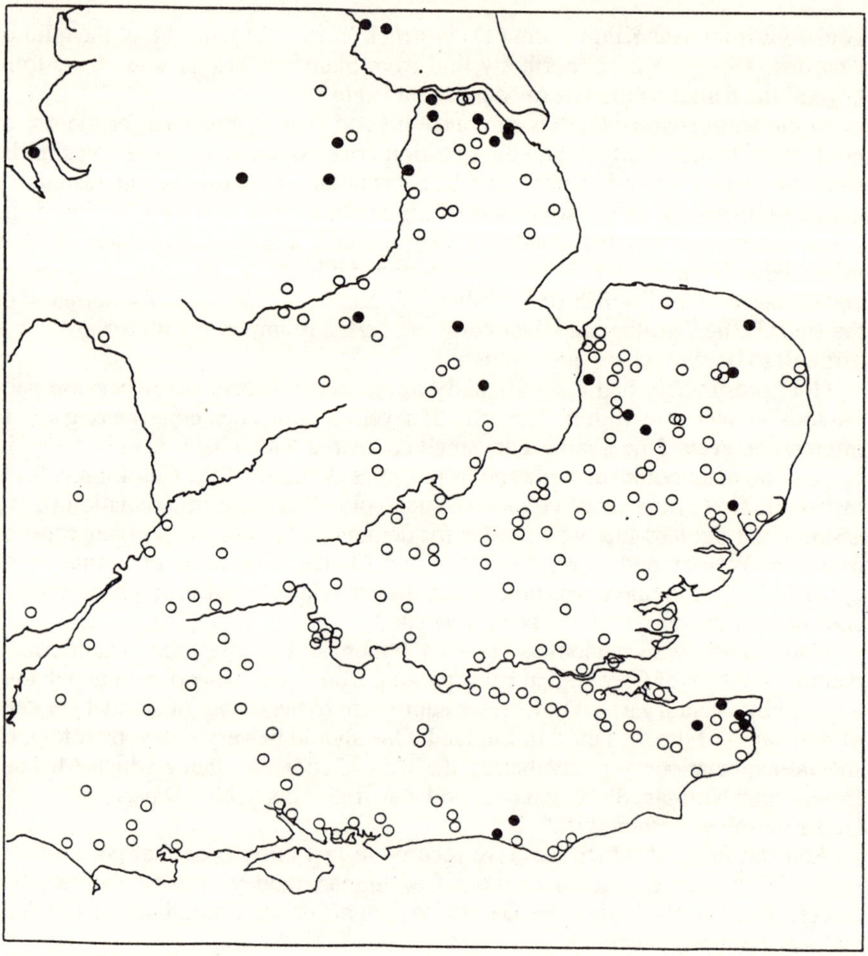

Fig. 5. Find localities of Northumbrian stycas south of the Humber-Mersey line (essentially from the second half of the ninth century; cf. Fig. 3)

penny – or even a moderately good silver penny, for we should remember that some ninth-century silver was quite debased.[10]

One was brought up to believe that stycas and silver pennies did not mix in circulation; and certainly they were not hoarded together in the south. But metal-detector finds of the last few years have made it increasingly clear that stycas were lost in southern England.

Once again we can (and should) distinguish several strands in the topographical pattern of the finds (Fig. 5), namely:

(1) a south Yorkshire, north Lincolnshire region where stycas make up a high

10 Metcalf and Northover, 'Coinage alloys'.

proportion of all the finds, and where they may have been the normal currency for much of the ninth century, even though south of the Humber;

(2) finds from Norfolk (reinforced by seven finds from Heacham, which are presumed to be a small hoard rather than single finds), quite probably dating from after the Danish conquest (there are various finds from Thetford, from different sites, making an interesting contrast with Ipswich, from where there is in effect very good negative evidence);

(3) finds from Reculver, Richborough, and Sandwich, those from Richborough being perfectly well attested. The geographical isolation of this group of finds points to the likelihood of their having arrived by sea, and to the shores of the Wantsum Channel still being, in the ninth century, an international emporium;

(4) finds from Brighton and Lewes, which one should hesitate to dismiss as modern losses;

(5) finds from Meols and Caernarfon which belong to a wider pattern of the circulation of stycas in the Irish Sea coastlands.[11]

A couple of the finds are suggestive of north-south travel by inland routes, namely Winteringham on the south bank of the Humber, where sceattas have also been found, and a site near Sixhills, on the line of the A1 on the northern border of Leicestershire.

There is a problem in knowing whether stycas had a higher loss-rate than pennies. In East Anglia they may well have become unacceptable after the introduction of the St Edmund Memorial coinage, but we should hesitate to suppose that people would then have simply thrown them away or given them to their children to play with: brass had a market value and would have been recycled, even if it was not worth recovering the small amounts of silver from the alloy.

Did the monetization of the economy vary in different kingdoms?

Carolingian coins and stycas are each an instructive special case. Let us now return to an analysis of the whole body of ninth-century material, beginning with the varying numbers of coin-finds per locality. This yields a distinctive pattern, of a large number of places from which only one or two coins are recorded, and a very few localities which have been prolific in ninth-century finds. *Hamwic* and Ipswich head the list, as towns which have been intensively excavated. York is in the same league if one includes stycas, which have not been taken into account here for sites north of the Humber. London and its area have yielded a good number of finds, and would doubtless yield many more if the ninth-century commercial district could be excavated more thoroughly. Finds are plentiful from various centres in east Kent. The only remaining prolific sites are Thetford and Royston. Northampton and Tilbury are in the middle rank. After that, we come down to places from which only twos and threes of coins are recorded – and those two or three not necessarily from the same field or the same site. The ninth-century coins are often part of a larger assemblage of Roman and medieval coins from a site. Where a particular field has yielded a good number of coins (of

11 Discussed in Metcalf, 'A topographical commentary'.

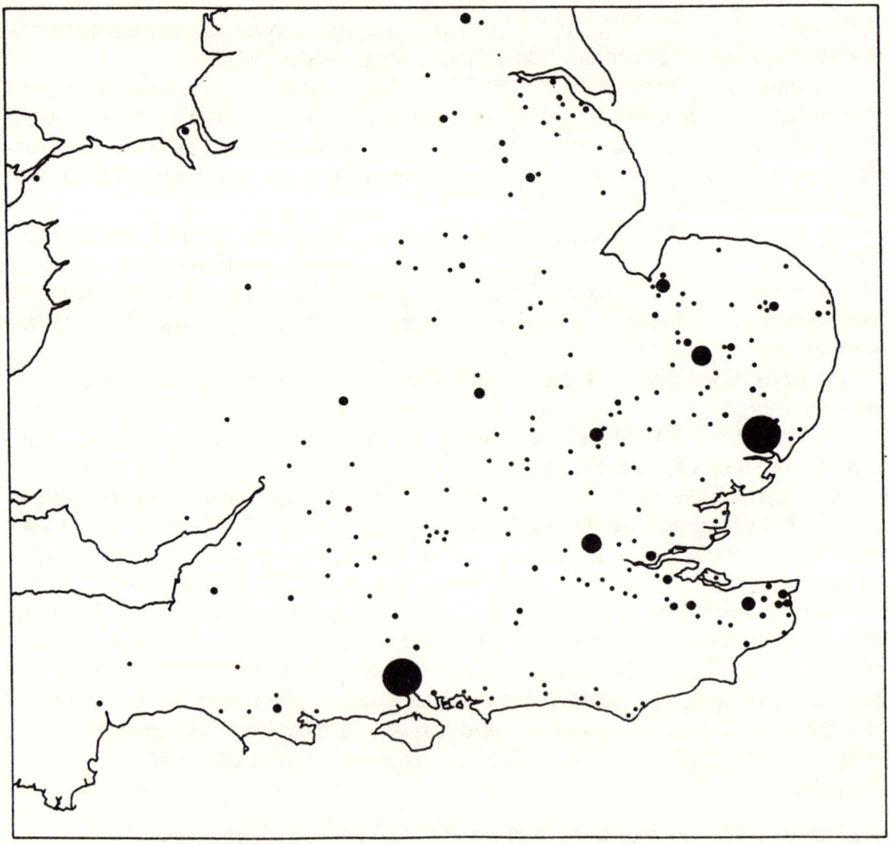

Fig. 6. Localities from which more than one find is recorded (the size of the symbols is related to the numbers of finds)

various periods) as a result of searching by metal-detectorists over the last ten or fifteen years, it may be assumed – and this is an important guarantee as to the nature of the evidence – that success will have spurred the finders on. Fig. 6 is intended to give a visual impression of the numbers of ninth-century coins from each locality. The map conveys a general impression of finds thinning out to some extent towards the west and north-west. The hobby of metal-detecting being widespread, and encouraged by success, we may accept its evidence as valid, if imprecise. We may construe it in terms of a greater monetization of the economy in the east. Set against the political frontiers of the time, this means that there was a contrast between Kent and East Anglia on the one hand, and Mercia on the other, Mercia being significantly less monetized – with whatever social and political consequences that may have had.

Next let us add some political boundaries to our base map (Fig. 7), and consider what proportion of the finds from each kingdom are of the local ruler. Notice that by talking about proportions within each kingdom we are avoiding

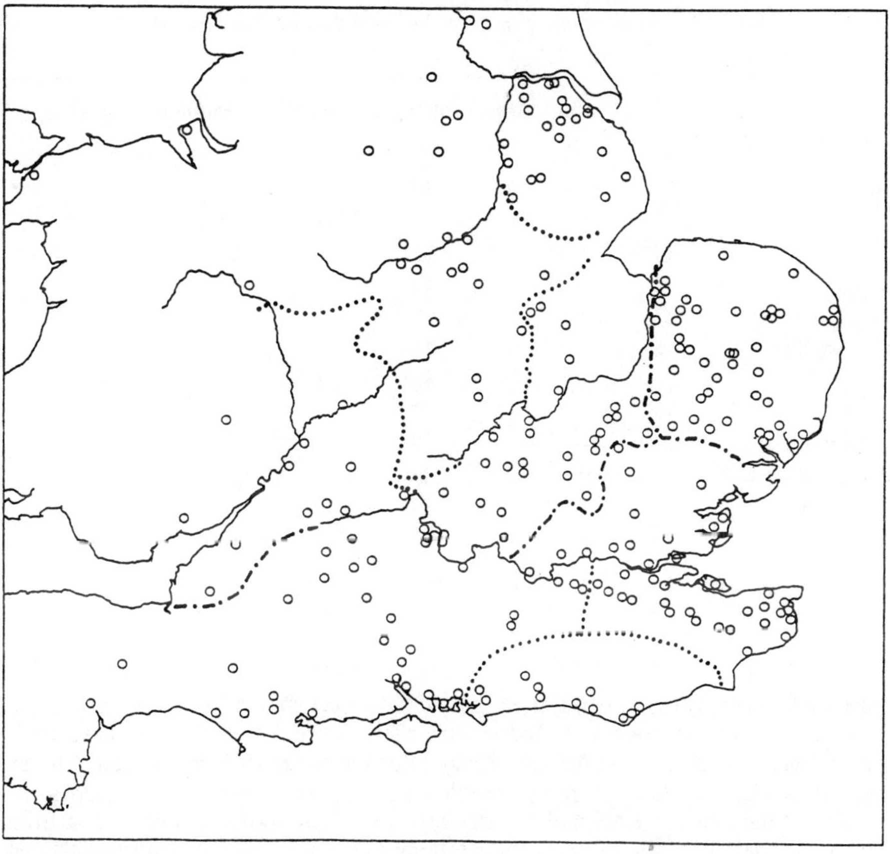

Fig. 7. Political boundaries (after C. R. Hart). The bold lines show the groupings assumed in Tables 1 and 2 for 'greater Mercia' and 'greater Wessex'

what may be a systematic defect of the evidence. In spite of what has just been said, it may be that coin finds are more plentiful in some regions than others, because more people have been interested in searching for them, or because the soil conditions favour their survival or recovery, or for various other reasons which we cannot measure. If we speak about proportions, however, we should automatically discount these unknown factors.

How many coins moved between one kingdom and another?

The hegemonies of Wessex and Mercia changed during the ninth century, e.g. as regards control of Essex, but it is desirable to keep the analysis simple by looking at the coin evidence for the century as a whole. If one tries to break it down into shorter periods, one runs into the difficulty that the exact date of loss of each single find is unknowable, and also the totals become so small as to be statistically

TABLE 1. Regional occurence by issuing authorities (number of coins)

Region where found	Wessex	Kent	Abps	Mercia	E. Anglia	Northern	Foreign	Total
Wessex	29	14	10	30	3	–	9	95
Sussex	3	–	2	3	–	2	1	11
Kent	17	4	9	13	2	6	–	51
Essex	14	4	6	14	1	–	–	39
GREATER WESSEX	63	22	27	60	6	8	10	196
Middle Anglia	8	7	4	14	5	3	3	44
Mercia	–	1	2	8	8	1	2	22
Hwiccia	3	1	3	7	2	–	–	16
Lincolnshire	8	–	–	9	1	10	–	28
GREATER MERCIA	19	9	9	38	16	14	5	110
EAST ANGLIA	11	7	3	30	39	14	14	118
Northern	2	–	1	5	1	11	6	26
TOTAL	95	38	40	133	62	47	35	450

unsatisfactory. Table 1, using the regional divisions shown in Fig. 7, shows that only a third of the finds from Mercia are Mercian, and only a third of the finds from East Anglia are East Anglian. Only a third of the finds from Greater Wessex are West Saxon, although the proportion rises to over half if one includes the issues of the kings of Kent and the archbishop of Canterbury. It is very clear from the table that although efforts were presumably made to exclude Carolingian and Northumbrian coins from the currency of most parts of England, most of the time, and with something like a 95 per cent success-rate or better no attempt was made to confine West Saxon, Mercian, and East Anglian coins to their own territories. Presumably they were accepted at par. Hoards tell the same story as the single finds. The fact that the different issues were so thoroughly mixed in circulation throughout southern England helps to confirm the assumption that losses were random in respect of the issuing authority. It seems reasonable to accept, on our random hypothesis, that this is unbiassed evidence, and that only a third of the *currency* of Mercia was Mercian, and so on. That implies, not just possibly but inescapably, that millions of coins, or perhaps one had better merely say the coins struck from hundreds of dies, were continuously crossing political frontiers and rapidly becoming thoroughly mingled. If the use of money had been largely restricted to an aristocratic elite, we might have expected fewer large-scale transfers and therefore a somewhat different regional pattern, and we might also have looked for hoards containing more batches of coin that had stayed together since they had been minted.

Because Mercian coins might be struck in Canterbury, Rochester, London, or East Anglia, we shall learn more about how coins were moving around if we substitute the mint-place for the issuing authority, and look at what proportion of the

TABLE 2. Regional occurrence by mints (number of coins)

egion where found	Canterbury	E. Anglia	London	Rochester	Wessex	Southern?	Northern	Foreign	Total
'essex	40	5	13	10	7	11	–	9	95
ıssex	5	–	–	1	1	1	3	1	10
ent	28	7	7	2	1	2	6	–	53
ssex	18	3	11	2	–	4	–	–	38
REATER WESSEX	91	15	31	15	8	17	9	10	196
iddle Anglia	24	5	4	–	1	2	3	3	42
ercia	2	9	6	–	–	–	1	2	20
wiccia	8	3	4	1	–	1	–	–	17
ncolnshire	9	3	7	1	–	1	10	–	31
REATER MERCIA	43	20	21	2	1	4	14	5	110
ıst Anglia	21	47	12	3	2	5	14	14	118
orthern	3	1	4	1	–	–	11	6	26
TOTAL	158	83	68	21	11	26	48	35	450

coins produced in each mint-place (for no matter which ruler) have been found in each region. Virtually all ninth-century pence can be reliably attributed to their mint, thanks to the researches of Blunt, Lyon and Stewart, Pagan, and Blackburn and Keynes. The few finds in the data-base for which no mint can be proposed are either contemporary counterfeits, or coins about which very little detail is available. The latter can be assumed to be random in respect of mint-place, and will not distort the statistics.

The conclusion is, in general terms, the same as before: coins of all mints circulated very widely, and some of all kinds were to be found in almost every region (Table 2). Given that that is so, the total numbers of finds for each of the various mints should be quite a reliable short cut to estimating the relative output of the mints (Fig. 8). It has the important technical advantage that it does not rely on the assumption that average die-output was the same at different mints.

The ranking of the mints

Canterbury is by far the dominant mint, with 35 per cent of the total, and the figure would be even higher in the first half of the century. Canterbury was not the main seat of royal power: its importance as a mint-place must be assumed to arise from the reminting of Carolingian and possibly other foreign silver brought in by trade across the Channel, as was certainly the case later in the middle ages. Ships made landfall in the Wantsum Channel, and it was at the nearby city of Canterbury that merchants sought the services of moneyers, and there that the Mercian and then the West Saxon kings chose to have their coins minted. The tiny volume of silver minted in Wessex, which presumably equates with the foreign bullion

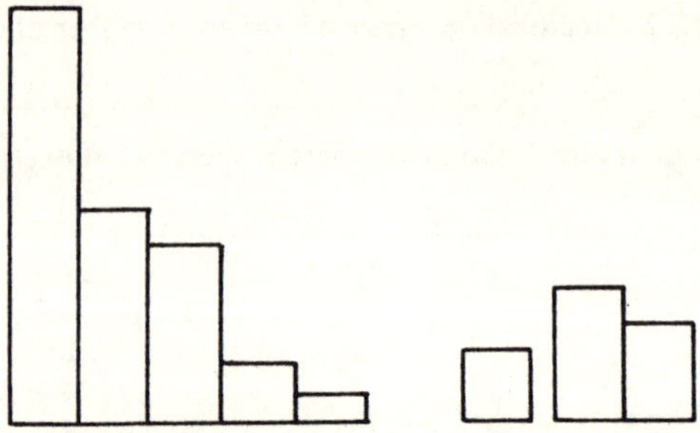

Fig. 8. Relative volume of output of the mints, as measured by the proportions among the single finds, for the ninth century as a whole (Canterbury, East Anglia, London, Rochester, Wessex, unattributed southern English, Northern/Danelaw, various Foreign)

coming into *Hamwic*, is in sharpest contrast with the volume coming into Canterbury, and this contrast is a significant feature in the pattern of bullion flows through most of the Anglo-Saxon period. For the ninth century it is again a useful general argument for saying that minting was not undertaken primarily from political motives, or to serve the interest of an aristocratic elite. Would not the powerful West Saxon kings otherwise have minted more coinage at Winchester?

London, which from the eleventh century onwards, and perhaps already from the mid-tenth, rivalled Canterbury as a major mint, falls surprisingly far behind it in the ninth century – especially if one disregards the prolific coinage of Burgred. The rise of London as a great trading city may be largely a late ninth- and tenth-century phenomenon. Nevertheless the proportions are puzzling, because they are more evenly balanced in the mid-eighth century.[12] It seems that quite sharp fluctuations in minting were possible, on a time-scale of decades.

The East Anglian mint or mints also come a poor second to Canterbury – the more so if one discounts the contribution of the St Edmund Memorial pence to the total. Rochester and Winchester, even in the first half of the ninth century, are minor mints. Chester at the very end of the ninth century was just beginning its meteoric rise as a mint-place. Similarly, one or more small mints may have been opened in the Danelaw late in the century, presaging the more complex patterns of mint-activity of the tenth century.

Fig. 9 shows the ranking of the mints in the second half of the ninth century. The main contrast with the statistics for the century as a whole is in the decline of Canterbury as a mint-place, with a corresponding rise at London. The percentages are heavily influenced by three distinctive coinages which are not as directly comparable as one could wish. They are the debased pennies of Burgred, the

12 This statement rests on a survey of single finds of sceattas, and on the arguments by which Series K and L are attributed to east Kent and London respectively (Metcalf, *Thrymsas and Sceattas*), III, pp. 368–83.

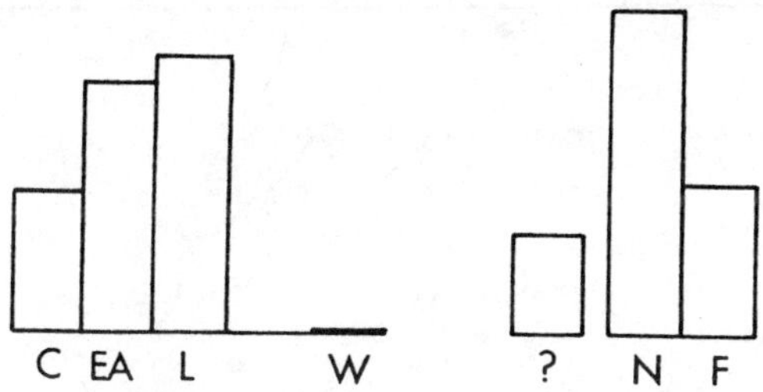

Fig. 9. Relative volume of output of the mints, as measured by the proportions among the single finds for the period from the mid-ninth century onwards (symbols as on Fig. 8)

even more debased stycas, and the St Edmund Memorial pennies which, in effect, belong to the next chapter of monetary history. If they were omitted from the survey, East Anglia would appear to share the decline which affected Canterbury. There, too, debasement was a significant development in the second half of the century. It has been related to a decline in the Carolingian coinage, which persisted until the Edict of Pitres in 864.[13] In England, the restoration of high silver standards was undertaken by Alfred in the 870s; his example was followed in the Danelaw in the 880s.[14]

If minting everywhere in the third quarter of the century was affected by the economic downturn, the area in the English hinterland within which the coinage circulated was not. We have already seen (Fig. 3) that the distribution of finds from the second half of the century is essentially the same as in the first half. The extent of the area over which the finds are scattered perhaps conveys a slightly misleading impression: the long-distance movements of Canterbury and London coins westwards, in the context of inter-regional trade, may have been to some extent disrupted. Monetary circulation, which had been quite strongly unified throughout England south of the Humber, was exhibiting a tendency to break down into regional isolation, in three or four broad regions. There is, however, too little evidence to yield more than a general suspicion of changed circumstances.

Mapping the single finds of coins of particular mints

In order to enjoy the statistical benefits of a large sample, we do best to continue to look at a 'long' ninth century as a whole – while remembering that our conclusions will be weighted towards the first half of the century, from which most of the finds come. Even in that perspective, some degree of localization is apparent in the circulation of the issues of the various mints. East Anglian coins tended to remain in East Anglia (Fig. 10). In preparing the map, the St Edmund Memorial coins were plotted separately, and compared. It seems fair to say that their range

13 Metcalf and Northover, 'Coinage alloys'.

14 Metcalf and Northover, 'Carolingian and Viking coins'.

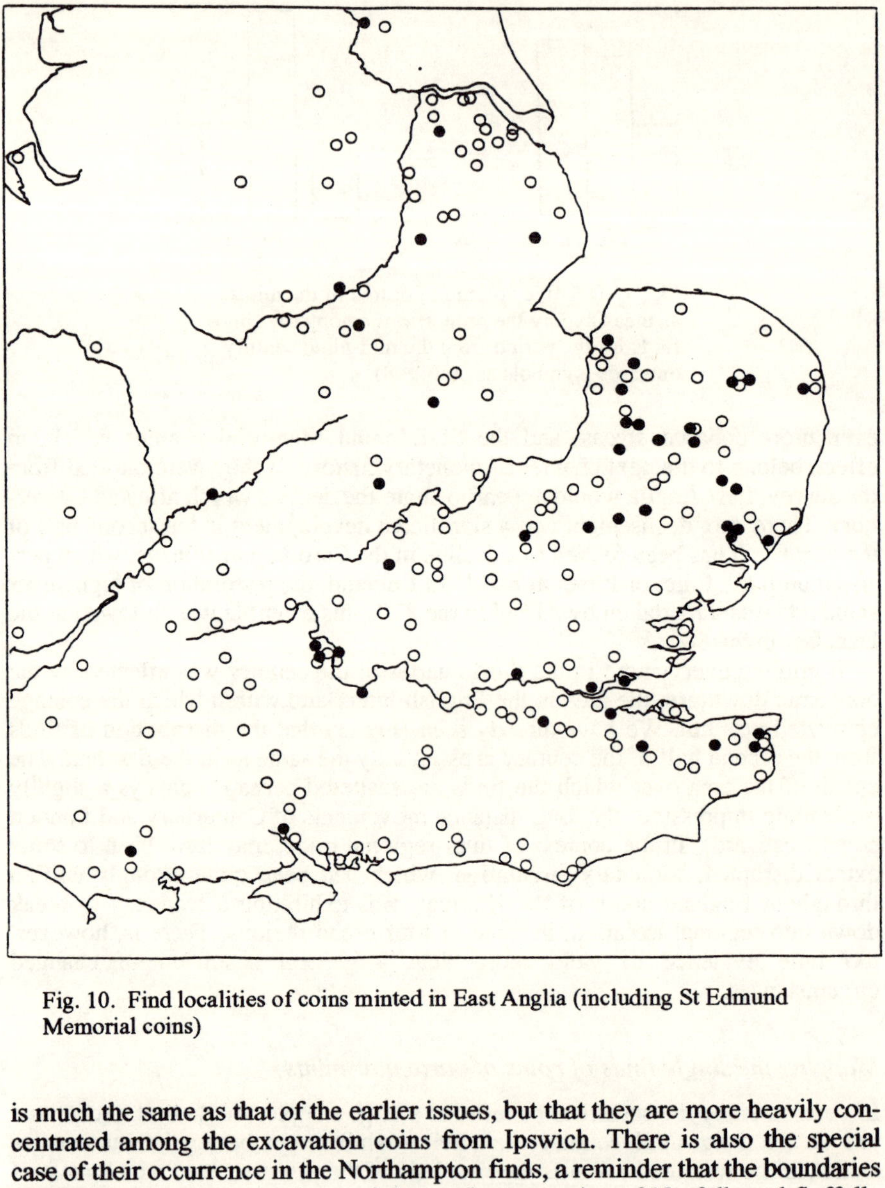

Fig. 10. Find localities of coins minted in East Anglia (including St Edmund Memorial coins)

is much the same as that of the earlier issues, but that they are more heavily concentrated among the excavation coins from Ipswich. There is also the special case of their occurrence in the Northampton finds, a reminder that the boundaries of East Anglia were not those of the modern counties of Norfolk and Suffolk. The later ninth-century evidence for the East Anglian coinage thus hints at some sort of quantitative retreat in the use of money to the urban centres.

This retreat seems to be characteristic throughout the Danelaw – not only at Ipswich and Northampton, but at Thetford and probably at Lincoln. We can quantify it by calculating, for the two halves of the ninth century, the proportions of single finds from the major sites, expressed as a percentage of all the listed finds (Table 3). *Hamwic* and London do not follow the same pattern.

TABLE 3. Coins from major sites as a percentage of all finds, for (a) the period to *ca* 850; (b) the period after *ca* 850.

	Before *ca* 850	After *ca* 850
Ipswich	4.25%	11.3%
Thetford	1.5%	6.5%
London	4.5%	5.35%
Hamwic	12.5%	8.1%

TABLE 4. Finds from north and south of the Thames of coins minted at Canterbury and London (numbers, followed by percentages in parentheses).

	Canterbury	London
North of Thames	86 (53%)	48 (71%)
South of Thames	75 (47%)	20 (29%)
	(100%)	(100%)

Canterbury coins, interestingly, tend to be more plentiful south of the Thames (Fig. 11). In the monetary circulation of the eighth century there is a pronounced tendency for particular types of secondary sceattas to show either a north-of-the-Thames or a south-of-the-Thames distribution, and one can detect a similar tendency in the ninth century. It is not very apparent to the eye when the data are mapped, but the statistics reveal the ratios clearly enough (Table 4). It will be interesting to see, on another occasion, how this compares with the intervening coinage of King Offa, the attribution of whose moneyers to Canterbury or London remains to some extent a grey area. And it will be of very real historical interest to see how the ninth-century pattern compares with that for the eleventh century. But in order to make these comparisons across the centuries we have to find standard numerical ways of describing the complex pattern of monetary circulation which are fair and appropriate to the comparison that is intended. The best way seems to be to make a simple regression analysis, by calculating the proportion of the local coins in progressive zones up to 25, 50, 75, 100km and so on away from each mint. One might expect the proportion to be highest in the vicinity of the mint-place, and to decline with distance. It is the exact way in which the proportion declines with distance that will give us clues to the characteristic role of each mint, as revealed by the differences between them.

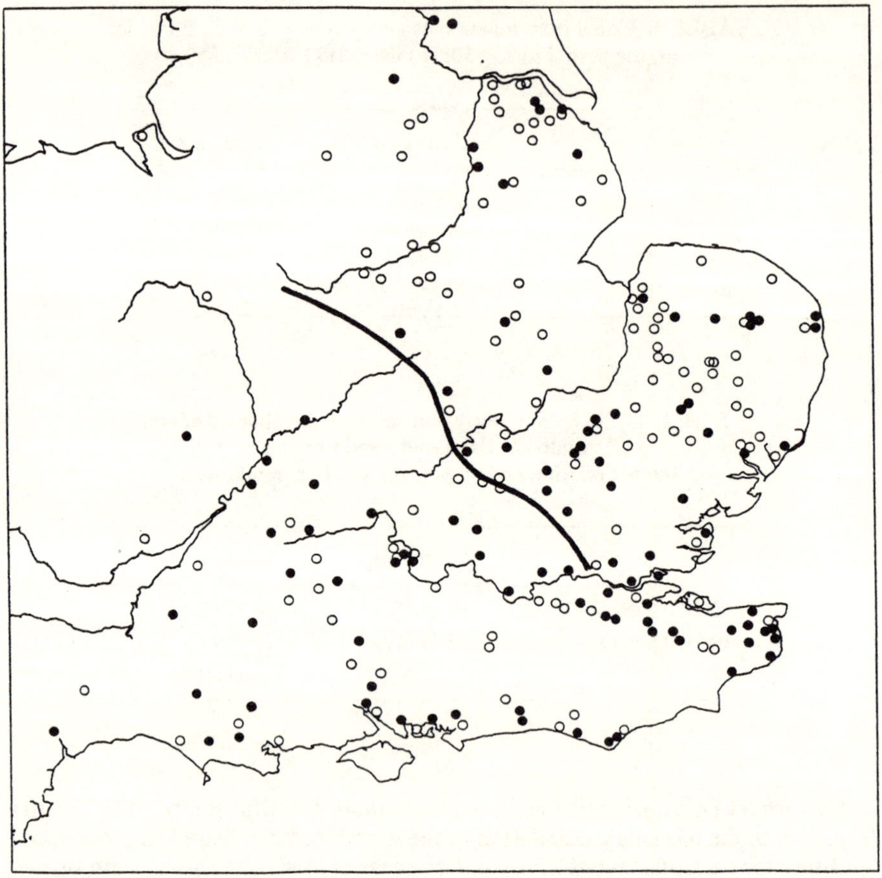

Fig. 11. Find localities of coins minted at Canterbury

Regression analysis

We draw concentric circles around each mint, to divide the country into zones 25km wide at an increasing distance from the mint (Fig. 12). The area of each zone will increase as we go further from the mint, and the number of coins falling into each zone will vary widely. The zone that includes Ipswich, for example (which will be a different zone for each mint), will immediately accumulate the thirty-two finds from that place. But the variation does not in principle affect the result, because we express the proportion for each zone of coins from the mint at the centre as a percentage – and the percentages are directly comparable. We can then plot the percentages on a graph, against distance from the mint, to obtain a line, a profile, which should reflect the way in which the coins are becoming diffused through the processes of circulation. All this is, of course, a familiar form of spatial analysis so far as geographers and archaeologists are concerned. They would expect to be able to show, for example, that high-class pottery had a

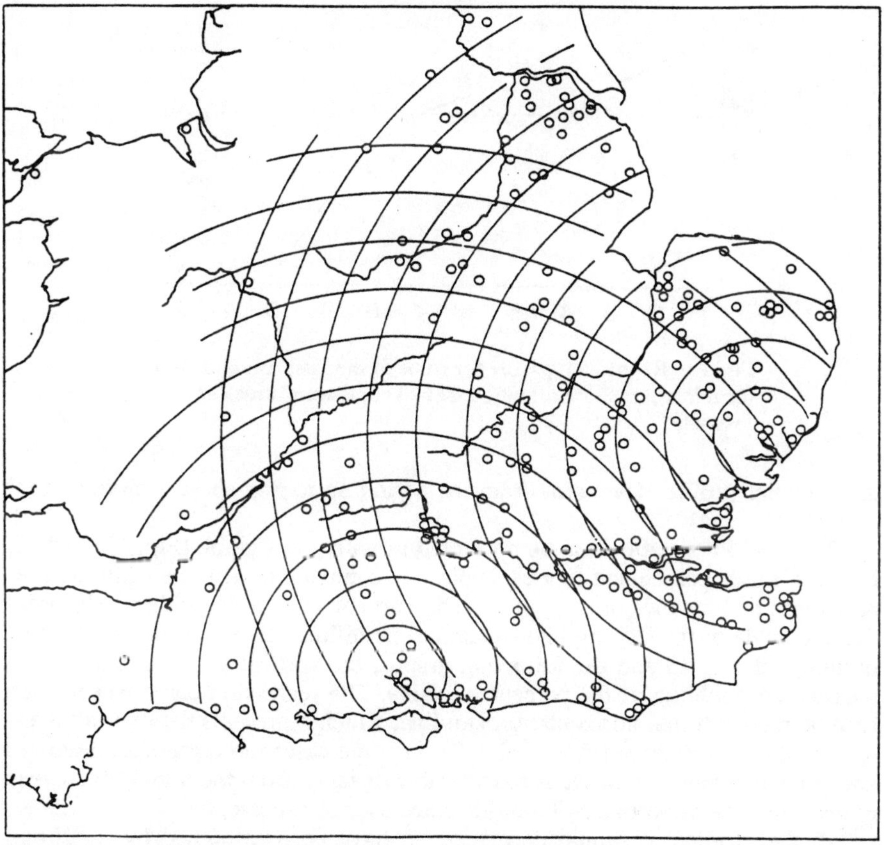

Fig. 12. Examples of 25km zoning around mint-places

different profile of dispersion from everyday coarse ware: the former was carried further than the latter. What the method allows us usefully to do is to compare one mint with another.

The profile for the East Anglian mint or mints (assumed for the purposes of drawing the concentric circles to be at Ipswich) is much as one might naively have imagined it should be: very high in the vicinity of the mint itself, and halving within 60 or 80km.

Zone	1	2	3	4	5	6	7	8	9	10	11	12
%	45	34	27	18	16	23	19	13	7	3	5	8

There is a blip in zone 6, which is obviously caused by the large number of St Edmund Memorial pennies excavated in Northampton. We do not know where that series was minted, and it is an open question whether there was more than one mint. Certainly, the number of moneyers involved was extremely large. If the St Edmund Memorial coins were struck (for example) partly in Middle Anglia, the form of regression analysis used here is inappropriate. That might account for

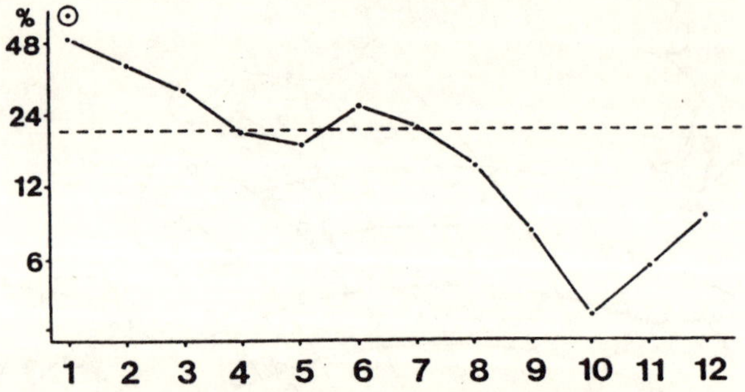

Fig. 13. Regression profile for coins of the East Anglian mint (or mints), on the assumption that all coins were struck at Ipswich

the irregular profile. The coins from the period up to 869 show a more normal regression.

The same information can be presented visually, as a graph (Fig. 13), which, because it uses percentage figures, is directly comparable with the similarly prepared graphs for other mints, below. The vertical scale is logarithmic (in order that the angle of the sloping line should not be influenced by the size of the proportion). In Fig. 13 and the following graphs, the vertical unit is standard, and measures a doubling of the percentage value. The regression curve can in each case be related to the horizontal broken line, which represents the over-all average for the mint (derived from Table 2). In some cases the regression line rises above the average in zones at a considerable distance from the mint. That serves to underline the importance of long-distance uses of coinage.

All the profiles, it should be explained, have been smoothed by weighting each percentage with half the percentage from the zone on either side. One could have achieved a similar result by weighting the actual numbers of coins, but as the totals can vary erratically from one zone to the next, because of the distribution of the major sites, it is probably more appropriate to smooth the graph using percentages. What one is plotting is, in effect, a convenient approximation to the data for a series of overlapping 50km zones. The unsmoothed percentage for zone 1 is ringed. It indicates a starting-point.

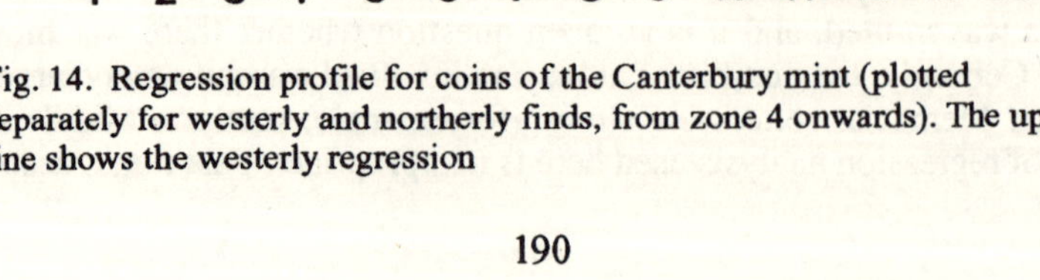

Fig. 14. Regression profile for coins of the Canterbury mint (plotted separately for westerly and northerly finds, from zone 4 onwards). The upper line shows the westerly regression

The profile for the Canterbury mint (Fig. 14) is much flatter and longer. Canterbury coins make up an almost identical proportion of the finds in any zone up to 300km away. This is, up to a point, what one might expect. Canterbury's dominance, with an average 35 per cent of all the finds, was difficult to dent, and once the coins had passed westwards beyond the immediate influence of London, there were no competing influences for them to encounter. However, what is unexpected but very clear is that there is no local concentration in the zone closest to the mint-place itself. The unsmoothed figure (the ringed dot) is no higher. From Canterbury itself we have nine single finds of which probably only three are of the local mint. One is reminded of Lafaurie's powerful analysis of single finds of Merovingian tremisses,[15] which led him to detect a contrast between mints whose coins are found locally, and other, prolific mints whose issues are scattered far and wide. He set this difference into a context of commercial routes, visible to us mainly as monetary routes, and he spoke of economic axes, monetary currents, zones to which money was attracted, and so on.

The large available sample of single finds of the Canterbury mint presents us with the opportunity to press the regression analysis one stage further, by distinguishing the *direction* in which the coins had travelled. On the map of Canterbury finds (Fig. 11), the line of the A5 trunk road (i.e. the line of Watling Street, and the Danelaw boundary) has been marked. Each zone (other than zones 1–3) is thus divided into a westerly and a northerly vector. When the percentages are calculated separately for the westerly and northerly halves of the dispersion, both profiles are strikingly flat and extended – and different.

Zone	1	2	3	4	5	6	7	8	9	10	11	12	13	14
% Westerly	48	52	49	42	42	44	43	41	46	52	50	39	25	33
% Northerly	–	–	–	25	29	25	25	25	25	26	24	27	34	31

The general implication of the figures, which are presented graphically in Fig. 14, is that Canterbury is, in Lafaurie's terms, one of those mints whose coins are found far and wide. Its coins were, obviously, put to a multiplicity of uses, but the topographical pattern is dominated by their use over long distances – doubtless in inter-regional trade. The westerly predominance is to some extent explained by competition from the London mint in regions to the north. The contrast between the vectors is nevertheless remarkably clear-cut. Zones 10 and 11 in a westerly direction take us as far as the Cotswolds and the Severn valley, where wool-production and export may provide the context for long-distance trade. The blip in zones 10 and 11, which takes the proportion above that in the immediate vicinity of Canterbury itself, gives a useful clue, but it cannot be by any means the whole story, when the graph is so level in all the intervening zones as well.

One ventures to press the claim, against those who are still inclined to think that the primary function of the coinage was to serve an aristocratic elite, that data which can be processed to reveal contrasts such as that between Figs 13 and

15 Lafaurie, 'Les routes commerciales', p. 267. A formal regression analysis of an updated list of single finds would, it is evident, be of lively interest.

14 points us in quite another direction. The primary function of the coins minted at Canterbury, or perhaps one should say the topographically dominant function, seems to have been inter-regional trade. Aristocratic uses of coinage might in principle be submerged within the evidence, as a secondary function, and they might in principle produce blips in the analytical diagrams. So far, none has come to light, unless one considers that Northampton might be something of the sort.

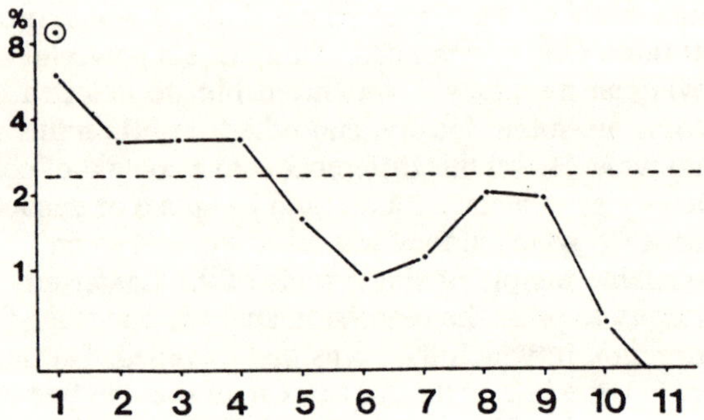

Fig. 15. Regression profile for the coins of the Wessex mint (assumed to be located at Winchester)

The profile for the West Saxon mint (Fig. 15) should not be relied upon for novel ideas, because it rests on only 11 single finds (in the context, of course, of a large body of negative evidence). The differences between the zones may well be unreliable, simply because of the wide margins of statistical uncertainty which will attach to them.

Zone	1	2	3	4	5	6	7	8	9	10	11
%	6.0	3.3	3.3	3.3	1.6	0.9	1.1	2.0	1.9	0.6	0

The mint-place has been assumed to be Winchester. From *Hamwic* (which lies within zone 1) the evidence is fortunately clear: only three coins of the local mint, among forty-seven listed. In the rest of zone 1, two out of seven single finds are local, which – if their evidence is at all representative – hints that the local coins were in some way preferred, and that there was a contrast in the functions or uses of money as between the commercial site of the *wic*, and the surrounding countryside.

The drift of the West Saxon issues appears to be predominantly north-eastwards (Fig. 16), and there is certainly no concentration of the local issues in western Wessex, such as would point towards a political interpretation of the work of the local mints. It may be that, once they had been carried as far as the middle Thames valley, the West Saxon coins were swept up among a much larger currency, and simply followed the patterns of movement of that currency.

From Rochester and its immediate vicinity there are four finds, none of which is of the local mint. The profile (Fig. 17) is intermediate between those for Canterbury and Wessex.

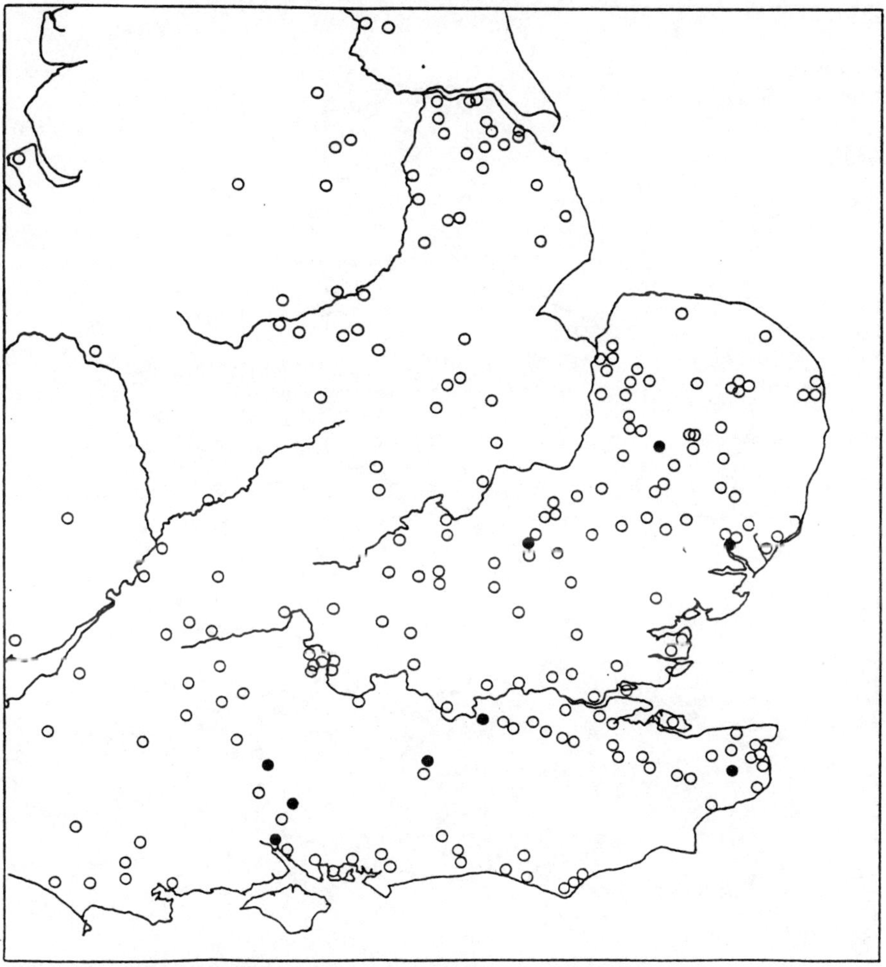

Fig. 16. Find localities of coins minted in Wessex

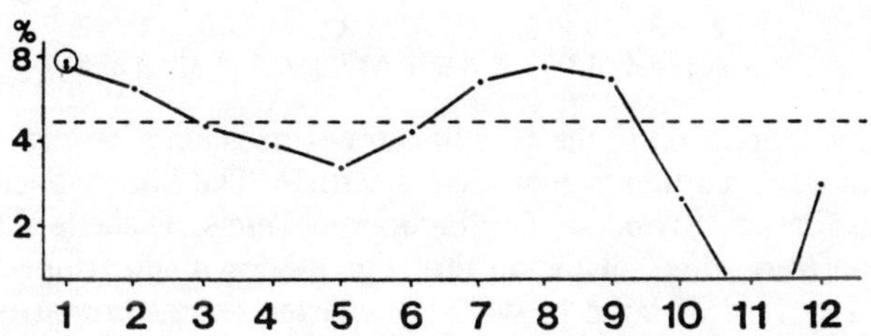

Fig. 17. Regression profile for coins of the Rochester mint

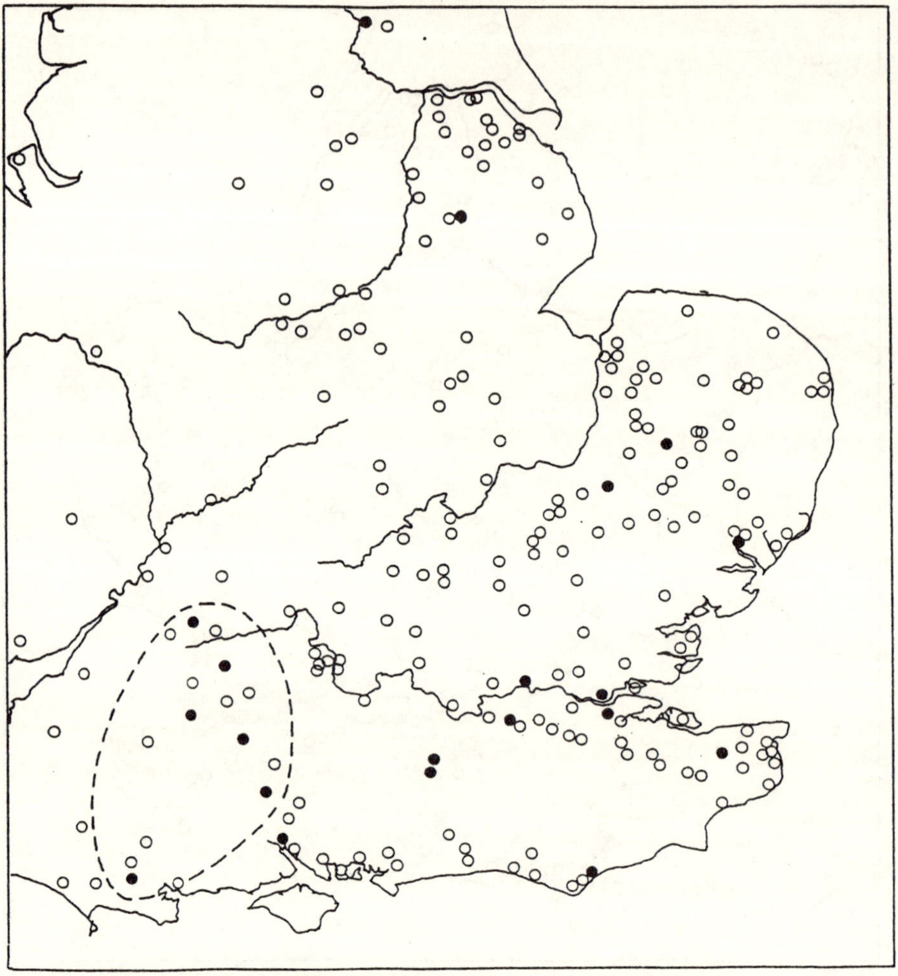

Fig. 18. Find localities of coins minted at Rochester (the ringed localities are referred to in the text; the symbols include one unlocated find from Hampshire

Zone	1	2	3	4	5	6	7	8	9	10	11	12
%	7.3	6.1	4.6	3.9	3.2	4.3	6.5	7.2	6.6	2.5	0	2.8

A dwindling proportion in the first five zones rises again in zones 7, 8, and 9. That is presumably a pointer to long-distance trade. The finds that cause the peak are from Cirencester, Swindon, Collingbourne Ducis, Bishops Cannings, and Bere Regis, an intriguing cluster on the edge of downland (ringed in Fig. 18). Again, there is a hint of trade in wool. Rochester served primarily a south-of-Thames, West Saxon hinterland, consonant with its right-bank location in the Thames estuary.

The profile for London (Fig. 19) shows a similar long-distance peak.

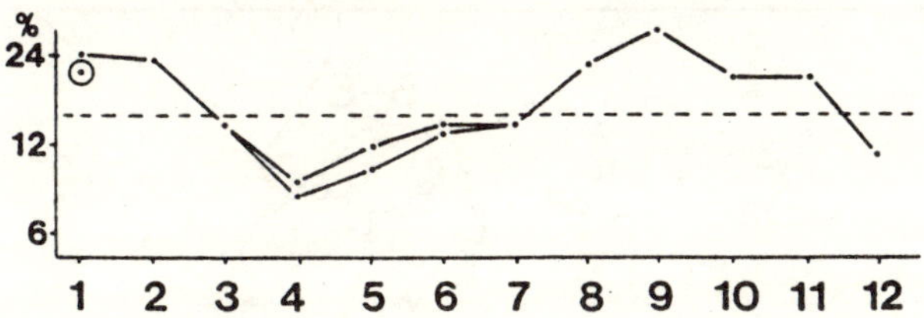

Fig. 19. Regression profile for coins of the London mint

Zone	1	2	3	4	5	6	7	8	9	10	11	12
%	24	23	14	8	10	13	14	22	29	20	20	11

In detail, the finds of London coins (Fig. 20) are rather difficult to interpret, and one suspects that local peculiarities would emerge more clearly from a larger sample. The northerly and westerly components do not show any significant contrasts, such as is found for Canterbury. The coinage of the time of Burgred, which makes up nearly half the London sample, is markedly peripheral in its distribution, and raises the suspicion that some coins were carried to distant places and lost, in circumstances which are perhaps not strictly comparable with those of the first half of the ninth century. One may mention finds from Caerleon (Fig. 20, 1), Cheddar Palace (2), Stoke Gifford (3), Stoke Bardolph (4), Barton-upon-Humber, and Barrow-upon-Humber (5, 6), as well as Southampton and York. Seven finds from *Hamwic* may, one suspects, reflect a hoard from the first half of the nineteenth century, for the same concentration has not been repeated in the modern excavations. If they were accepted as genuine single finds they would raise the percentages in zones 4, 5, and 6 to 9, 12, and 14 respectively (three zones are affected because of the smoothing procedure). It is clear from the diagram (Fig. 19) that the alternative does not greatly affect our understanding of the dispersion of London coins.

Coins minted in London are virtually absent among the Ipswich finds, and their distribution in East Anglia is curiously restricted. All in all, one hesitates to say much about the behaviour of London coins, except that they seem to exemplify the kind of mint-place that Lafaurie alluded to when he spoke of 'une circulation monétaire locale associée â une fonction économique plus étendue'.[16]

The main result to emerge from the regression analysis is of two contrasting types of mint-profile. Canterbury, Rochester, and London, which together account for two-thirds of the finds, seem to be much more involved with long-distance trade. The mints of East Anglia and especially Wessex stand aside from this commercial axis reaching up the Thames basin and into the Midlands: they have a more local function. Because foreign coins which reached England were in principle recycled, we have virtually no evidence for the continental destinations of the trade which passed via the Thames estuary and the Wantsum channel. The ports of the Rhine mouths were no doubt the major partners.

16 Lafaurie, 'Les routes commerciales', p. 269.

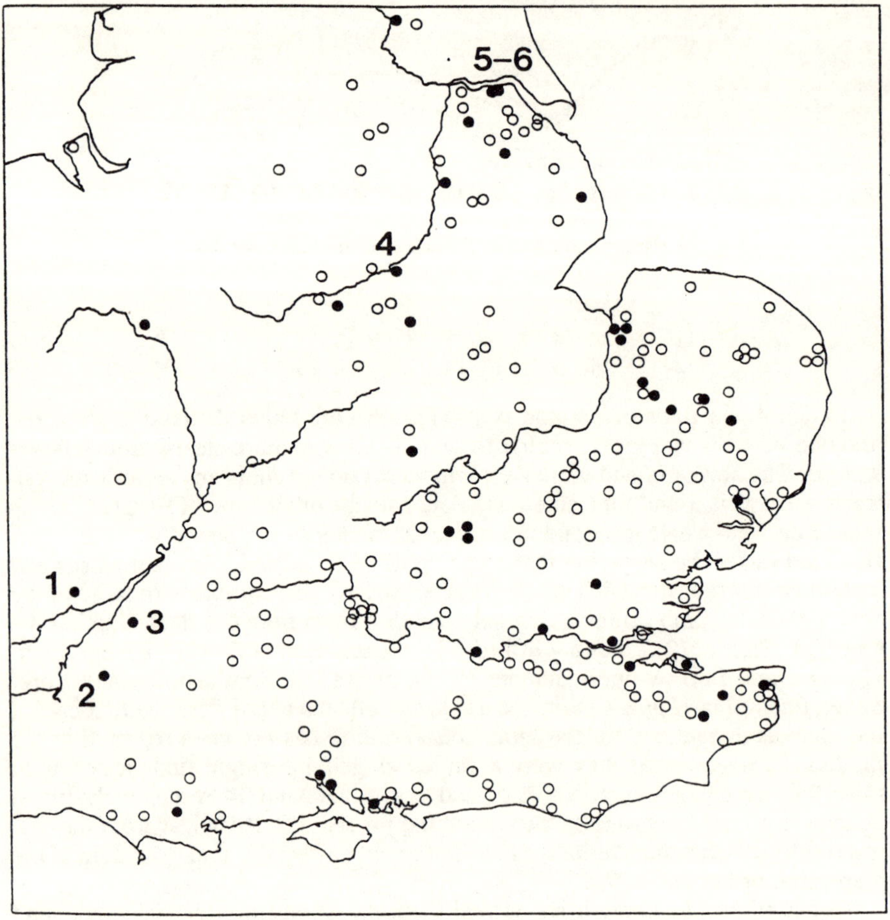

Fig. 20. Find localities of coins minted at London

Seven arguments against minimalism

To sum up: a topographical analysis of the find evidence offers at least an indirect rebuttal of the minimalist position. We have looked at the relation between town and country; the fringe penetration of Carolingian and Northumbrian coins; the easterly distribution of productive sites; the way in which coins freely crossed political frontiers; the balance between the mints, with Canterbury dominant and Wessex tiny; changes in the ranking of the mints during the ninth century in the context of North Sea trade; and finally we have compared the profiles of the various mints by a simple regression analysis. Had the use of coinage not been widespread through society, many of these patterns would have looked different. None of the arguments has relied on assumptions about the average output of a die or the overall volume of mint-output.

There are many other questions that we could frame, and then proceed to test against the data-base. Were West Saxon coins, minted in Kent, relatively more plentiful in Wessex than non-West Saxon coins minted in Kent? Are there any regional differences of emphasis in circulation between coins of the kings of Kent, and the archbishops? And so on.

Coexistence of a monetized and a non-monetary economy is normal

We had better be as precise as possible about how far the argument has carried us. A self-contained, non-monetized economy of agricultural estates, royal manors, and so on existed, of course, and will have left virtually no trace on the numismatic evidence. The rich lands of the Severn basin, for example, were relatively untouched by a money economy. But among the purposes that money *was* used for, long-distance trade seems to have been important. An assessment of the balance between the money economy, in all its aspects, and the non-monetized economy cannot be reached by way of the arguments we have been following. Let us be clear about that. It is probably always going to be very difficult to be sure about it. The scale of the currency is not in itself evidence for the level of monetary activity, even if one could agree on the average output of a die. Long-term trends in the rate of stray losses are more interesting, but it is very difficult to establish comparability across major social changes such as the growth of towns. Long-term trends revealed by the similarities or differences of regression profiles seem to be a promising way forward, and I hope on another occasion to try to find ways of drawing profiles for the period *ca* 973–1086, in order to see whether the eleventh century looks any different from the ninth.

IX

SINGLE FINDS OF NINTH-CENTURY COINS FROM SOUTHERN ENGLAND: A LISTING

Michael Bonser

The following list of ninth-century single-coin finds from south of the Humber has been gleaned, in the main, from published reports and works of reference, information from excavators, and reports from metal-detector users. Wherever possible a publication-reference is given for each coin; however, some of the excavation-finds are as yet unpublished and the details incomplete. Most of the metal-detector finds are from the past decade; some are already published, many are in the course of publication at the time of writing, and some are very recent finds awaiting future publication. The coins are listed by the kingdom and then the ruler for whom they were struck, rather than by the mint-place. Within each reign the arrangement is alphabetical by find-spot.

Coin-finds of the last few years of the eighth century, after Offa's death (796), have been included here because this date forms a more natural division for the coinage than an arbitrary 800. A listing of single finds from the reign of Offa is in preparation by Mr Derek Chick. All known single-coin finds of the St Edmund Memorial issue have also been included, despite the fact that many were struck in the early tenth century because a firm chronology is lacking, and because many of those noted here have insufficient detail to enable them to be classified as early or late examples. Foreign coins of the ninth century – many of which come from areas with a Scandinavian presence – have been included in the list.

It was decided in principle to exclude from the listing the base Northumbrian 'stycas' since they were listed in detail by Elizabeth Pirie in 1986, and because they are a distinctive coinage that circulated mainly in Northumbria to the exclusion of southern silver pennies. The present listing does not, then, include 'stycas' found in Northumbria or Scotland. However, the number of 'stycas' found south of the Humber has grown in recent years and a distinctive pattern is emerging for Lincolnshire and East Anglia. It has therefore been decided to include a section on these finds.

Few silver pennies or foreign coins have been found in Northumbria, Scotland or Wales, and for convenience they have been included here under the relevant kings, although they are not strictly within the scope of this paper.

This list was closed in September 1991, and, although finds have continued to occur at a significant rate, I have resisted the temptation to include them. To have done so would have required the redrawing of the accompanying histograms and maps, which have been painstakingly prepared by Derek Chick, and the revision of many tables and maps in Michael Metcalf's paper which draws its data from this listing. In any event no catalogue of coin-finds is ever complete. It is no more than a sample, however hard one tries to record new material or to search for all accounts. Further work, for example, on county Sites and Monuments Records or in the archives of local museums and archaeological units, would no doubt yield some relevant finds. Nonetheless the present tally of some five hundred ninth-century finds (including fifty 'stycas') is a far larger and richer body of material than has ever been available before to monetary historians.

The number of metal-detector users, excavators and numismatists who have brought finds to my attention over the last decade or more is too large for me to list, but my debt to them is fundamental. I must also acknowledge the care and skill which Derek Chick has kindly lavished on the accompanying histograms and maps. Mark Blackburn and David Dumville, as editors, have also spent a great deal of time pulling into shape the manuscript, which has been typed and revised several times by Ruth Johnson of the Department of Anglo-Saxon, Norse, and Celtic at Cambridge.

KINGS OF EAST ANGLIA

Eadwald (ca 796–ca 800)

BIDFORD-ON-AVON, Warwicks., 27 April 1991. *Circumscription obverse* type (unpublished type), East Anglia, Eadnoth. 1.28g, 0°. 'Coin Register' 1990, no. 196.

BIDFORD-ON-AVON, Warwicks., April 1986. *Three-line/quatrefoil* type (BLS Ea 1), East Anglia, Eadnoth. Two joining fragments, 0.34g, 270°. 'Coin Register' 1988, no. 142, as 'Offa, king of Mercia(?)'; Chick & Seaby, 'A new variant', p. 221.

BRANDON, near, Suffolk, 1989. *Circumscription obverse* type (unpublished type), East Anglia, Eadnoth. 1.38g. Christies, 10 October 1989, lot 457 (illustrated). To be published by Blackburn, Bonser and Chick.

CRINGLEFORD, near Norwich, Norfolk, March 1991. *Three-line/quatrefoil* type (BLS Ea 1), East Anglia, Eadnoth. Fragment, weight and die-axis not recorded. To be published.

IPSWICH (Buttermarket), Suffolk. Type not specified, East Anglia, Lul. Excavation-find. Information from Suffolk Archaeological Unit.

IPSWICH, north of, Suffolk, 27 December 1989. *Three-line/cross fourchée* type (BLS Ea 3 var.), East Anglia, Wihtred. Information J. Sadler.

NORWICH AREA, Norfolk, before 1983. *Three-line/quatrefoil* type (BLS Ea 1), East Anglia, Eadnoth. 1.31g, 270°. Blackburn & Bonser, 'Single finds – 2', no. 51. (Fitzwilliam Museum, Blunt collection)

OXBOROUGH, near, Methwold, Norfolk, 1985. *Three-line/quatrefoil* type (BLS –), East Anglia, Wo(del)? 0.34g, fragment, *ca* 225°. Blackburn & Bonser, 'Single finds – 2', no. 66, where it is listed under 'Thetford region, or more probably King's Lynn region, Norfolk'. (Private collection)

RAMSHOLT, near Woodbridge, Suffolk, August 1989. *Three-line/cross* type (unpublished type), East Anglia, moneyer uncertain, but probably Botred. 0.48g, fragment. Information from Suffolk Archaeological Unit.

RICHBOROUGH, Kent, 1924. *Three-line/quatrefoil* type (BLS Ea 2), East Anglia, Lul. 1.43g. Excavation-find. Dolley, *Anglo-Saxon Pennies*, plate 1, 3. (British Museum)

TILBURY, Essex, 1986/7. *Three-line/quatrefoil* type (BLS Ea 2), East Anglia, Lul. 1.33g, 180°. *Numismatic Circular* July 1987, no. 4363. To be published by Blackburn and Bonser.

WETHERINGSETT-CUM-BROCKFORD, near Stowmarket, Suffolk, 1987. *Three-line/cross fourchée* type (BLS Ea 3 var.), East Anglia, Wihtred. 1.09g, 20% of coin missing, 180°. *Numismatic Circular* September 1987, no. 5087; 'Coin Register' 1987, no. 116. (Private collection)

Æthelstan (ca 825 – ca 845)

BULWICK, Northants., *ca* 1864. *Cross moline* type (N 442), East Anglia, Torthelm. 1.34g, 270°. *SCBI* Copenhagen I, 93.

DEBENHAM, near Stowmarket, Suffolk, 1989. East Anglia, Athelhelm. 1.22g. Information from Suffolk Archaeological Unit.

GARBOLDISHAM, Norfolk, before 1919. *Non-portrait* type (N 446 var.), East Anglia, Monn. Found at an old maltings. Pagan, 'The coinage', p. 61, v.

HOCKWOLD, near Feltwell, Norfolk, 1981. *Cross and wedges* type (N 445), East Anglia, Æthelhelm. Weight not recorded, 0°. 'Coin Register' 1987, no. 117.

HUNDON, Suffolk, before 1949. *Non-portrait* type (N 441), East Anglia, Reghere. 1.23g chipped. Pagan, 'The coinage', p. 62, I, 1. (British Museum)

OXBOROUGH, near, Methwold, Norfolk, 1980s. Fragment. Information from Norfolk Archaeological Unit.

ROCHESTER, near, Kent, before 1874. *Non-portrait* type (N 447), East Anglia, Monn. 1.28g, 0°. *SCBI* Copenhagen I, 95.

ROYSTON, near, Herts., 1985. *Non-portrait* type (N 445), East Anglia, Æthelhelm. 0.92g chipped, 180°. Blackburn & Bonser, 'Single finds – 3', no. 57. (With the finder)

ROYSTON, near, Herts., December 1988. *Non-portrait* type (N 442), East Anglia, Torthelm. 1.23g, chipped, 320°. To be published by Blackburn and Bonser. (With the finder)

SIX HILLS, near, Leics., 14 September 1986. *Non-portrait* type (N 440), East Anglia, Torthelm. 1.21g, edge chips, 270°. *Numismatic Circular* July 1987, no. 4364. Slight differences in published weights are due to small pieces breaking away from the edge. To be published by Blackburn, Bonser and Chick.

WEST HARLING, near East Harling, Norfolk, 1977. *Ship* type (N 449/1), East Anglia, Eadgar. 1.27g, *ca* 0°. Archibald, 'A ship type'. (Castle Museum, Norwich)

Æthelweard (ca 845 – ca 855)

IPSWICH, Suffolk, 1957/8. *Cross-crosslet* type (N 455), East Anglia, Twicga, 1.24g. *SCBI* East Anglia 1071.

IPSWICH, Suffolk, *ca* 1966. *Letter A/cross pattée* type (N 450), East Anglia, Dudda. Excavation-find. Information from T. H. McK. Clough.

Edmund (ca 855 – 869)

BARHAM, Ipswich, Suffolk, July 1981. *Omega/cross pattée* type (N 462), East Anglia, Twicga. 0.96g. *Ipswich Numismatic Society Notes* 5 (1984), pp. 9–11. (Private collection)

BLEWBURY, near Didcot, Oxon., January 1989. *Letter A/cross and pellets* type (N 456), East Anglia, Eadberht. Weight and die-axis not recorded. To be published by Blackburn, Bonser and Chick.

ERISWELL, Mildenhall, Suffolk, *ca* February 1964. No details known except that, 'the coin was found in a garden'. *Seaby's Coins & Medals Bulletin* 1964, p. 136.

IPSWICH (Buttermarket), Suffolk. Excavation-find. Information Suffolk Archaeological Unit.

IPSWICH (Franciscan Way), Suffolk. Excavation-find. Information Suffolk Archaeological Unit.

READING, Berks., before 1919. *Cross and crescents/cross and wedges* type (N 457), East Anglia, Ethelwulf. *Numismatic Circular*, November–December 1919, no. 76229.

THETFORD, Norfolk, 1988. *Cross and crescents/cross and wedges* type (N 457), East Anglia, Ethelwulf. 1.16g, 90°. Found during construction of the by-pass. To be published by Blackburn, Bonser and Chick.

KINGS OF KENT

Eadberht Præn (796 – ca 798)

BAWSEY, near King's Lynn, Norfolk, March–April 1990. *Three-line* type (BLS Ep 2), Canterbury, Ethelmod. 0.31g, fragment, *ca* 70°. To be published by Blackburn, Rogerson and Margeson.

BAWSEY, near King's Lynn, Norfolk, two pieces found separately in 1988 and 1989. *Three-line* type (BLS Ep 1), Canterbury, Babba. 1.14g, edge chipped, 180°. To be published by Blackburn, Rogerson and Margeson.

HELLESDON, Norwich, Norfolk, 1846. *Three-line* type (BLS Ep 1), Canterbury, Babba. 1.32g. *BMC* 2; BLS Ep 1a.

LETCHWORTH?, Herts., before 1956. *Two-line* type (BLS Ep 4), Canterbury, Ethelnoth. 1.35g. This coin has not been included on the maps; it was bought at Letchworth in 1956 and very possibly found locally, but this is speculative. *Archaeologia Cantiana* 71 (1957), pp. 162–6; BLS Ep 4.

MAIDSTONE?, Kent, before 1869. *Three-line* type (BLS Ep 2), Canterbury,

Ethelmod. 1.03g, slight edge chip. BLS Ep 2e; Mack sale II (Glendining, 23 March 1977), lot 71. As there is some doubt about the find-spot, it has not been included on the distribution-maps. The coin is variously described as having been acquired in Copenhagen or found at Maidstone.

SANDWICH, near, Kent, before 1882. *Three-line* type (BLS Ep 2), Canterbury, Ethelmod. 1.20g, 90°. BLS Ep 2a. (British Museum)

SWAFFHAM, Norfolk, December 1990. *Two-line* type (BLS —), Canterbury, Duda. Weight and die-axis not recorded. Information from D. S. Chick.

WEST HYTHE, near Lympne, Kent, 1950s. *Three-line* type (BLS Ep 2), Canterbury, Ethelmod. 1.27g, 0°. Blackburn & Bonser, 'Single finds – 2', no. 71. (Private collection)

Cuthred (798–807)

ANDOVER, Hants., before 1886. *Cross moline* type (BLS Cd 9), *ca* 802 x *ca* 804, Canterbury, Eaba. 1.23g. Brooke, 'Anglo-Saxon acquisitions II', no. 159; BLS Cd 9a.

BEDFORDSHIRE, before 1873. *Double tribrach* type (BLS Cd 8), *ca* 802 x *ca* 804, Canterbury, Eaba. 1.30g. 'Probably found in Beds.'. Hawkins, *The Silver Coins*, p. 33; BLS Cd 8a. (British Museum)

BLEDLOW AREA, Bucks., November 1989. *Portrait* type (BLS Cd 20), *ca* 804x807, Canterbury, Sigeberht. To be published by Blackburn, Bonser and Chick.

BRIXWORTH, Northants., 1879. *Portrait* type (BLS Cd 16), *ca* 804x807, Canterbury, Eaba. 1.44g, 270°. *SCBI* Midlands Museums 95.

BURROW HILL, Butley, Suffolk, 1980/1. *Portrait* type (BLS Cd 15 var.), *ca* 804x807, Canterbury, Duda. 1.35g. Excavation-find. Sherlock, 'The coins', no. 13.

CAMBRIDGE, near, before 1886. *Portrait* type (BLS Cd 15), *ca* 804x807, Canterbury, Duda. 1.23g. Brooke, 'Anglo-Saxon acquisitions II', no. 158; BLS Cd 15b.

HERTFORDSHIRE, before 1909. *Portrait* type (BLS Cd 15), *ca* 804x807, Canterbury, Duda. 1.17g. BLS Cd 15g.

?LONDON (?Billingsgate excavation spoil), before September 1986. *Tribach* type (BLS Cd 5), *ca* 802 x *ca* 804, Canterbury, Sigeberht. 0.73g, chipped, *ca* 125°. 'Coin Register' 1987, no. 98, where it is noted, 'Find-spot not reported, but "lacey" corrosion is reminiscent of some finds from the Billingsgate, London, soil dumps in Essex.'

LONDON, before 1890. *Tribrach* type (BLS Cd 2), *ca* 802 x *ca* 804, Canterbury, Eaba. Fragment. *BMC* 12 (the actual coin).

RECULVER, Kent, before 1783. *Triple tribrach* type (BLS Cd 1), *ca* 802 x *ca* 804, Canterbury, Duda. 1.46g. BLS Cd 1b. There is a query as to whether this is the actual specimen from Reculver.

ROYSTON, near, Herts., 1985. *Triple tribrach* type (BLS Cd 2), *ca* 802 x *ca* 804, Canterbury, Eaba. 1.14g, 330°. Blackburn & Bonser, 'Single finds – 3', no. 53. (With the finder)

ROYSTON, near, Herts., 1985/6. *Triple tribrach* type (BLS Cd 1–2), *ca* 802 x *ca* 804, Canterbury, Duda or Eaba? 0.91g, fragment, 300°. Blackburn & Bonser, 'Single finds – 3', no. 54. (With the finder)

SOUTHAMPTON (St Mary's), before 1864. *Tribrach* type, *ca* 802 x *ca* 804, Canterbury, Werheard. Pagan, 'The older finds', p. 64, 9.

SOUTHAMPTON, 1825–65. *Tribrach* type (BLS Cd 4), *ca* 802 x *ca* 804, Canterbury, Werheard. Found during brickearth digging. Pagan, 'The older finds', p. 64, no. 9.

SOUTHAMPTON (Six Dials), 1977–9. *Single tribrach* type (BLS Cd 11) *ca* 802 x *ca* 804, Canterbury, Sigeberht. 0.81g, broken. Excavation-find. Metcalf, 'The coins', p. 53, no. 137; *SCBI* South-Eastern Museums 623.

SOUTHAMPTON (Stoner Motors), 1982. *Portrait* type (BLS Cd 22), *ca* 804x807, Canterbury, Werheard. 1.32g. Excavation-find. Metcalf, 'The coins', p. 53, no. 138; *SCBI* South-Eastern Museums 624.

SOUTHMINSTER, near, Essex, 1984. *Portrait* type (BLS Cd 16), *ca* 804x807, Canterbury. No letters of the moneyer's name are visible, but the obverse die-links with Cd 16c, a coin of Eaba. 0.75g, in two fragments. Bispham, 'Recent metal detector finds', p. 185, no. E8. (With the finder)

TOCKENHAM, near Wootton Bassett, Wilts., 1985. *Portrait* type (BLS Cd 23), *ca* 804x807, Canterbury, Werheard. 1.10g. BLS Cd 23e.

WESTBURY, Wilts., 1865. *Double tribrach* type (BLS Cd 7), *ca* 802 x *ca* 804, Canterbury, Werheard. 1.39g. Brooke, 'Anglo-Saxon acquisitions II', no. 163; BLS Cd 7b.

Canterbury Anonymous Regal Issue (ca 822/3)

EYNSHAM ABBEY, Oxford, 1854. *Bare head* type (BLS An 7), Canterbury, Werheard. 1.41g. BLS An 7. (Fitzwilliam Museum, Blunt collection)

SOUTHAMPTON. *Bare head* type (BLS An 3), Canterbury, Oba. 1.26g. Excavation-find. Metcalf, 'The coins', p. 53, no. 139; *SCBI* South-Eastern Museums 624.

SOUTHAMPTON, *ca* 1825. Canterbury, Diormod. 1.43g. Pagan, 'The older finds', p. 63, no. 6.

Baldred (ca 823–825)

AYLESFORD, near, Kent, before 1874. *Cross pattée* type (BLS Ba 15), Canterbury, Tidbearht. 1.23g. BLS Ba 15e. (Fitzwilliam Museum, Blunt collection)

EAST COKER, near Yeovil, Somerset, 1860x1870. *Cross pattée* type (BLS Ba 16), Canterbury, Werheard. 1.23g. Found in the churchyard. BLS Ba 16b.

FAIRFORD (Claydon Pike), Glos., 1982. *Cross pattée* type (BLS Ba 10), Canterbury, Oba. 1.24g, chipped and holed through centre, 0°. Excavation-find. *CBA Report* January–February 1983.

GUILDFORD, near, Surrey, *ca* 1850. *Portrait/cross moline* type (BLS Ba 18), Rochester, Dunun. 1.09g, 0°. *SCBI* Mack 648.

HUNCOTE, near, Leics., 1984. *Portrait ('Bonnet')* type (BLS Ba 2 var.), Canterbury, Diormod. 1.27g, 45°. Blackburn & Bonser, 'Single finds – 1', no. 12. (Fitzwilliam Museum, Blunt collection)

LONDON (R. Thames at Lambeth), 1973. *Portrait ('Bonnet')* type (BLS Ba 1 obv., Ba 7 rev.), Canterbury, Diormod. 1.12g. Blunt, 'A new coin of Baldred'.

SWINDON ('Old Swindon'), Wilts., 1903. *Portrait/'Wheel'* type (BLS Ba 19), Rochester, Dunun. 1.35g. BLS Ba 19. (Ashmolean Museum) This coin has not been included on the distribution-maps, as some doubt has lately been cast on the find-spot; cf. *Wiltshire Archaeological Magzine* 1972–3, p. 197, n. 10.

THETFORD, Norfolk, 1983. *Portrait/crooked cross* type (BLS Ba –), Rochester, Ealhstan. Blackburn & Bonser, 'Single finds – 1', no. 26.

ARCHBISHOPS OF CANTERBURY

Æthelheard (without reference to the king, 796 x ca 798?)

SUFFOLK, north east?, before 1989. *Circumscription/moneyer's name* type (BLS –; N 231/1), Canterbury, Eadgar. 1.23g. Chick, 'A remarkable new penny'.

Æthelheard (under Cenwulf, ca 798–804)

BERE REGIS, near, Dorset, 1987. *Circumscription/letter M* type (BLS Æ 2), Canterbury. Weight and die-axis not recorded.

BIDFORD-ON-AVON, Warwicks., October 1988. *Circumscription/letter M* type (BLS Æ 2), Canterbury. 1.17g, slight chipping, 0°. 'Coin Register' 1988, no. 140.

CISSBURY, N. of Worthing, Sussex, before 1916. *Circumscription/letter M* type (BLS Æ 2), Canterbury. 1.37g. *SCBI* Cambridge 437; Grierson & Blackburn, *Medieval European Coinage* 1, no. 1140.

EASTRY, Kent, before 1886. *Circumscription/letter M* type (BLS Æ 2), Canterbury. 1.23g. BLS Æ 2a. (British Museum)

'ESSEX', 1988. *Circumscription/letter M* type (BLS Æ 2), Canterbury. 1.27g, 180°. Bought by Spink.

IPSWICH (School St), Suffolk. Excavation-find. Information from Suffolk Archaeological Unit.

ROCHESTER CATHEDRAL, Kent, before 1876. *Circumscription/tribrach* type (BLS Æ 1), Canterbury. BLS Æ 1e.

SOUTHAMPTON (Six Dials). *Circumscription/letter M* type (BLS Æ 2), Canterbury. 1.29g. Metcalf, 'The coins', p. 53, no. 140; *SCBI* South-Eastern Museums 624.

SOUTHAMPTON (Six Dials), 1982. *Circumscription/letter M* type (BLS Æ 2), Canterbury. 1.10g. Metcalf, 'The coins', p. 53, no. 141; *SCBI* South-Eastern Museums 625.

STANSTED (New Stansted Hall), Essex, 1870. *Circumscription/tribrach* type (BLS Æ 1), Canterbury. 1.08g, chipped, 330°. Found in earth dug out for the foundations of the Hall. *SCBI* Mack 652.

STOKE DOWN, N.W. of West Stoke, near Chichester, Sussex, 1936. *Circumscription/letter M* type (BLS Æ 2), Canterbury. 1.11g. *SCBI* Norweb 85.

Wulfred (805–832)

BARMBY, N. Humberside, 1984. Group II (BLS Wu 3), *ca* 810, Canterbury, Swefherd. To be published by Blackburn, Bonser and Chick.

BAWSEY, near King's Lynn, Norfolk, March–April 1990. Group I, *Alpha-Omega* type (BLS Wu 2), *ca* 805 x *ca* 810, Canterbury, without moneyer's name. 0.76g, fragment, 0°. To be published by Blackburn, Rogerson and Margeson. (Fitzwilliam Museum)

BOXLEY, near Maidstone, Kent, November 1989. *Regular monogram* type (N 240/1), *ca* 815x823, Canterbury, Sæberht. Weight and die-axis not recorded. To be published.

DARTFORD, Kent, before 18 June 1979. *Anonymous* issue (BLS Wu 14), *ca* 823, Canterbury, Wilnoth. 1.31g, 180°. 'Coin Register' 1987, no. 105.

DEAL, near, Kent, 24 March 1991. *Anonymous* issue (BLS Wu 12), *ca* 823, Canterbury, Swefherd. 0.97g, chipped, 180°. To be published.

DOVER, at or near, Kent, before 1836. Group VI, *Baldred* type (BLS Wu 17), *ca* 823 x *ca* 825, Canterbury, Swefherd. 1.35g. *BMC* 28 (this coin); information from C. E. Blunt.

(GREAT?) LIMBER, Lincs., before 1766. Group III, *Regular monogram* type (BLS Wu 6), *ca* 810 x *ca* 823, Canterbury, Saeberht. '21+ gr.'. Blackburn *et al.*, *Early Medieval Coins from Lincoln*, pp. 7, 8.

GREAT MISSENDEN, Bucks., February 1988. Group I, *Cross-crosslet* type (BLS Wu 1), *ca* 805 x *ca* 810, Canterbury. 1.33g, 180°. Christies, 28 February 1989, lot 200.

HOLLINGBOURNE, Kent, 1986. Group III, *Regular monogram* type (BLS Wu 7A), *ca* 810 x *ca* 823, Canterbury, Swefherd. 1.40g, 270°. To be published by Blackburn, Bonser and Chick.

LONDON BRIDGE, March 1824. Group III, *Regular monogram* type (BLS Wu 4D), *ca* 810 x *ca* 823, Canterbury, Sæberht. Stott, 'Saxon and Norman coins', no. 60.

LOUTH, near, Lincs., 1987. Group II/III, *Transitional* type (BLS Wu –), *ca* 810, Canterbury, Swefherd. 1.25g. To be published by Blackburn, Bonser and Chick. (Private collection)

MELBOURN, Cambs., September 1984. Group II, *Transitional monogram* type (BLS Wu 3), *ca* 810, Canterbury, Sæberht. 1.37g, 230°. Blackburn & Bonser, 'Single finds – 1', no. 19. (With the finder)

NORTH ESSEX, *ca* 1980x1983. *Second monogram* type (BLS Wu 19), *ca* 825x832, Canterbury, Swefherd? Large fragment, weight and die-axis not recorded. 'Coin Register' 1987, no. 103.

SOUTHAMPTON, *ca* 1825x1865. Group IV, *Anonymous* issue (BLS Wu 13), *ca* 823, Canterbury, Luning. Pagan, 'The older finds', p. 64, no. 9.

WALLINGFORD, Oxon., before 1886. Group III, *Regular monogram* type (BLS Wu 8), *ca* 810 x *ca* 823, Canterbury, Swefherd. 1.24g. Brooke, 'Anglo-Saxon acquisitions II', no. 200; BLS Wu 8f.

WESTBURY, Wilts., before 21 August 1974. *Regular monogram* type (BLS Wu 4A), *ca* 810 x *ca* 823, Canterbury, Saeberht. 1.34g, 0°. Said to have been found on the White Horse of Westbury. 'Coin Register' 1987, no. 101.

Ceolnoth (833–870)

CANVEY ISLAND, Essex, 1988. *Chi-Rho monogram* type (N 242), *ca* 843 x *ca* 848, Canterbury, moneyer uncertain. 0.78g, very corroded, 0°(?). 'Coin Register' 1988, no. 141.

EXETER (Cathedral), Devon, 1932. *Dorovernia Ca monogram* type (N 241), *ca* 833 x *ca* 839, Canterbury, Biornmod. Excavation-find from the Deanery gardens. The coin was subsequently lost in a War-time air-raid. Dolley & Shiel, 'A Carolingian *denarius*', p. 11.

FARNBOROUGH, Kent, after 1984. *DORBC monogram* type (N 241), *ca* 833 x *ca* 839, Canterbury, Biornmod. 0.80g, fragmentary. To be published by Blackburn, Bonser and Chick. (With the finder)

FLIXBOROUGH, N. Lincs., 1990/91. *Portrait/Dorovernia Ca monogram* type (N 241), *ca* 839 x *ca* 843. Excavation-find. Blackburn, 'Coin finds in Lindsey', p. 87.

GLOUCESTER, before 1795. *Dorovernia Ca monogram* type (N 241), *ca* 839 x *ca* 843, Canterbury, Wunhere. 1.30g, 270°. *SCBI* Oxford 49.

HOLLINGBOURNE, Kent, March 1990. *DORBC monogram* type (N —), *ca* 833 x *ca* 839, Canterbury, Biornmod. 0.88g, fragment, 0°. To be published by Blackburn, Bonser and Chick.

KIRMINGTON, Lincs., *ca* 1987. *Lunettes* type (N 249), *ca* 866 x *ca* 870, Canterbury, Hebeca. 1.07, 270°. 'Coin Register' 1987, no. 104. (With the finder)

MILTON KEYNES, near, Bucks., 1989. *Chi-Rho monogram* type (N 242), *ca* 843 x *ca* 848, Canterbury, Biornmod. Weight and die-axis not recorded. *Treasure Hunting* May 1990, p. 54, where the coin is illustrated but without find-spot.

ROYSTON, near, Herts., 1985. *DORBC monogram* type (N —), *ca* 833 x *ca* 839, Canterbury, Biornmod. 0.47g, fragment, 180°. Blackburn & Bonser, 'Single finds – 3', no. 58. (With the finder)

SOUTHAMPTON (Six Dials), 1980/1. *Inscribed cross* type (N 245), *ca* 852 x *ca* 862, Canterbury, Liabing. 0.68g, broken and chipped. Excavation-find. Metcalf, 'The coins', p. 53, no. 142.

SOUTHAMPTON (Edinburgh Hotel), *ca* 1855. *Dorovernia Ca monogram* type (N 241), *ca* 839 x *ca* 843, Canterbury, Wunhere. Pagan, 'The older finds', pp. 63–4, no. 7.

Æthelred (870–888)

TETBURY, near, Glos. *Cross and lozenge* type (N 251), *ca* 875 x *ca* 880, Canterbury, Torhtmund. 1.32g. *SCBI* Cambridge 446; Grierson and Blackburn, *Medieval European Coinage* 1, no. 1353; Blackburn & Keynes, above, no. 19.

Plegmund (890–923)

There are no recorded single finds of coin of Archbishop Plegmund. Two coins, one of them fragmentary, found on the Thames foreshore at Southwark in 1974/5, may be part of an early tenth-century hoard.

KINGS OF MERCIA

Cenwulf (796–821)

ALDWORTH, Berks., before April 1988. *Tribrach* type (BLS Cn 11), *ca* 798 x *ca* 802, Canterbury, Ethelmod. 1.34g, 270°. 'Coin Register' 1988, no. 154.

ALFORD, near, Lincs., 1980s. *Tribrach* type (BLS Cn 21), *ca* 798 x *ca* 804, London, Wighard. 1.32g, 160°. Bispham, 'Recent metal detector finds', p. 185, L6. (With the finder)

BAWSEY, near King's Lynn, Norfolk, *ca* 1980x1986. *Tribrach* type (BLS Cn 5–22), *ca* 798 x *ca* 804. Moneyer's name not recorded. To be published by Blackburn, Rogerson and Margeson.

BAWSEY, *ca* 1980x1986. *Portrait/cross and wedges* type (BLS Cn 23–30), *ca* 807 x *ca* 810. Moneyer's name not recorded. To be published by Blackburn, Rogerson and Margeson.

BAWSEY, *ca* 1980x1986. Fragment. Moneyer's name not recorded. No details. To be published by Blackburn, Rogerson and Margeson.

BAWSEY, *ca* 1980x1986. *Portrait/cross and wedges* type (N 44), *ca* 807 x *ca* 810. Canterbury, Sigeberht. To be published by Blackburn, Rogerson and Margeson.

BAWSEY, *ca* 1980x1986. No details, but the moneyer is said to be unrecorded in North, *English Hammered Coinage*. To be published by Blackburn, Rogerson and Margeson.

BEACHY HEAD, East Sussex, 1932. *Portrait/cross crosslet* type (BLS Cn 53), *ca* 810x821, Canterbury, Dealla. *SCBI* South-Eastern Museums 643.

BERE REGIS, Dorset, 1986. *Tribrach* type (BLS Cn 7), *ca* 798 x *ca* 802, Canterbury, Duda. 1.38g, 0°. 'Coin Register' 1987, no. 110.

BERE REGIS, near, Dorset, 23 September 1989. *Tribrach* type (BLS Cn 21), *ca* 798 x *ca* 804, London, Wighard. Weight and die-axis not recorded. To be published.

BIDFORD-ON-AVON, Warwicks, 1978. *Portrait/cross crosslet* type (BLS Cn 103), *ca* 805x821, East Anglia, Wihtred. 1.22g, 30°. Excavation-find. Seaby, 'A Coenwulf penny'.

BIDFORD-ON-AVON, Warwicks., August 1985. *Portrait/cross and wedges* type (BLS Cn 23–30), *ca* 807 x *ca* 810, Canterbury. Fragment. 'Coin Register' 1988, no. 156.

BOTTISHAM, Cambs., 1983. *Tribrach* type (BLS Cn 12), *ca* 798 x *ca* 802, Canterbury, Seberht. 1.27g, 290°. Blackburn, 'A penny of Coenwulf'; Grierson & Blackburn, *Medieval European Coinage* 1, no. 1139.

BOWTHORPE, Norfolk, 1991. *Portait* type (BLS Cn 100), *ca* 800–821, East Anglian mint, Botred. 'Coin Register' 1991, no. 124.

BRADWELL-ON-SEA, Essex, before 1865. *Triple tribrach* type, *ca* 798 x *ca* 804, 'TVR'. No other details. *Numismatic Chronicle* 1865, Proceedings, pp. 7–8.

BREEDON-ON-THE-HILL, Leics., *ca* 1952. *Tribrach* type (BLS Cn 16), 796 x *ca* 804, London, Ibba. BLS Cn 16b.

CAISTOR-ON-THE-WOLDS, N. Lincs., April 1990. *Cross fourchée* type (BLS

Cn 62), *ca* 810 x *ca* 821, Canterbury, Swefherd. Fragment; weight and die-axis not recorded. To be published.

CANTERBURY (St Augustine's), Kent, 1921. *Portrait/quatrefoil* type (BLS Cn 97), *ca* 800 x *ca* 810, East Anglia, Lul. BLS Cn 97c. (Thought to have been stolen from Canterbury Museum)

CANTERBURY, near, Kent, October 1985. *Three-line/tribrach* type (*BMC* –, BLS –), 796 x *ca* 798, London, Ibba. 1.39g, 0°. To be published. (Private collection)

CANVEY ISLAND, Essex, 1989. A lead flan with incuse retrograde impressions, the obverse being of Cenwulf's East Anglian *Portrait* series, the reverse of the East Anglian moneyer Wihtred's *Lozenge cross* type, *ca* 805x821. 1.55g, chipped and poorly struck, 90°. To be published by Blackburn, Bonser and Chick. (British Museum)

CHALK, near Gravesend, Kent, April 1984. *Portrait/cross potent* type (BLS Cn 82), *ca* 820, Rochester, Ealhstan. 1.40g. *Archaeologia Cantiana* 1984, pp. 373–4.

CHIPPING ONGAR, near, Essex, 14 September 1988. *Tribrach* type (BLS Cn 21), *ca* 798 x *ca* 804, London, Wighard. 1.31g. 'Coin Register' 1988, no. 155.

CIRENCESTER, near, Glos., August 1986. *Portrait/cross-and-crescents* type (BLS Cn 79), *ca* 820, Rochester, Ealhstan. Pierced in the centre. Blackburn & Bonser, 'Single finds – 3', no. 85.

COLNEY, near Norwich, Norfolk, 1983. *Portrait/cross and wedges* type (BLS –; N 344), 807 x *ca* 810, Canterbury, Duda. 1.40g. The coin has been struck with an altered obverse die of Cuthred. Blackburn & Bonser, 'Single finds – 1', no. 6. (With the finder)

EASTBOURNE, near, Sussex, 26 August 1987. *Portrait/large cross moline* type (BLS Cn 65), *ca* 810x821, Canterbury, Oba. 1.39g, 180°. 'Coin Register' 1987, no. 113.

EASTRY, near, Kent, 1980s. *Portrait/quatrefoil* type (as BLS Cn 98, but with left-facing bust), *ca* 800 x *ca* 810, East Anglia, Lul. About a quarter of the coin missing. Information from P. Weir, Dover.

EMSWORTH, Hants., before 1918. *Tribrach* type (BLS Cn 12), *ca* 798 x *ca* 802, Canterbury, Seberht. Carlyon-Britton sale (Sotheby) 1918, lot 1608b.

HASLINGFIELD, Cambs., before 1876. *Portrait/large cross moline* type (BLS Cn 65), *ca* 815x821, Canterbury, Oba. 1.13g, pierced and chipped. *SCBI* Cambridge 400; Grierson & Blackburn, *Medieval European Coinage* 1, no. 1151.

'HOD', 1867. *Portrait/pincer-cross* type (BLS Cn 46), *ca* 810x821, Canterbury, Werheard. Information from C. E. Blunt, whose reference says: ' "Hod" 1867. Ploughed up. = ?Hod Hill, Blandford.'

HOLLINGBOURNE, Kent, 1986. *Portrait/quatrefoil* type (BLS Cn 98), *ca* 800 x *ca* 810, East Anglia, Lul. 1.29g, 180°. To be published by Blackburn, Bonser and Chick.

HOLLINGBOURNE, Kent, October 1987. *Portrait/cross crosslet* type (BLS Cn 101), *ca* 805x821, East Anglia, Hereberht. 1.09g, very badly damaged, 0°. To be published by Blackburn, Bonser and Chick. (With the finder)

IPSWICH, Suffolk, before 1980. Excavation-find from Tower Ramparts site.

Proceedings of the Suffolk Institute of Archaeology and History 34 (1980), p. 295.

KENT, before 1933. *Tribrach* type (BLS Cn 10), *ca* 798 x *ca* 802, Canterbury, Ethelmod. 1.01g, broken, 330°. *SCBI* Mack 577.

KENT, before 1886. *Tribrach* type (BLS Cn 11), *ca* 798 x *ca* 802, Canterbury, Ethelmod. 1.31g. Brooke, 'Anglo-Saxon acquisitions I', no. 101; BLS Cn 11b.

KENT, before 1865. *Portrait/annulet cross* type (BLS Cn 111), *ca* 805x821, East Anglia, Wodel. 1.14g. BLS Cn 111d. (Fitzwilliam Museum, Blunt collection)

KETTON (Geeston), near Stamford, Lincs., 1970. *Portrait/pincer-cross* type (BLS Cn 38), *ca* 810 x *ca* 815, Canterbury, Tidbearht. 1.33g, pierced, 90°. Found below the floor of a house. Blackburn *et al.*, *Early Medieval Coins from Lincoln*, p. 6, no. 7.

LEIGHTON BUZZARD, near, Beds., 1986. *Tribrach* type (BLS Cn 16), *ca* 798 x *ca* 804, London, Ibba. Chipped and corroded, 300°. Blackburn & Bonser, 'Single finds – 3', 110.

LONDON (Billingsgate excavation-spoil), 1980s. No details of type or moneyer. Stott, 'Saxon and Norman coins', no. 58.

LONDON (Fleet Street), 1914. *Tribrach* type (BLS Cn 11), *ca* 798 x *ca* 802, Canterbury, Ethelmod. 1.30g. BLS Cn 11c; Stott, 'Saxon and Norman coins', no. 56.

LONDON (Maiden Lane), 1986. *Tribrach* type (BLS Cn 16), *ca* 798 x *ca* 804, London, Ibba. 1.09g. Excavation-find. Stott, 'Saxon and Norman coins', no. 57.

LOUDWATER, Bucks., before 21 February 1980. *Portrait/pincer-cross* type (BLS Cn 44), *ca* 815x821, Canterbury, Diormod. 1.39g, 180°. 'Coin Register' 1987, no. 112.

METHWOLD, Norfolk, August 1985. *Portrait/cross-crosslet* type (BLS –, cf. Cn 95; N 45 var.), *ca* 810x821, London, Ælhun. 1.34g, 0°. Blackburn & Bonser, 'Single finds – 2', no. 48. (Fitzwilliam Museum, Blunt collection)

NOTTINGHAM, near, 15 June 1991. *Portrait/cross-crosslet* type (BLS Cn 101), *ca* 805x821, East Anglia, Hereberht. 1.33g, 180°. To be published.

PEACEHAVEN, Sussex, before 1963. *Portrait/pincer-cross* type (BLS Cn 45), *ca* 810x821, Canterbury, Tidbearht. 1.39g. *SCBI* South-Eastern Museums 642.

PONTEFRACT, near, S. Yorks., January 1988. *Portrait/cross and wedges* type (BLS Cn 28 or 29), 807 x *ca* 810, Canterbury, Sigeberht. Large fragment, weight not recorded, 0°. To be published by Blackburn, Bonser and Chick.

PORTCHESTER (Portchester Castle), Hants., 1844. *Portrait/letter A* type (BLS Cn 61), *ca* 810x821, Canterbury Sigestef. 1.09g, chipped. *BMC* 79.

ROYSTON, near, Herts., 1985. *Tribrach* type (BLS Cn 9), *ca* 798 x *ca* 802, Canterbury, Eoba. 1.25g, 90°. Blackburn & Bonser, 'Single finds – 3', no. 51. (With the finder)

ROYSTON, near, Herts., 1983. *Tribrach* type (BLS Cn 6), *ca* 798 x *ca* 802, Canterbury, Duda. 1.38g. Blackburn & Bonser, 'Single finds – 3', no. 50; Spink Auction 36 (30 May 1984), lot 811.

ROYSTON, near, Herts., 1985. *Tribrach* type (BLS Cn 12), *ca* 798 x *ca* 802,

Canterbury, Seberht. 1.28g, chipped, 170°. Blackburn & Bonser, 'Single finds – 3', no. 52. (With the finder)

ROYSTON, near, Herts., after 1976. *Portrait/cross and wedges* type (BLS Cn 29), 807 x *ca* 810, Canterbury, Sigeberht? 0.88g, fragment, 240°. Blackburn & Bonser, 'Single finds – 3', no. 55. (With the finder)

ROYSTON, near, Herts., after 1976. *Portrait/cross and wedges* type (BLS Cn 30), 807–*ca* 810, Canterbury, Werheard. 1.23g, chipped, 45°. Blackburn & Bonser, 'Single finds – 3', no. 56. (With the finder)

SHROPSHIRE, before 1955. *Tribrach* type (BLS Cn 16), *ca* 798 x *ca* 804, London, Ibba. 0.99g, chipped. BLS Cn 16a. (British Museum)

SHROPSHIRE, before 1963. *Tribrach* type (BLS Cn 18), *ca* 798 x *ca* 804, London, Diola. 1.17g, chipped. BLS Cn 18a; Seaby, 'A Coenwulf penny', p. 29. (Shrewsbury Museum and Art Gallery)

SOUTHAMPTON (Clifford Street North), 1968/9. Contemporary forgery?, *Tribrach* type (BLS Cn –), *ca* 798 x *ca* 804, moneyer Dan? Metcalf, 'The coins', no. 134; *SCBI* South-Eastern Museums 639.

SOUTHAMPTON (St Mary's Street), before 30 June 1983. *Tribrach* type (BLS Cn –; N 342), *ca* 798 x *ca* 802, Canterbury, Winoth. 0.97g, 180°. 'Coin Register' 1987, no. 111.

SOUTHAMPTON, *ca* 1825x1865. *Tribrach* type (BLS Cn 12), *ca* 798 x *ca* 802, Canterbury, Seberht. Found while digging brickearth. Pagan, 'The older finds', p. 64, no. 9.

SOUTHAMPTON (Kingsland), 1949. *Tribrach* type (BLS Cn 10), *ca* 798 x *ca* 802, Canterbury, Ethelmod. Addyman & Hill, 'Saxon Southampton I', p. 91, no. 87; BLS Cn 10e.

SOUTHAMPTON (Clifford Street), 1974. *Tribrach* type (BLS Cn 10), *ca* 798 x *ca* 802, Canterbury, Ethelmod. 1.31g. Metcalf, 'The coins', no. 133; *SCBI* South-Eastern Museums 640.

SOUTHAMPTON, *ca* 1825x1865. *Portrait/cross and quatrefoil* type (BLS Cn 31), *ca* 810x821, Canterbury, Duda. Found while digging brickearth. Pagan, 'The older finds', p. 64, no. 9.

SOUTHAMPTON, *ca* 1825x1865. *Portrait/cross-crosslet* type (BLS Cn 101), *ca* 805x821, East Anglia, Hereberht. Found while digging brickearth. The actual coin can no longer be identified. Pagan, 'The older finds', p. 64, no. 9.

SOUTHAMPTON (Northam Station), 1921. No details of type or moneyer. Addyman & Hill, 'Saxon Southampton I', p. 90, no. 77; Pagan, 'The older finds', p. 64, no. 12.

SOUTHAMPTON, *ca* 1825x1855. No details of type or moneyer. Found while digging brickearth. Pagan, 'The older finds', p. 63, no. 2.

STAINES, near, Middx, 1980. *Tribrach* type (BLS Cn 19), *ca* 798 x *ca* 804, London, Eanmund. 1.20g, chipped, 0°. Excavation-find on the north bank of the Thames. 'Coin Register' 1988, no. 153a.

STAINES, Middx, *ca* 1983. *Portrait/cross and wedges* type (BLS Cn 67), 807 x *ca* 810, Canterbury, Oba. 0.98g, chipped, broken and repaired, 180°. Blackburn & Bonser, 'A portrait coin'.

SUFFOLK, before 1949. *Portrait/rosette of pellets* (BLS Cn 102), *ca* 805 x *ca* 821, East Anglia, Hereberht. BLS Cn 102b.

SUFFOLK, before 1949. *Tribrach* type (BLS Cn 9), *ca* 798 x *ca* 802, Canterbury, Eoba. BLS Cn 9f.

TEWKESBURY, near, Glos., before July 1988. *Tribrach* type (BLS Cn 6), *ca* 798 x *ca* 802, Canterbury, Duda. 1.24g, chipped, 0°. To be published by Blackburn, Bonser and Chick.

THETFORD AREA, Norfolk, *ca* 1988. *Portrait/cross and wedges* type (BLS 103 var.), *ca* 805x821, East Anglia, Wihtred. 1.17g, 0°. Possibly from the by-pass earthmoving. *Numismatic Circular* October 1988, no. 6303.

TILBURY, Essex, November 1987. Early issue, *Cross and ?wedges* type (BLS Cn 70, var.), *ca* 810x821, Rochester, Ealhstan. 1.30g, 0°. To be published by Blackburn & Bonser.

TILBURY, Essex, November 1987. *Tribrach* type (BLS Cn 7 var.), *ca* 798 x *ca* 802, Canterbury, Duda. 1.23g, 0°. To be published by Blackburn & Bonser.

TORKSEY, Lincs., before March 1988. *Tribrach* type (BLS Cn 15), *ca* 798 x *ca* 804, London, Eama. 1.07g. To be published by Blackburn, Bonser and Chick.

UPMINSTER, Essex, October 1984. *Tribrach* type (BLS Cn 10), *ca* 798 x *ca* 802, Canterbury, Ethelmod. Two-thirds of the coin, in fragments, 0°. Blackburn & Bonser, 'Single finds – 1', no. 32.

WASHINGBOROUGH, Lincs., 1922. *Portrait/cross moline* type (BLS Cn 72), *ca* 810x821, Rochester, Ealhstan. 1.37g, 0°. *SCBI* Lincolnshire Collections 1622; Blackburn *et al.*, *Early Medieval Coins from Lincoln*, p. 6, no. 6.

WEST HYTHE, near Lympne, Kent, 1950s. *Tribrach* type (BLS Cn 8), *ca* 798 x *ca* 802, Canterbury, Eaba. 1.32g, 210°. Blackburn & Bonser, 'Single finds – 2', no. 72.

WINTERBORNE WHITECHURCH, Dorset, 1986. Later East Anglian issue, *Portrait/cross-crosslet* type (BLS Cn 113 var.), *ca* 805x821, East Anglia, Wodel. 1.11g, chipped, 90°. 'Coin Register' 1987, no. 109.

WOOD WALTON (Monk's Wood), near Huntingdon, Cambs., 1936. *Portrait/cross and wedges* type (BLS Cn 67), 807 x *ca* 810, Canterbury, Oba. 1.30g. *SCBI* South-Eastern Museums 644.

WROTHAM, Kent, before 1885. *Portrait/cross and quatrefoil* type (BLS Cn 31), *ca* 810x821, Canterbury, Duda. BLS Cn 31e.

YAXHAM, Norfolk, 1961. *Portrait/cross moline* type (BLS Cn 40), *ca* 810x821, Canterbury, Tidbearht. 1.50g. BLS Cn 40. (Fitzwilliam Museum, Blunt collection)

Ceolwulf I (821–823)

BISHOP'S CANNINGS, Wilts., 1853. *Portrait/letter A* type (BLS Cl 10), Rochester, Eanwulf. 1.30g, chipped. Brooke, 'Anglo-Saxon acquisitions – 1', no. 107; BLS Cl 10. The Montagu sale catalogue (Sotheby, 18 November 1895, lot 259), perhaps pinpoints the find-spot in saying 'Found at West Kennet'.

DUDDENHOE END, near, Chrishall, Saffron Walden, Essex, before 1843. *Portrait/letter A* type (BLS Cl 2), Canterbury, Sigestef. *Numismatic Chronicle* 1843, Proceedings, p. 5.

GREAT YARMOUTH (Burgh Castle), before 1845. *Portrait/three-line* type (BLS Cl 29), East Anglia, Werbald. 1.24g. *BMC* 109; BLS Cl 29a.

HAMPSHIRE, before 1848. *Portrait/cross and crescents* type (BLS Cl 9), Rochester, Ealhstan. 1.23g. BLS Cl 9c; Blunt, 'Grangerized copies'. (Fitzwilliam Museum, Blunt Collection)

HAVERHILL, near, Suffolk ('but just in South Cambs.'), 3 September 1991. *Cross-crosslet* type (BLS Cl 21), London, Aelhun. Chipped. To be published.

IPSWICH (School St), Suffolk. *East Anglian* type? Excavation-find. Information from Suffolk Archaeological Unit.

IXWORTH, near, Suffolk, before 1885. *Portrait/three-line* type (BLS Cl 1), Canterbury, Oba. 1.52g, 180°. *SCBI* American Collections 195.

LINCOLNSHIRE, North, before 1866. *Portrait/annulet-cross* type (BLS Cl 25), East Anglia, Fotred (Botred?). 1.31g. Brooke, 'Anglo-Saxon acquisitions – 1', no. 117; BLS Cl 25.

LONDON (City), before 1854. *Portrait/three-line* type (BLS Cl 29), East Anglia, Werbald. BLS Cl 29b; Stott, 'Saxon and Norman coins', no. 59.

NEWMARKET, near, Suffolk, before 1981. *Portrait/cross and crescents* type (BLS Cl 9), Rochester, Ealhstan. 1.10g. Information from C. E. Blunt. (Fitzwilliam Museum, Blunt collection)

SWINDERBY, near, Lincs., 1980s. *Three-line reverse* type (BLS Cl 28), East Anglia, Hereberht. 1.33g, *ca* 40°. To be published by Blackburn, Bonser and Chick.

TODDINGTON, Beds., before 1886. *Portrait/cross-crosslet* type (BLS Cl 21), London, Ælhun. 1.28g. *SCBI* South-Eastern Museums 645.

Beornwulf (823–826)

BARTLOW, Cambs., before 1844. *Three-line* type (BLS Be 1), East Anglia, Werbald. 1.35g. BLS Be 1d. (British Museum) There is some doubt as to whether this is the coin from Bartlow. In view of this, and the fact that the find-spot of the coin below, Hadstock, is only one and a half miles away, one is perhaps entitled to wonder if the two reports are of the same coin-find. *Victoria County History* says, 'Ashdon (Hadstock)'. Ashdon lies between Bartlow and Hadstock and shares their parish-boundaries.

HADSTOCK, Essex, before 1838. *Three-line* type (BLS Be 1), East Anglia, Werbald. 1.44g. *BMC* 115; BLS Be 1c. See comments above.

IPSWICH (15–17 Lower Brook Street), Suffolk, 1975. *Cross-crosslet* type (BLS Be 2), East Anglia, Fucga (Eacga). 1.14g, 225°. Excavation-find (IAS 55020497). Unpublished note by M. M. Archibald and T. H. McK. Clough.

OTLEY, near Ipswich, Suffolk, 1991. *Cross-crosslet* type (BLS Be 2), East Anglia, Eacga. Information J. Newman.

THETFORD, Norfolk, late 1988. *Three-line* type (BLS Be 1; N 94, bust 2), East Anglia, Werbald. 1.03g, chipped. Found in mud dredged from the Little Ouse river north of the town. To be published by Blackburn, Bonser and Chick.

WETHERINGSETT-CUM-BROCKFORD, Suffolk, 1987. *Three-line* type (BLS Be 1), East Anglia, Werbald. 1.32g, small edge chip, 90°. 'Coin Register' 1988, no. 157.

Wiglaf (827–829, 830–840)

SOHAM, Cambs., 1990. *'A'/three-line* type (BLS –; N 401/1), London, Redmund. 1.22g, chipped and broken into several pieces, 170°. To be published by Blackburn, Bonser and Chick. (Fitzwilliam Museum)

GRAVESEND, near, Kent, 1991. *Cross/three-line* type (BLS –; N 401/2), London, Redmund. Chipped. Glendining, 11 March 1992, lot 359.

Berhtwulf (840–852)

References are given to Booth's corpus of Berhtwulf's coinage, above.

BAWSEY, near King's Lynn, Norfolk, *ca* 1980x1986. Unspecified type and moneyer, London mint. To be published by Blackburn, Rogerson and Margeson; Booth no. 13 or 60.

FLIXBOROUGH, N. Lincs., 1990/1. *Portrait* type, London, Oswulf. Excavation-find. Blackburn, 'Coin finds in Lindsey', p. 87.

HOXNE, Suffolk, before October 1985. *Portrait/cross-crosslet* type, *ca* 845, London, Oswulf. 0.70g, chipped, 0°. The coin is possibly a contemporary forgery. Blackburn & Bonser, 'Single finds – 2', no. 32; Booth no. 11.

MIDDLE HARLING, near East Harling, Norfolk, before 31 July 1987. *Portait/cross-crosslet* type, *ca* 845, London, Oswulf. 0.69g, chipped, 0°. 'Coin Register' 1987, no. 115; Booth no. 9.

NETLEY (near the Abbey), near Southampton, 1861. *Portrait/cross-crosslet* type, *ca* 845, London, Oswulf. Weight and die-axis not recorded. Pagan, 'The older finds', p. 64, no. 13; Booth no. 10.

NORTHAMPTON (St Peter's Street), 1973–76. *Portrait* type, *ca* 848?, London, Eanred. Excavation-find. Archibald in Williams, *St Peter's Street*, p. 244, no. 7; Booth no. 61.

RICHBOROUGH, Kent. *Portrait* type, *ca* 850?, London, Eama (Eanna). Brooke, 'Anglo-Saxon acquisitions 1', no. 134; Booth no. 76.

SCAWBY (Greetwell Crossroads), South Humberside (North Lincs.), October 1982. *Portrait/cross-crosslet* type, *ca* 845, London, Oswulf. 1.23g, 90°. Blackburn *et al.*, *Early Medieval Coins from Lincoln*, p. 7, no. 10; Booth no. 12.

SOUTHAMPTON (Grove Street), 1946. Group I, *Portrait/cross and wedges* type, *ca* 848?, London, Burnwald. 1.10g. Blunt, 'Saxon coins from Southampton', pp. 256–9; Metcalf 1989, no. 135; Booth no. 36.

SOUTHAMPTON (Kingsland), 1946–50. *Portrait/alpha-omega* type, *ca* 850?, London, Sigeheah. Metcalf, 'The coins', no. 136; Booth no. 74.

THETFORD, Norfolk, 1988. *Portrait/alpha-omega* type, *ca* 850?, London, Burnwald. 1.10g, 90°. Found during the by-pass earthmoving. To be published by Blackburn, Bonser and Chick; Booth no. 77.

TILBURY, Essex, 1986/7. *Portrait/cross-crosslet over quatrefoil* type, *ca* 850?, London, Sigeheah. 0.79g, fragment, 270°. To be published by Blackburn & Bonser; Booth no. 67.

TILBURY, Essex, 1986/7. *Non-Portrait, Chi-Rho/letter M* type, London, Burnwald. 0.80g, fragment, 0°. To be published by Blackburn & Bonser; Booth no. 85.

Burgred (852–874)

BARROW-UPON-HUMBER (St Chad's), South Humberside (North Lincs.), 1978. *Lunettes* type (N 423), *ca* 865x874, London, Hussa. Excavation-find. Blackburn *et al.*, *Early Medieval Coins from Lincoln*, p. 37, no. 12.

BRANDON, Suffolk, before 1980. *Lunettes* type, *ca* 865x874. *Proceedings of the Suffolk Institute of Archaeology* 34/4 (1980), p. 293.

CAERLEON, Gwent, Wales, 1751. *Lunettes* type, *ca* 865x874, London, Cenred. Dykes, *Anglo-Saxon Coins*, p. 27, no. 2.

CANTERBURY (St George's Gate), Kent, before 1988. *Lunettes* type (N 425 or 426), *ca* 866 x *ca* 868, London, Ealinc? *Archaeologia Cantiana* (1988), p. 155.

CHEDDAR PALACE, Somerset, 1960–2. *Lunettes* type (N 423), *ca* 865x874, London, Berheah. 1.04g, fragmentary, 0°. Excavation-find. *SCBI* West Country Museums 340.

CHEDDAR PALACE, Somerset, 1960–2. *Lunettes* type (N 423), *ca* 865x874, London, Eadwulf. Fragmentary and repaired, 0°. *SCBI* West Country Museums 345.

CORBRIDGE, Northumberland, before 1865. Found in the church under the chancel floor (grave find?). *Lunettes* type, *ca* 860x874, moneyer not specified. Metcalf, 'Some finds', p. 107, no. 86.

KIRKBY BELLARS (churchyard), Leics., 1965. *Lunettes* type (N 423), *ca* 865x874, London, Heawulf. 0.97g, 90°. *SCBI* Midland Museums 90.

LONDON (Northumberland Avenue), before 1889. *Lunettes* type (N 425), *ca* 865 x *ca* 868, London, Hugered. Pagan, 'Coinage in the age of Burgred', p. 22.

MIDDLETON, near King's Lynn, Norfolk, before October 1990. *Lunettes* type (N 426), *ca* 865x874, London, Tata. 1.15g, 0°. To be published.

NORMANBY-LE-WOLD, Lincs., 1909. *Lunettes* type (N 423), *ca* 865x874, London, Eadwulf. 1.15g, 90°. *SCBI* Lincolnshire Collections, 1624; Blackburn *et al.*, *Early Medieval Coins from Lincoln*, p. 37, no. 11.

OXBOROUGH, near, Methwold, Norfolk, 1989. *Lunettes* type (N 423), *ca* 865x874, London?, Ethel___. 0.39g, fragment, 90°. To be published by Blackburn, Bonser and Chick. (Fitzwilliam Museum)

SOUTHAMPTON, before 1864. *Lunettes* type (N 423), *ca* 860, London, Tatel. Found while digging brickearth. Pagan, 'The older finds', p. 64, no. 9.

SOUTHAMPTON (near St Mary's Churchyard), 1825. *Lunettes* type (N 423), *ca* 860, London, Tatel. '20 grains'. *Gentleman's Magazine* 1825, p. 261; Pagan, 'The older finds', p. 63, no. 6.

SOUTHAMPTON, before 1864. *Lunettes* type (N 423), *ca* 865x874, London, Berhthelm. Found while digging brickearth. Pagan, 'The older finds', p. 64, no. 9.

SOUTHAMPTON, before 1837. *Lunettes* type (N 423), *ca* 865x874, London, Diarulf. 1.17g. *BMC* 219, this coin. Pagan, 'The older finds', p. 64, no. 11.

SOUTHAMPTON, before 1837. *Lunettes* type (N 426), *ca* 865x874, London, Cenred. 1.33g. *BMC* 184, this coin. Pagan, 'The older finds', p. 64, no. 11.

SOUTHAMPTON, 1825x1855. No details. Pagan, 'The older finds', p. 63, no. 2.

SOUTHAMPTON (Lower St Mary's Road), before 1855. *Lunettes* type, *ca* 865x874, London, Dudwine. Pagan, 'The older finds', p. 64, no. 8.

STOKE BARDOLPH, Nottingham, 1955. *Lunettes* type (N 427), *ca* 865x874, London, Ecgulf. Excavation-find. *SCBI* Midland Museums 94.

STOKE GIFFORD, Glos., before 1863. *Lunettes* type (N 423), *ca* 865x874, London, Tidhelm. 1.23g, chipped. *SCBI* West Country Museums 338.

THETFORD, Norfolk, before 1779. 'Enred'. No other details. Martin, *History of Thetford*, 1779, pp. 279–81.

THETFORD, Norfolk, before 1779. 'Beagia' (Beagstan?). No other details. Martin, *History of Thetford*, 1779, pp. 279–81.

TILBURY, Essex, 1986/7. Trial striking on lead flan, *Lunettes* type (N 423), *ca* 865x874, London, Lulla. 3.79g. To be published by Blackburn & Bonser. (Fitzwilliam Museum, Blunt collection)

TORKSEY, Lincs., 1989–91. *Lunettes* type, London, Tata, *ca* 870. Blackburn, 'Coin finds in Lindsey', p. 89.

YORK (21–33 Aldwark), 1973. *Lunettes* type (N 423), *ca* 868x874, Eanred, but name inverted, blundered and barbarous. Chipped, 180°? Excavation-find. Pirie, *Post-Roman Coins*, p. 53, no. 37.

YORK (58–9 Skeldergate), 1974. *Lunettes* type (N 426), *ca* 865x874, London, Diarwulf. 0.74g, 340°. Excavation-find. Pirie, *Post-Roman Coins*, p. 53, no. 38.

YORK (Tanner Row), 1961. *Lunettes* type (N 423), *ca* 865x874, London, Diga. 0.89g, chipped, broken and repaired, 0°. *SCBI* Yorkshire 959.

KINGS OF WESSEX

Beorhtric (786–802)

ANDOVER (within two miles of), Hants., April 1854. *Alpha-omega/omega* type (N 559), *ca* 796x802, Winchester or Southampton, Peochthun. 22 gr. Shaw, 'New coin of Beorchtric'.

GUILDFORD, near, Surrey, before 1783. *Letter A/cross* type (N 558), *ca* 796x802, Winchester or Southampton, Ecghard. 1.34g, 240°. *SCBI* Glasgow 528.

SUNBURY, Middx, 1865. *Letter A/cross* type (N 558), *ca* 796x802, Winchester or Southampton, Ecghard. 1.17g. *BMC* 36; Dolley & Strudwick, 'The provenances', p. 41.

Ecgberht (802–839)

BERE REGIS, near, Dorset, 12 March 1988. *Cross potent/cross potent* type (N 579), *ca* 828x839, Rochester, Beagmund. Weight reported as 1.11g, chipped, 0°. To be published.

BLANDFORD FORUM, near, Dorset, August 1991. *Portrait/DOROB C* type (N 573), *ca* 828x839, Canterbury, Dealla. Weight and die-axis not recorded. A piece broken off. To be published.

BOXLEY, near Maidstone, Kent, July 1989. *Portrait/DOROB C* type (N 573), *ca* 828x839, Canterbury, Diormod. 1.19g, 270°. To be published by Blackburn, Bonser & Chick.

BURY ST EDMUNDS, near, Suffolk, before 1909. *Portrait/DOROB C* type (N 573), *ca* 828x839, Canterbury, Biornmod. Walters Sale, Sotheby, 26 May 1913, lot 6.

CAISTER-ON-SEA, Norfolk, 1954. *Portrait/DOROB C* type (N 573), *ca* 828x839, Canterbury, Swefheard. Grave-find from excavations. *SCBI* East Anglia 1108.

CODICOTE, near Welwyn, Herts., 1926. *Portrait/DOROB C* type (N 573), *ca* 828x839, Canterbury, Oba. *East Herts. Archaeological Soc. Transactions* 7, p. 179.

COLLINGBOURNE DUCIS, Wilts., 1984. *Cross potent/cross potent* type (N 579), *ca* 828x839, Rochester, Beagmund. 1.09g, chipped, 270°. Blackburn & Bonser, 'Single find – 2', no. 23.

GILLINGHAM, Kent, May 1992. *St Andrews* type (N 588), *ca* 828x839, Rochester (episcopal mint). 1.00g, large fragment. To be published.

GODALMING, near, Surrey, *ca* 1855. *Cross pattée on saltire/cross potent* type (N 582), *ca* 828x839, Rochester, Beagmund. 1.28g. Whitbourn, 'On two unpublished coins'.

GRIMSBY, near, S. Humberside (N. Lincs.), September 1988. *Portrait/DOROB C* type (N 573), *ca* 828x839, Canterbury, Tidbearht. Weight not recorded. Die-axis *ca* 75°. To be published by Blackburn, Bonser and Chick.

HURSLEY, Hants., 1986. *Portrait/DOROB C* type (N 573), *ca* 828x839, Canterbury, Bosel. Found on construction-site near the IBM offices. Reverse only illustrated in *Treasure Hunting*, November 1987, p. 5.

IPSWICH, near, Suffolk, before 1955. *Portrait/cross* type (N 574), *ca* 825 x *ca* 828, Rochester, Dunun. 1.09g, broken. *SCBI* Mack 701.

IPSWICH AREA, Suffolk, 1989. *SAXON* type (N 589), *ca* 828x839, Winchester or Southampton, Beornehart. 1.20g, chipped, 180°. To be published.

KENT, before 1923. *Six limb/five limb* type (N 567), *ca* 825 x *ca* 828, Canterbury, Werheard. 1.30g. Brooke, 'Anglo-Saxon acquisitions IV', no. 411.

KENT, *ca* 1847. *Saxon* type (N 589), *ca* 828x839, Winchester or Southampton, Tideman. Blunt, 'Grangerized copies'.

LONDON (Westminster Abbey), 1986. *Portrait/Cross with two arms potent* type (N 576 var.), *ca* 825 x *ca* 828, Rochester, Ethelmod. Excavation-find. Stott, 'Saxon and Norman coins', no. 62.

'LONDON, WEST OF', mid-1980s. *Early portrait/cross-crosslet* type (N 562), *ca* 825 x *ca* 828, Canterbury, Oba. Weight and die-axis not recorded. Information from J. Linzalone.

LOWER SLAUGHTER, Glos., November 1957. *Early portrait/wedges* type (N 560), *ca* 825 x *ca* 828, Canterbury, Tidbearht. 1.29g, 180°. Found in the Slaughter Brook during work on a new bridge. Blunt, 'The coinage of Ecgbeorht', p. 467. (British Museum)

MITCHAM, Surrey, before 1974. *Portrait/cross potent* type (N 576), *ca* 825 x *ca* 828, Rochester, Dunun. Described 'As BMA 394', in a manuscript note in D.F. Allen's copy of Hawkins, *The Silver Coins of England* (1887).

PEVENSEY, E. Sussex, 1946. *Crescent cross/plain cross* type (N 583), *ca* 828x839, Rochester, Cobba. Chipped. Blunt, 'The coinage of Ecgbeorht', p. 470, no. 20. (British Museum)

ROCHESTER, Kent, pre-1862. *Mercian Cross potent/monogram* type (N 585), *ca* 829, London, Redmund. 0.97g, large fragment. Whitbourne, 'On two unpublished coins'. (Fitzwilliam Museum, Blunt collection)

ROYSTON, near, Herts., July 1986. *SAXONIORUM* type (N 590), *ca* 828x839, Winchester or Southampton, Eanwald. 0.72g, large fragment. To be published by Blackburn and Bonser. (With the finder)

SOUTHAMPTON (Gaol site), 1825x1855. *SAXON* type (N 589), *ca* 828x839, Winchester or Southampton, Tideman. Pagan, 'The older finds', p. 63, no. 1; *SCBI* Oxford 233.

SOUTHAMPTON (Lower St Mary's Road), before 1855. *Plain cross/five limb* type (N 568), *ca* 825–*ca* 828, Canterbury, Swefheard. Pagan, 'The older finds', p. 64, no. 8. (Fitzwilliam Museum, Blunt collection)

SOUTHAMPTON (Six Dials), 1981. *Early portrait/cross-crosslet* type (N 562), *ca* 825 x *ca* 828, Canterbury, Diormod. 1.29g. Excavation-find. Metcalf, 'The coins', p. 54, no. 143.

SOUTHAMPTON (Chapel Road), 1973. *Portrait* type, *ca* 825 x *ca* 828, Rochester, Dunun. 0.71g, chipped. Excavation-find. Metcalf, 'The coins', p. 54, no. 144.

SOUTHAMPTON (71 Clifford Street), April 1950. *SAXON* type (N 589), *ca* 828x839, Winchester or Southampton, Tilred. 0.74g, chipped. Blunt, 'Saxon coins from Southampton', p. 259; Metcalf, 'The coins', p. 54, no. 145.

STREATLEY, near, Berks., 1989. *Early portrait/cross-crosslet* type (N 562), *ca* 825 x *ca* 828, Canterbury, Oba. 1.35g, 180°. Information from D. M. Metcalf.

THETFORD AREA, Norfolk, *ca* 1988. *SAXON* type (N 589), *ca* 828x839, Winchester or Southampton, Ifa. 1.20g, 180°. Possibly from the by-pass earthmoving. Acquired by Spink.

YORK (Minster), 1971. *Portrait/DOROB C* type (N 573), *ca* 828x839, Canterbury, Tidbearht. 0.83g, large fragment, corroded. Excavation-find. Information from Miss M.M. Archibald.

Æthelwulf (839–858)

BARKING (Abbey), London. *DORB/CANT* type (N 614), *ca* 848 x *ca* 851, moneyer uncertain. 0.56g, fragment. Excavation-find. Stott, 'Saxon and Norman coins', no. 64. (Passmore Edwards Museum)

CANTERBURY, Kent. *Early portrait* type (N 600?), *ca* 843 x *ca* 848, Rochester, Ethelhere. 0.35g, repaired fragments. Excavation-find. Information from D. Dawson.

CANTERBURY, Kent. *DORB/CANT* type (N 614), *ca* 848 x *ca* 851, Canterbury, Ealgmund. 1.26g, small chip. Excavation-find. Information from Miss M. M. Archibald.

CHEDDAR PALACE, Somerset, 1960–2. *SAXONIORUM* type (N 596), 839 x *ca* 843, Canterbury. Fragment. Excavation-find. *SCBI* West Country Museums 377.

FLIXBOROUGH, N. Lincs., 1990/1. *Open cross* type (N 618), *ca* 852x858. Excavation-find. Blackburn, 'Coin finds in Lindsey', p. 87.

IPSWICH (Buttermarket), Suffolk. Excavation-find. Information from Suffolk Archaeological Unit.

IPSWICH (St Peters St.), Suffolk. Phase II. Excavation-find. Information from Suffolk Archaeological Unit.

LONDON (London Wall), 1837. *SAXONIORUM* type (N 596), 839 x *ca* 843, Canterbury, moneyer D___ probably Diar. Discovered by 'workmen employed in a sewer in London Wall, near the end of Winchester Street' on '15th inst.', but month unclear, possibly September in which case this may be same find as next entry. *Numismatic Journal* 2 (1837–8), p. 109.

LONDON (R. Thames), 14 September 1837. No details of moneyer or type. Stott, 'Saxon and Norman coins', no. 63 (citing Roach Smith journals).

SANDWICH, near, Kent, 1989. *SAXONIORVM* type (N 596), 839 x *ca* 843, Canterbury, Osmund. To be published.

SOUTHAMPTON, 1825x1855. No details. Found while digging brickearth. Pagan, 'The older finds', p. 63, no. 3.

SOUTHAMPTON. *Early portrait/cross moline* type (N 591 var.), 839 x *ca* 843, Rochester, Dun. 1.08g, chipped. Excavation-find. Metcalf, 'The coins', p. 54, no. 146.

'SUFFOLK', 1988. *Portrait/cross and wedges* type (N 612), *ca* 843 x *ca* 848, Canterbury, Ethelmund. 1.15g, 180°. *Numismatic Circular* December 1988, no. 7794.

YORK (Clementhorpe), 1976. *DORB/CANT* type (N 614), *ca* 848 x *ca* 851, Rochester, Wealheard. 1.06g, 270°. Excavation find. Pirie, *Post-Roman Coins*, p. 54, no. 39.

Æthelberht (858–865; king of Kent, 855–858)

CANTERBURY (St Augustine's Abbey), Kent, 1984. *Open cross* type (N 620), 858 x *ca* 863, a Kentish mint, moneyer illegible. Excavation-find. *Archaeologia Cantiana* 103 (1986), p. 113.

FLIXBOROUGH, N. Lincs., 1990/91. *Open cross* type (N 620), 858 x *ca* 863. Excavation-find. Blackburn, 'Coin finds in Lindsey', p. 87.

FLIXBOROUGH, N. Lincs., 1990/91. *Open cross* type (N 620) 858 x *ca* 863. Excavation-find. Blackburn, 'Coin finds in Lindsey', p. 87.

FORDINGTON, Dorchester, Dorset, before 18 June 1982. *Open cross* type (N 620), 858 x *ca* 863, a Kentish mint, Æthelhere. 'Coin Register' 1987, no. 121.

LENHAM, near, Kent, 1989. *Open cross* type (N 620), 858 x *ca* 863, a Kentish mint, moneyer uncertain, but probably Degberht (DEG[ ]). Fragment, 0.29g, 90°. To be published.

SHOREHAM, Kent, 1933. *Floriated cross* type (N 621), *ca* 862x865, a Kentish mint, Dudda. *Archaeologia Cantiana* 1934, pp. 198–9.

SOUTHAMPTON (Lower St Mary's Road), before 1855. *Open cross* type (N 620), 858 x *ca* 863, a Kentish mint, Degberht. Pagan, 'The older finds', p. 64, no. 8.

SOUTHAMPTON, 1825x1865. *Open cross* type (N 620), 858 x *ca* 863, a Kentish mint, Beagmund. Found while digging brickearth. Pagan, 'The older finds', p. 64, no. 9.

WASHINGTON, Sussex, 1866. *Open cross* type (N 620), 858 x *ca* 863, Canterbury?, Ethelred. 1.11g, chipped. Brooke, 'Anglo-Saxon acquisitions IV', no. 433.

Æthelred I (865–871)

GAINSBOROUGH, near, Lincs., November 1989. *Lunettes* type (N 622–3), Blackburn, 'Coin finds in Lindsey', p. 87.

LINCOLN (St Paul-in-the-Bail), 1978. *Lunettes* type (N 622), a Kentish mint, Dudda. 0.50g, fragment, 180°. Excavation-find. *SCBI* Lincolnshire Collections, 1944; Blackburn *et al.*, *Early Medieval Coins from Lincoln*, p. 10, no. 14.

Alfred (871–899)

ALDBOURNE, Wilts. *Lunettes* type (N 625), 871 x *ca* 875, Canterbury, Eadwulf. Information from C. E. Blunt.

BARROW-UPON-HUMBER (St Chad's Church), S. Humberside (N. Lincs.), 1978. *Lunettes* type (N 627), 871 x *ca* 875, London?, Dudwine. 0.83g, corroded, 0°. Blackburn *et al.*, *Early Medieval Coins from Lincoln*, p. 37, no. 13.

BARTON-ON-HUMBER, S. Humberside (N. Lincs.), March 1991. *Lunettes* type (N 625), 871 x *ca* 875, London?, Beagstan? Weight and die-axis not recorded. Blackburn, 'Coin finds in Lindsey', p. 87.

BAWSEY, near King's Lynn, Norfolk, October/November 1989. *Cross-and-lozenge* type (cf. N 629), possibly an imitation *ca* 875 x *ca* 880, Lulla. 0.37g, fragment, 270°. Blackburn & Keynes, above, no. 55. (Fitzwilliam Museum)

BEDFORD, 1986. *London monogram* type (N 645), *ca* 880, London. Halfpenny, 0.27g, 180°. Excavation-find from the northern Anglo-Saxon defences. 'Coin Register' 1987, no. 124.

BURGHEAD, Morayshire, ?1861. *Lunettes* type (N 625), 871 x *ca* 875, (Dud?)wine. Pierced twice. *SCBI* Edinburgh 81.

CANTERBURY, Kent, *ca* 1955. *Cross-and-lozenge* type (N 629), *ca* 875 x *ca* 880, Canterbury, Diarmund. 1.40g. Excavation-find in the city centre. Blackburn and Keynes, above, no. 11. (Canterbury Museum)

CANTERBURY (St Augustine's), Kent, 1964. *Lunettes* type (N 625), 871 x *ca* 875, Hubearn. 0.87g. Information from Miss M. M. Archibald.

CROYDON (Palace), Surrey, before 1888. *Two Emperors* type (N 632), *ca* 875. Mint uncertain, Cenred, 1.30g. Brooke, 'Anglo-Saxon acquisitions IV', no. 476; Blackburn & Keynes, above, no. 5. (British Museum)

DUNSTABLE (Downs), Beds., 1932. *London monogram* type (N 463 var. or 645), *ca* 880, London, irregular? *SCBI* South-Eastern Museums 759.

EASTRY, Kent, 1832. *Two-line* type (N 635), *ca* 880x899, Canterbury, Diarvald. Large piercing. (Fitzwilliam Museum, Blunt collection.)

FAIRFORD (Claydon Pike), Glos., 1982. *Lunettes* type (N 627), 871 x *ca* 875, uncertain mint, Ealmod. 0.56g, badly chipped, 180°. Information from D. M. Metcalf.

FLIXBOROUGH, N. Lincs., 1990/91. *Lunettes* type (N 625–8), 871 x *ca* 875, moneyer uncertain. Excavation-find. Blackburn, 'Coin finds in Lindsey', p. 87.

FLIXBOROUGH, N. Lincs., 1990/91. *Lunettes* type (N 625–8), 871 x *ca* 875, Eadmund. Excavation-find. Blackburn, 'Coin finds in Lindsey', p. 87.

GREAT SHELFORD, Cambs., July 1980. *Lunettes* type (N 625), 871 x *ca* 875, uncertain mint and moneyer, [ ]MVND. 0.40g, fragment. Grierson & Blackburn, *Medieval European Coinage* 1, no. 1350A.

HEREFORD, 1972x1976. *Two-line* type (N 635), *ca* 880x899, Canterbury, Tirwald. Excavation-find, in poor condition. *CBA Research Report* 56 (1985) p. 33 (report on microfiche).

IPSWICH (Buttermarket). *Two-line* type (N 635–9), *ca* 880x899, Ludiman. Excavation-find. Information from J. Newman, Suffolk Archaeological Unit.

IPSWICH (Buttermarket). *London monogram* type, halfpenny (N 645?), *ca* 880 or later. It is not yet known whether the coin is official or a Viking imitation. Excavation-find. Information from J. Newman, Suffolk Archaeological Unit.

LINCOLN (St Paul-in-the-Bail), 1978. *Lunettes* type (N 626), 871 x *ca* 875, Canterbury, Wine. 0.76g, slightly chipped, 90°. Excavation-find. *SCBI* Lincolnshire collections 1946; Blackburn *et al.*, *Early Medieval Coins from Lincoln*, p. 34, 2.

LONDON (Threadneedle Street), before 1854. *London monogram* type (N 644), *ca* 880, London. Stott, 'Saxon and Norman coins', no. 70.

LONDON (R. Thames near Lambeth Bridge), 1974. *Lunettes* type (N 625), 871 x *ca* 875, Canterbury, Hebeca. 0.98g. Stott, 'Saxon and Norman coins', no. 67.

LONDON (City), before 5 May 1839. *Lunettes* type (N 625), 871 x *ca* 875, Canterbury, Dunn. Stott, 'Saxon and Norman coins', no. 68.

LONDON (Thames Exchange spoil), 1988–9. *Lunettes* type, (N 626), 871 x *ca* 875, Herebeald. 0.96g, 0°. The coin is said to be copper with a silver surface. Acquired by Spink.

LONDON, before 1890. *DORO* type (N 638), *ca* 895, Canterbury, Dunninc. (British Museum: Roach Smith 1935–4–9–19)

LONDON (Thames Exchange spoil), 1990/91. Three separate losses, *London monogram* type (N 645), halfpennies, one with left-facing portrait. 0.48g, 0.71g and 0.49g. Information from D. S. Chick.

LONDON (11–19 St Thomas Street), 1977. *London monogram* type (N 645), *ca* 880, London. 0.68g, halfpenny. Stott, 'Saxon and Norman coins', no. 71.

LOUTH, near, Lincs., 1987. *Two-line* type (N 635–9), *ca* 880x899, small fragment. Blackburn, 'Coin finds in Lindsey', p. 88.

MIDDLE HARLING, near, East Harling, Norfolk, 1980s. *Two-line* type (N 636), *ca* 880x899, London, Tilwine. 0.35g, fragment. Found in the same general area as the hoard of Beonna's coins, but not directly connected with them. Archibald, 'The coinage of Beonna', p. 17.

POOLE, near, Dorset, before 1826. Offering piece (N 648). 10.5g. *BMC* 158; Martin, 'Some remarks', pp. 230–1.

PORTSMOUTH, near, Hants., September 1988. *London monogram* type (N 646), *ca* 880, London, Tilwine. Unconfirmed verbal report.

PULBOROUGH, Sussex. *Two-line* type, *ca* 880x899, a West Mercian mint, Cuthberht. *SCBI* South-Eastern Museums 760.

ROCHESTER (Castle), Kent, July 1976. *Cross-and-lozenge* type (N 629), *ca* 875 x *ca* 880, London, Ciolwulf. 0.55g, corroded and broken, *ca* 150°. Excavation-find. Archibald, 'An Alfred penny'; Blackburn & Keynes, above, no. 20.

SHEPPEY, ISLE OF, Kent, before 1904. *London monogram* type (N 644), *ca* 880, London. Brooke, 'Anglo-Saxon acquisitions IV', no. 451. [Record of provenance mislaid]

SOUTHAMPTON, 1949. *Two Emperors/Cross-and-Lozenge* mule? (N 632/629), *ca* 875. Uncertain mint, 'Eth-----'. Excavation-find. Metcalf, 'The coins', no. 147; Blackburn & Keynes, above, no. 7. (British Museum)

STANTON ST JOHN, Oxon., *ca* 1985. *Cross-and-Lozenge* type (N 629), *ca* 875 x *ca* 880. Uncertain mint, Luceman. Blackburn & Keynes, above, no. 50. (Ashmolean)

TORKSEY (bank of River Trent), Lincs., 1984. *Lunettes* type (N 628), 871 x *ca* 875, Canterbury, Biarnred. Weight and die-axis not recorded. 'Coin Register' 1987, no. 122.

WESTWELL, Kent, before 1908. *Two-line* type (N 639), *ca* 880x899, Winchester, Wulfred. 1.46g. Brooke, 'Anglo-Saxon acquisitions IV', no. 488.

WINCHESTER (Cathedral Green), Hants., 1964. *Cross-and-Lozenge* type (N 629), *ca* 875 x *ca* 880. Uncertain mint, Lulla. Excavation-find. Dolley and Blunt, 'Coins from the Winchester excavations', no. 2; Blackburn & Keynes, above, no. 53. (Winchester Museum)

WINCHESTER, Hants., 1989. *Two-line* type (N 639), *ca* 880x899, Winchester, Athelulf. Excavation-find. 1.73g, uncleaned and severely corroded. Information from M. Blackburn.

WYE, near, Kent, before 1849. *Cross-and-Lozenge* type (N 629), *ca* 875 x *ca* 880, London, Hereferth. 'Found on the Downs near Wye.' *British Archaeological Association Sixth Annual Mtg., Chester, 1849, A Catalogue of the Museum of Antiquities Exhibited at the King's School, Chester*, (1849), p. 27; Blackburn & Keynes, above, no. 20.

VIKINGS OF THE DANELAW

(a) Imitations of 'Alfred'

DONCASTER, Yorks., 1987. Imitative *London monogram* type (N 466), after *ca* 880, Danelaw. 1.14g, chipped, 180°. Archibald, 'A Viking copy'.

FORNCETT ST PETER, near Forncett St Mary, Norfolk, 1987. Viking imitation of halfpenny of *DORO* type (cf. N 640), 890s, Danelaw, Byrnvald (blundered). 0.70g. *Numismatic Circular* 1987, no. 7076.

GRIMSTON, Norfolk, 1990. Imitation of Alfred's *Two-line* type, *ca* 880x899, 'London', 'Ludig'. 1.04g, chipped, 180°. To be published by Blackburn, Bonser and Chick.

IPSWICH (Buttermarket). Imitation of Alfred. Excavation-find. Information from J. Newman, Suffolk Archaeological Unit.

IPSWICH (Tower Ramparts). Imitation of Alfred, halfpenny, 'late type'. Excavation-find. Information from J. Newman, Suffolk Archaeological Unit.

LINCOLN region, before 1842. Imitative *Two-line* type (N 475/1), *ca* 880x899, moneyer, 'Ida'. 1.30g, 70°. Blackburn *et al.*, *Early Medieval Coins from Lincoln*, p. 12, fig. 20; *BMC* no. 345.

LINCOLN (Flaxongate), 1976. Imitative *Two-line* type (N 475/1), *ca* 880x899, 'London', 'Ludig'. 0.93g, 135°. Excavation-find. *SCBI* Lincolnshire Collections 1947; Blackburn *et al.*, *Early Medieval Coins from Lincoln*, p. 11, fig. 18.

STAMFORD (Castle), Lincs., 1976. Imitative *Two-line* type (N 475/1), *ca* 880x899, 'London', 'Ludig'. 1.15g, chipped, 315°. Excavation-find. *SCBI* Lincolnshire Collections 1625a; Blackburn *et al.*, *Early Medieval Coins from Lincoln*, p. 11, fig. 19.

(b) St Edmund Memorial Coins

CHOLSEY, near Wallingford, Oxon., before 1893. *ca* 895 x *ca* 918 (N 483). The provenance has been doubted. Metcalf, 'Continuity and change I', p. 48.

CONGHAM, near King's Lynn, Norfolk, 1990. *ca* 895 x *ca* 918 (N 483). To be published by Blackburn, Bonser and Chick.

EAST KIRKBY, Lincs., before 1884. Cuerdale type, *ca* 895 x *ca* 905 (N 483), moneyer 'Boleti'. Blackburn *et al.*, *Early Medieval Coins from Lincoln*, p. 38, no. 16.

The following 15 coins are all Ipswich excavation-finds. Information courtesy of J. Newman, Suffolk Archaeological Unit. To be published by M. M. Archibald.

IPSWICH (Buttermarket). Post-Cuerdale type.
IPSWICH (Buttermarket). Lead 'struck as customs token'. Post-Cuerdale type.
IPSWICH (Buttermarket). Post-Cuerdale type.
IPSWICH (Buttermarket). Late/post-Cuerdale type.
IPSWICH (Buttermarket). Late/post-Cuerdale type.
IPSWICH (Buttermarket).
IPSWICH (Buttermarket).
IPSWICH (Foundation St). Late type.
IPSWICH (Foundation St). Late type.
IPSWICH (School St). Late Cuerdale type.
IPSWICH (School St).
IPSWICH (School St). Cuerdale type.
IPSWICH (Lower Brook St). Cuerdale type, moneyer? Iohannes.
IPSWICH (Smart St). Post-Cuerdale type.
IPSWICH (Fore St). Late Cuerdale type.

LINCOLN (Flaxengate), 1974. Post-Cuerdale type, *ca* 905 x *ca* 918 (N 483), moneyer uncertain. Excavation-find. 0.26g, fragment. *SCBI* Lincolnshire Collections 1943; Blackburn *et al.*, *Early Medieval Coins from Lincoln*, p. 12–13, fig. 22.

LINCOLN (Flaxengate), 1976. Post-Cuerdale type, *ca* 905 x *ca* 918 (N 483), moneyer 'Icam'. Excavation-find. 1.37g, 180°. *SCBI* Lincolnshire Collections 1942; Blackburn *et al.*, *Early Medieval Coins from Lincoln*, p. 12, fig. 21.

LONG WITTENHAM, near Abingdon, Oxon., before 1893. *ca* 895 x *ca* 918. The provenance has been doubted. Metcalf, 'Continuity and change I', p. 48

MIDDLE HARLING, Norfolk, 1980–3. Post-Cuerdale type, *ca* 905 x *ca* 918 (N 483). 1.03g. Found in the general area of the Middle Harling hoard of Beonna coins, but not directly connected with them. Archibald, 'The coinage of Beonna', p. 17.

MURSLEY, near Bletchley, Bucks., *ca* 1981. (N 483), *ca* 895 x *ca* 918, moneyer 'Aboncio'. 1.16g, *ca* 180°. Metcalf, 'A bent St Edmund Memorial penny'.

NARFORD, near Swaffham, Norfolk, 1959, *ca* 895 x *ca* 918 (N 483). Rigold, 'Finds of St Edmund Memorial Coins', p. 190. (Narford is a deserted medieval village, about five miles N.W. of Swaffham. Only the Hall and church now survive. The coin was found near the Hall. *Medieval Archaeology* 4 (1960), p. 136.)

NORTHAMPTON (Castle site), 1879–81. Cuerdale type, *ca* 895 x *ca* 905 (N 483), moneyer uncertain. 0.82g, fragment. *SCBI* Midlands Museums 98.

NORTHAMPTON (Castle site), 1879–81. Cuerdale type, *ca* 895 x *ca* 905 (N 483), moneyer uncertain. The coin has an obverse legend reading +NORDVICO, which has been interpreted as perhaps Norwich. 1.00g, fragment. *SCBI* Midlands Museums 100.

NORTHAMPTON (Castle site), 1879–81. *ca* 895 x *ca* 918 (N 483), moneyer uncertain. The flan is small, but is probably a penny rather than a halfpenny. 0.33g, fragment. *SCBI* Midlands Museums 105.

NORTHAMPTON (St Peter's Street), 1973–76. Two, possibly three, St Edmund Memorial coins, one post-Cuerdale type (N 483), found in excavations. Archibald in Williams, *St Peter's Street*, p. 444, nos Nu 8–10.

NORTHAMPTON (Marefair), 1977. Post-Cuerdale type (N 483), *ca* 905 x *ca* 918. *Northants. Archaeology* 14 (1979), p. 69. (Excavation-find from Phase 7. A fragment of another ninth-century coin – possibly a St Edmund Memorial penny – was found in Phase 5.)

NORTHAMPTON (Chalk Lane), before 1981. Excavation-finds of three single coin losses of St Edmund Memorial pennies, *ca* 895 x *ca* 918 (N 483), from Phase 3A, 3A/C and 'probably 3C'. *Northants. Archaeology* 16 (1981), p. 118.

NORTH CREAKE, Norfolk, August/September 1990. *ca* 895 x *ca* 918 (N 483), moneyer uncertain. Fragmentary. To be published.

NORWICH (Barn Rd.), Norfolk, 1954. Probably Cuerdale type, *ca* 895 x *ca* 905 (N 483), moneyer uncertain. Weight not recorded, fragmentary and pierced. Excavation-find. *SCBI* East Anglia 1103.

OXBOROUGH, near Swaffham, Norfolk, 1991. Early post-Cuerdale type, *ca* 905 x *ca* 910 (N 483), moneyer Berner. 1.20g, broken and chipped. To be published by Blackburn, Bonser and Chick. (Fitzwilliam Museum)

OXBOROUGH, near Swaffham, Norfolk, 1991. Another St Edmund Memorial coin (N 483) reported from the same site as the last, but not seen. To be published by Blackburn, Bonser and Chick.

OXBOROUGH, near Swaffham, Norfolk, before September 1987. Halfpenny, *ca* 895 x *ca* 918 (N 485), moneyer uncertain. 0.21g. Fragment, corroded and broken. *ca* 50°. 'Coin Register' 1987, no. 119. (Fitzwilliam Museum)

PLAYFORD, near Ipswich, Suffolk, before November 1987. Late Cuerdale type, *ca* 905 x *ca* 910 (N 483), moneyer uncertain. 1.37g, 270°. 'Coin Register' 1987, no. 120.

ROYSTON, near, Herts., *ca* 1979–8. Post-Cuerdale type, *ca* 905 x *ca* 918 (N 483), moneyer 'Coinnoi'. 1.25g, chipped, 250°. Blackburn & Bonser, 'Single finds – 3', no. 59.

ROYSTON, near, Herts., 1985. Halfpenny, *ca* 895 x *ca* 918 (N 485), moneyer uncertain. 0.42g, fragment. Blackburn & Bonser, 'Single finds – 3', no. 60.

ROYSTON, near, Herts., December 1988. Probably Post-Cuerdale type, *ca* 905 x *ca* 910 (N 483), moneyer 'Boici'. 1.34g, 0°. To be published by Blackburn & Bonser.

ROYSTON, near, Herts., 1987–9. Post-Cuerdale type, *ca* 905 x *ca* 918, moneyer uncertain. 0.62g, fragment, 0°. To be published by Blackburn and Bonser.

THETFORD (St Mary), Norfolk, 1948–52. Post-Cuerdale type, *ca* 905 x *ca* 918 (N 483), moneyer uncertain. 1.18g, 90°. Excavation-find no. 842. *SCBI* East Anglia 1101.

THETFORD (St Mary), Norfolk, 1948–52. Post-Cuerdale type, *ca* 905 x *ca* 918 (N 483/1), 1.04g, 335°. Excavation-find. *SCBI* East Anglia 1102.

THETFORD (St Mary), Norfolk, 1948–52. *ca* 895 x *ca* 918 (N 483), moneyer uncertain. 0.66g, fragment. Excavation-find no. 990. *SCBI* East Anglia 110.

THETFORD (St Mary), Norfolk, 1948–52. Halfpenny, Cuerdale type, *ca* 895 x *ca* 905 (N 485), moneyer Otbert. 0.55g, 165°. Excavation-find. *SCBI* East Anglia 1106.

THETFORD (St Mary), Norfolk, 1948–52. Halfpenny, Cuerdale type, *ca* 895 x *ca* 905 (N 485), moneyer uncertain. 0.52g, 150°. Excavation-find. *SCBI* East Anglia 1107.

THETFORD, Norfolk, *ca* 1991. Halfpenny, Post-Cuerdale type (N 485), *ca* 905 x *ca* 918, moneyer uncertain. To be published

WEETING (Hereward Way), near Brandon, Suffolk, *ca* 1988. Post-Cuerdale type (described as 'late'), *ca* 905 x *ca* 918 (N 483). Found while digging a garden. Norfolk Sites and Monuments Record, no. 24891; information A. Rogerson.

WYMESWOLD, near Loughborough, Leics., September 1986. Post-Cuerdale type, *ca* 905 x *ca* 918 (N 483), moneyer 'Ioialvei'. 180°. 'Coin Register' 1987, no. 118.

VIKINGS OF YORK

DERBY (St Alkmund's church). *Mirabilia fecit* type, *ca* 900, York. Excavation-find. Exhibited at the British Numismatic Society (*British Numismatic Journal* 36 (1967), p. 214).

SOUTHOE, Hunts. (Cambs.), December 1985. *Cnut-Cunnetti* type (N 501), *ca* 900, York. 1.07g, chipped and cracked, 330°. Blackburn & Bonser, 'Single finds – 2', no. 63.

LONDON (Cornhill), *ca* 1858. *Cnut-Cunnetti* type (N 501), *ca* 900, York. 'Exhumed in making a sewer in one of the courts in Cornhill'. Stott, 'Saxon and Norman Coins', no. 72 (as 'from a hoard?').

NINTH-CENTURY CAROLINGIAN AND OTHER FOREIGN COINS

BARDWELL, near Ixworth, Suffolk. Carolingian, obol, Charles the Bald, 840x877. Information from J. Newman, Suffolk Archaeological Unit.

BEACHAMWELL, near Swaffham, Norfolk, 1987. Carolingian, Charles the Bald, *Gratia Di Rex* type, 864x877 or later (*MEC* 1:860–7), Courcessin. 1.53g, 100°.

CAERNARFON, Gwynedd, Wales, 2 May 1988. Carolingian, Pepin II of Aquitaine, *Monogram* type (*MEC* 1:814), 845x848, Melle. Weight reported as 1.45g. To be published by Blackburn, Bonser and Chick.

CAMBRIDGE (River Cam near Magdalene Bridge), before 1904. Frisian imitative gold solidus of Louis I (the Pious), *ca* 830 x *ca* 850. Grierson & Blackburn, *Medieval European Coinage* 1, no. 753.

CHICHESTER, Sussex, before 1981. Carolingian, Charles the Bald, 840x877, Chichester excavation report, Miss M. M. Archibald, 1981.

CONGHAM, near King's Lynn, Norfolk, 11 March 1990. Anonymous Carolingian gold denier, *ca* 867 x *ca* 925, reverse struck from a regular die of Chartres, period Charles the Bald or later. Blackburn & Bonser, 'A Carolingian gold coin'.

COXWOLD, N. Yorks., April 1988. Carolingian, Charles the Bald, *Karolus monogram* type (*MEC* 1:924–33), 840x877, Melle. 1.56g, 90°. To be published by Blackburn, Bonser and Chick.

CULM DAVEY, near Hemyock, Devon, *ca* 1900. Carolingian, Charles the Bald, *Karolus monogram* type (*MEC* 1:923–33), *ca* 848 x *ca* 900, Melle. Dolley & Shiel, 'A Carolingian *denarius*'.

DOWNHAM MARKET, near, Norfolk, 1980s. Carolingian, Louis the Pious, *Christiana Religio* type (*MEC* 1:793–808), 822x840, unspecified Frankish mint. Weight and die-axis not recorded. To be published by Blackburn, Bonser and Chick.

ELGIN, Morayshire, before 1864. Imitative gold solidus of Louis the Pious, *ca* 830 x *ca* 850. 4.31g. Grierson, 'The gold solidus', p. 25, I (a). (British Museum)

EXETER, Devon, before 1984. A base metal imitation of a solidus of Louis the Pious, *ca* 830 x *ca* 850. Excavation-find. Archibald, 'The Coins'.

HINDRINGHAM, near Fakenham, Norfolk, 1988. Plated forgery of an imitative gold solidus, Louis the Pious. Cut half. To be published by Blackburn, Bonser and Chick.

IPSWICH (Buttermarket). Carolingian, Charles the Bald, *Gratia Dei Rex* type, 864x877, St Quentin. Excavation-find. Information from J. Newman, Suffolk Archaeological Unit.

IPSWICH (School St). Carolingian, Charles the Bald, type unspecified, 840x877, Beauvais. Excavation-find. Information from J. Newman, Suffolk Archaeological Unit.

IPSWICH (School St). Carolingian, obol, Charles the Bald, type unspecified, 840x877. Quentovic. Excavation-find. Information from J. Newman, Suffolk Archaeological Unit.

IPSWICH (St Peter's St). Carolingian, Charles the Bald, type and mint unspecified, 840x877. Excavation-find. Information from J. Newman, Suffolk Archaeological Unit.

LAKENHEATH, Suffolk, 1978. Denmark, penny Hedeby (Malmer KG5), *Facing bust/stag* type. 0.89g. Archibald, 'Against the tide', no. 3; Blackburn *et al.*, *Early Medieval Coins*, p. 24 (then thought wrongly to have been found at Lavenham, Suffolk).

LEWES, Sussex, 1884. Imitative gold solidus of Louis the Pious, *ca* 830 x *ca* 850. Grierson, 'The gold solidus', p. 34, XVI d. (Ashmolean Museum)

MIDDLE HARLING, Norfolk, before 1985. An imitation of a Samanid dirhem of Isma'il b.Ahmad, AD 892–907, with the name of Caliph al-Mu'tadid in the area and that of his predecessor al-Mu'tamid in the margin. Found in the general area of the Middle Harling hoard of coins of Beonna, but not directly connected with them. Archibald, 'The coinage of Beonna', p. 17, no. 6.

OXBOROUGH, near Swaffham, Norfolk, 1986/87. Two fragmentary dirhems: a. Umayyad, Wasit, *ca* AH 120–8 (AD 737–46), 0.79g; b. Abbasid, Al Muhammadiyyah, *ca* AH 198 (AD 813), 0.55g. *Fitzwilliam Museum, Annual Report* 1991, pp. 37–8.

PIN'S KNOLL, Litton Cheyney, Dorset. Imitative obol of Lothar II, 855x869, Palace mint. Dolley & Morrison, 'Finds of Carolingian coins', pp. 75–7.

PORTCHESTER, Hants, 1832. Imitative gold solidus of Louis the Pious, *ca* 830 x *ca* 850. Sotheby's sale 25 March 1850, lot 247.

PRESHUTE, Marlborough, Wilts. Carolingian, Charles the Bald, 840x877, Rouen. Shortt, 'A denier'.

REPTON, near, Derbys., May 1985. Carolingian, Louis the Pious, *Christiana Religio* type, 822x840 (*MEC* 1:793–808), unspecified Frankish mint. 180°. Blackburn & Bonser, 'Single finds – 3', no. 122.

ROYSTON, near, Herts, 31 August 1989. Carolingian, Odo, *Misericordia Dei* type (*MEC* 1:983), 888x897, Tours. 0.87g, fragment, 0°. To be published by Blackburn and Bonser.

SETTLE (Attemire Cave), West Yorks., mid-late 19th century. Carolingian, Lothaire I, 840x855, Dorestadt. Pirie, 'Finds of "sceattas" ', p. 79, no. 75. (Pigyard Museum, Settle)

SOUTHAMPTON. Denier of Louis the Pious, *Christiana Religio* type, 822x840. Metcalf, 'The Coins', p. 55, no. 149.

SOUTHAMPTON. Carolingian, Charles the Bald, 840x877, Toulouse (Morrison and Grunthal 1100). Metcalf, 'The Coins', p. 55, no. 150.

SOUTHAMPTON. Imitative gold solidus of Louis the Pious, *ca* 830 x *ca* 850. 4.56g. Metcalf, 'The Coins', p. 54, no. 148.

SOUTHAMPTON. Islamic dirhem, *ca* AD 765–815, Umayyad, probably Cordoba mint. 0.56g, cut fragment, holed. Metcalf, 'The Coins', p. 57, no. 216.

STAMFORD BRIDGE, Yorks., early 1940s. Imitative gold solidus of Louis the Pious, *ca* 830 x *ca* 850. Christie's sale 17 November 1970, lot 46a ('found at Stamford Bridge').

THERFIELD, near Royston, Herts., before 1860. Imitative gold solidus of Louis the Pious, *ca* 830 x *ca* 850. 4.59g, 0°. Dolley Morrison, *The Carolingian Coins*, no. 78; Pagan, 'The imitative Louis the Pious solidus', p. 71. (British Museum)

THETFORD, Norfolk, *ca* 1980. Carolingian, Charles the Bald, *Gratia Di Rex* type, 864x877 or later (*MEC* 1:860–7), Quentovic. Found in mud dredged from the river Thet. Blackburn & Bonser, 'Single finds – 1', no. 22.

WYMESWOLD, near, Leics., 3 January 1987. Islamic dirhem, Abbasid, Caliph al-Mu'tamid, mint of Bardha'ah, AD 890x892. 2.52g. Blackburn & Bonser, 'Single finds – 3', no. 137.

YORK (Coppergate), 1980. Denmark, Hedeby, *Facing bust/Stag* type (Malmer KG 5), *ca* 850. 0.11g, fragment. Excavation-find. Pirie, *Post-Roman Coins*, no. 45.

YORK (Coppergate), 1981. Carolingian, Charles the Bald, obol, Palace mint, 864x877. 0.45g, corroded. Excavation-find. Pirie, *Post-Roman Coins*, no. 46.

NINTH-CENTURY NORTHUMBRIAN 'STYCAS' FOUND SOUTH OF THE HUMBER AND IN WALES

ANSTON (Moses Seat), near Worksop, S. Yorks., 1980. Æthelred II, 840x848?, moneyer Fordred. Pirie, 'Finds', no. 125.

APPLEBY, S. Humberside (N. Lincs.), before 1874. Æthelred II, 840x848?, moneyer Leofthegn. Pirie, 'Finds', no. 112.

BRANDON (Staunch Meadow), Suffolk, 1981. Æthelred II, 840x848?, moneyer Alghere. Excavation-find. Pirie, 'Finds', no. 121.

BRIGHTON, Sussex, before 1940. Eanred, 810x840?, moneyer Monne. Some doubt has been cast on the provenance, but recent finds from Kent and Sussex make it plausible. Pirie, 'Finds', 136. (Ashmolean Museum)

CADEBY (Pot Ridings Wood), near Doncaster, S. Yorks., 1980–2. Three coins of Æthelred II, 840x848?, moneyers Eanred, Leofthegn and Odilo. Pirie, 'Finds', no. 124.

CAERNARVON (Roman fort), Gwynedd, Wales, 1922. Eanred, 810x840?, moneyer Ulfheard. Pirie, 'Finds', no. 128.

CANTERBURY, near, Kent, October 1986. Eanred, 810x840?, moneyer Fordred. 0.99g, 140°. To be published.

CASTLETON (Castle Hill), Derbys., before 1848. An uncertain number of single finds, only one specifically identified; Æthelred II (2nd reign), 844x848?, moneyer Eardwulf. Pirie, 'Finds', no. 126.

DOWNHAM MARKET, near, Norfolk, 1980s. Æthelred II?, moneyer Eardwulf. To be published.

FLIXBOROUGH, Lincs., 1990/91. 22 Northumbrian 'stycas'. Excavation-finds. Blackburn, 'Coin finds in Lindsey', p. 87.

GAINSBOROUGH, near, Lincs., 1989. Æthelred II, *ca* 840 x *ca* 848, moneyer Monne. 1.31g, 180°. Blackburn, 'Coin finds in Lindsey', p. 87.

GRIMSBY, near, S. Humberside (N. Lincs.), 1983. Mid-9th-century imitation of Æthelred I, moneyer Tidwulf. 0.65g, 300°. Blackburn & Bonser, 'Sceattas, a styca, and other coin finds', pp. 236–7, illustrated in Blackburn & Bonser, 'Single finds – 1', pl. 1, no. 9A.

GRIMSTHORPE, near Bourne, Lincs., 1894. Æthelred II (1st reign), 840x844?, moneyer Eanred. Pirie, 'Finds', no. 114. (Peterborough City Museum)

HASKETON, near Woodbridge, Suffolk, 1981. Osbert, 848x867?, moneyer Winiberht. Pirie, 'Finds', no. 122.

HEACHAM, near Hunstanton, Norfolk, 1977–9. Listed as seven single-coin finds, but subsequent enquiries into the circumstances of recovery suggest the possibility of a small hoard or purse loss. a. Eanred, 810x840?, moneyer Fordred; b-c. Æthelred II, 840x848?, one coin each of the moneyers Monne and ?Leofthegn; d. Archbishop Wigmund, 837x854?, moneyer Coenred; e-g. three irregular coins, *ca* 840 x *ca* 848. Pirie, 'Finds', no. 116. (Casts in Norwich Castle Museum)

IRBY, S. Humberside (N. Lincs.), before 1984. Æthelred II, 840x848?, moneyer Fordred. Blackburn & Bonser, 'Single finds – 1', no. 11 (as unknown site near Grimsby).

KEELBY, Lincs., 1991. Two 'stycas': a. Æthelred II (2nd reign), 844x848?, moneyer Eardwulf; b. irregular issue, mid-9th cent. Blackburn, 'Coin finds in Lindsey', p. 88.

KIRMINGTON, S. Humberside (N. Lincs.), 1979. Eanred, 810x840?, moneyer Wilheah. Pirie, 'Finds', no. 113.

LEWES, Sussex, 21 June 1990. Æthelred II (2nd reign), 840x848?, moneyer Eardwulf. To be published.

LINCOLNSHIRE (North-eastern area), before 1984. Æthelred II, 840x848?, moneyer Monne. 1.20g, 70°. Blackburn & Bonser, 'Single finds – 1', no. 17.

MEOLS SANDS, Wirral, Cheshire, before 1863. Three single finds: a. Æthelred II, moneyer Fordred; b. Redwulf, moneyer Coenred; c. uncertain 'styca'. Pirie, 'Finds', no. 127.

NORTH WALSHAM, Norfolk. Æthelred II, 840x848?, moneyer Monne. 1.10g, 315°. *SCBI* East Anglia 1030; Pirie, 'Finds', no. 117.

NORWICH (Towlers Court, Elm Hill), Norfolk, before 1894. Æthelred II (1st reign), 840x844?, moneyer Odilo. *SCBI* East Anglia (supplement C); Pirie, 'Finds', no. 118.

PETERBOROUGH (Park Rd), Cambs., 1962. Æthelred II (1st reign), 840x844?, moneyer Wendelberht. Pirie, 'Finds', no. 115. (Peterborough City Museum)

RECULVER, Kent, before 1756. Eanred, 810x840?, moneyer Ulfheard. Rigold and Metcalf, 'A Revised Check-list'. The provenance has been doubted. Pirie, 'Finds', no. 131.

RICHBOROUGH, Kent. Three single finds from the Roman fort: a. Æthelred II (1st reign), 840x844?, moneyer Eanred; b. Æthelred II (1st reign), 840x844?, moneyer Fordred; c. Eanred, 810x840?, moneyer Aldates. a and b found before 1851; c found in excavations 1931–8. Pirie, 'Finds', no. 123.

SANDWICH, near, Kent, May 1988. Æthelred II (2nd reign), 844x848?, moneyer Eardwulf. 0.79g, 90°. To be published by Blackburn, Bonser and Chick.

SIX HILLS, near, Leics., November 1987. Æthelred II (1st reign), 840x844?, moneyer Brother. To be published by Blackburn, Bonser and Chick.

STOW, Lincs., before March 1990. Irregular issue, mid-ninth century. Blackburn, 'Coin finds in Lindsey', p. 89.

THETFORD (Bury Rd Allotment), Norfolk, 1975. Æthelred II (1st reign), 840x844?, moneyer Eanred. 1.00g, 270°. *SCBI* East Anglia 1020; Pirie, 'Finds', no. 119.

THETFORD (Saxon defences), Norfolk, 1977. Æthelred II (1st reign), 840x844?, moneyer Hnifula. Excavation-find. Pirie, 'Finds', no. 120. (Thetford Museum)

THETFORD, Norfolk, 30 June 1988. Æthelred II, 840x848?, moneyer Monne. 1.01g, 90°. Found during construction of the Thetford by-pass. To be published by Blackburn, Bonser and Chick.

THETFORD, Norfolk, 1990. Æthelred II, 840x848?, moneyer Wulfred. To be published.

THETFORD, Norfolk, 1989. Wigmund, archbishop of York, 837x854?, moneyer Cenred. 0.72g, chipped and corroded, 90°. Found during construction of the by-pass. Information from A. Rogerson, Norfolk Archaeological Unit.

TORKSEY, Lincs., 1989–91. Seven Northumbrian 'stycas': a. Æthelred II (1st reign), moneyer Fordred; b. Æthelred II (2nd reign), moneyer Eardwulf; c. Archbishop Wigmund, 837x854?, moneyer Coenræd; d. Archbishop Wigmund, moneyer Æthelweard; e–g. three 'stycas', irregular series, mid-ninth cent. Blackburn, 'Coin finds in Lindsey', p. 89.

TORKSEY or TORKSEY REGION ('north-west of Lincoln, on or near the east bank of the River Trent'), before January 1989. Eight Northumbrian 'stycas': a. Archbishop Eanbald II, 796x830?, moneyer Eadwulf; b. Eanred, *ca* 835?, moneyer Monne; c. Archbishop Wigmund, 837x854?, moneyer Hunlaf; d. Æthelred II, moneyer Brother?; e. Redwulf, 844?, moneyer Brother; f-h. three 'stycas', irregular series, mid-ninth century. Blackburn, 'Coin finds in Lindsey', p. 89.

WINTERINGHAM, S. Humberside (N. Lincs.), 1750. Eanred, *ca* 810 x *ca* 840, moneyer Cunwulf. Pirie, 'Finds', no. 111.

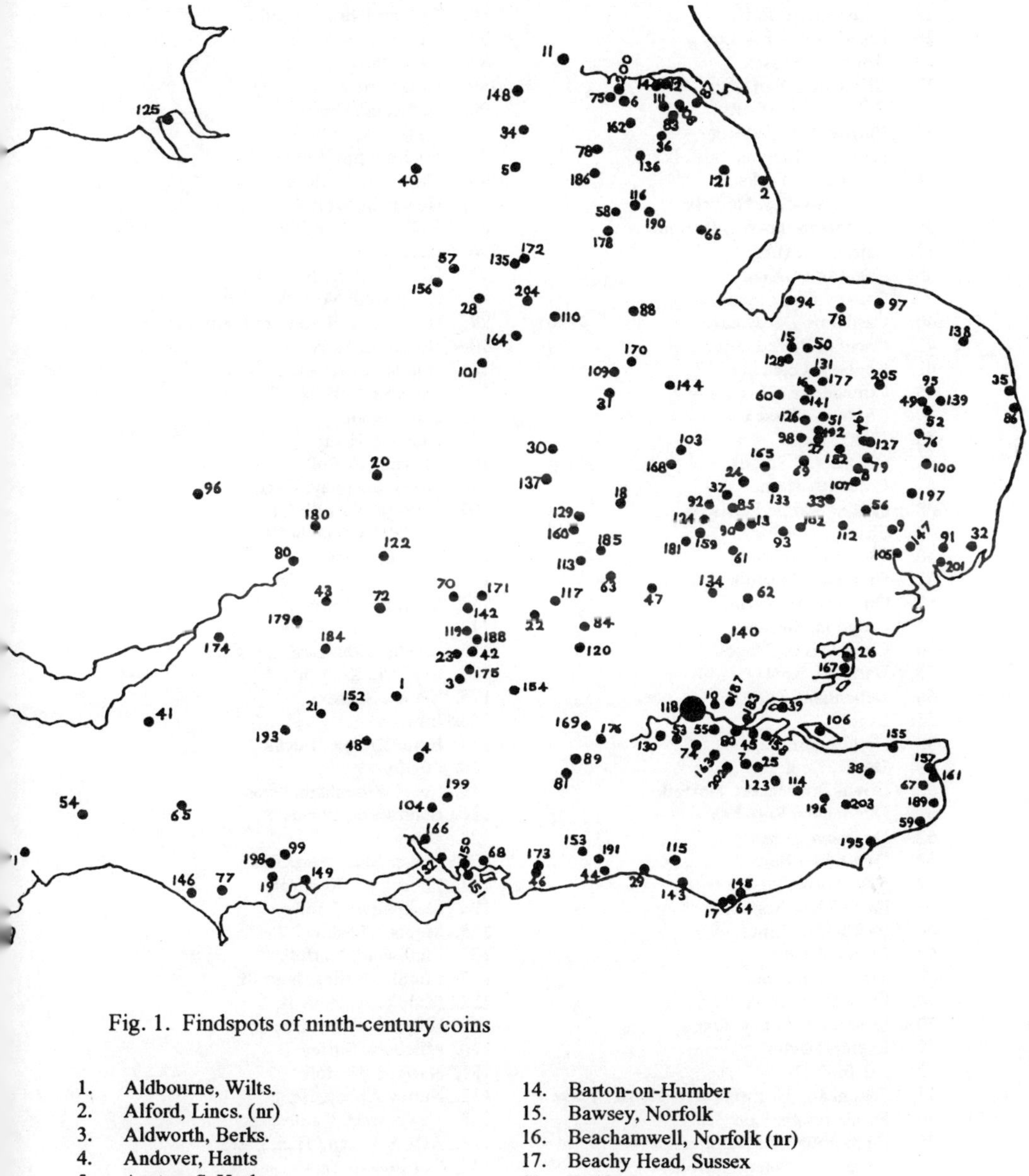

Fig. 1. Findspots of ninth-century coins

1. Aldbourne, Wilts.
2. Alford, Lincs. (nr)
3. Aldworth, Berks.
4. Andover, Hants
5. Anston, S. Yorks.
6. Appleby, S. Humberside
7. Aylesford, Kent (nr)
8. Bardwell, Suffolk
9. Barham, Suffolk
10. Barking Abbey, Essex
11. Barmby, N. Humberside
12. Barrow-on-Humber
13. Bartlow, Cambs.
14. Barton-on-Humber
15. Bawsey, Norfolk
16. Beachamwell, Norfolk (nr)
17. Beachy Head, Sussex
18. Bedford
19. Bere Regis, Dorset
20. Bidford-on-Avon, Warks.
21. Bishop's Cannings, Wilts.
22. Bledlow, Bucks.
23. Blewbury, Oxon.
24. Bottisham, Cambs.
25. Boxley, Kent
26. Bradwell, Essex

27. Brandon, Suffolk
28. Breedon-on-Hill, Leics.
29. Brighton, Sussex
30. Brixworth, Northants
31. Bulwick, Northants
32. Burrow Hill, Suffolk
33. Bury St Edmunds, Suffolk (nr)
34. Cadeby, S. Yorks.
35. Caister-by-Sea, Norfolk
36. Caistor-on-the-Wolds, Lincs.
37. Cambridge (nr)
38. Canterbury, Kent
39. Canvey Isle, Essex
40. Castleton, Derbyshire
41. Cheddar Palace, Somerset
42. Cholsey, Oxon.
43. Cirencester, Glos. (nr)
44. Cissbury, Sussex
45. Chalk, Kent
46. Chichester, Sussex
47. Codicote, Herts.
48. Collingbourne Ducis, Wilts.
49. Colney, Norfolk
50. Congham, Norfolk
51. Cranwich, Norfolk
52. Cringleford, Norfolk
53. Croydon, Surrey
54. Culm Davey, Devon
55. Dartford, Kent
56. Debenham, Suffolk
57. Derby
58. Doddington, Lincs. (nr)
59. Dover, Kent
60. Downham Market, Norfolk
61. Duddenhoe End, Essex
62. Dunmow, Essex
63. Dunstable, Beds.
64. Eastbourne, Sussex
65. East Coker, Somerset
66. East Kirby, Lincs.
67. Eastry, Kent
68. Emsworth, Hants
69. Eriswell, Suffolk
70. Eynesham Abbey, Oxon.
71. Exeter, Devon
72. Fairford, Glos.
73. Fakenham, Norfolk (nr) – North Creake
74. Farnborough, Kent
75. Flixborough, S. Humberside
76. Forncett St Peter, Norfolk
77. Fordington, Dorset
78. Gainsborough, Lincs.
79. Garboldisham, Norfolk
80. Gloucester
81. Godalming, Surrey (nr)
82. Gravesend, Kent (nr)
83. Gt Limber, Lincs.
84. Gt Missenden, Bucks. (nr)
85. Gt Shelford, Cambs.
86. Gt Yarmouth, Suffolk
87. Grimsby, S. Humberside
88. Grimsthorpe, Lincs.
89. Guildford, Surrey (nr)
90. Hadstock, Essex
91. Hasketon, Suffolk
92. Haslingfield, Cambs.
93. Haverhill, Suffolk
94. Heacham, Norfolk
95. Hellesdon, Norfolk
96. Hereford
97. Hindringham, Norfolk
98. Hockwold, Norfolk
99. Hod Hill & Blandford Forum, Dorset
100. Hoxne, Suffolk
101. Huncote, Leics. (nr)
102. Hundon, Suffolk
103. Huntingdon
104. Hursley, Hants
105. Ipswich, Suffolk
106. Isle of Sheppey, Kent
107. Ixworth, Suffolk (nr)
108. Keelby, S. Humberside
109. Ketton, Lincs.
110. Kirby Bellars, Leics.
111. Kirmington, Lincs.
112. Lavenham, Suffolk
113. Leighton Buzzard, Beds. (nr)
114. Lenham, Kent (nr)
115. Lewes, Sussex
116. Lincoln
117. Little Kimble, Bucks.
118. London
119. Long Wittenham, Oxon.
120. Loudwater, Bucks.
121. Louth, Lincs.
122. Lower Slaughter, Glos.
123. Maidstone, Kent (nr)
124. Melbourne, Cambs.
125. Meols, Cheshire
126. Methwold, Norfolk
127. Middle Harling, Norfolk
128. Middleton, Norfolk
129. Milton Keynes, Bucks.
130. Mitcham, Surrey
131. Narford, Norfolk
132. Netley Abbey, Hants
133. Newmarket, Cambs. (nr)
134. New Stanstead Hall, Essex
135. Nottingham (nr)
136. Normanby-le-Wold, Lincs.
137. Northampton
138. North Walsham, Norfolk
139. Norwich, Norfolk
140. Ongar, Essex
141. Oxborough, Norfolk (nr)
142. Oxford
143. Peacehaven, Sussex
144. Peterborough, Cambs.

145. Pevensey, Sussex
146. Pin's Knoll, Dorset
147. Playford, Suffolk
148. Pontefract, S. Yorks. (nr)
149. Poole, Dorset
150. Portchester (Castle) Hants
151. Portsmouth, Hants
152. Preshute, Wilts.
153. Pulborough, Sussex
154. Reading, Berks.
155. Reculver, Kent
156. Repton, Derbyshire (nr)
157. Richborough, Kent
158. Rochester, Kent
159. Royston, Herts
160. Salden, Bucks.
161. Sandwich, Kent (nr)
162. Scawby, S. Humberside
163. Shoreham, Kent
164. Six Hills, Leics. (nr)
165. Soham, Cambs.
166. Southampton, Hants
167. Southminster, Essex
168. Southoe, Hunts
169. Staines, Middx
170. Stamford, Lincs.
171. Stanton St John, Oxon.
172. Stoke Bardolph, Notts.
173. Stoke Down, Sussex
174. Stoke Gifford, Glos.
175. Streatley, Berks.
176. Sunbury, Middx
177. Swaffham, Norfolk
178. Swinderby, Lincs.
179. Tetney, Glos. (nr)
180. Tewkesbury, Glos. (nr)
181. Therfield, Herts
182. Thetford, Norfolk
183. Tilbury, Essex (nr)
184. Tockenham, Wilts.
185. Toddington, Beds.
186. Torksey, Lincs.
187. Upminster, Essex
188. Wallingford, Oxon.
189. Walmer, Kent
190. Washingborough, Lincs.
191. Washington, Sussex
192. Weeting, Suffolk
193. Westbury, Wilts.
194. West Harling, Norfolk
195. West Hythe, Kent
196. Westwell, Kent
197. Wetheringsett-cum-Brockford, Suffolk
198. Whitechurch, Dorset
199. Winchester, Hants
200. Winteringham, S. Humberside
201. Woodbridge, Suffolk (nr)
202. Wrotham, Kent
203. Wye, Kent
204. Wymeswold, Lincs.
205. Yaxham, Norfolk

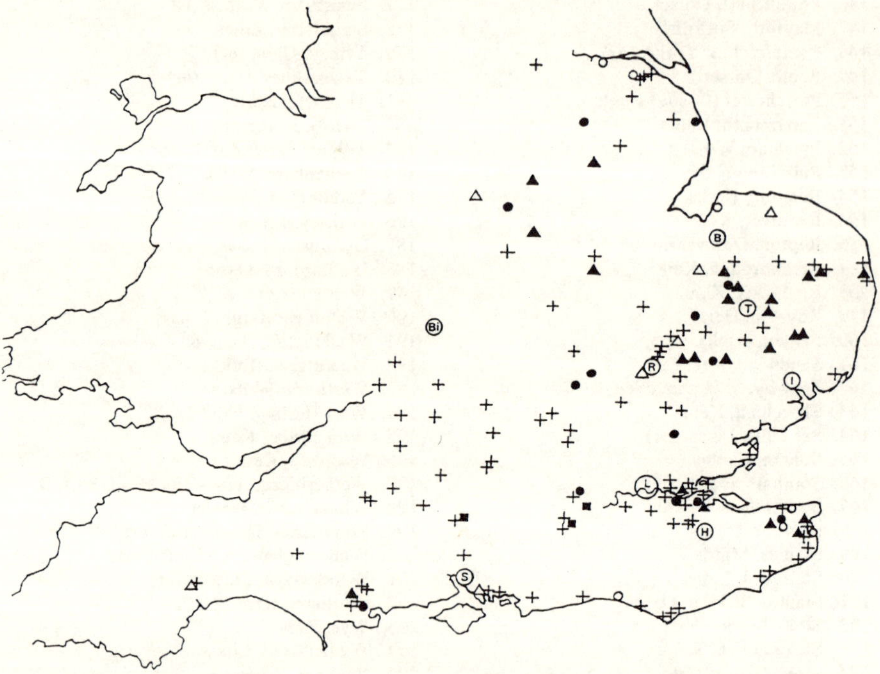

Fig. 2. Finds of coins struck 796–840

Canterbury/Rochester:	+
London:	●
East Anglia:	▲
Southampton/Winchester:	■
Stycas:	○
Foreign:	△
Unidentified:	×

London:	(L)	$+^{7}$	$●^{1}$	$▲^{1}$	$×^{1}$		
Southampton:	(S)	$+^{16}$	$●^{1}$	$▲^{1}$	$■^{2}$	$△^{3}$	$×^{5}$
Thetford:	(T)	$+^{1}$	$▲^{2}$	$■^{1}$			
Bawsey:	(B)	$+^{2}$	$×^{3}$				
Bidford-on-Avon:	(Bi)	$+^{2}$	$▲^{3}$				
near Royston:	(R)	$+^{8}$	$▲^{2}$	$■^{1}$			
near Maidstone:	(H)	$+^{2}$	$▲^{2}$				
Ipswich:	(I)	$+^{2}$	$▲^{3}$	$■^{1}$	$×^{1}$		

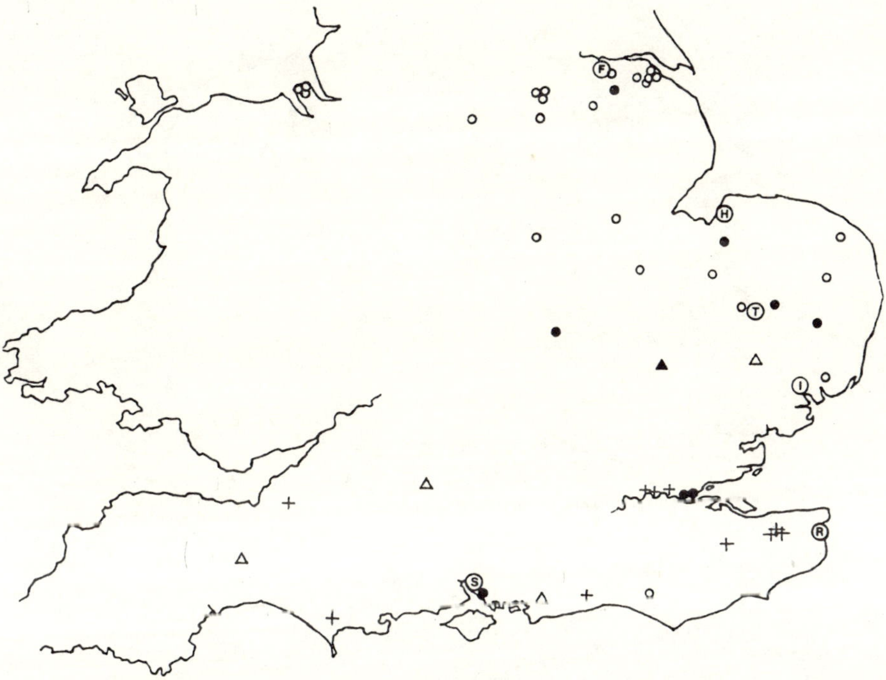

Fig. 3. Finds of coins struck 840–860

Canterbury/Rochester: +
London: ●
East Anglia: ▲
Southampton/Winchester: ■
Stycas: ○
Foreign: △
Unidentified: ×

Southampton: Ⓢ +^{6} ●^{4} △^{1}
Heacham: Ⓗ ○^{6}
Thetford: Ⓣ ●^{1} ○^{5}
Ipswich: Ⓘ +^{2} ▲^{2}
Richborough: (with Sandwich) Ⓡ ●^{1} ○^{2}
Flixborough: Ⓕ +^{5} ○^{22}

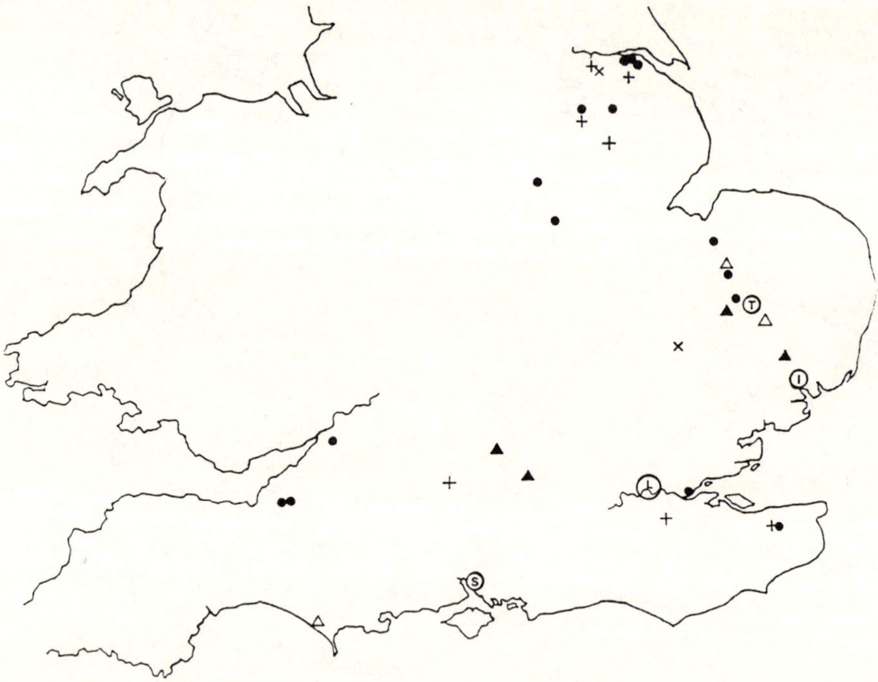

Fig. 4. Finds of coins struck 860–875

Canterbury/Rochester:	+
London:	●
East Anglia:	▲
Southampton/Winchester:	■
Stycas:	○
Foreign:	△
Unidentified:	×

London:	Ⓛ	+²	●¹	
Southampton:	Ⓢ	●⁵		
Thetford:	Ⓣ	●²	▲¹	△¹
Ipswich:	Ⓘ	▲²	△⁴	

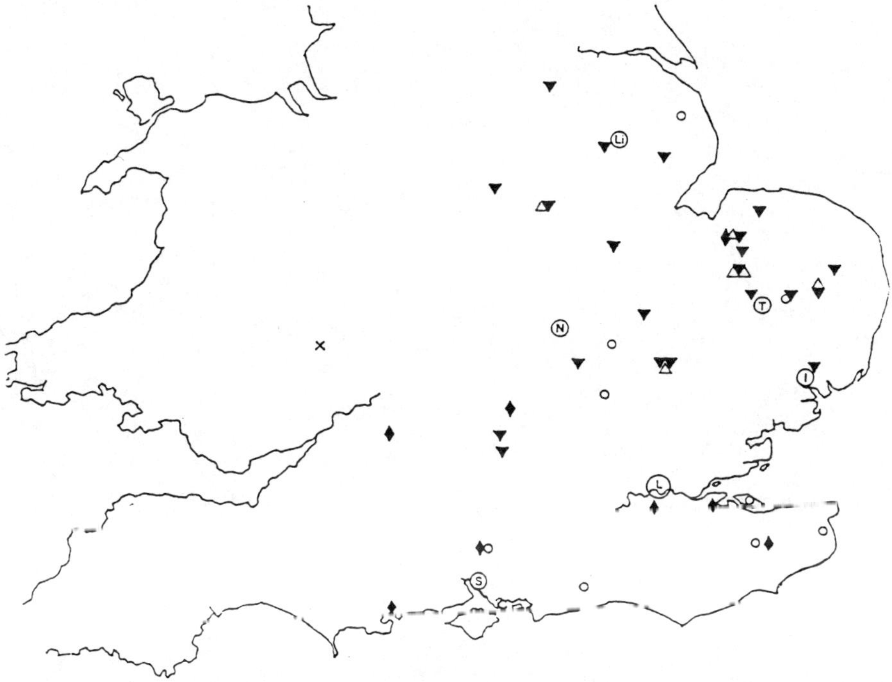

Fig. 5. Finds of coins struck 875–900

Cross-and-Lozenge and minor types:	♦
Two-line and mint – signed types:	○
Viking issues (York Royal, Alfred imitat- ions and St Edmund:	▼
Foreign:	△

London:	Ⓛ	○^{6}	▼^{1}	
Southampton:	Ⓢ	♦^{1}	×^{2}	
Northampton:	Ⓝ	▼^{7}		
Thetford:	Ⓣ	▼^{6}		
Lincoln:	(Li)	○^{2}	▼^{2}	
Ipswich:	Ⓘ	○^{1}	▼^{17}	×^{1}

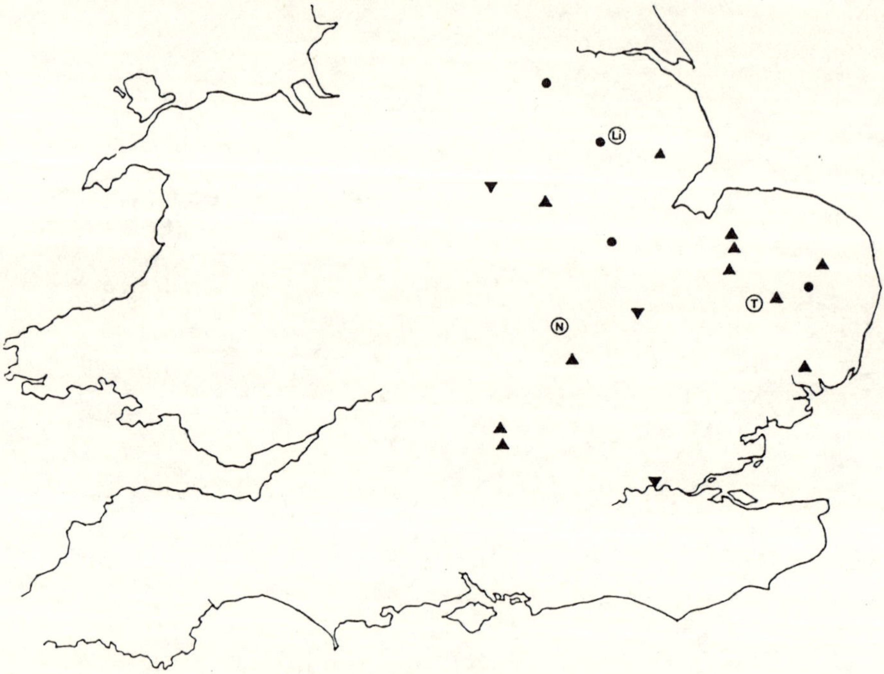

Fig. 6. Finds of Viking coins

Alfred imitations: ●
St Edmund: ▲
York Royal: ▼

Thetford: (T) ▲5
Lincoln: (Li) ●2 ▲2
Northampton: (N) ▲7

Fig. 7. Finds of foreign coins

Carolingian, excluding solidi: △
Solidi: +
Gold denier: ⨺
Danish: ▼
Arabic: □

Southampton: Ⓢ △[2] +[1] □[1]

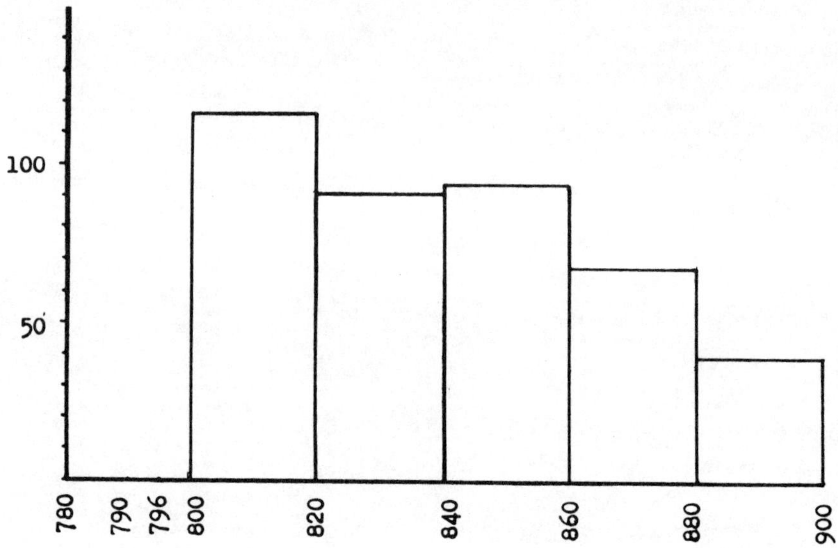

Fig. 8. Histogram of all finds 780–900, including 'stycas' and foreign coins, plotted according to the date of striking (source: above listing, and for coins 780–796 unpublished work of D. Chick)

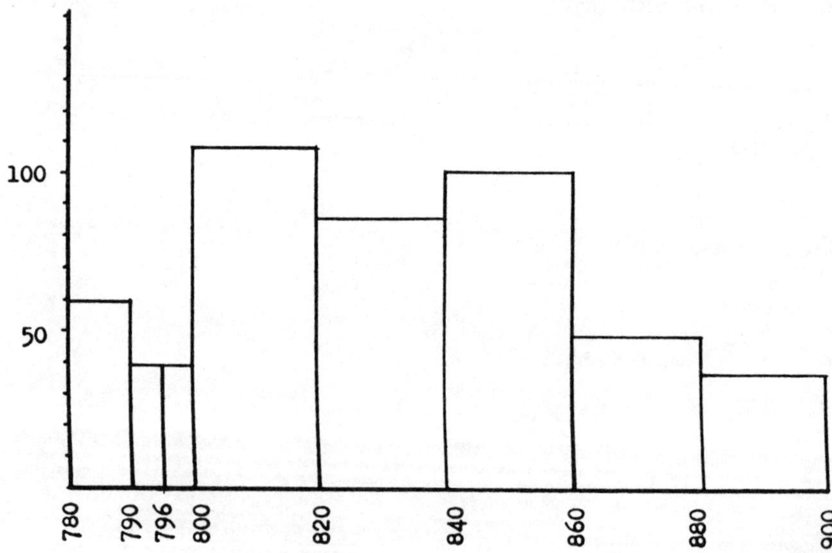

Fig. 9. Histogram of all finds 800–900, adjusted to reflect the date of loss by assuming that one third of the coins lost in any one period were struck in an earlier period, as discussed in Blackburn, 'What factors', p. 19

BIBLIOGRAPHY

Abbreviations

The following concise abbreviations are used throughout this volume. Full references can be found in the bibliography below.

BLS	Blunt, Lyon & Stewart, 'The coinage of southern England'
BMA	Brooke, 'Anglo-Saxon acquisitions', I–V
BMC	Keary & Grueber, *A Catalogue of English Coins*
'Coin Register'	Annual listings of finds in *British Numismatic Journal* from volume 57 (1987)
EHD	Whitelock, *English Historical Documents, 1*
MEC	Grierson & Blackburn, *Medieval European Coinage, 1*
N	North, *English Hammered Coinage, I*
S	Sawyer, P. H. *Anglo-Saxon Charters*
SCBI	*Sylloge of Coins of the British Isles*
SCBI Cambridge	Grierson, *Fitzwilliam Museum, Cambridge*
SCBI Copenhagen	Galster, *Royal Collection, Copenhagen*
SCBI East Anglia	Clough, *Museums in East Anglia*
SCBI Glasgow	Robertson, *Hunterian and Coats Collections*
SCBI Lincolnshire	Gunstone, *Coins in Lincolnshire Collections*
SCBI Mack	Mack, *R. P. Mack Collection*
SCBI Midlands	Gunstone, *Ancient British, Anglo-Saxon and Norman Coins*
SCBI Norweb	Blunt *et al.*, *Collection of Ancient British, Romano-British and English Coins*
SCBI Oxford	Thompson, *Ashmolean Museum, Oxford*
SCBI South-Eastern Museums	Gunstone, *South-Eastern Museums*

ABELS, R. 'King Alfred's peace-making strategies with the Vikings', *Haskins Society Journal* 3 (1991) 23–34

ABRAMS, Lesley *Anglo-Saxon Glastonbury: Church and Endowment* (Woodbridge 1996)

ADDYMAN, P. V. & HILL, D. H. 'Saxon Southampton: a review of the evidence, part I', *Proceedings of the Hampshire Field Club and Archaeological Society* 25 (1968) 61–93

ALLAN, J. P. *et al.* (edd.) *Medieval and Post-Medieval Finds from Exeter 1971–1980*, Exeter Archaeological Report 3 (Exeter 1984)

ANDREWS, P. (ed.) *Southampton Finds, I, The Coins and Pottery from Hamwic* (Southampton 1988)

ANGENENDT, Arnold *Kaiserherrschaft und Königstaufe. Kaiser, Könige und Päpste als geistliche Patrone in der abendländischen Missionsgeschichte* (Berlin 1984)

ARCHIBALD, M. M. 'A ship type of Athelstan I of East Anglia', *British Numismatic Journal* 52 (1982) 34–40

ARCHIBALD, M. M. 'A Viking copy of an Alfred London Monogram penny from Doncaster', *Yorkshire Numismatist* 1 (1988) 9–11

ARCHIBALD, M. M. 'Against the tide: coin-movement from Scandinavia to the British Isles in the Viking age', *NNF-Nytt* (1991) 19–22

ARCHIBALD, M. M. 'An Alfred penny from Rochester', *Archaeologia Cantiana* 94 (1978) 55–9

ARCHIBALD, M. M. 'Pecking and bending: the evidence of British finds', in *Sigtuna Papers*, edd. K. Jonsson & B. Malmer (Stockholm 1990), pp. 11–24

ARCHIBALD, M. M. 'The coinage of Beonna in the light of the Middle Harling hoard', *British Numismatic Journal* 55 (1985) 10–54

ARCHIBALD, M. M. 'The coins', in *Medieval and Post-Medieval Finds from Exeter 1971–1980*, edd. J. P. Allan *et al.* (Exeter 1984), pp. 250–1

ASTILL, G. 'Medieval ceramics and urban development: a review', *Archaeological Journal* 146 (1989) 559–70

AYRE, J. *et al.* 'Æthelred's hythe to Queenhithe: the origin of a London dock', *Medieval Life* 5 (Summer 1996) 14–25

BAINES, A. H. J. 'Monks Risborough: new light from Islington', *Records of Buckinghamshire* 36 (1994) 98–102

BAINES, A. H. J. 'The boundaries of Monks Risborough', *Records of Buckinghamshire* 23 (1981) 76–101

BAINES, A. H. J. 'The Danish wars and the establishment of the borough and county of Buckingham', *Records of Buckinghamshire* 26 (1984) 1–27

BAINES, A. H. J. 'The origins of the borough of Newport Pagnell', *Records of Buckinghamshire* 28 (1986) 128–37

BAINES, A. H. J. 'Wynflæd v. Leofwine: a Datchet lawsuit of 990', *Records of Buckinghamshire* 32 (1990) 63–75

BETHMANN, L. & WAITZ, Georg (edd.) *Scriptores Rerum Langobardicarum et Italicarum Saec. VI–IX* (Hanover 1878)

BEUMANN, Helmut (ed.) *Karl der Grosse: Persönlichkeit und Geschichte*, in *Karl der Grosse*, ed. W. Braunfels (4 vols, Düsseldorf 1965), I

BIDDLE, M. *et al.* 'Coins of the Anglo-Saxon period from Repton, Derbyshire', in *Anglo-Saxon Monetary History*, ed. M. A. S. Blackburn (Leicester 1986), pp. 111–32

BIDDLE, M. *et al.* 'Coins of the Anglo-Saxon period from Repton, Derbyshire II', *British Numismatic Journal* 56 (1986) 16–34

BIDDLE, M. 'London on the Strand', *Popular Archaeology* 6.1 (1984) 23–7

BIRD, J. *et al.* (edd.) *Collectanea Londiniensia* (London 1978)

BISPHAM, J. 'Recent metal detector finds from Essex and Lincolnshire', *British Numismatic Journal* 56 (1986) 183–5

BJÖRKMAN, E. *Nordische Personennamen in England* (Halle 1910)

BLACKBURN, M. A. S. & BONSER, M. J. 'A Carolingian gold coin struck from a die of Chartres and found at Congham, Norfolk', *Numismatic Circular* 98 (1990) 304–6

BLACKBURN, M. A. S. 'A penny of Coenwulf and a small hoard of Cnut from Bottisham, Cambridgeshire', *British Numismatic Journal* 53 (1983) 176–7

BLACKBURN, M. A. S. & BONSER, M. J. 'A portrait coin of Coenwulf found near Stains', *Numismatic Circular* 92 (1984) 113

BLACKBURN, M. A. S. & PAGAN, H. 'A revised check-list of coin hoards from the British Isles *c.* 500–1100', in *Anglo-Saxon Monetary History*, ed. M. A. S. Blackburn (Leicester 1986), pp. 291–313

BLACKBURN, M. A. S. (ed.) *Anglo-Saxon Monetary History. Essays in Memory of Michael Dolley* (Leicester 1986)

BLACKBURN, M. A. S. 'Coin finds and coin circulation in Lindsey *c.* 600–900', in *Pre-Viking Lindsey*, ed. A. Vince (Lincoln 1993), pp. 80–90

BLACKBURN, M. A. S. *et al. Early Medieval Coins from Lincoln and its Shire* c. *770–1100*, Archaeology of Lincoln VI–1 (London 1983)

BLACKBURN, M. A. S. 'Mints, burhs, and the Grately Code cap. 14.2', in *The Defence of Wessex*, edd. D. Hill & A. R. Rumble (Manchester 1996), pp. 160–75

BLACKBURN, M. A. S. & BONSER, M. J. 'Sceattas, a styca, and other coin finds from a site in north east Lincolnshire', in *Sceattas in England and on the Continent*, edd. D. Hill & D. M. Metcalf (Oxford 1984), pp. 233–9

BLACKBURN, M. A. S. & BONSER, M. J. 'Single finds of Anglo-Saxon and Norman coins –1', *British Numismatic Journal* 54 (1984) 63–73

BLACKBURN, M. A. S. & BONSER, M. J. 'Single finds of Anglo-Saxon and Norman coins –2', *British Numismatic Journal* 55 (1985) 55–78

BLACKBURN, M. A. S. & BONSER, M. J. 'Single finds of Anglo-Saxon and Norman coins –3', *British Numismatic Journal* 56 (1986) 64–101

BLACKBURN, M. A. S. 'The Ashdon (Essex) hoard and the currency of the southern Danelaw in the late ninth century', *British Numismatic Journal* 59 (1989) 13–38

BLACKBURN, M. A. S. 'The earlist Anglo-Viking coinage of the southern Danelaw (late 9th cent.)', in *Proceedings of the 10th International Congress of Numismatics, London September 1986,* ed. I. A. Carradice (London 1989), pp. 341–8

BLACKBURN, M. A. S. 'What factors govern the number of coins found on an archaeological site?', in *Coins and Archaeology*, edd. H. Clarke & E. Schia (Oxford 1989), pp. 15–24

BLAIR, John *Anglo-Saxon Oxfordshire* (Stroud 1994)

BLUNT, C. E. 'A new coin of Baldred, king of Kent', *British Numismatic Journal* 44 (1974) 75–6

BLUNT, C. E. 'A new type for Alfred', *British Numismatic Journal* 26 (1949–51) 213–15

BLUNT, C. E. 'A small parcel from the Dorking (1817) hoard', *British Numismatic Journal* 41 (1972) 179

BLUNT, C. E., STEWART, B. H. I. H. & LYON, C. S. S. *Coinage in Tenth-Century England from Edward the Elder to Edgar's Reform* (Oxford 1989)

BLUNT, C. E. *et al. Collection of Ancient British, Romano-British and English Coins formed by Mrs. Emery May Norweb* (SCBI 16, Oxford 1973)

BLUNT, C. E. 'Grangerized copies of Ruding's Annals', *Numismatic Circular* 84 (1976), 226–7

BLUNT, C. E. 'Saxon coins from Southampton and Bangor', *British Numismatic Journal* 27 (1952–4) 256–62

BLUNT, C. E. 'The Anglo-Saxon coinage and the historian', *Medieval Archaeology* 4 (1960) 1–15

BLUNT, C. E. 'The coinage of Athelstan, 924–939. A survey' *British Numismatic Journal* 42 (1974) 35–160

BLUNT, C. E. 'The coinage of Æthelred, archbishop of Canterbury, 870–89', *British Numismatic Journal* 31 (1962) 43–4

BLUNT, C. E. 'The coinage of Ecgbeorht, king of Wessex, 802–39', *British Numismatic Journal* 28 (1955–7) 467–76

BLUNT, C. E. 'The coinage of Offa', in *Anglo-Saxon Coins*, ed. R. H. M. Dolley (London 1961), pp. 39–62

BLUNT, C. E., LYON, C. S. S. & STEWART, B. H. I. H. 'The coinage of southern England, 796–840', *British Numismatic Journal* 32 (1963) 1–74

BLUNT, C. E. & DOLLEY, R. H. M. 'The hoard evidence for the coins of Alfred', *British Numismatic Journal* 29 (1958/9) 220–47

BLUNT, C. E. 'The Sevington hoard of 1834', *British Numismatic Journal* 41 (1972) 7–13

BOGNETTI, Gian Piero *L'età longobarda* (4 vols, Milan 1966–8)

BORETIUS, A. & KRAUSE, V. (edd.) *Capitularia regum Francorum* (2 vols, Hanover 1883/97)

BRAUNFELS, Wolfgang (ed.) *Karl der Grosse: Lebenswerk und Nachleben* (4 vols, Düsseldorf 1965)

BROMWICH, Rachel & EVANS, D. Simon (edd.) *Culhwch and Olwen: An Edition and Study of the Oldest Arthurian Tale* (Cardiff 1992)

BROOKE, C. N. L. & KERR, G. *London 800–1216: The Shaping of a City* (London 1975)

BROOKE, C. N. L. *et al.* (edd.) *Studies in Numismatic Method presented to Philip Grierson* (Cambridge 1983)

BROOKE, G. C. 'Anglo-Saxon acquisitions of the British Museum. I. Thrymsa and sceatta series; Mercia', *Numismatic Chronicle*, 5th S., 2 (1922) 214–44

BROOKE, G. C. 'Anglo-Saxon acquisitions of the British Museum. II. Kent; archbishops of Canterbury; East Anglia', *Numismatic Chronicle*, 5th S., 3 (1923) 243–59

BROOKE, G. C. 'Anglo-Saxon acquisitions of the British Museum. III. Northumbria', *Numismatic Chronicle*, 5th S., 4 (1924) 86–95

BROOKE, G. C. 'Anglo-Saxon acquisitions of the British Museum. IV. Wessex; Ecgberht to Æthelred I', *Numismatic Chronicle*, 5th S., 4 (1924) 239–53

BROOKE, G. C. 'Anglo-Saxon acquisitions of the British Museum. V. Alfred to Edwig', *Numismatic Chronicle*, 5th S., 5 (1925) 343–65

BROOKE, G. C. *English Coins* (3rd edn, London 1950)

BROOKS, N. 'Epilogue', in *Coinage in Ninth-Century Northumbria*, ed. D. M. Metcalf (Oxford 1987), pp. 397–401

BROOKS, N. P. 'The administrative background to the Burghal Hidage', in *The Defence of Wessex*, edd. D. Hill and A. R. Rumble (Manchester, 1996), pp. 128–50

BROOKS, Nicholas *The Early History of the Church of Canterbury. Christ Church from 597 to 1066* (Leicester 1984)

CALMETTE, J. *La diplomatie carolingienne* (Paris 1917)

CAMPBELL, A. *Old English Grammar* (Oxford 1959)

CAMPBELL, A. (ed. & transl.) *The Chronicle of Æthelweard* (Edinburgh 1962)

CAMPBELL, J. 'Asser's *Life of Alfred*', in *The Inheritance of Historiography 350–900*, edd. C. Holdsworth and T. P. Wiseman (Exeter 1986), pp. 115–35

CAMPBELL, James (ed.) *The Anglo-Saxons* (Oxford 1982)

CAMPBELL, J. 'The late Anglo-Saxon state: a maximum view', *Proceedings of the British Academy* 87 (1995) 39–65

CARRADICE, I. A. (ed.) *Proceedings of the 10th International Congress of Numismatics, London, September 1986* (London 1989)

CASEY, J. & REECE, R. *Coins and the Archaeologist* (2nd edn, London 1988)

CHICK, D. & SEABY, W. 'A new variant for Eadwald/Eadnoth(?)', *Numismatic Circular* 99 (1991) 221

CHICK, D. 'A remarkable new penny of Archbishop Aethelheard of Canterbury', *Numismatic Circular* 100 (1992) 188–200

CLARKE, H. & SCHIA, E. (edd.) *Coins and Archaeology* (Oxford 1989)

CLARKE, Helen & AMBROSIANI, Björn *Towns in the Viking Age* (Leicester 1991)

CLOUGH, T. H. McK. *Museums in East Anglia* (SCBI 26, Oxford 1980)

COLLINS, Roger *Early Medieval Europe 300–1000* (London 1991)

COLMAN, Fran *Money Talks. Reconstructing Old English* (Berlin 1992)

COMBE, T. 'An account of some Anglo-Saxon pennies found at Dorking in Surrey', *Archaeologia* 19 (1821) 109–19, plates IX–X

COWDREY, H. E. J. 'Bede and the "English people" ', *Journal of Religious History* 11 (1981) 501–23

COX, B. 'Rutland and the Scandinavian settlements: the place-name evidence', *Anglo-Saxon England* 18 (1989) 135–48

DARLINGTON, R. R. & McGURK, P. (edd.) *The Chronicle of John of Worcester*, II: *The Annals from 450 to 1066* (Oxford 1995)

DAVIS, R. H. C. 'Alfred and Guthrum's frontier', *English Historical Review* 97 (1982) 803–10

DAVIS, R. H. C. 'Alfred the Great: propaganda and truth', *History*, N.S., 56 (1971) 169–82

DE COURSON, A. *Cartulaire de l'abbaye de Redon en Bretagne*, Documents inédits sur l'histoire de France (Paris 1863)

DESHUSSES, J. & DAVRAGON, B. *Concordances et tableaux pour l'étude des grands sacramentaires*, Spicilegium Friburgense, Subsidia, 9–11 (Freiburg/Schweiz 1982–)

DESHUSSES, J. (ed.) Le Sacramentaire Grégorien. *Ses principales formes d'après les plus anciens manuscrits. Étude comparative*, Spicilegium Friburgense, XVI, XXIV, XXVIII (Freiburg/Schweiz 1971–82)

D'HAENENS, A. *Les invasions normandes en Belgique au ixe siècle* (Louvain 1967)

DÖLGER, F. *Byzanz und das europäische Staatenwelt: ausgewählte Vorträge und Aufsätze* (Darmstadt 1964)

DÖLGER, F. 'Die "Familie der Könige" im Mittelalter', in *Byzanz und das euroäpische Staatenwelt*, F. Dölger (Darmstadt 1964), pp. 34–69

DOLLEY, R. H. M. & SHIEL, N. 'A Carolingian *denarius* with a Devonshire provenance', *British Numismatic Journal* 50 (1980) 7–11

DOLLEY, R. H. M. 'A new type and moneyer for Eadbearht "Præn" ', *British Numismatic Journal* 28 (1955–7) 243–8

DOLLEY, R. H. M. 'A piedfort lead trial-piece of Edward the Confessor', *British Numismatic Journal* 27 (1953) 175–8

DOLLEY, R. H. M. (ed.) *Anglo-Saxon Coins. Studies presented to F. M. Stenton on the Occasion of his 80th Birthday* (London 1961)

DOLLEY, R. H. M. *Anglo-Saxon Pennies* (London 1964)

DOLLEY, R. H. M. 'An unpublished hoard-provenance for a penny of Ceolwulf II of Mercia', *British Numismatic Journal* 32 (1963) 88–90

DOLLEY, R. H. M. 'Ælfred the Great's abandonment of the concept of periodic recoinage', in *Studies in Numismatic Method presented to Philip Grierson*, edd. C. N. L. Brooke *et al.* (Cambridge 1983), pp. 153–60

DOLLEY, R. H. M. & MORRISON, K. F. 'Finds of Carolingian coins from Great Britain and Ireland', *British Numismatic Journal* 32 (1963) 75–87

DOLLEY, R. H. M. & MORRISON, K. F. *The Carolingian Coins in the British Museum* (London, 1966)

DOLLEY, R. H. M. & BLUNT, C. E. 'The chronology of the coins of Ælfred the Great 871–99', in *Anglo-Saxon Coins*, ed. R. H. M. Dolley (London 1961), pp. 77–95

DOLLEY, R. H. M. & SKAARE, K. 'The coinage of Æthelwulf, king of the West Saxons, 839–58', in *Anglo-Saxon Coins*, ed. R. H. M. Dolley (London 1961), pp. 63–76

DOLLEY, R. H. M. & STRUDWICK, J. S. 'The provenances of the Anglo-Saxon coins recorded in the two volumes of the British Museum catalogue', *British Numismatic Journal* 28 (1956) 26–59

DORNIER, ANN (ed.) *Mercian Studies* (Leicester 1977)

DOWNER, L. J. (ed.) *Leges Henrici Primi* (Oxford 1972)

DUCHESNE, L. & VOGEL, C. (edd.) *Liber Pontificalis* (3 vols, Paris 1886–1956)

DUEMMLER, Ernest (ed.) *Epistolae Karolina Aevi II* (Berlin 1895)

DUGGAN, A. J. (ed.) *Kings and Kingship in Medieval Europe* (London 1993)

DUMVILLE, David N. & KEYNES, S. (gen. edd.) *The Anglo-Saxon Chronicle: a Collaborative Edition* (23 vols, Cambridge 1983–)

DUMVILLE, D. N. 'The treaty of Alfred and Guthrum', in *Wessex and England from Alfred to Edgar*, D. N. Dumville (Woodbridge 1992), pp. 1–27

DUMVILLE, David N. *Wessex and England from Alfred to Edgar. Six Essays on Political, Cultural, and Ecclesiastical Revival* (Woodbridge 1992)
DYKES, D. W. *Anglo-Saxon Coins in the National Museum of Wales* (Cardiff [1976])
DYSON, T. 'King Alfred and the restoration of London', *London Journal* 15 (1990) 99–110
DYSON, T. & SCHOFIELD, J. 'Saxon London', in *Anglo-Saxon Towns in Southern England*, ed. J. Haslam (Chichester 1984), pp. 285–313
DYSON, T. 'Two Saxon land grants for Queenhithe', in *Collectanea Londiniensia*, edd. J. Bird *et al.* (London 1978), pp. 200–15
ECKHARDT, Karl August (ed.) *Pactus Legis Salicae* (Hanover 1962)
EDWARDS, Heather *The Charters of the Early West Saxon Kingdom* (Oxford 1988)
ERNST, Raimund *Die Nordwestslawen und das fränkische Reich* (Berlin 1976)
ERNST, R. 'Karolingische Nordostpolitik zur Zeit Ludwigs der Frommen', in *Östliches Europa*, edd. C. Goehrke *et al.* (Wiesbaden 1977), pp. 81–107
FARAL, Edmond (ed. & transl.) *Ermold le Noir: Poème sur Pouis le Pieux et épitres au roi Pépin* (Paris 1932)
FENWICK, V. 'Insula de Burg, excavations at Burrow Hill, Butley, Suffolk 1978–1981', *Anglo-Saxon Studies in Archaeology and History* 3 (1984) 35–54
FINBERG, H. P. R. (ed.) *Gloucestershire Studies* (Leicester 1957)
FINBERG, H. P. R. (ed.) *Scandinavian England* (Chichester 1975)
FOOT, S. 'The making of *Angelcynn*: English identity before the Norman Conquest', *Transactions of the Royal Historical Society*, 6th S., 6 (1996) 25–49
FRYDE, E. B. *et al.* (edd.) *Handbook of British Chronology* (3rd edn, London 1986)
GALSTER, Georg *Royal Collection, Copenhagen. Part 1. Ancient British and Anglo-Saxon Coins before Æthelred II* (SCBI 4, Oxford 1964)
GODDEN, Malcolm & LAPIDGE, Michael (edd.) *The Cambridge Companion to Old English Literature* (Cambridge 1991)
GODMAN, P. & COLLINS, R. *Charlemagne's Heir: New Perspectives on the Reign of Louis the Pious (814–840)* (Oxford 1990)
GOEHRKE, C. *et al.* (edd.) *Östliches Europa: Spiegel der Geschichte. Festschrift für Manfred Hellmann zur 65. Geburtstag* (Wiesbaden 1977)
GRANT, L. (ed.) *Medieval Art, Architecture and Archaeology in London* (London 1990)
GREENWAY, Diana (ed.) *Henry, Archdeacon of Huntingdon: 'Historia Anglorum' The History of the English People* (Oxford 1996)
GRIERSON, Philip *Fitzwilliam Museum, Cambridge. Part 1. Ancient British and Anglo-Saxon Coins* (SCBI 1, London 1958)
GRIERSON, P. 'Halfpennies and third-pennies of King Alfred', *British Numismatic Journal* 28 (1955–7) 477–93
GRIERSON, Philip & BLACKBURN, Mark *Medieval European Coinage, with a Catalogue of the Coins in the Fitzwilliam Museum, Cambridge, 1, The Early Middle Ages (5th–10th centuries)* (Cambridge 1986)
GRIERSON, P. 'The gold solidus of Louis the Pious and its imitations', *Jaarboek voor Munt- en Penningkunde* 38 (1951) 1–41
GUNSTONE, A. J. H. *Ancient British, Anglo-Saxon and Norman Coins in Midlands Museums* (SCBI 17, Oxford 1971)
GUNSTONE, Anthony *Coins in Lincolnshire Collections* (*SCBI* 27, Oxford 1981)
GUNSTONE, A. J. H. *South-Eastern Museums. Ancient British, Anglo-Saxon and Later Coins to 1279* (*SCBI* 42, Oxford 1992)
HALL, R. A. 'The five boroughs of the Danelaw: a review of present knowledge', *Anglo-Saxon England* 18 (1989) 149–206
HAMILTON, N. E. S. A. (ed.) *Willelmi Malmesbiriensis Monachi De Gestis Pontificum Anglorum Libri Quinque* (London 1870)

HARE, Michael *The Two Anglo-Saxon Minsters of Gloucester,* Deerhurst Lecture 1992 (Deerhurst 1993)
HARMER, F. E. (ed. & transl.) *Select English Historical Documents of the Ninth and Tenth Centuries* (Cambridge 1914)
HART, C. 'Athelstan "Half King" and his family', *Anglo-Saxon England* 2 (1973) 115–44, reprinted (with revisions) in his *The Danelaw* (London 1992), pp. 569–604
HART, Cyril *The Danelaw* (London 1992)
HART, C. 'The ealdordom of Essex', in *An Essex Tribute*, ed. K. Neale (London 1987), pp. 57–84, reprinted (with revisions) in his *The Danelaw* (London 1992), pp. 115–40
HART, Cyril *The Early Charters of Northern England and the North Midlands* (Leicester 1975)
HART, C. 'The kingdom of Mercia', in *Mercian Studies,* ed. A. Dornier (Leicester 1977), pp. 43–61
HASLAM, Jeremy (ed.) *Anglo-Saxon Towns in Southern England* (Chichester 1984)
HAUCK, K. 'Der Missionsauftrag Christi und das Kaisertum Ludwigs des Frommen', in *Charlemagne's Heir,* edd. P. Godman & R. Collins (Oxford 1990), pp. 275–96
HAWKINS, E. 'An account of some Saxon pennies, and other articles, found at Sevington, North Wilts', *Archaeologia* 27 (1838) 301–5
HAWKINS, E. *The Silver Coins of England* (3rd edn, ed. R. L. Kenyon, London 1887)
HEARNE, Thomas (ed.) *A Collection of Curious Discourses Written by Eminent Antiquaries* (2nd edn, 2 vols, London 1771)
HEARNE, Thomas (ed.) *Hemingi Chartularium ecclesiæ Wigorniensis* (2 vols, Oxford 1723)
HILL, D. 'Gazeteer of Burghal Hidage sites', in *The Defence of Wessex*, edd. D. Hill & A. R. Rumble (Manchester 1996), pp. 189–231
HILL, D. & METCALF, D. M. (edd.) *Sceattas in England and on the Continent*, BAR British Series 128 (Oxford 1984)
HILL, David & RUMBLE, Alexander R. (edd.) *The Defence of Wessex: The Burghal Hidage and Anglo-Saxon Fortifications* (Manchester 1996)
HOBLER, F. *Records of Roman History . . . as Exhibited on the Coins* (1860)
HOBLEY, Brian *Roman and Saxon London: a Reappraisal*, Museum of London Annual Archaeology Lecture 1985 (London 1986)
HOLDSWORTH, Christopher & WISEMAN, T. P. (edd.) *The Inheritance of Historiography 350–900* (Exeter 1986)
HUNTER BLAIR, P. 'The Northumbrians and their Southern Frontier', *Archaeologia Aeliana*, 4th S., 26 (1948) 98–126, reprinted in *Anglo-Saxon Northumbria*, edd. M. Lapidge and P. Hunter Blair (London 1984)
ISENBERG, Gabriele 'Die Würdigung Wilfrieds von York in der Historia Gentis Anglorum Bedas und der Vita Wilfridi des Eddius' (dissertation, Münster 1978)
JANKUHN, H. 'Karl der Grosse und der Norden', in *Karl der Grosse*, ed. H. Beumann (Düsseldorf 1965), pp. 699–707
JOHN, Eric *Orbis Britanniae and Other Studies* (Leicester 1966)
JOHN, Eric *Reassessing Anglo-Saxon England* (Manchester 1996)
JOHN, E. 'The age of Edgar', in *The Anglo-Saxons*, ed. J. Campbell (Oxford 1982), pp. 160–89
JONES, A. E. E. *Anglo-Saxon Worcester* (Worcester 1958)
JONSSON, Kenneth & MALMER, Brita (edd.) *Sigtuna Papers. Proceedings of the Sigtuna Symposium on Viking Age Coinage 1–4 June 1989* (Stockholm 1990)
KEARY, Charles Frances & GRUEBER, Herbert A. *A Catalogue of English Coins in the British Museum. Anglo-Saxon Series* (2 vols, London 1887/93)
KEENE, D. 'London in the early middle ages', *London Journal* 20 (1995) 9–21
KELLY, S. E. (ed.) *Charters of Selsey*, Anglo-Saxon Charters 6 (Oxford 1997)

KELLY, S. E. (ed.) *Charters of St Augustine's Abbey, Canterbury, and Minster-in-Thanet*, Anglo-Saxon Charters 4 (Oxford 1995)
KEYNES, S. 'A charter of King Edward the Elder for Islington, *Historical Research* 66 (1993) 303–16
KEYNES, Simon & LAPIDGE, Michael *Alfred the Great: Asser's* Life of King Alfred *and Other Contemporary Sources* (Harmondsworth 1983)
KEYNES, S. *An Atlas of Attestations in Anglo-Saxon Charters* c. *670–1066* (Cambridge 1993)
KEYNES, S. 'Anglo-Saxon entries in the *Liber Vitae* of Brescia', in *Alfred the Wise*, edd. J. Roberts & J. L. Nelson (Cambridge 1997), pp. 99–119
KEYNES, S. 'England, 700–900', in *The New Cambridge Medieval History*, II, ed. R. McKitterick (Cambridge 1995), pp. 18–42
KEYNES, S. 'England, 900–1016', in *The New Cambridge Medieval History*, III, ed. Timothy Reuter (Cambridge forthcoming)
KEYNES, S. 'King Athelstan's books', in *Learning and Literature in Anglo-Saxon England*, edd. M. Lapidge & M. Gneuss (Cambridge 1985), pp. 143–201
KEYNES, S. 'On the authenticity of Asser's *Life of King Alfred*', *Journal of Ecclesiastical History 47* (1996) 529–51
KEYNES, S. 'Royal government and the written word in late Anglo-Saxon England', in *The Uses of Literacy in Early Mediaeval Europe*, ed. R. McKitterick (Cambridge 1990), pp. 226–57
KEYNES, S. 'The age of Alfred', in *The Making of England*, edd. L. Webster & J. Backhouse (London 1991), pp. 254–6
KEYNES, S. 'The control of Kent in the ninth century', *Early Medieval Europe* 2 (1993) 111–31
KEYNES, S. *The Councils of Clofesho*, Brixworth Lecture 1993, University of Leicester, Department of Adult Education, Vaughan Paper 38 (Leicester 1994)
KEYNES, S. 'The Fonthill letter', in *Words, Texts and Manuscripts*, ed. M. Korhammer (Cambridge 1992), pp. 53–97
KEYNES, Simon (ed.) *The Liber Vitae of the New Minster and Hyde Abbey, Winchester*, Early English Manuscripts in Facsimile 26 (Copenhagen 1996)
KEYNES, S. 'The West Saxon charters of King Æthelwulf and his sons', *English Historical Review* 109 (1994) 1109–49
KING, Margot H. & STEVENS, W. M. (edd.) *Saints, Scholars and Heroes. Studies in Medieval Culture in Honour of Charles W. Jones* (2 vols, Collegeville, Minn. 1979)
KIRBY, D. P. 'Asser and his Life of King Alfred', *Studia Celtica* 6 (1971) 12–35
KIRBY, D. P. *The Earliest English Kings* (London 1991)
KORHAMMER, Michael (ed.) *Words, Texts and Manuscripts: Studies in Anglo-Saxon Culture presented to Helmut Gneuss on the Occasion of his Sixty-fifth Birthday* (Cambridge 1992)
KRUSCH, Bruno (ed.) *Chronicarum quae dicuntur Fredegarii Scholastici Libri IV cum Continuationibus* (Hanover 1888)
KRUSCH, Bruno & LEVISON, W. (edd.) *Gregorii episcopi Turonensis Libri historiarum* X (Hanover 1937–51)
LAFAURIE, J. 'Les routes commerciales indiquées par les trésors et trouvailles monétaires mérovingiens', *Moneta e scambi nell'alto medioevo* (Spoleto 1961), pp. 231–78
LAPIDGE, Michael & GNEUSS, H. (edd.) *Learning and Literature in Anglo-Saxon England. Studies presented to Peter Clemoes on the Occasion of his Sixty-fifth Birthday* (Cambridge 1985)
LAPIDGE, Michael & HUNTER BLAIR, P. (edd.) *Anglo-Saxon Northumbria* (London 1984)

LAUER, Philippe (ed. & transl.) *Nithard: Histoire des fils de Louis le Pieux* (Paris 1926)
LEMARIGNIER, J.-F. *Recherches sur l'hommage en marche et les frontiers féodales*, Travaux et mémoires de l'Université de Lille, N.S. Droit et lettres XXIV (Lille 1945)
LEVISON, W. *England and the Continent in the Eighth Century* (Oxford 1946)
LIEBERMANN, Felix (ed. & transl.) *Die Gesetze der Angelsaschsen* (3 vols, Halle a.S. 1898–1916)
LINDSAY, John *A View of the Coinage of the Heptarchy to which is added a List of Unpublished Mints and Moneyers* (Cork 1842)
LLOYD, John Edward *A History of Wales from the Earliest Times to the Norman Conquest* (3rd edn, 2 vols, London 1939)
LOT, Ferdinand *Recueil des travaux historiques de Ferdinand Lot, avec un avant-propos par Ch. Samaran* (3 vols, Geneva 1968/1970/1973)
LOT, F. 'Roric. Ses incursions', in his *Recueil des travaux historiques de Ferdinand Lot, avec un avant-propos par Ch. Samaran* (3 vols, Geneva 1968), II. 678–85
LOYN, Henry *The Vikings in Britain* (London 1977)
LYNCH, Joseph H. *Godparents and Kinship in Early Medieval Europe* (Princeton, N.J. 1986)
LYON, C. S. S. 'Historical problems of Anglo-Saxon coinage – (2). The ninth century – Offa to Alfred', *British Numismatic Journal* 37 (1968) 216–38
LYON, C. S. S. 'Historical problems of Anglo-Saxon coinage – (4). The Viking age', *British Numismatic Journal* 39 (1970) 193–204
LYON, C. S. S. 'Some problems in interpreting Anglo-Saxon coinage', *Anglo-Saxon England* 5 (1976) 173–224
McGURK, Patrick 'The metrical calendar of Hampson', *Analecta Bollandiana* 104 (1986) 79–125
McKITTERICK, Rosamond *The Frankish Kingdoms under the Carolingians, 751–987* (London 1983)
McKITTERICK, Rosamond (ed.) *The New Cambridge Medieval History*, II: c. *700*– c. *900* (Cambridge 1995)
McKITTERICK, Rosamond (ed.) *The Uses of Literacy in Early Mediaeval Europe* (Cambridge 1990)
MACK, R. P. *R. P. Mack Collection. Ancient British, Anglo-Saxon and Norman Coins* (*SCBI* 20, Oxford 1973)
MAGISTRETTI, M. *Monumenta veteris liturgiae Ambrosianae*, III, *Manuale Ambrosianum* (Milan 1904)
MANVILLE, Harrington E. & ROBERTSON, Terrance J. *British Numismatic Auction Catalogues 1710–1984* (London 1986)
MARTIN, J. S. 'Some remarks on eighteenth-century numismatic manuscripts and numismatists', in *Anglo-Saxons Coins*, ed. R. H. M. Dolley (London 1961), pp. 227–40
MARTIN, Thomas *The History of the Town of Thetford* (London 1779)
MERRIFIELD, R. 'The contribution of archaeology to our understanding of pre-Norman London, 1973–1988', in *Medieval Art, Architecture and Archaeology in London*, ed. L. Grant (London 1990), pp. 1–15
METCALF, D. M. 'A bent St Edmund Memorial penny from Mursley, Bucks.', *Seaby Coin and Medal Bulletin* (1981) 196–7
METCALF, D. M. 'A topographical commentary on the coin finds from ninth-century Northumbria (c. 780–c. 870)', in *Coinage in Ninth-Century Northumbria,* ed. D. M. Metcalf (Oxford 1987), pp. 361–82
METCALF, D. M. & NORTHOVER, J. P. 'Carolingian and Viking coins from the Cuerdale hoard: an interpretation and comparison of their metal contents', *Numismatic Chronicle* 148 (1988) 97–116

METCALF, D. M. & NORTHOVER, J. P. 'Coinage alloys from the time of Offa and Charlemagne to *c.* 864', *Numismatic Chronicle* 149 (1989) 101–20

METCALF, D. M. (ed.) *Coinage in Ninth-Century Northumbria* (Oxford 1987)

METCALF, D. M. 'Continuity and change in English monetary history *c.* 973–1086', *British Numismatic Journal* 50 (1980) 20–49; 51 (1981) 52–90

METCALF, D. M. & NORTHOVER, J. P. 'Debasement of the coinage in southern England in the age of King Alfred', *Numismatic Chronicle* 145 (1985) 150–76

METCALF, D. M. 'Monetary expansion and recession: interpreting the distribution-patterns of seventh- and eighth-century coins', in *Coins and the Archaeologist*, edd. J. Casey & R. Reece (2nd edn, London 1988), pp. 230–53

METCALF, D. M. 'Some finds of medieval coins from Scotland and the north of England', *British Numismatic Journal* 30 (1960–1) 88–123

METCALF, D. M. 'The coins', in *Southampton Finds, I,* ed. P. Andrews (Southampton 1988), pp. 17–59

METCALF, D. M. 'The monetary history of England in the tenth century viewed in the perspective of the eleventh century', in *Anglo-Saxon Monetary History*, ed. M. A. S. Blackburn (Leicester 1986), pp. 133–57

METCALF, D. M. *Thrymsas and Sceattas in the Ashmolean Museum Oxford* (3 vols, London 1993–4)

MILLS, J. 'Before King Alfred: the Saxons in town and country', *Current Archaeology* 11.4 (1991) 170–3

MOMMSEN, Theodor (ed.) *Chronica Minora Saec. IV. V. VI. VII.* (3 vols, Berlin 1891–8)

NEALE, Kenneth (ed.) *An Essex Tribute: Essays presented to Frederick G. Emmison* (London 1987)

NELSON, J. L. ' "A king across the sea": Alfred the Great in a continental perspective', *Transactions of the Royal Historical Society*, 5th S., 36 (1986) 45–68

NELSON, Janet L. *Politics and Ritual in Early Medieval Europe* (London 1986)

NELSON, J. L. 'Reconstructing a royal family: reflections on Alfred, from Asser, Chapter 2', in *Peoples and Places in Northern Europe 500–1600*, edd. I. Wood & N. Lund (Woodbridge 1991) pp. 47–66

NELSON, Janet L. (transl.) *The Annals of St-Bertin* (Manchester 1991)

NELSON, J. L. 'The political ideas of Alfred of Wessex', in *Kings and Kingship in Medieval Europe*, ed. A. J. Duggan (London 1993), pp. 125–58

NELSON, J. L. 'The second English Ordo', in her *Politics and Ritual in Early Medieval Europe* (London 1986), pp. 361–74

NELSON, J. L. 'Wealth and wisdom: the politics of Alfred the Great', in *Kings and Kingship*, ed. J. Rosenthal, *Acta* 11 (1984) 31–52

NOBLE, T. F. X. 'Louis the Pious and the frontiers of the Frankish realm', in *Charlemagne's Heir*, edd. P. Godman & R. Collins (Oxford 1990), pp. 333–48

NORTH, J. J. *English Hammered Coinage, I, Early Anglo-Saxon to Henry II* (3rd edn, London 1994)

NORTH, J. J. 'The coinage of Berhtwulf of Mercia (840–852)', *Numismatic Circular* 69 (1961) 213–15

PAGAN, H. E. & STEWART, B. H. I. H. 'A new Mercian moneyer for Alfred's Lunettes type', *Numismatic Circular* 97 (1989) 8

PAGAN, H. E. 'An unpublished fragment of a coin of Ceolwulf II', *British Numismatic Journal* 41 (1972) 14–20

PAGAN, H. E. 'Coinage in southern England, 796–874', in *Anglo-Saxon Monetary History*, ed. M. A. S. Blackburn (Leicester 1986), pp. 45–65

PAGAN, H. E. 'Coinage in the age of Burgred', *British Numismatic Journal* 34 (1965) 11–27

PAGAN, H. E. 'The coinage of the East Anglian kingdom from 825 to 870', *British Numismatic Journal* 52 (1982) 41–83

PAGAN, H. E. 'The imitative Louis the Pious solidus from Southampton and finds of other related coins in the British Isles', in *Southampton Finds, I,* ed. P. Andrews (Southampton 1988), pp. 71–2

PAGAN, H. E. 'The older finds of Anglo-Saxon coins from Southampton', in *Southampton Finds, I,* ed. P. Andrews (Southampton 1988), pp. 60–70

PAGAN, H. E. 'Two groups of coins of Aelfred with the London Monogram', *Numismatic Circular* 91 (1983) 121

PAGAN, H. E. 'Two new coins in the names of Aethelred I and Alfred of Wessex', *Numismatic Circular* 99 (1991) 6

PETRIE, Henry & SHARPE, J. (edd.) *Monumenta Historica Britannica, or Materials for the History of Britain, from the Earliest Period* (London 1848)

PIRIE, E. J. E. 'Early Northumbrian coins at auction, 1981', *British Numismatic Journal* 51 (1981) 32–51

PIRIE, E. J. E. 'Finds of "sceattas" and "stycas" of Northumbria', in *Anglo-Saxon Monetary History*, ed. M. A. S. Blackburn (Leicester 1986), pp. 67–90

PIRIE, E. J. E. *Post-Roman Coins from York Excavations 1971–1981*, Archaeology of York 18:1 (London 1986)

PLUMMER, Charles *The Life and Times of Alfred the Great* (Oxford 1902)

PLUMMER, Charles (ed.) *Two of the Saxon Chronicles Parallel, with Supplementary Extracts from the Others. A Revised Text on the Basis of an Edition by John Earle* (2 vols, Oxford 1892/9; rev. imp., by D. Whitelock, 1952)

RADNER, Joan Newlon (ed.) *Fragmentary Annals of Ireland* (Dublin 1978)

RANDSBORG, K. *The Viking Age in Denmark* (London 1980)

RASHLEIGH, J. 'An account of Anglo-Saxon coins and gold and silver ornaments found at Trewhiddle, near St Austell, Cornwall, A.D. 1774', *Numismatic Chronicle,* 2nd S., 8 (1868) 137–57

RASHLEIGH, P. 'Account of antiquities discovered in Cornwall, 1774', *Archaeologia* 9 (1788) 187–8 + plate VIII

RASMUSSON, Nils Ludvig & MALMER, Brita (edd.) *Commentationes de nummis saeculorum IX–XI in Suecia repertis* II (Stockholm 1968)

RAU, R. *Quellen zur karolingischen Reichsgeschichte* (3 vols, Darmstadt 1955/1957/1960)

REUTER, Timothy (transl.) *The Annals of Fulda* (Manchester 1992)

REUTER, T. 'The end of Carolingian military expansion', in *Charlemagne's Heir*, edd. P. Godman & R. Collins (Oxford 1990), pp. 391–405

REUTER, Timothy (ed.) *The New Cambridge Medieval History*, III: *900–1024* (Cambridge forthcoming)

REYNOLDS, S. 'What do we mean by "Anglo-Saxon" and "Anglo-Saxons"?' *Journal of British Studies* 24 (1985) 395–414

RICHARDS, M. P. 'The manuscript contexts of the Old English laws: tradition and innovation', in *Studies in Earlier Old English Prose*, ed. P. E. Szarmach (Albany, N.Y. 1986), pp. 171–92

RIGOLD, S. E. 'Finds of St. Edmund Memorial and other Anglo-Saxon coins from excavations at Thetford', *British Numismatic Journal* 29 (1958–9) 189–90

ROACH SMITH, C. *Catalogue of the Illustrations of London Antiquities* (London, 1854)

ROBERTS, Jane & NELSON, Janet. L. (edd.) *Alfred the Wise: Studies presented to Janet Bately* (Cambridge 1997)

ROBERTSON, A. J. (ed. & transl.) *Anglo-Saxon Charters* (2nd edn, Cambridge 1956)

ROBERTSON, Anne S. *Hunterian and Coats Collections, University of Glasgow. Part 1. Anglo-Saxon Coins* (SCBI 2, Oxford 1961)

ROSENTHAL, J. (ed.) *Kings and Kingship*, *Acta* 11 (1984)

ROWELL, Geoffrey (ed.) *The English Religious Tradition and the Genius of Anglicanism* (Wantage 1992)

RUDING, Rev. Rogers *Annals of the Coinage of Great Britain and its Dependencies* (3rd edn, London 1840)

SAWYER, B. *et al.* (edd.) *The Christianization of Scandinavia* (Alingsas 1987)

SAWYER, P. H. *Anglo-Saxon Charters. An Annotated List and Bibliography* (London 1968)

SAWYER, P. H. & WOOD, I. N. *Early Medieval Kingship* (Leeds 1977)

SCHARER, A. 'The writing of history at King Alfred's court', *Early Medieval Europe* 5 (1996) 177–206

SCHÜTT, Marie 'The literary form of Asser's "Vita Alfredi" ', *English Historical Review* 72 (1957) 209–20

SCHOFIELD, John *The Building of London from the Conquest to the Great Fire* (London 1984)

SEABY, W. A. 'A Coenwulf penny of Wihtred from Bidford-on-Avon, Warwickshire', *British Numismatic Journal* 52 (1982) 29–33

SEARLE, William George *Onomasticon Anglo-Saxonicum. A List of Anglo-Saxon Proper Names from the Time of Beda to that of King John* (Cambridge 1897)

SHAW, S. 'New coin of Beorchtric', *Numismatic Chronicle*, 1st S., 17 (1855) 59–61

SHERLOCK, D. 'The coins', in V. Fenwick, 'Insula de Burg, excavations at Burrow Hill, Butley, Suffolk 1978–1981', *Anglo-Saxon Studies in Archaeology and History* 3 (1984) 35–54 at 44–53

SHORTT, H. 'A denier of Charles the Bald from Preshute', *Wiltshire Archaeological and Natural History Magazine* 64 (1969) 51–2

SMART, V. J. 'Moneyers of the late Anglo-Saxon coinage 973–1016', in *Commentationes de nummis saeculorum IX–XI in Suecia repertis* II, edd. N. L. Rasmusson & B. Malmer (Stockholm 1968), pp. 191–276

SMART, V. J. 'Moneyers of the late Anglo-Saxon coinage: the Danish dynasty 1017–42', *Anglo-Saxon England* 16 (1987) 233–308

SMART, V. 'Scandinavians, Celts, and Germans in Anglo-Saxon England: the evidence of moneyers' names', in *Anglo-Saxon Monetary History*, ed. M. A. S. Blackburn (Leicester 1986), pp. 171–84

SMART, Veronica *Sylloge of Coins of the British Isles, [vol.] 28, Cumulative Index of Volumes 1–20* (London 1981)

SMART, Veronica *Sylloge of Coins of the British Isles, [vol.] 41, Cumulative Index of Volumes 21–40* (Oxford 1992)

SMITH, J. M. *Province and Empire: Brittany and the Carolingians* (Cambridge 1992)

SMITH, Roach *The Antiquities of Richborough, Reculver, and Lympne* (London 1850)

SMYTH, Alfred P. *King Alfred the Great* (Oxford 1995)

STAFFORD, Pauline *The East Midlands in the Early Middle Ages* (Leicester 1985)

STAFFORD, Pauline *Unification and Conquest: a Political and Social History of England in the Tenth and Eleventh Centuries* (London 1989)

STENTON, D. M. (ed.) *Preparatory to Anglo-Saxon England* (Oxford 1970)

STENTON, F. M. *Anglo-Saxon England* (3rd edn, Oxford 1971)

STENTON, F. M. 'The Anglo-Saxon coinage and the historian', in *Preparatory to Anglo-Saxon England*, ed. D. M. Stenton (Oxford 1970), pp. 371–82

STENTON, F. M. *The Early History of the Abbey of Abingdon* (Reading 1913)

STENTON, F. M. *The Latin Charters of the Anglo-Saxon Period* (Oxford 1955)

STEPHENS, J. N. 'Bede's Ecclesiastical History', *History* 62 (1977) 1–14

STEVENSON, William Henry (ed.) *Asser's Life of King Alfred together with the Annals of Saint Neots erroneously ascribed to Asser* (Oxford 1904; rev. imp., by D. Whitelock, 1959)
STEWART, I. 'A solidus from Yorkshire', *British Numismatic Journal* 56 (1986) 182–3
STEWART, I. 'English numismatics – progress and prospects', *British Numismatic Journal* 58 (1988) 110–22
STEWART, I. 'Ministri and monetarii', *Revue Numismatique*, 6th S., 30 (1988) 166–75
STOTT, P. 'Saxon and Norman coins from London', *Aspects of Saxon and Norman London 2: Finds and Environmental Evidence*, London and Middlesex Archaeological Society Special Paper 12 (London 1991), pp. 279–325
STUBBS, William (ed.) *Willelmi Malmesbiriensis monachi De gestis regum Anglorum libri quinque; Historiæ novellæ libri tres* (2 vols, London 1887/9)
SWEET, Henry (ed.) *The Oldest English Texts* (London 1885)
SZARMACH, Paul. E. (ed.) *Sources of Anglo-Saxon Culture* (Kalamazoo MI, 1986)
SZARMACH, Paul E. (ed.) *Studies in Earlier Old English Prose* (Albany N.Y., 1986)
TATTON-BROWN, T. 'The topography of Anglo-Saxon London', *Antiquity* 60 (1986) 21–8
TAYLOR, C. S. 'The origin of the Mercian shires', *Gloucestershire Studies*, ed. H. P. R. Finberg (Leicester 1957), pp. 17–51
THACKER, A. T. 'Chester and Gloucester: early ecclesiastical organization in two Midland burhs', *Northern History* 18 (1982) 199–211
THACKER, A. T. 'Some terms for noblemen in Anglo-Saxon England, *c.* 650–900', *Anglo-Saxon Studies in Archaeology and History* 2 (1981) 201–36
THOMPSON, J. D. A. *Ashmolean Museum, Oxford. Anglo-Saxon Pennies* (*SCBI* 9, Oxford 1967)
THOMPSON, J. D. A. *Inventory of British Coin Hoards A.D. 600–1500*, Royal Numismatic Society Special Publications 1 (London 1956)
THOMSON, R. L. 'British Latin and English history: Nennius and Asser', *Proceedings of the Leeds Philosophical and Literacy Society*, Literature and History Section 18, pt 1 (1982) 38–53
THORPE, Benjamin (ed.) *Florentii Wigorniensis Monachi Chronicon ex Chronicis* (2 vols, London 1848/9)
TURNER, D. H. (ed.) *The Claudius Pontificals*, Henry Bradshaw Society 97 (London 1971)
VINCE, Alan (ed.) *Pre-Viking Lindsey*, Lincoln Archaeological Studies 1 (Lincoln 1993)
VINCE, Alan *Saxon London. An Archaeological Investigation* (London 1990)
VINCE, A. 'The Aldwych: Mid-Saxon London discovered?', *Current Archaeology* 8.10 (August 1984) 310–12
VOGEL, W. *Die Normannen und das fränkische Reich bis zur Gründung der Normandie* (799–911) (Heidelberg 1906)
VOLLRATH-REICHELT, Hanna *Königsgedanke und Königtum bei den Angelsachsen* (Cologne 1971)
WAINWRIGHT, F. T. 'Æthelflæd, Lady of the Mercians', in *Scandinavian England*, ed. H. P. R. Finberg (Chichester 1975), pp. 305–24
WALLACE-HADRILL, J. M. *Bede's Ecclesiastical History of the English People: A Historical Commentary* (Oxford 1988)
WALLACE-HADRILL, J. M. *Early Medieval History* (Oxford 1975)
WALLACE-HADRILL, J. M. 'The Franks and the English in the ninth century: some common historical interests', *History*, N.S., 35 (1950) 202–18, reprinted in his *Early Medieval History* (Oxford 1975), pp. 201–16

WEBSTER, Leslie & BACKHOUSE, Janet (edd.) *The Making of England. Anglo-Saxon Art and Culture AD 600–900* (London 1991)

WHITBOURNE, R. 'On two unpublished coins of Egbert', *Numismatic Chronicle*, 2nd S., 3 (1863) 46–7

WHITELOCK, Dorothy *Anglo-Saxon Wills* (Cambridge 1930)

WHITELOCK, Dorothy (transl.) *English Historical Documents* 1. c. *500–1042* (2nd edn, London 1979)

WHITELOCK, D. 'Some charters in the name of King Alfred', in *Saints, Scholars and Heroes*, edd. M. H. King & W. M. Stevens (2 vols, Collegeville, Minn. 1979), I.77–98

WHITELOCK, Dorothy *The Genuine Asser*, Stenton Lecture 1967 (Reading 1968)

WHITELOCK, Dorothy *The Importance of the Battle of Edington* (Edington [1978])

WILLIAMS, A. 'Some notes and considerations on problems connected with the English royal succession, 860–1066', *Proceedings of the Battle Conference* 1 (1979) 144–67 and 225–33

WILLIAMS, Ann 'The Vikings in Essex, 871–917', *Essex Archaeology and History* 27 (1996) 92–101

WILLIAMS, Ifor & BROMWICH, R. (edd.) *Armes Prydein. The Prophecy of Britain from the Book of Taliesin* (Dublin 1972)

WILLIAMS, John H. (ed.) *St Peter's Street Northampton Excavations: 1973–1976* (Northampton 1979)

WILSON, D. M. & BLUNT, C. E. 'The Trewhiddle hoard', *Archaeologia* 98 (1961) 75–120

WOOD, I. N. 'Christians and pagans in ninth-century Scandinavia', in *The Christianization of Scandinavia*, edd. B. Sawyer *et al.* (Alingsas 1987), pp. 36–67

WOOD, Ian & LUND, Niels (edd.) *Peoples and Places in Northern Europe 500–1600: Essays in Honour of Peter Hayes Sawyer* (Woodbridge 1991)

WOOD, Michael 'The making of King Aethelstan's empire: an English Charlemagne?', in *Ideal and Reality in Frankish and Anglo-Saxon Society*, edd. P. Wormald *et al.* (Oxford 1983), pp. 250–72

WORMALD, P. 'Anglo-Saxon society and its literature', in *The Cambridge Companion to Old English Literature*, edd. M. Godden & M. Lapidge (Cambridge 1991), pp. 1–22

WORMALD, P. 'Bede, the Bretwaldas, and the origins of the Gens Anglorum', in *Ideal and Reality in Frankish and Anglo-Saxon Society*, edd. P. Wormald *et al.* (Oxford 1983), pp. 99–129

WORMALD, P. 'Celtic and Anglo-Saxon kingship: some further thoughts', in *Sources of Anglo-Saxon Culture*, ed. Paul E. Szarmach (Kalamazoo MI, 1986), pp. 151–83

WORMALD, P. '*Engla Lond*: the making of an allegiance', *Journal of Historical Sociology* 7 (1994) 1–24

WORMALD, Patrick *et al.* (edd.) *Ideal and Reality in Frankish and Anglo-Saxon Society. Studies presented to J. M. Wallace-Hadrill* (Oxford 1983)

WORMALD, P. 'In search of King Offa's "law-code" ', in *Peoples and Places in Northern Europe 500–1600,* edd. I. Wood & N. Lund (Woodbridge 1991), pp. 25–45

WORMALD, P. '*Lex Scripta* and *Verbum Regis*: legislation and Germanic kingship, from Euric to Cnut', in *Early Medieval Kingship*, edd. P. H. Sawyer & I. N. Wood (Leeds 1977), pp. 105–38

WORMALD, P. 'The making of England', *History Today* (February 1995) 26–32

WORMALD, P. 'The ninth century', in *The Anglo-Saxons*, ed. J. Campbell (Oxford 1982), pp. 132–59

WORMALD, P. 'The Venerable Bede and the "Church of the English" ', in *The English Religious Tradition and the Genius of Anglicanism*, ed. G. Rowell (Wantage 1992), pp. 13–32

YORKE, B. 'Æthelwold and the politics of the tenth century', in *Bishop Æthelwold*, ed. B. Yorke (Woodbridge 1988), pp. 65–88

YORKE, Barbara (ed.) *Bishop Æthelwold: His Career and Influence* (Woodbridge 1988)

YORKE, Barbara *Kings and Kingdoms of Early Anglo-Saxon England* (London 1990)

YORKE, Barbara *Wessex in the Early Middle Ages* (Leicester 1995)

GENERAL INDEX